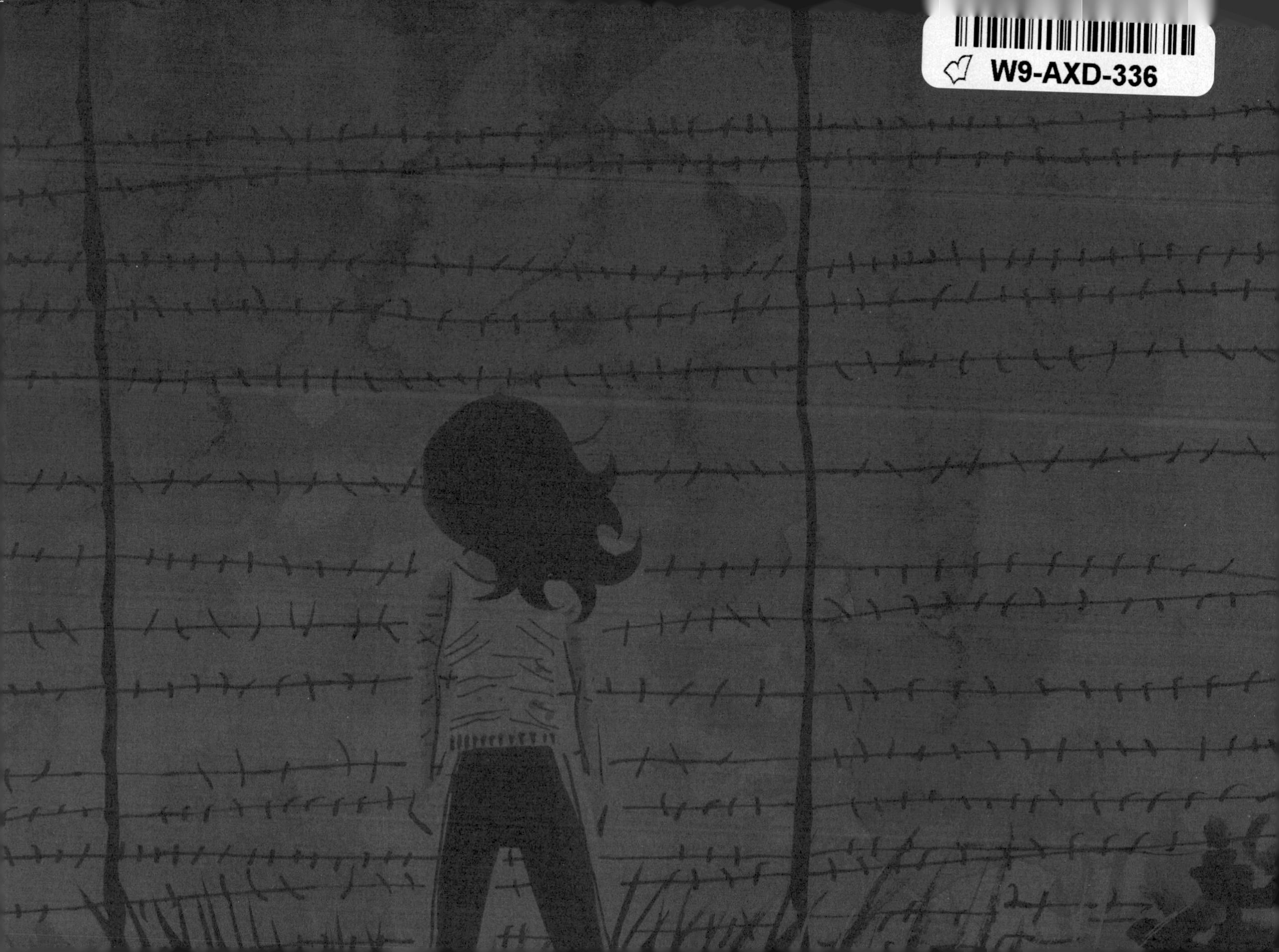

# AGAINST HOPE™

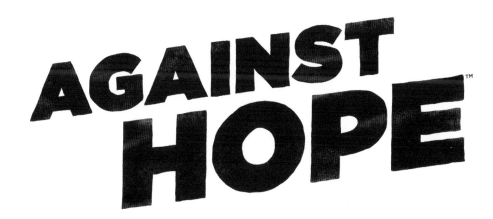

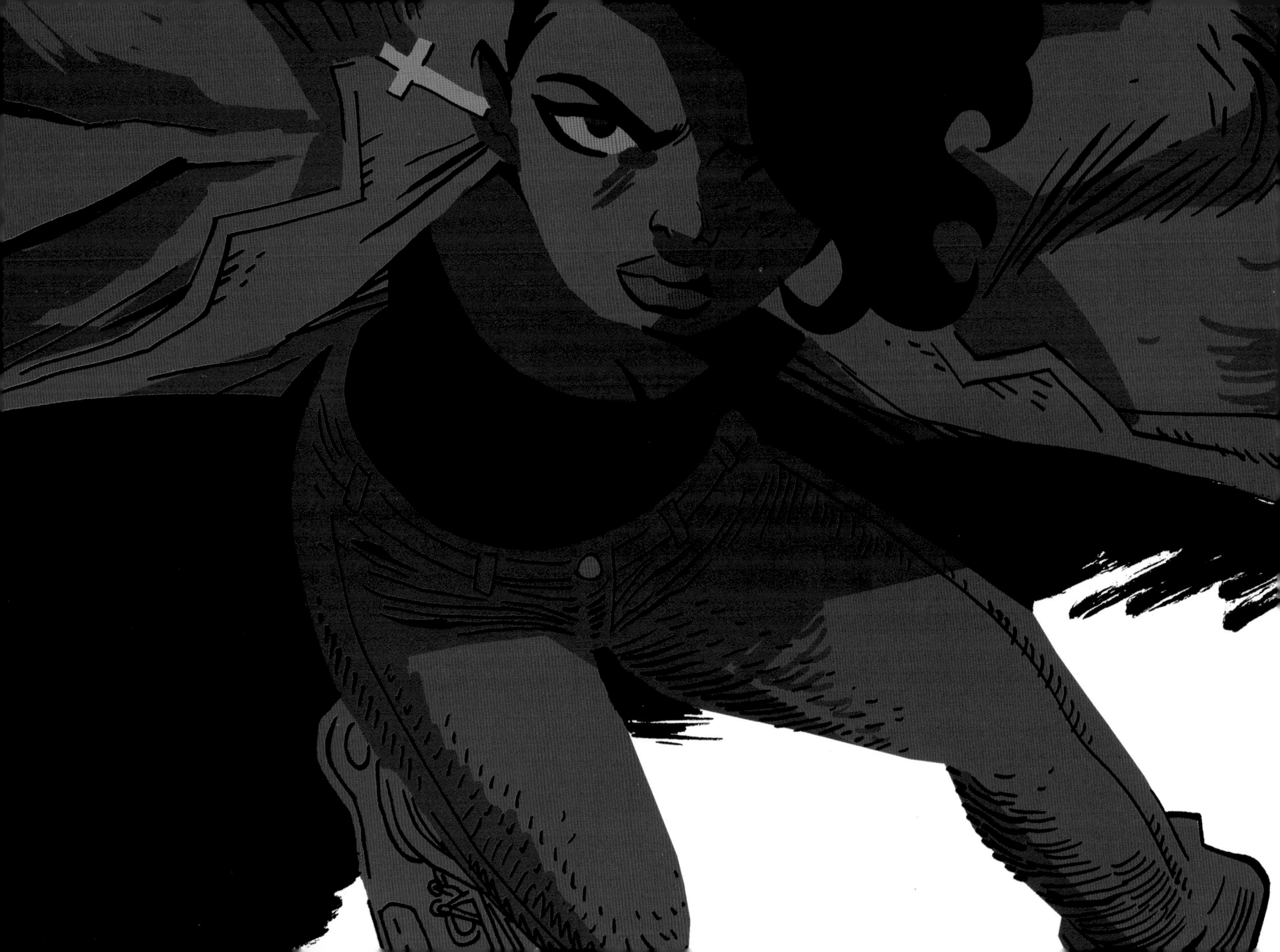

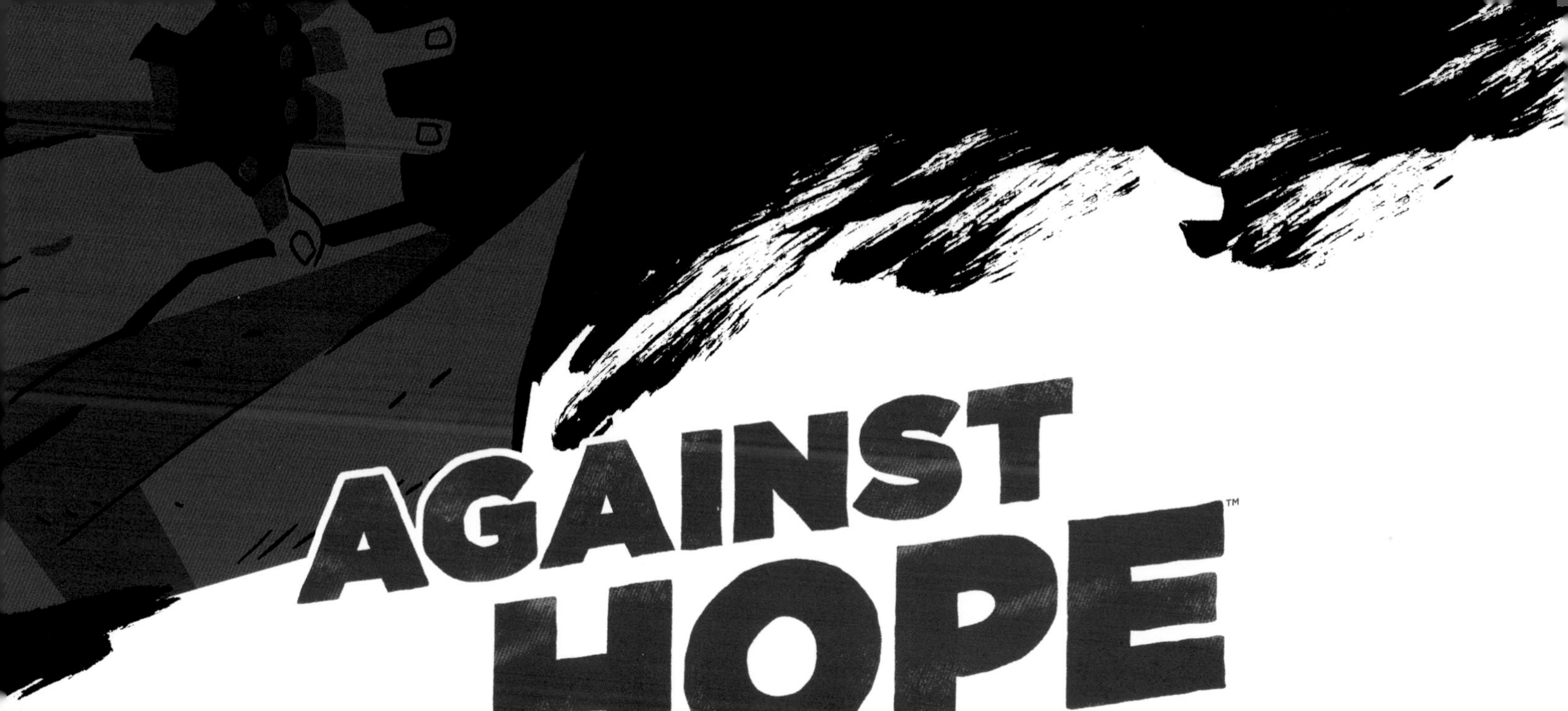

# AGAINST HOPE™

WRITTEN AND ILLUSTRATED BY

**VICTOR SANTOS**

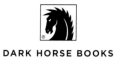

DARK HORSE BOOKS

PRESIDENT & PUBLISHER **MIKE RICHARDSON**   EDITOR **SPENCER CUSHING**

ASSISTANT EDITOR **KONNER KNUDSEN**   DESIGNER **ETHAN KIMBERLING**

DIGITAL ART TECHNICIAN **ALLYSON HALLER**

Published by Dark Horse Books
A division of Dark Horse Comics LLC
10956 SE Main Street
Milwaukie, OR 97222

DarkHorse.com

First edition: June 2020
ISBN 978-1-50671-796-8
Digital ISBN 978-1-50671-797-5

10 9 8 7 6 5 4 3 2 1
Printed in China

To find a comics shop in your
area, visit comicshoplocator.com

Neil Hankerson, Executive Vice President · **Tom Weddle** Chief Financial Officer **Randy Stradley,** Vice President of Publishing · **Nick McWhorter,** Chief Business Development Officer · **Dale LaFountain,** Chief Information Officer · **Matt Parkinson,** Vice President of Marketing · **Vanessa Todd-Holmes,** Vice President of Production and Scheduling · **Mark Bernardi,** Vice President of Book Trade and Digital Sales · **Ken Lizzi,** General Counsel · **Dave Marshall,** Editor in Chief **Davey Estrada,** Editorial Director · **Chris Warner,** Senior Books Editor · **Cary Grazzini,** Director of Specialty Projects · **Lia Ribacchi,** Art Director · **Matt Dryer,** Director of Digital Art and Prepress · **Michael Gombos,** Senior Director of Licensed Publications · **Kari Yadro,** Director of Custom Programs · **Kari Torson,** Director of International Licensing · **Sean Brice,** Director of Trade Sales

**Library of Congress Cataloging-in-Publication Data**

Names: Santos, Victor, 1977- author, illustrator.
Title: Against hope / Victor Santos.
Description: First edition. | Milwaukie, OR : Dark Horse Books, 2020. |
   Summary: "It has been years since an insane family of neo-Nazi's murdered her boyfriend and almost killed Hope, now she is tracking them down and exacting her bloody revenge"-- Provided by publisher.
Identifiers: LCCN 2020002507 | ISBN 9781506717968 (hardcover)
Subjects: LCSH: Graphic novels.
Classification: LCC PN6777.S29 A73 2020 | DDC 741.5/946--dc23
LC record available at https://lccn.loc.gov/2020002507

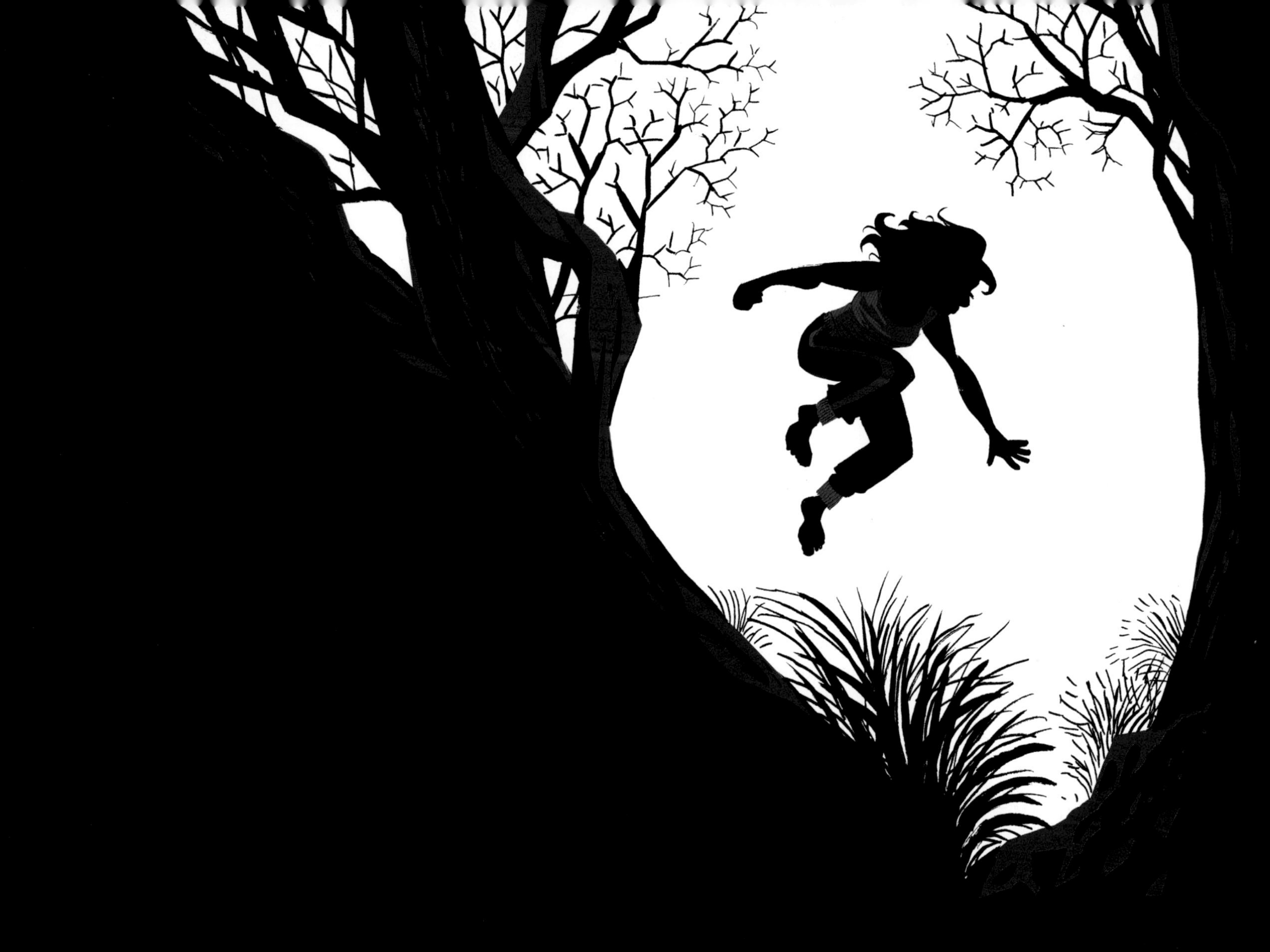

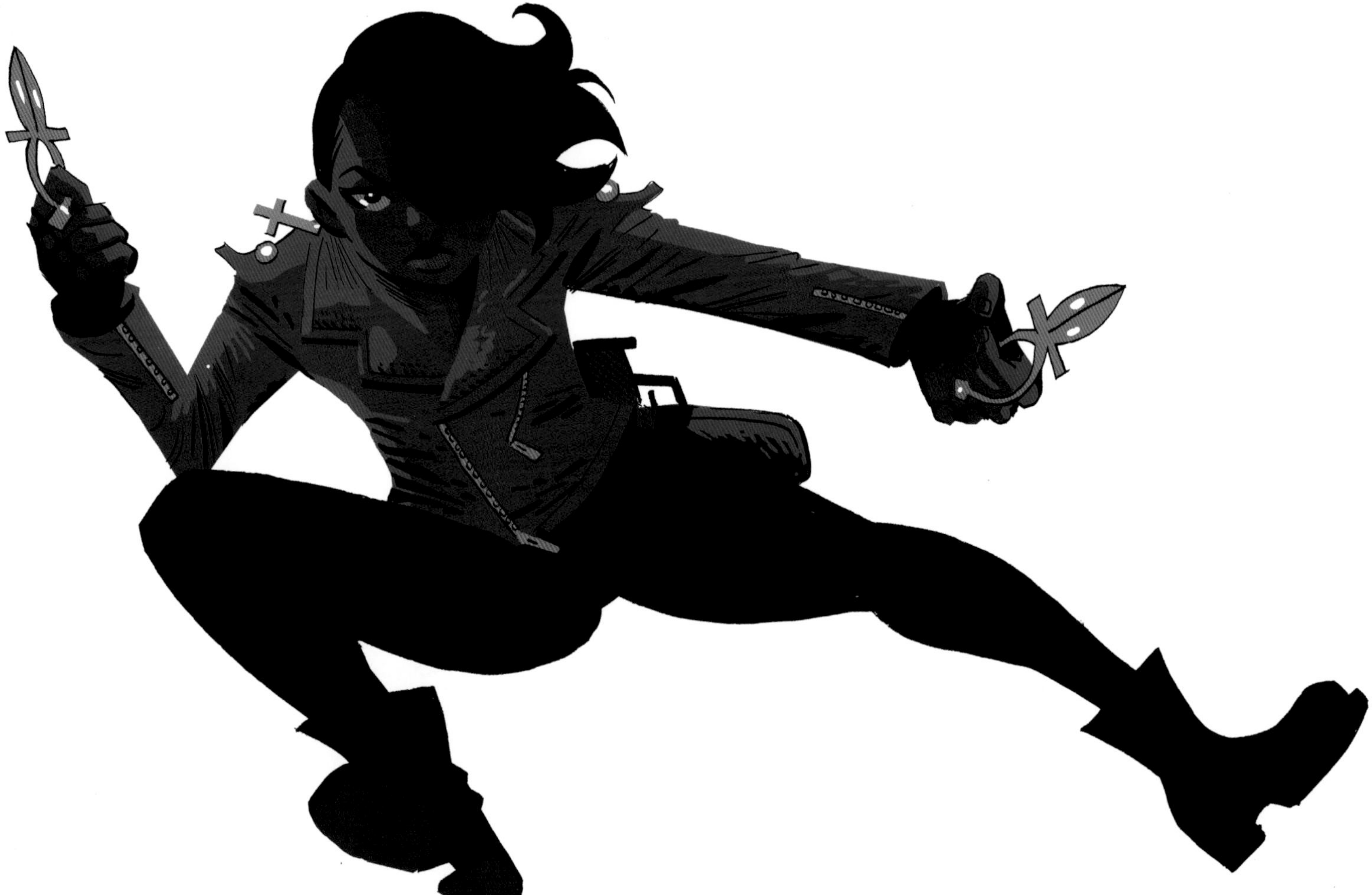

# PROLOGUE

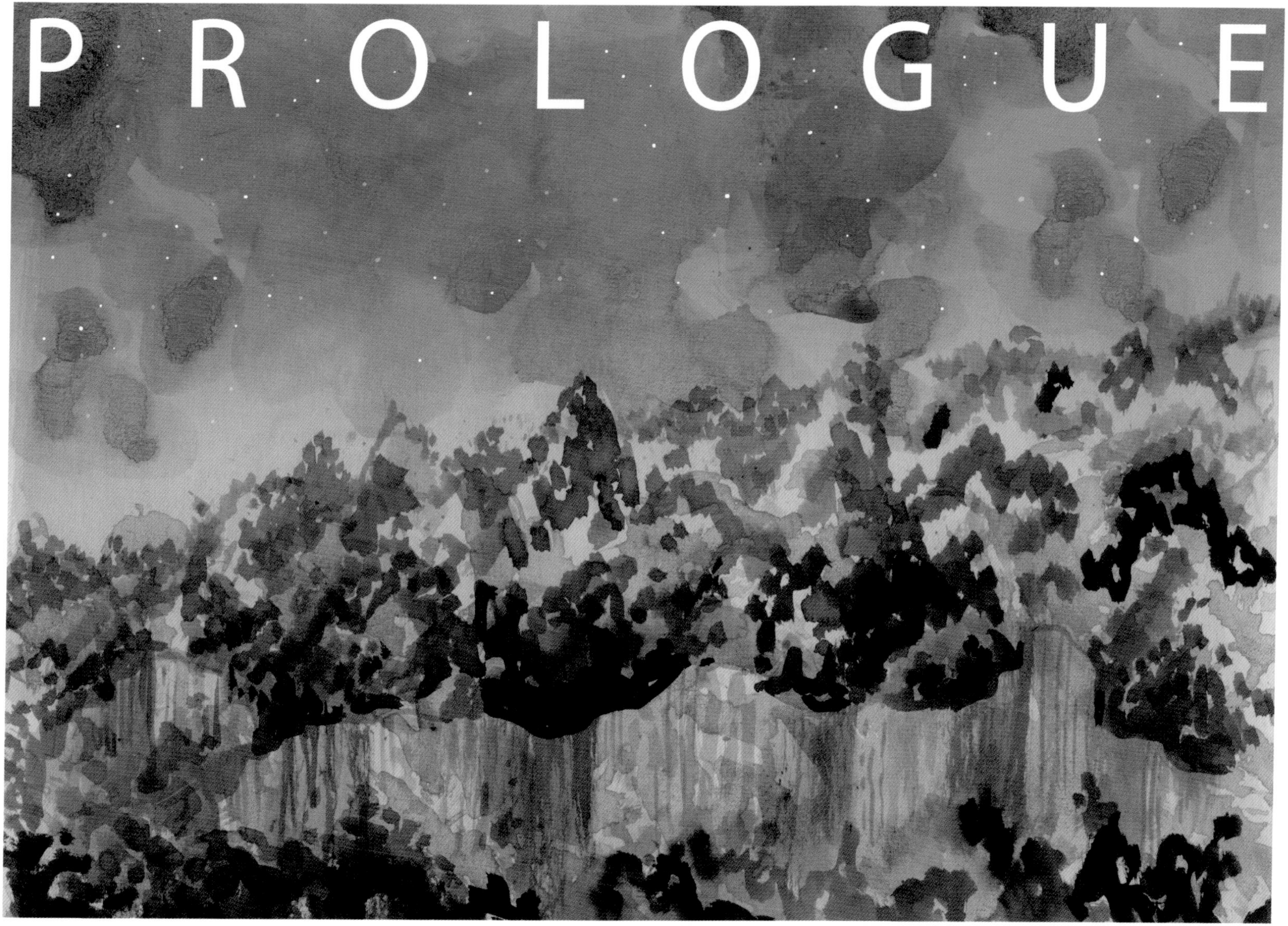

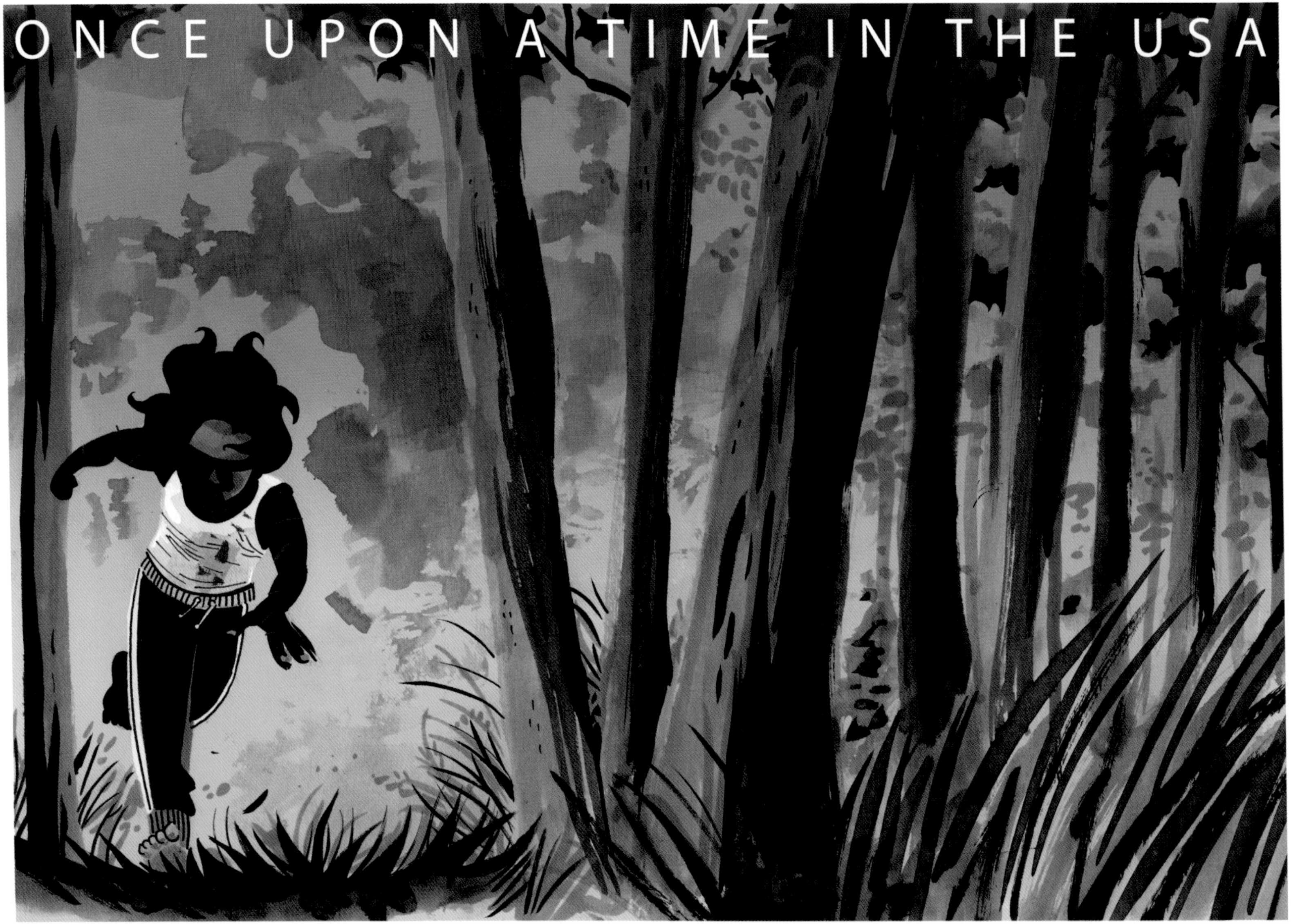
ONCE UPON A TIME IN THE USA

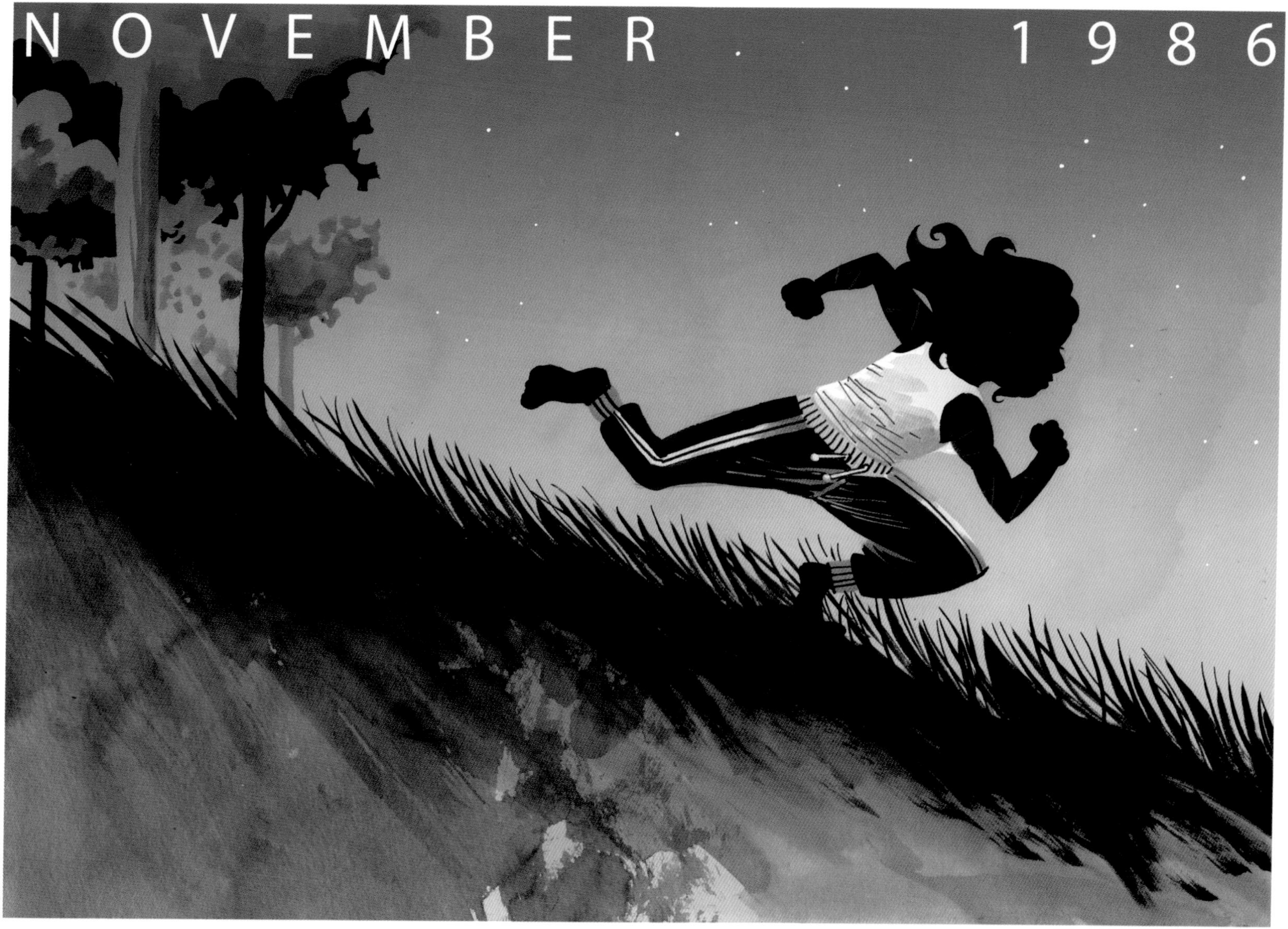
NOVEMBER 1986

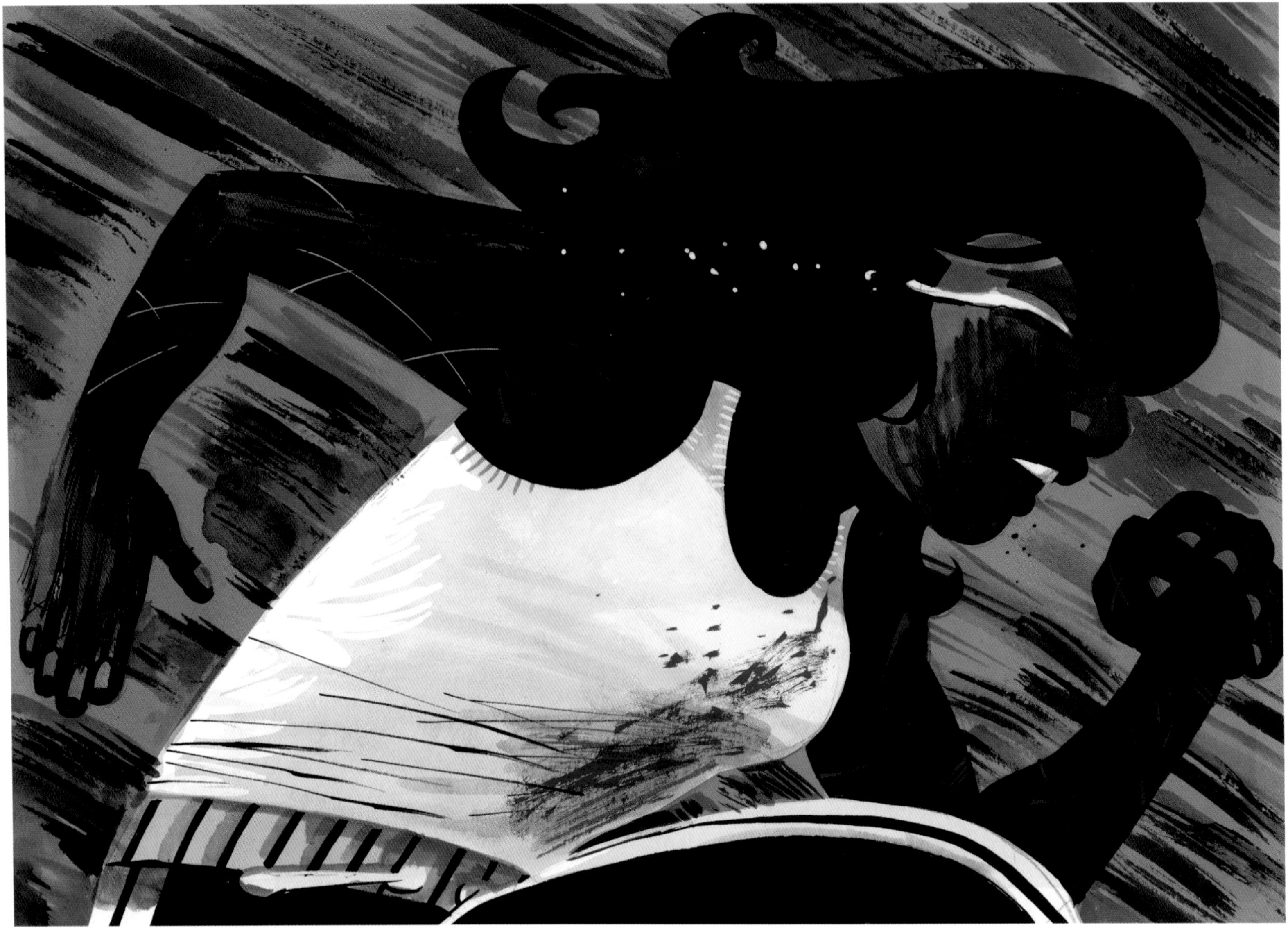

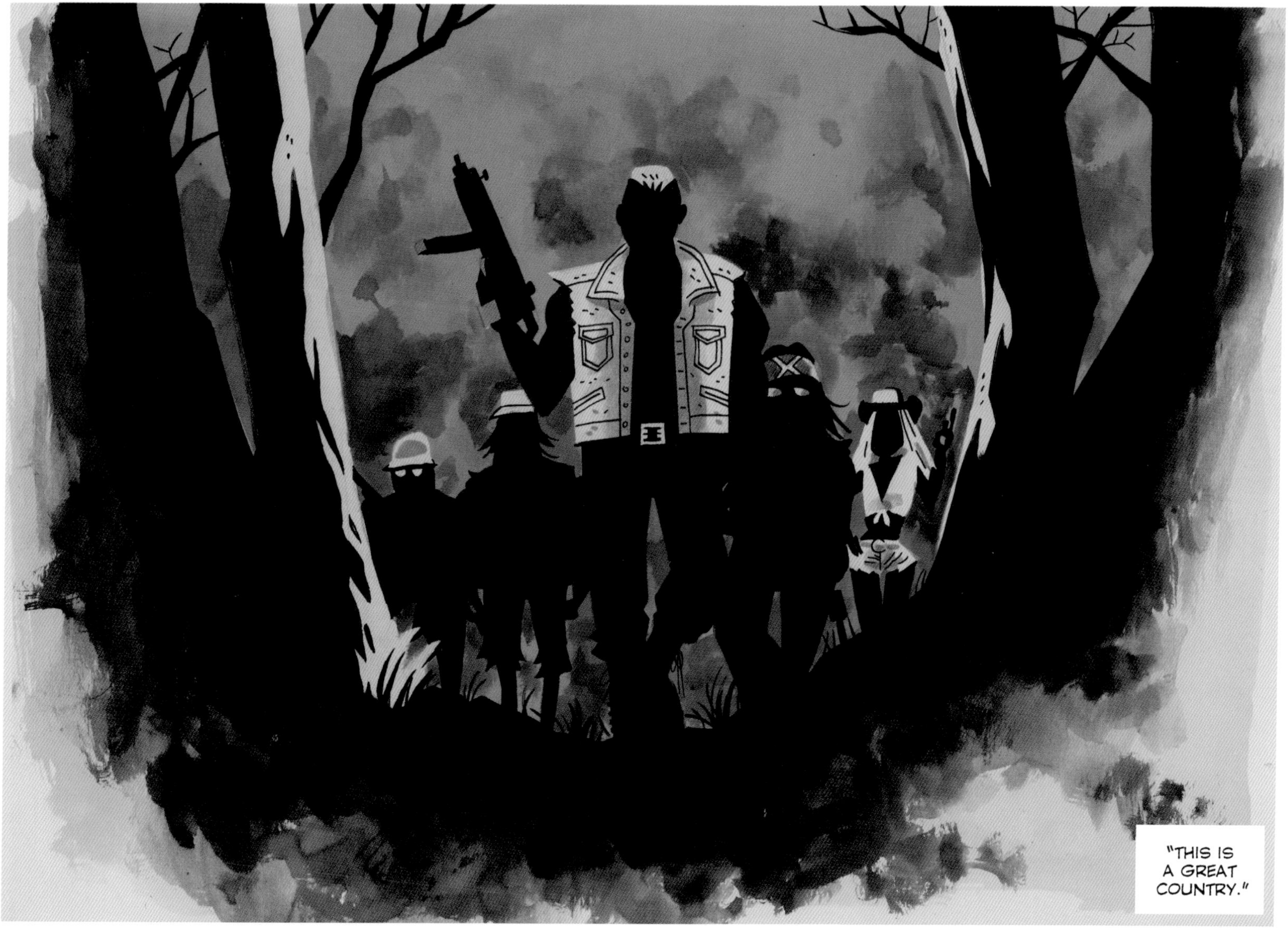
"THIS IS A GREAT COUNTRY."

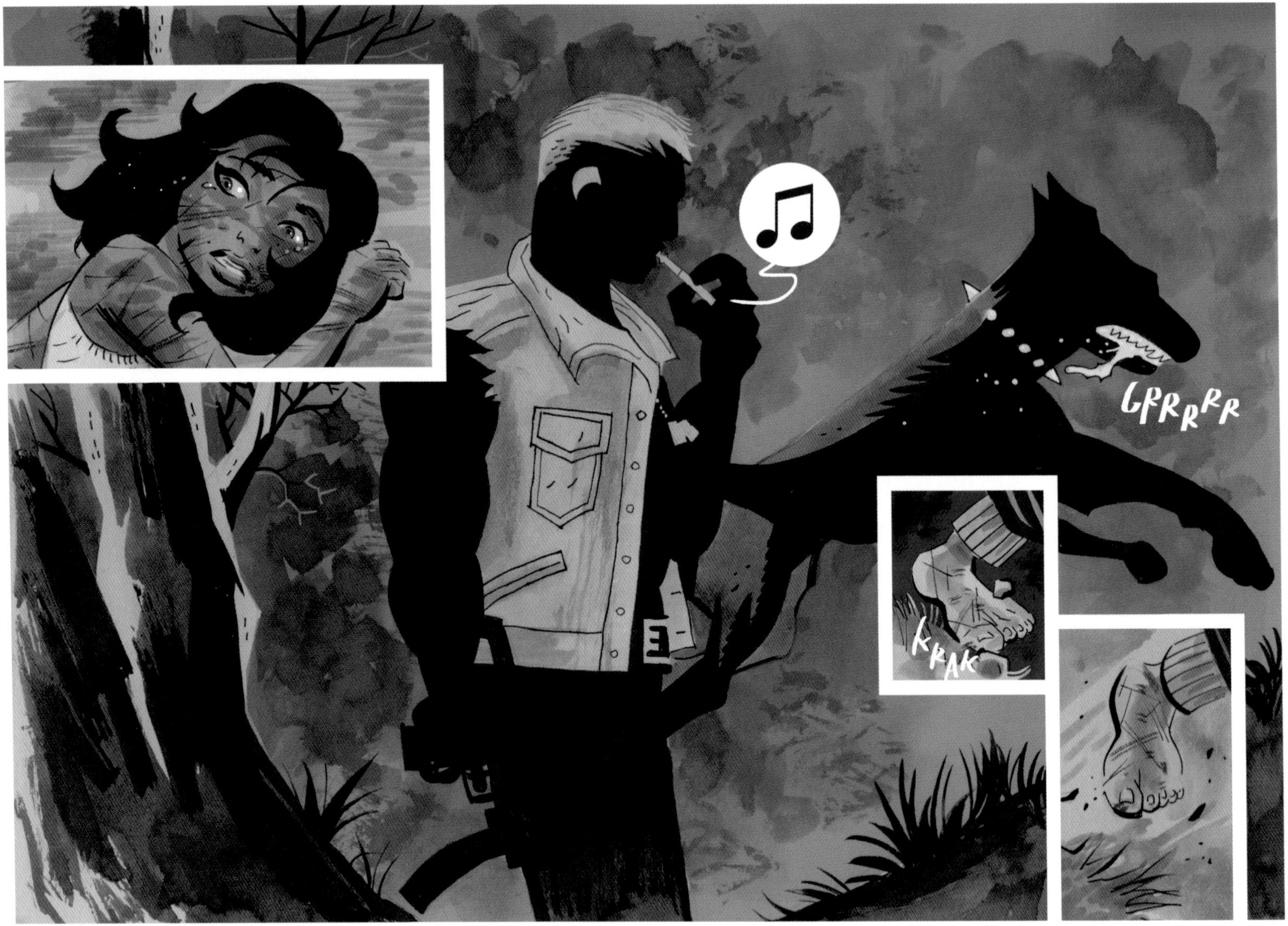
GRRRRR
KRAK

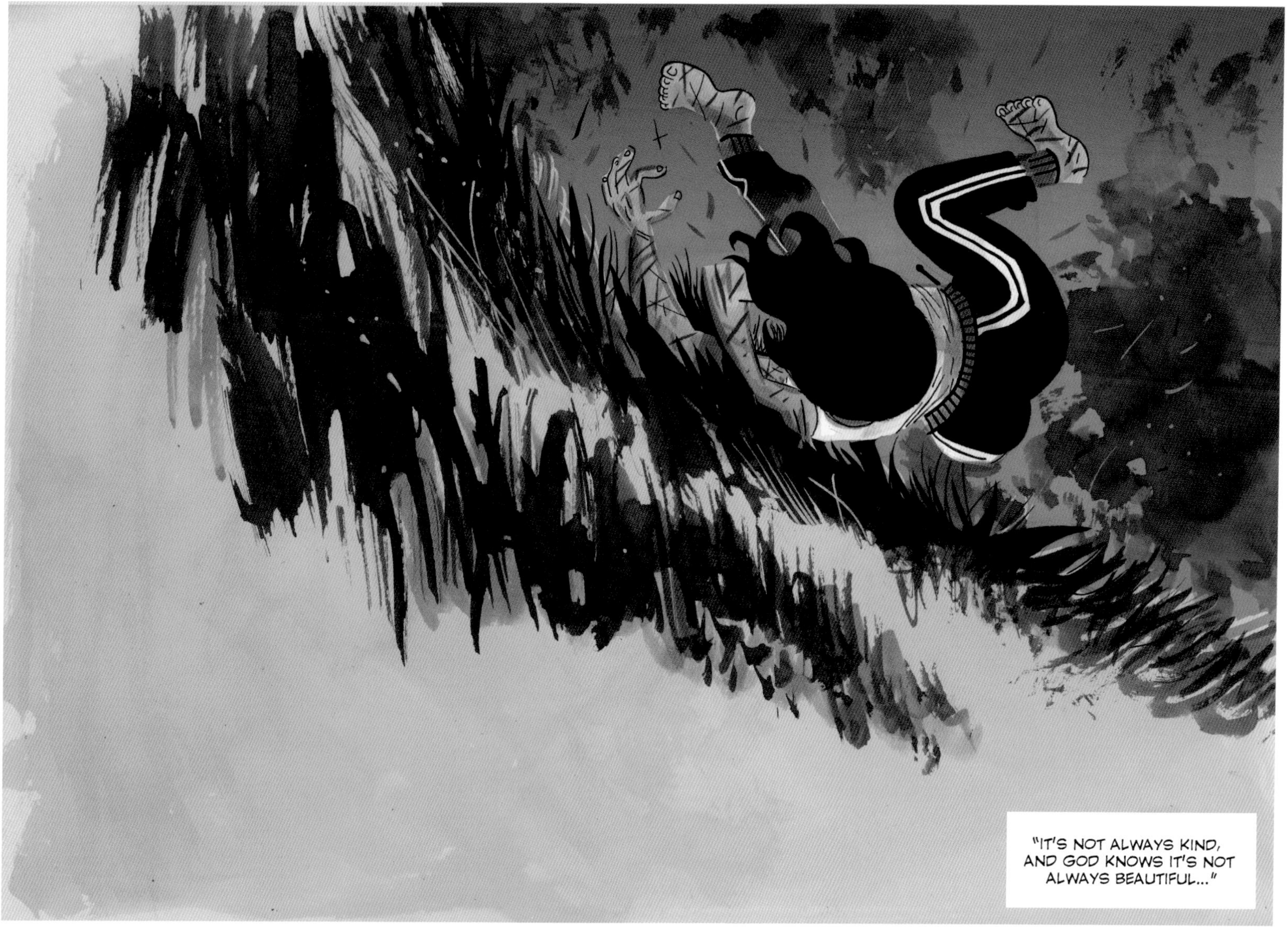
"IT'S NOT ALWAYS KIND,
AND GOD KNOWS IT'S NOT
ALWAYS BEAUTIFUL..."

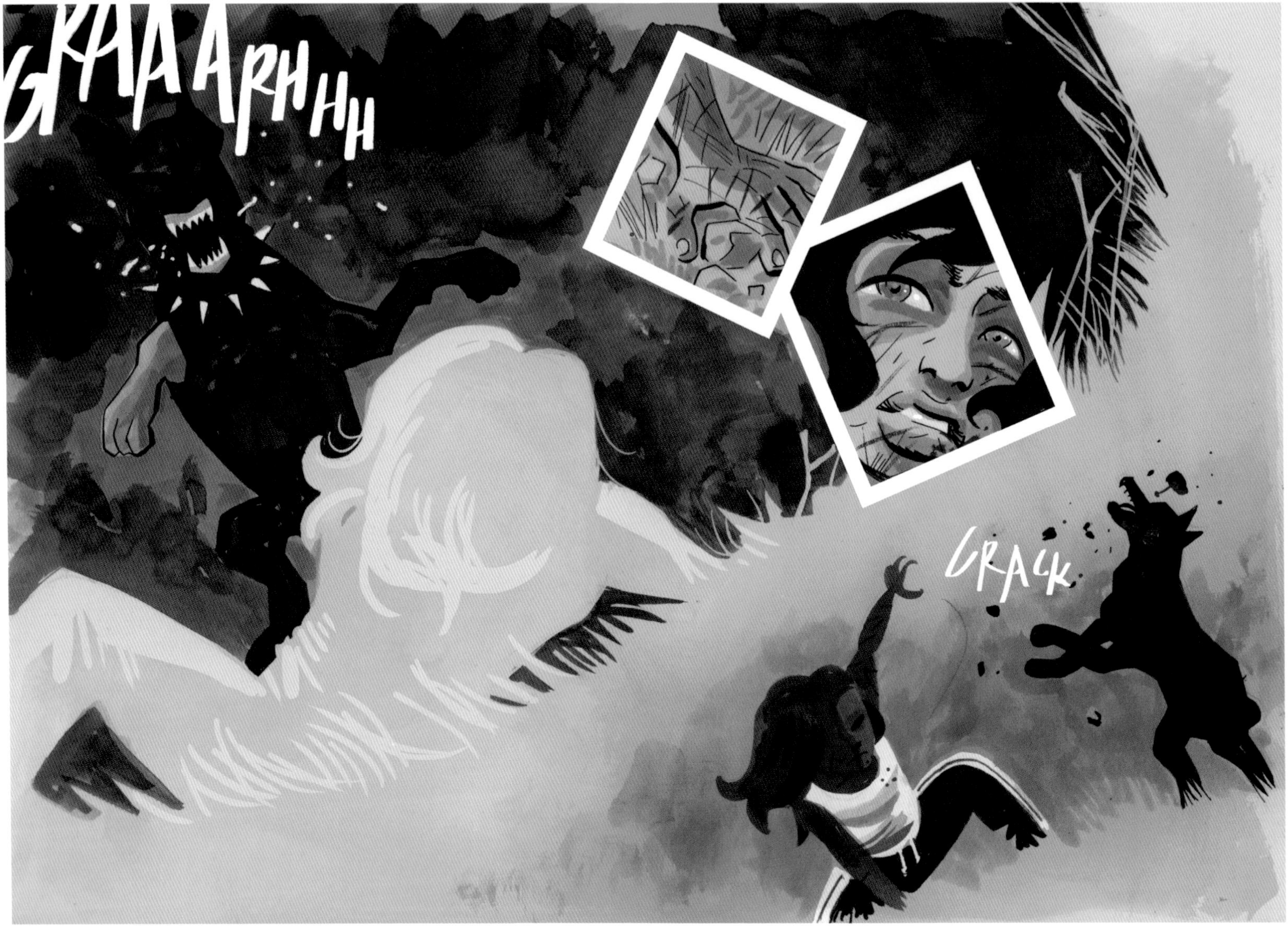
GRAAAARHHH
CRACK

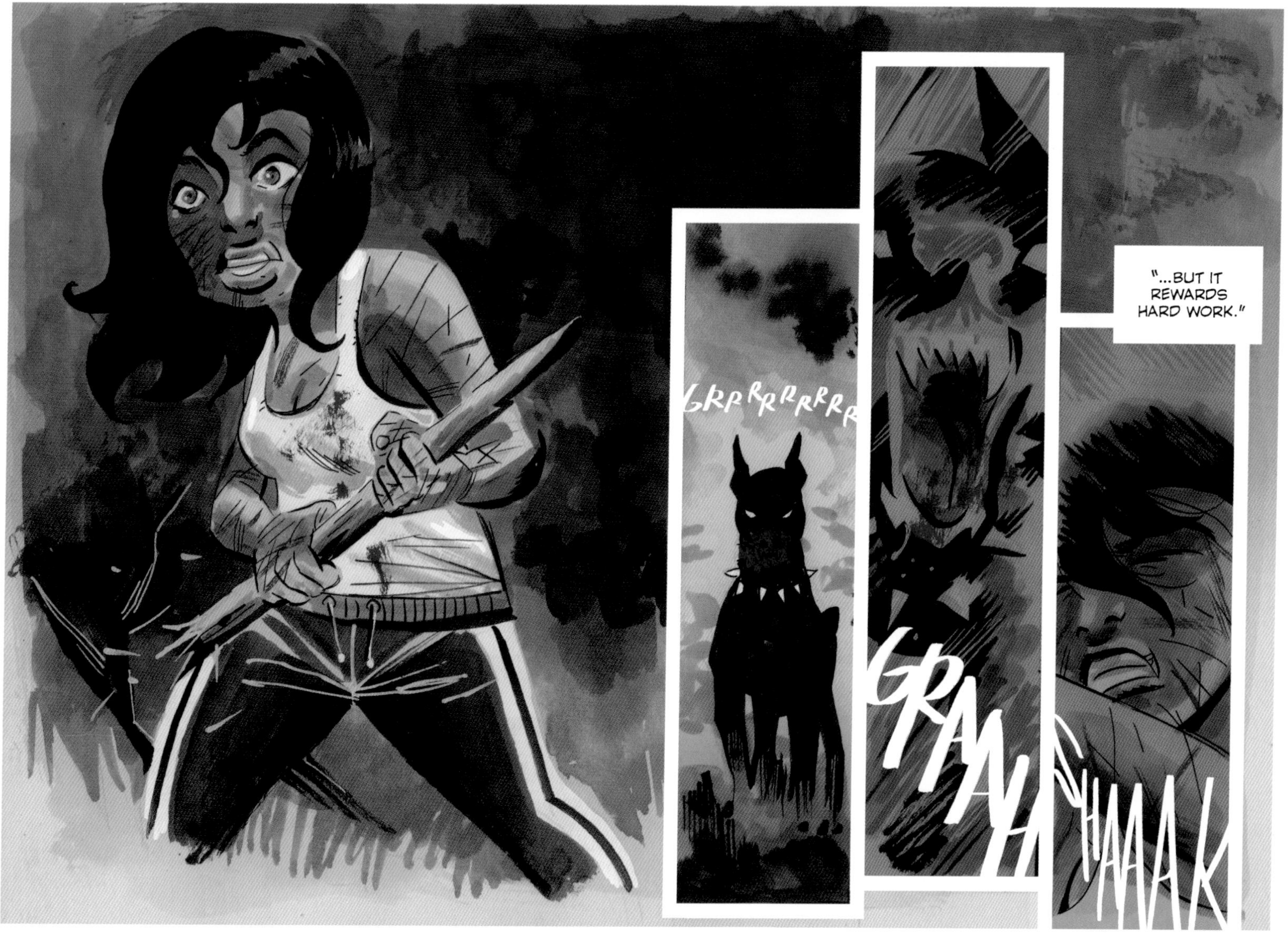

GRRRRRRRRR
GRAAAH
"...BUT IT REWARDS HARD WORK."
SHAAAK

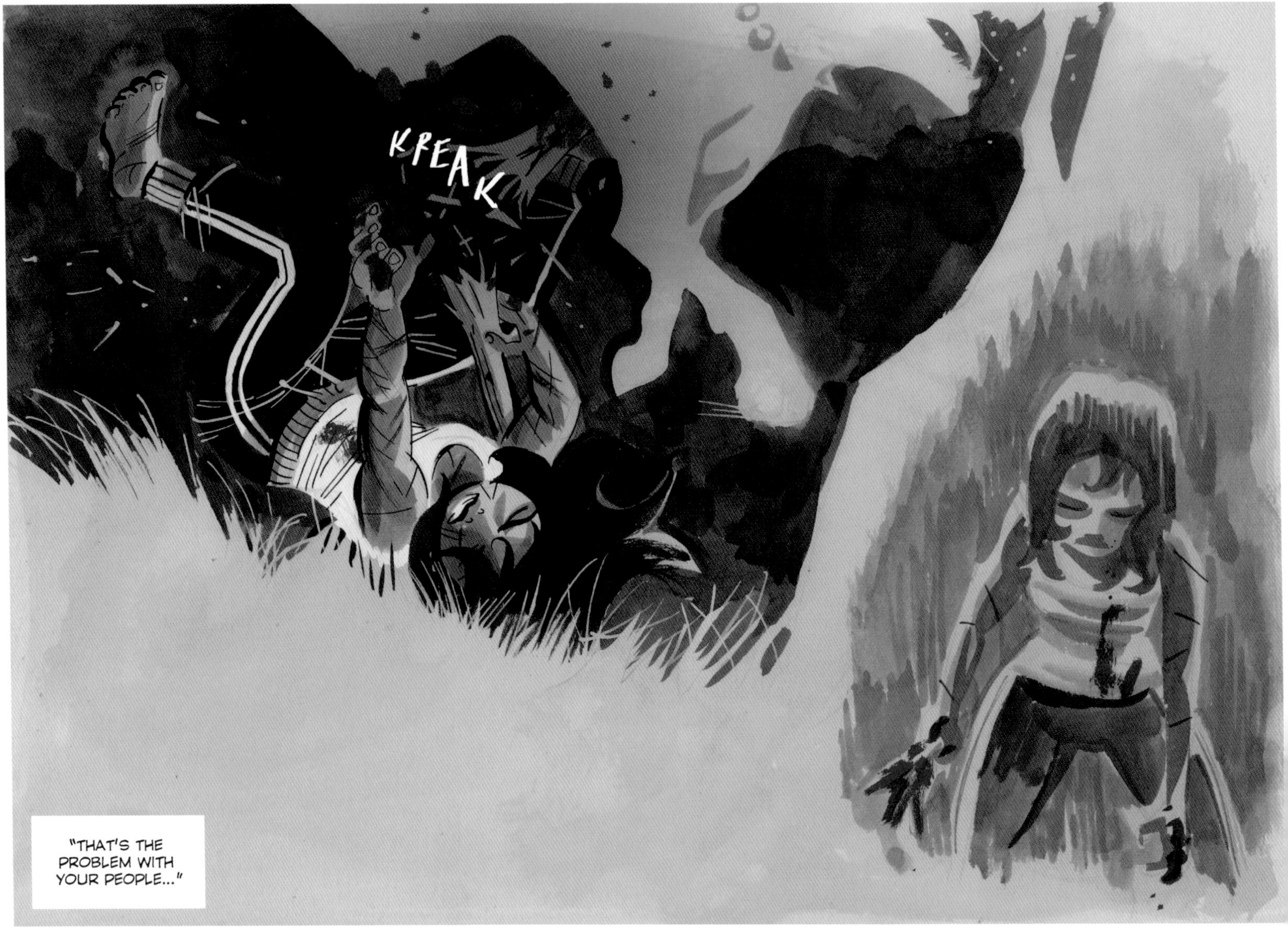
KREAK
"THAT'S THE PROBLEM WITH YOUR PEOPLE..."

# CHAPTER 1

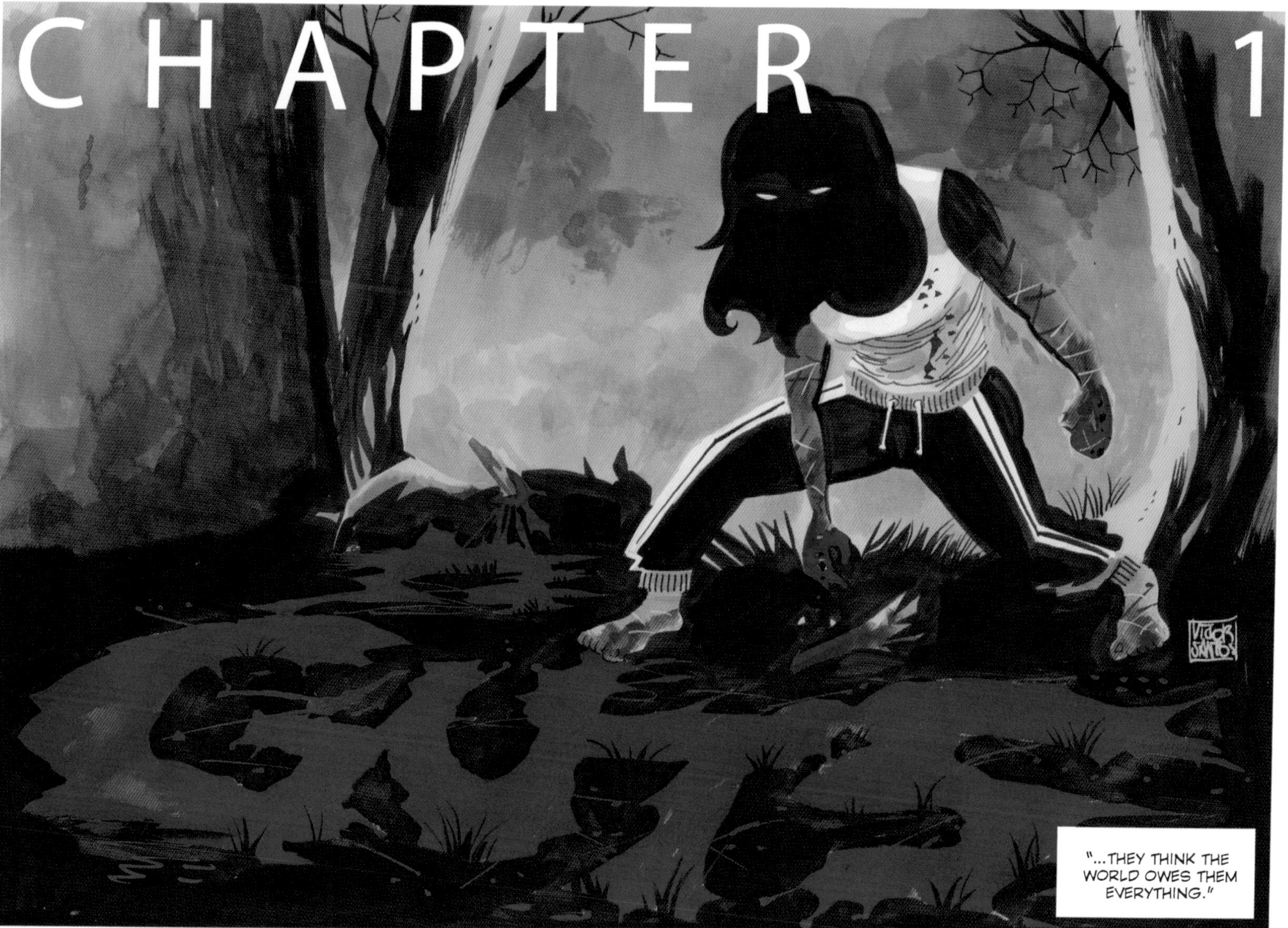
"...THEY THINK THE WORLD OWES THEM EVERYTHING."

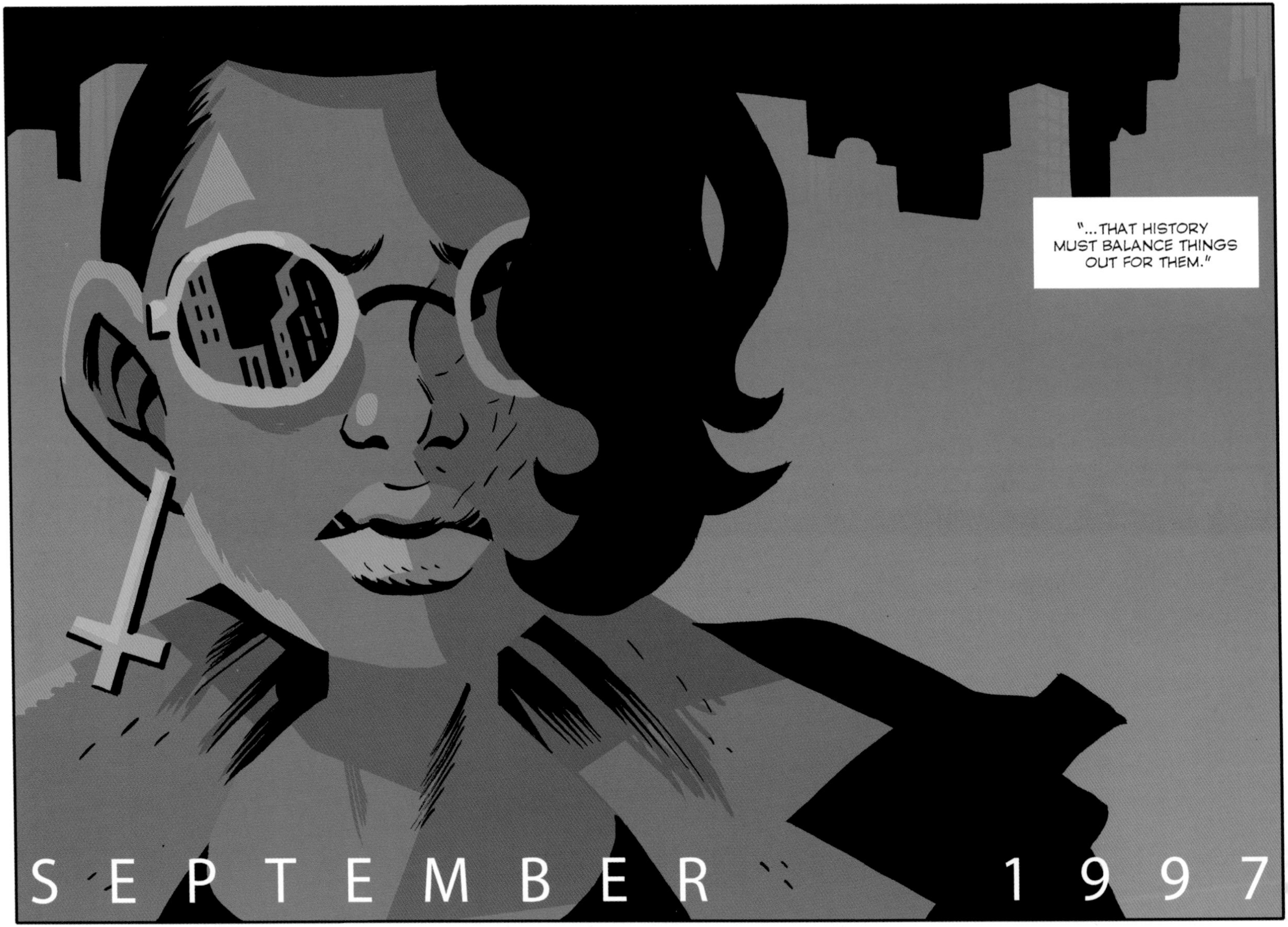
"...THAT HISTORY MUST BALANCE THINGS OUT FOR THEM."
SEPTEMBER 1997

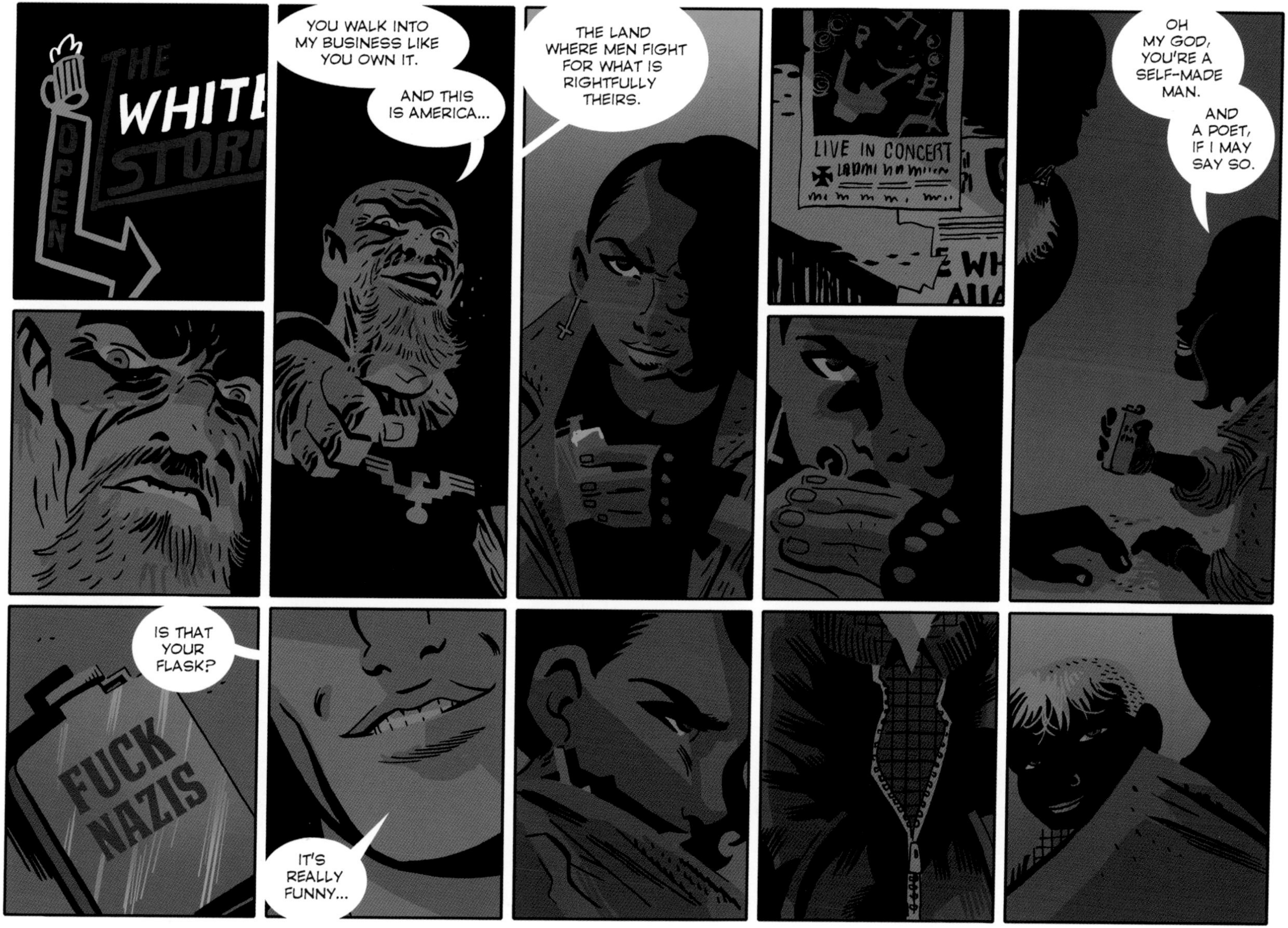
THE
WHITE
OPEN
YOU WALK INTO MY BUSINESS LIKE YOU OWN IT.
AND THIS IS AMERICA...
THE LAND WHERE MEN FIGHT FOR WHAT IS RIGHTFULLY THEIRS.
LIVE IN CONCERT
OH MY GOD, YOU'RE A SELF-MADE MAN.
AND A POET, IF I MAY SAY SO.
IS THAT YOUR FLASK?
FUCK NAZIS
IT'S REALLY FUNNY...

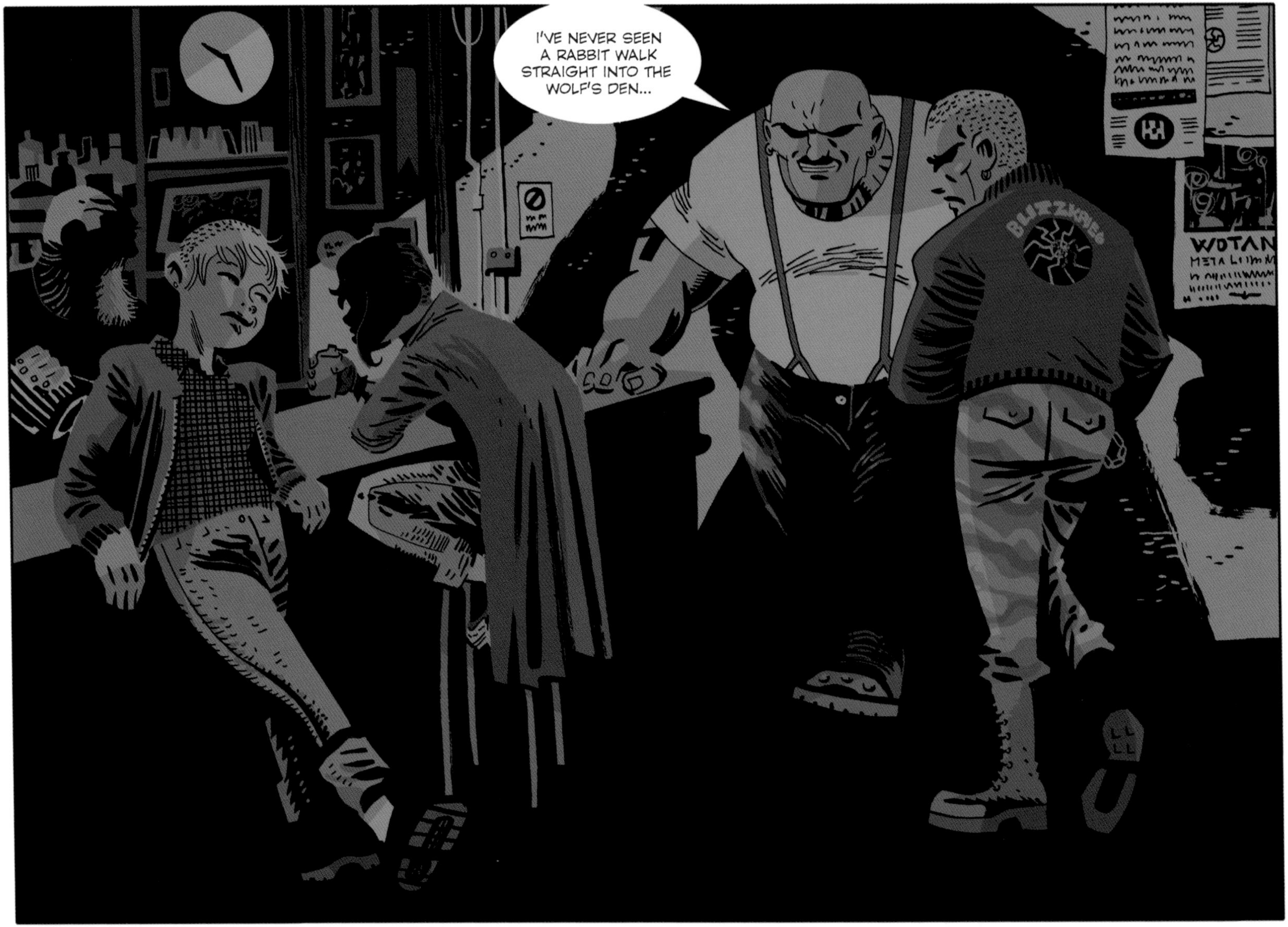
I'VE NEVER SEEN A RABBIT WALK STRAIGHT INTO THE WOLF'S DEN...
WOTAN

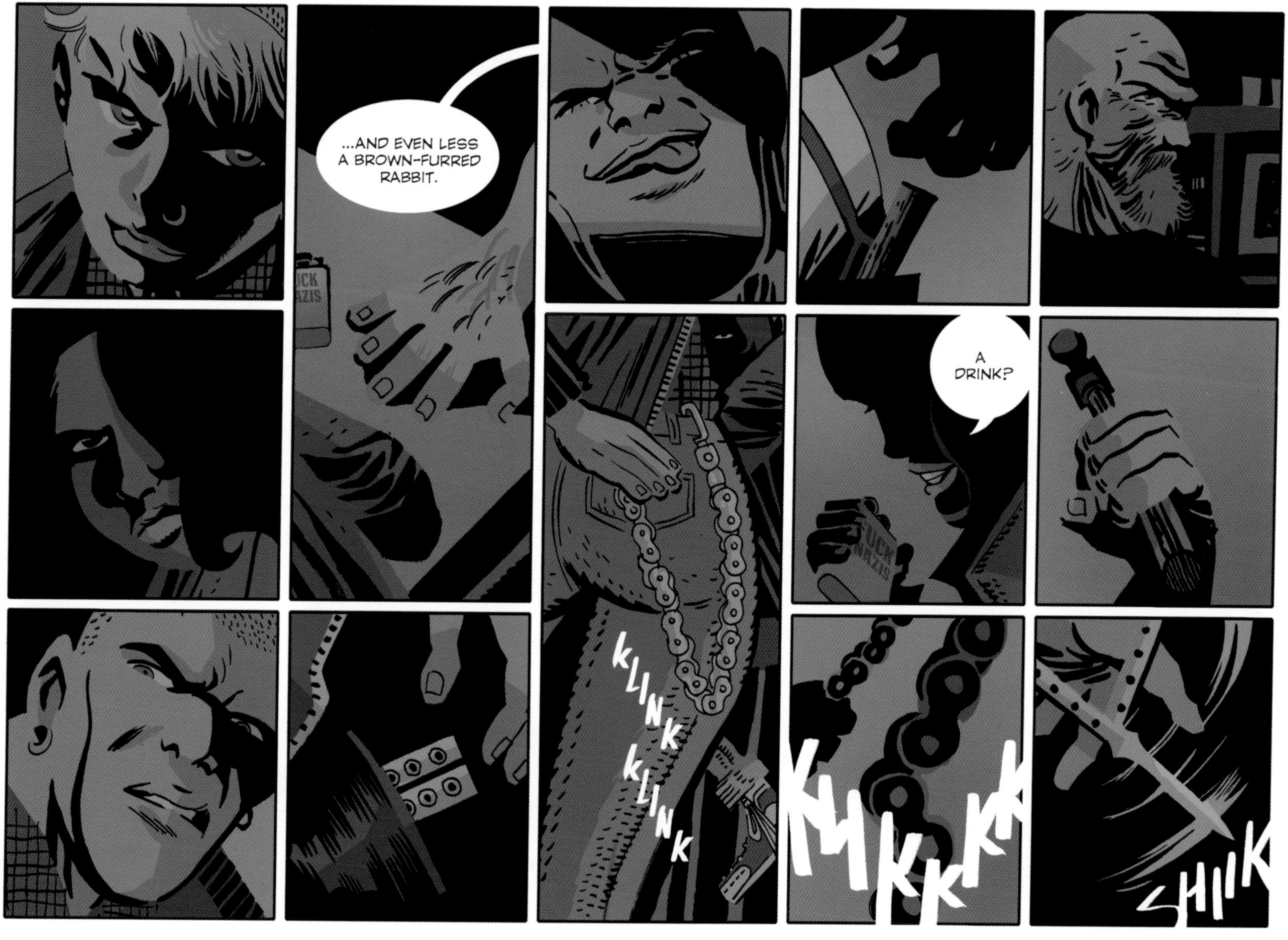
...AND EVEN LESS A BROWN-FURRED RABBIT.
A DRINK?
KLINK KLINK KLINK
SHIIK

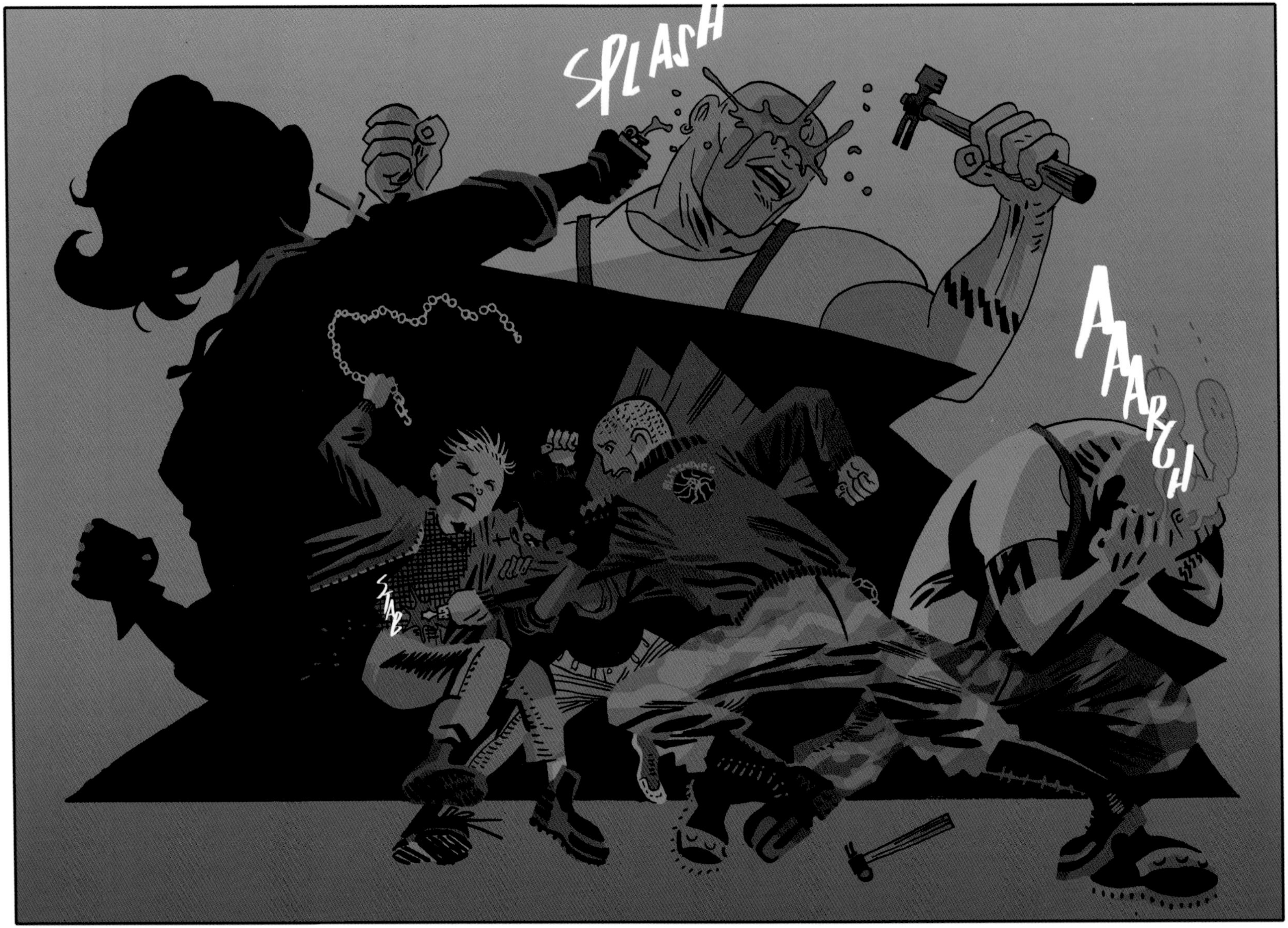
SPLASH
AAARGH
STAB

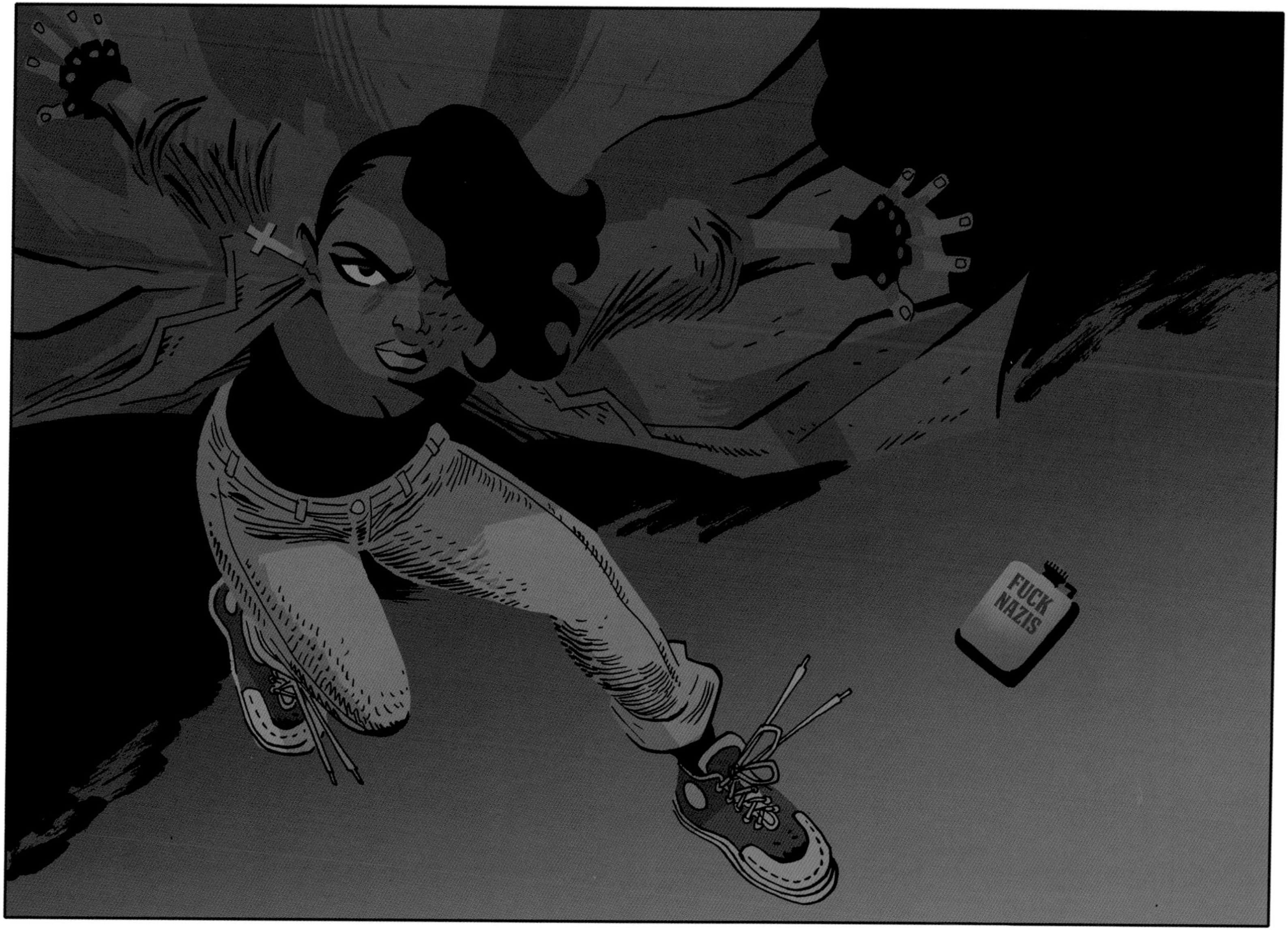
FUCK
NAZIS

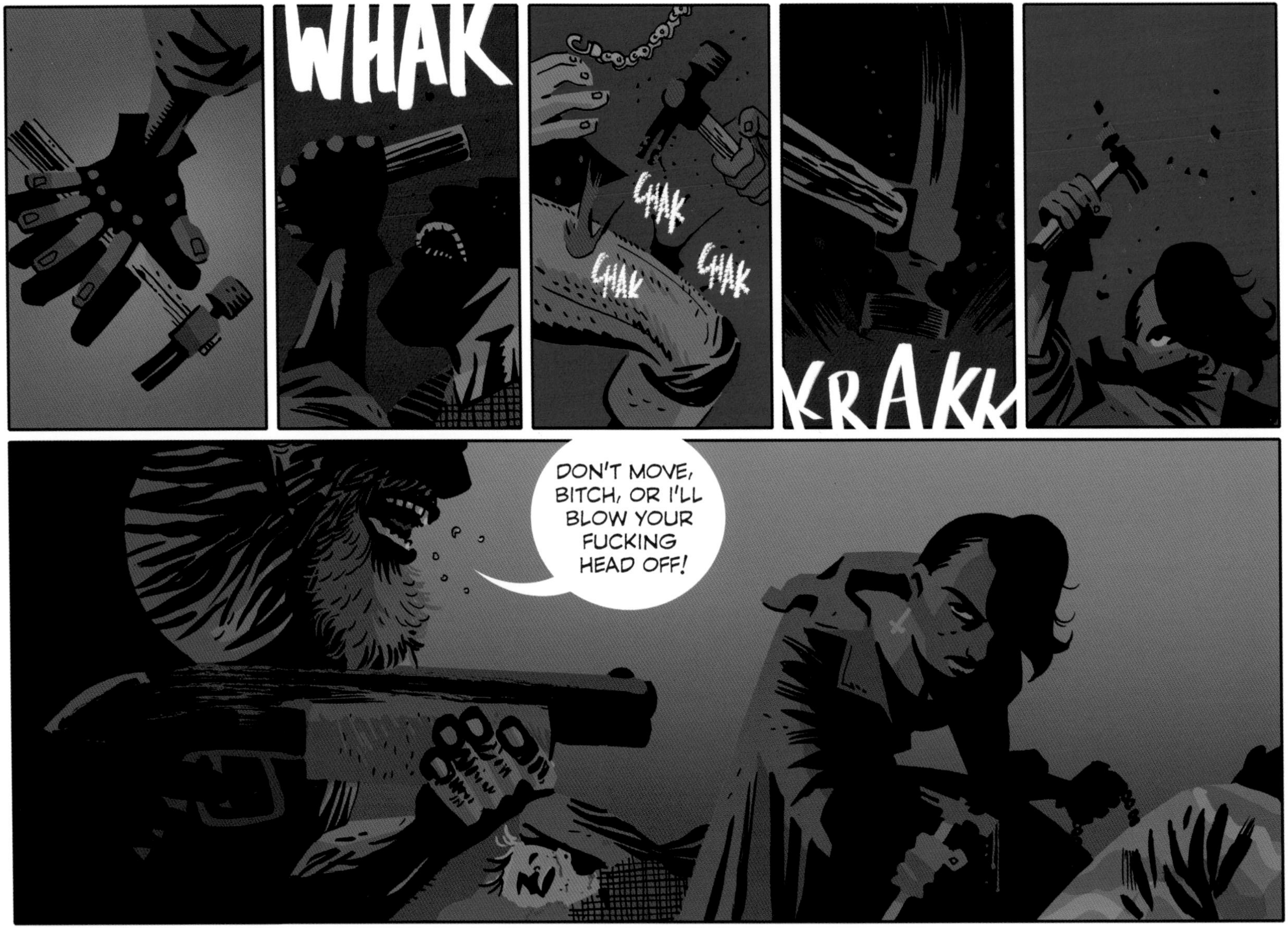
WHAK
CHAK
CHAK
CHAK
KRAKK
DON'T MOVE, BITCH, OR I'LL BLOW YOUR FUCKING HEAD OFF!

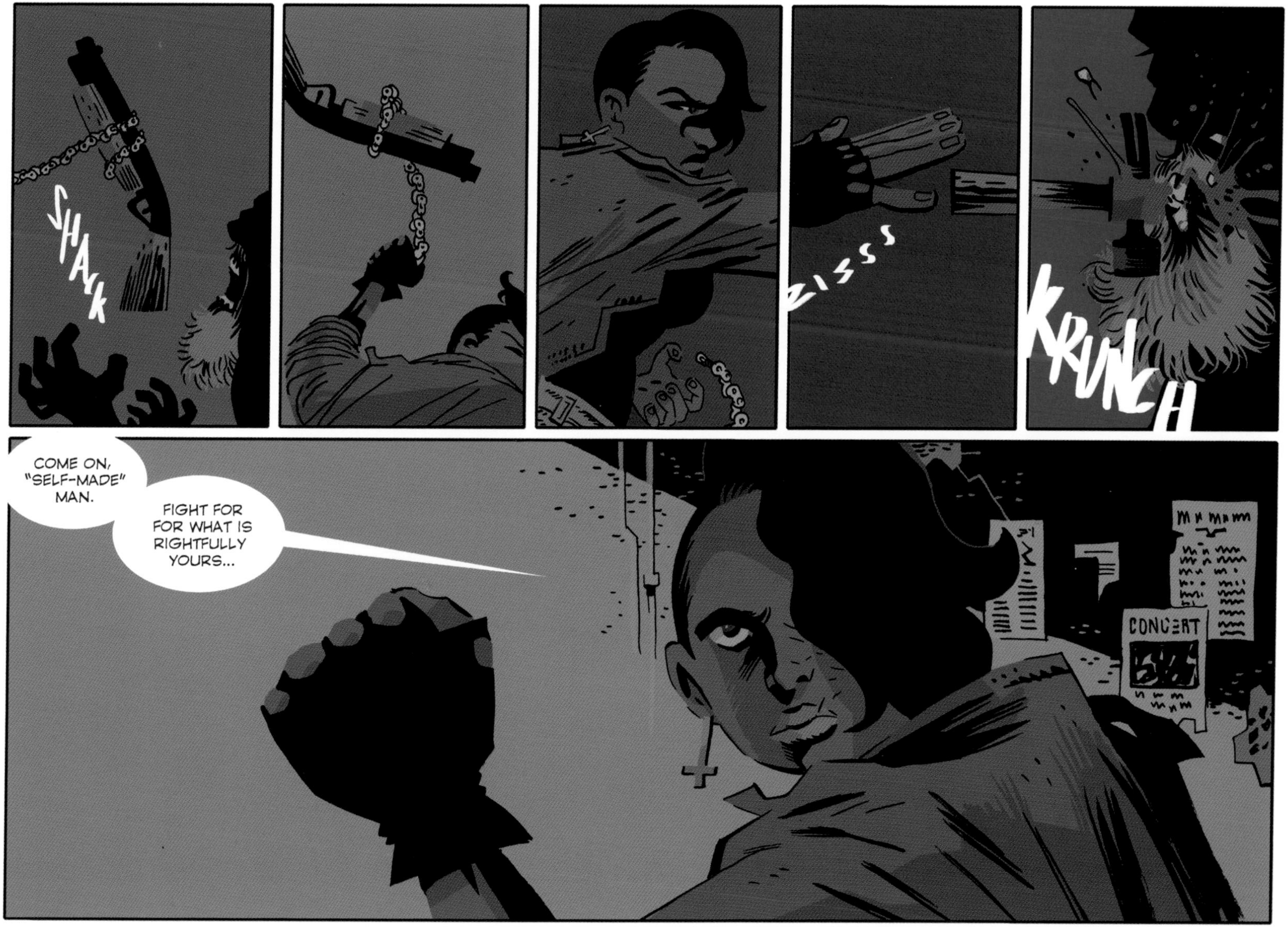
SHACK
ZISSS
KRUNCH
COME ON, "SELF-MADE" MAN.
FIGHT FOR FOR WHAT IS RIGHTFULLY YOURS...
CONCERT

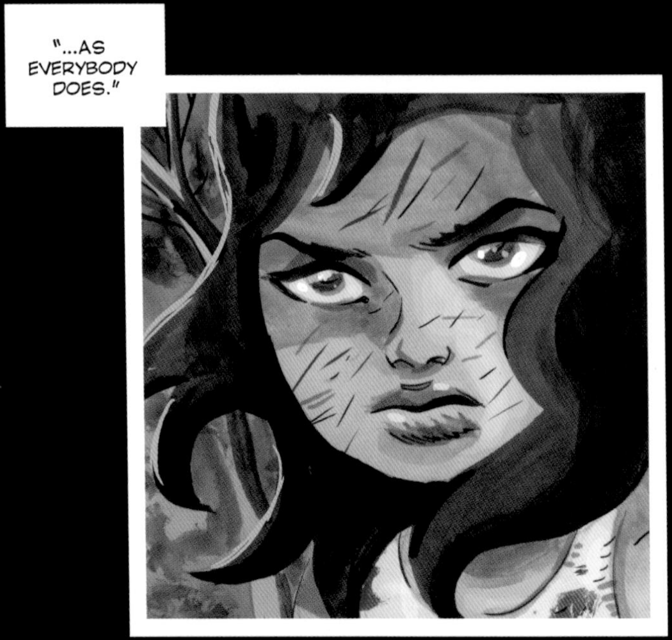
"...AS EVERYBODY DOES."

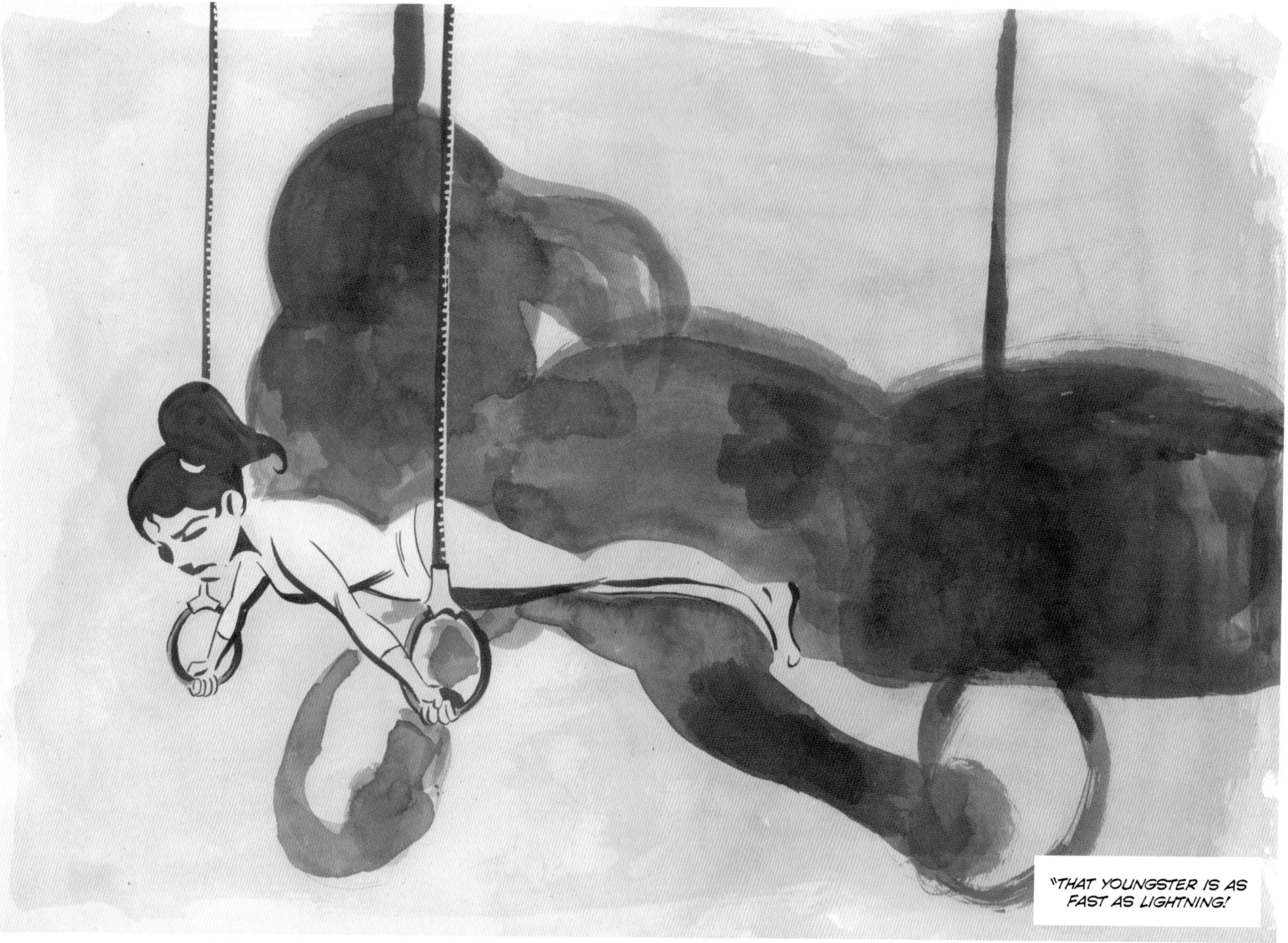
"THAT YOUNGSTER IS AS FAST AS LIGHTNING!

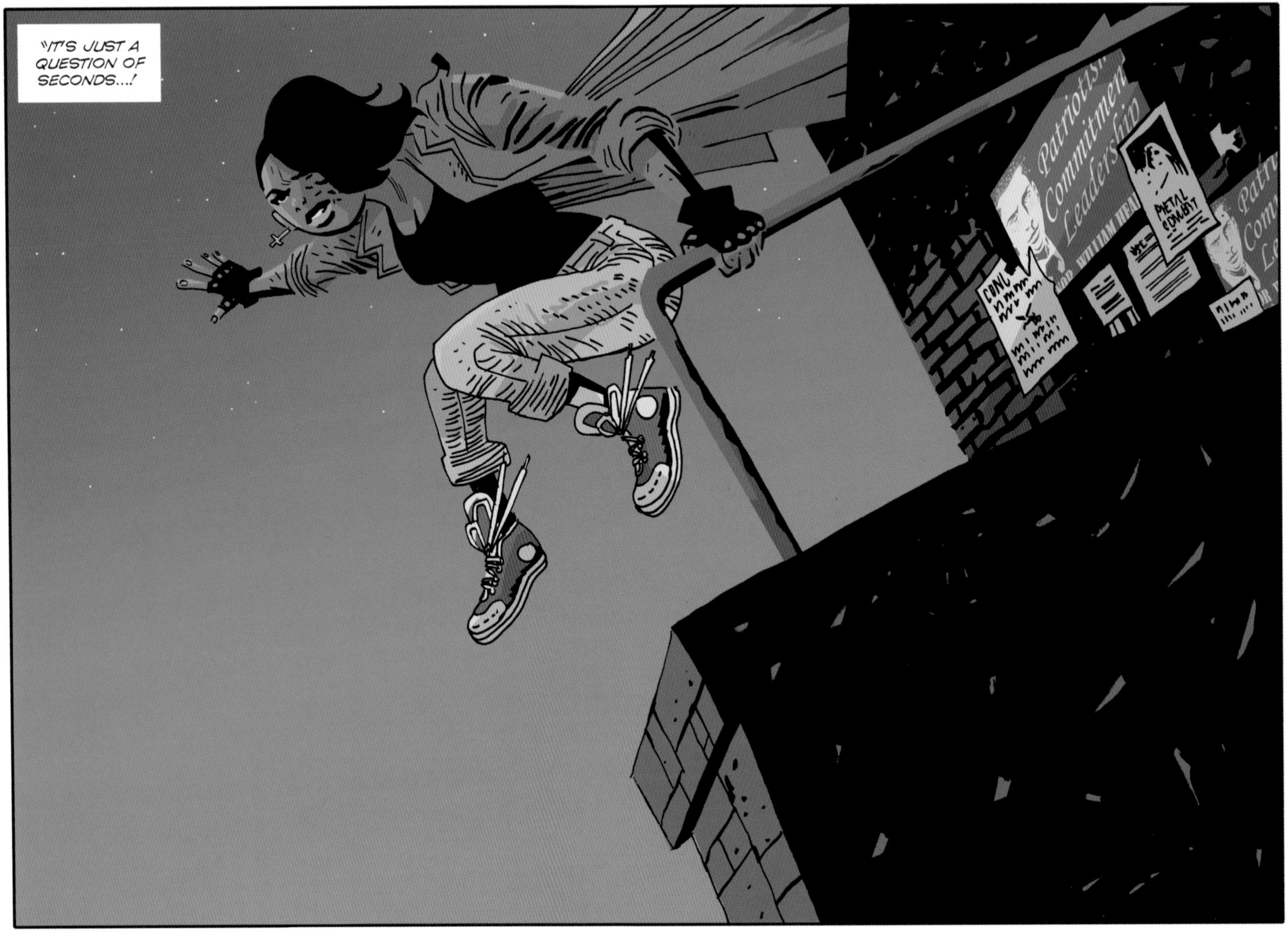
"IT'S JUST A QUESTION OF SECONDS...!
Leadership
WILLIAM

# CHAPTER 2

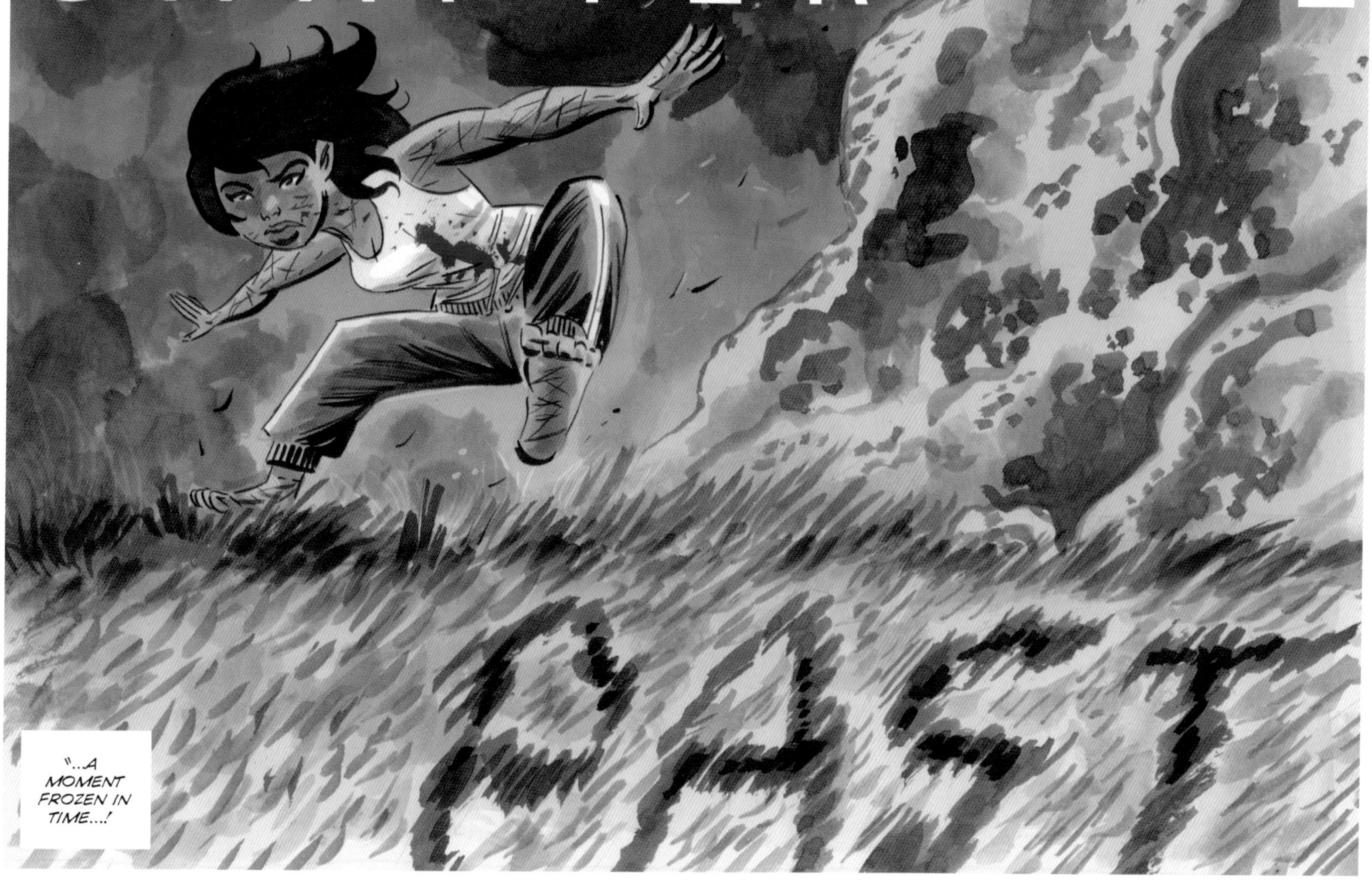
"...A MOMENT FROZEN IN TIME...!
PAST

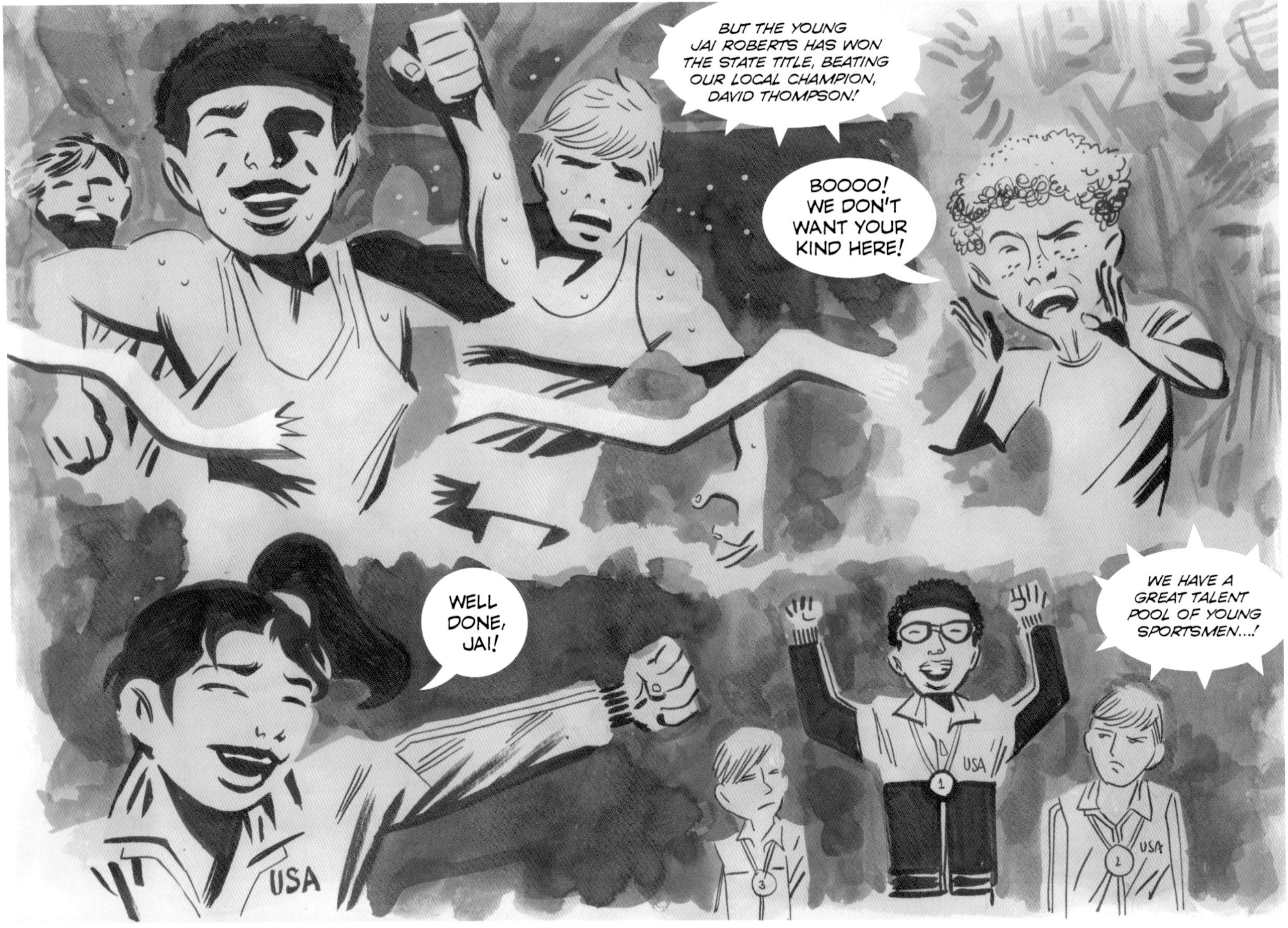
BUT THE YOUNG JAI ROBERTS HAS WON THE STATE TITLE, BEATING OUR LOCAL CHAMPION, DAVID THOMPSON!
BOOOO! WE DON'T WANT YOUR KIND HERE!
WELL DONE, JAI!
USA
WE HAVE A GREAT TALENT POOL OF YOUNG SPORTSMEN...!
USA
USA
USA

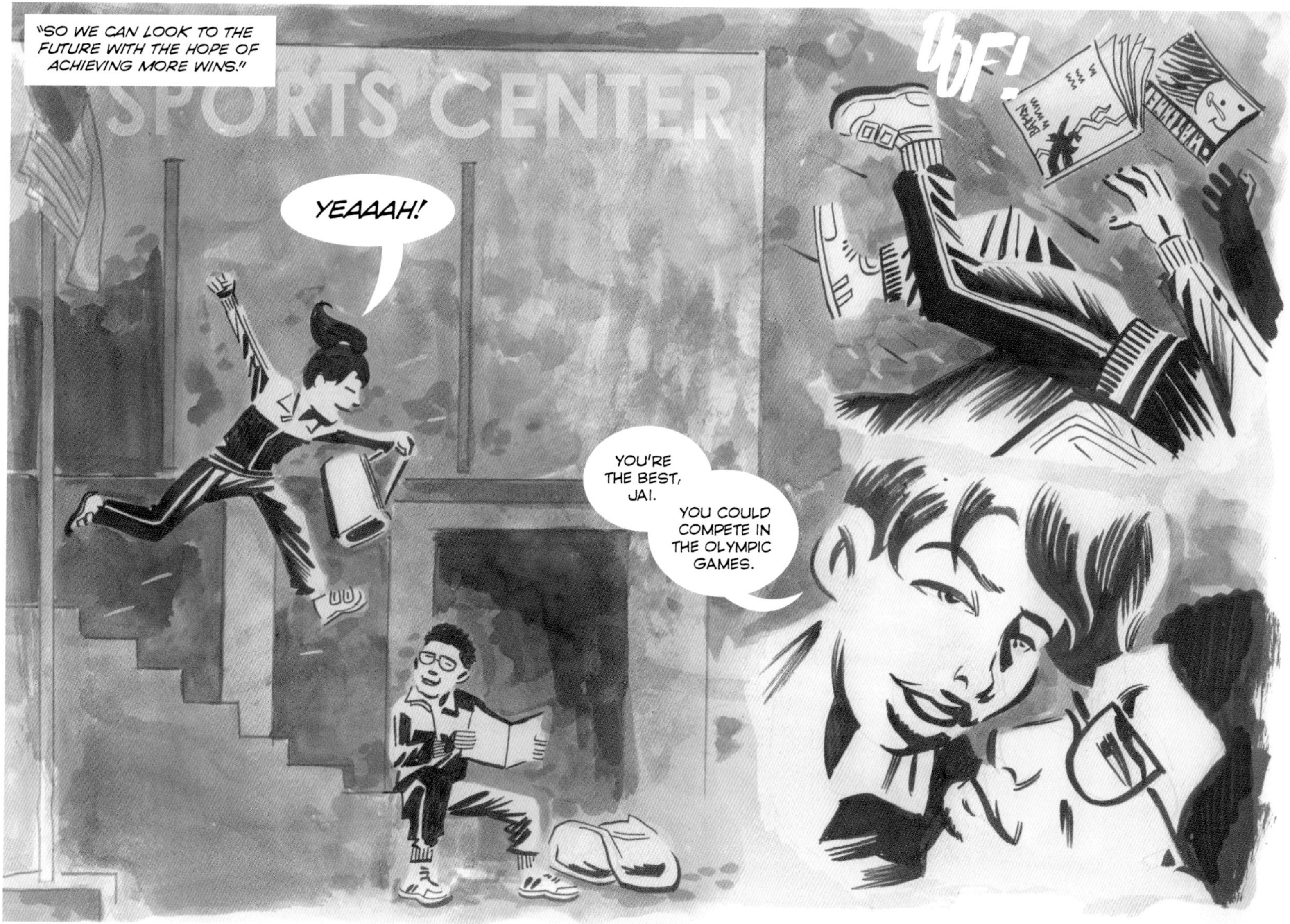
"SO WE CAN LOOK TO THE FUTURE WITH THE HOPE OF ACHIEVING MORE WINS."
SPORTS CENTER
YEAAAH!
OOF!
YOU'RE THE BEST, JAI.
YOU COULD COMPETE IN THE OLYMPIC GAMES.

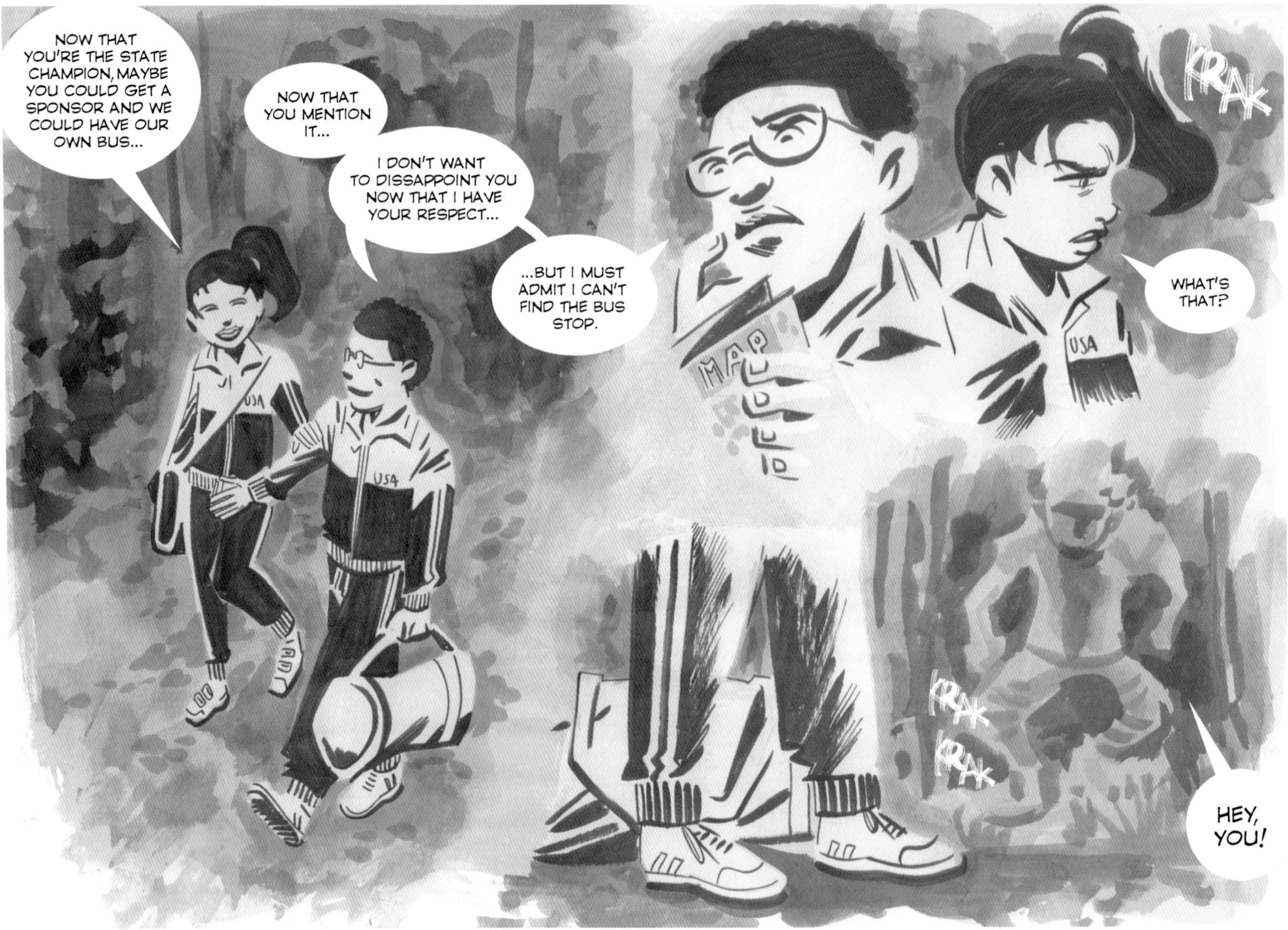
NOW THAT YOU'RE THE STATE CHAMPION, MAYBE YOU COULD GET A SPONSOR AND WE COULD HAVE OUR OWN BUS...
NOW THAT YOU MENTION IT...
I DON'T WANT TO DISSAPPOINT YOU NOW THAT I HAVE YOUR RESPECT...
...BUT I MUST ADMIT I CAN'T FIND THE BUS STOP.
MAP
KRAK
WHAT'S THAT?
KRAK
KRAK
HEY, YOU!

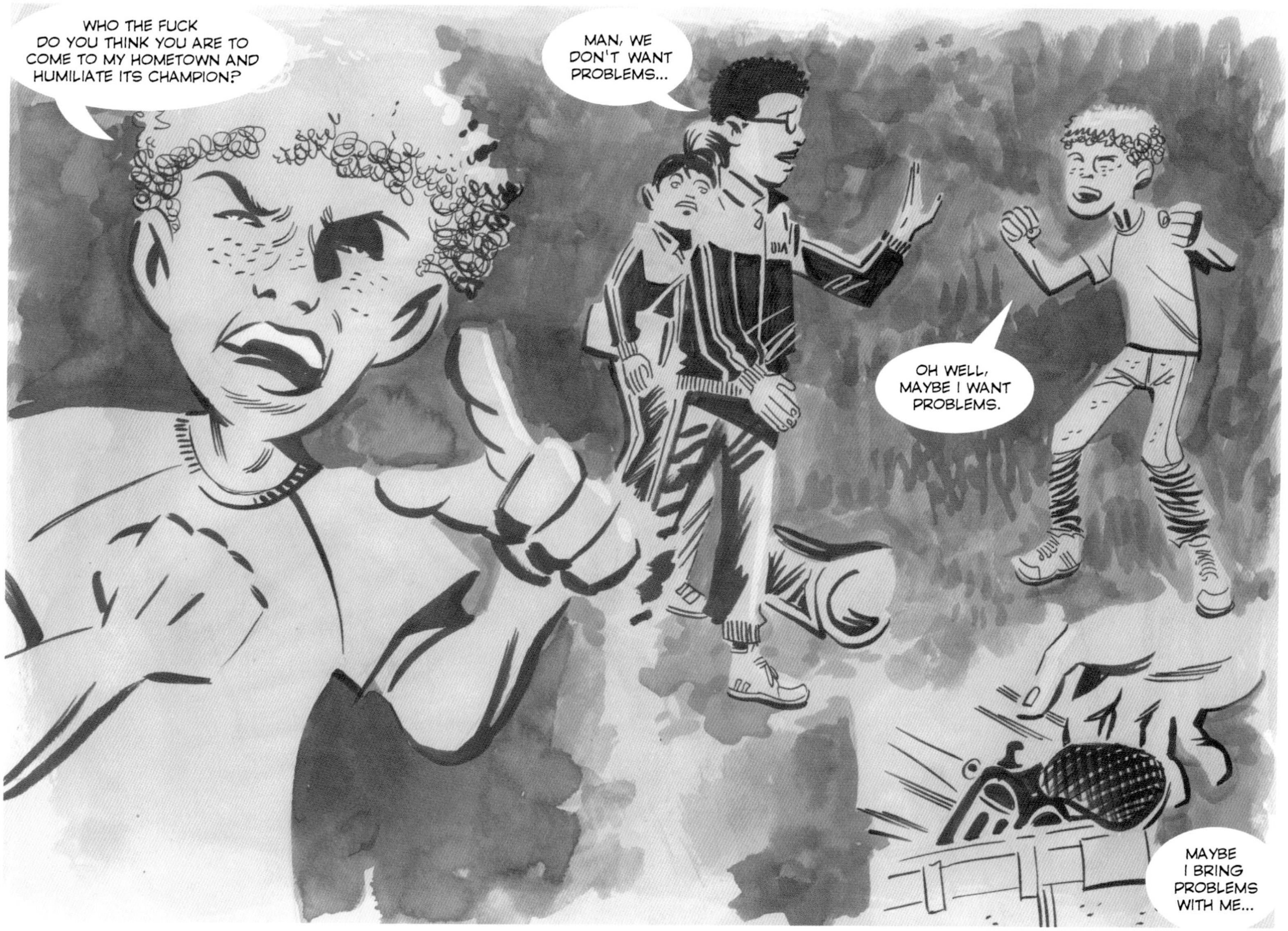
WHO THE FUCK DO YOU THINK YOU ARE TO COME TO MY HOMETOWN AND HUMILIATE ITS CHAMPION?
MAN, WE DON'T WANT PROBLEMS...
OH WELL, MAYBE I WANT PROBLEMS.
MAYBE I BRING PROBLEMS WITH ME...

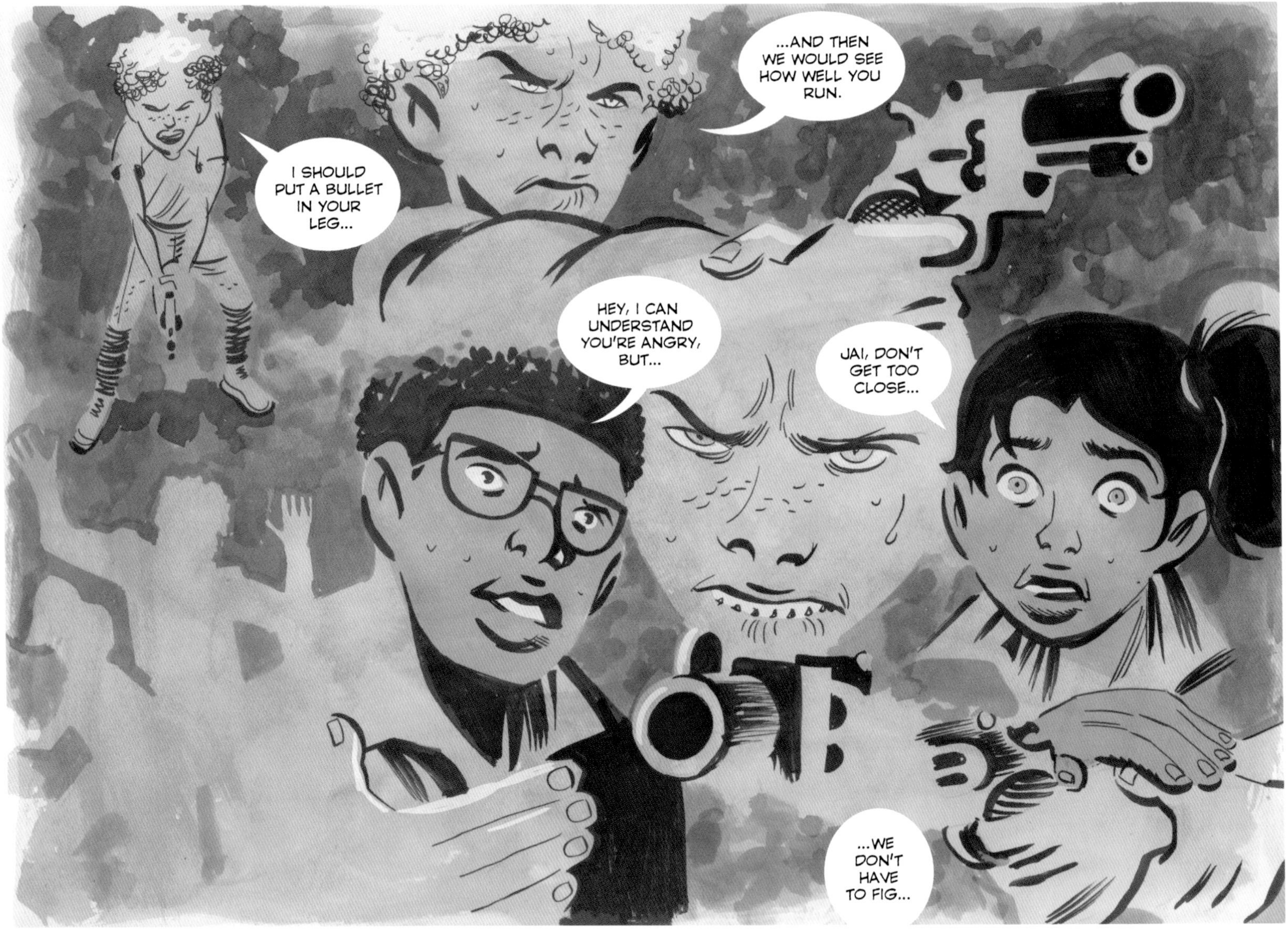
I SHOULD PUT A BULLET IN YOUR LEG...
...AND THEN WE WOULD SEE HOW WELL YOU RUN.
HEY, I CAN UNDERSTAND YOU'RE ANGRY, BUT...
JAI, DON'T GET TOO CLOSE...
...WE DON'T HAVE TO FIG...

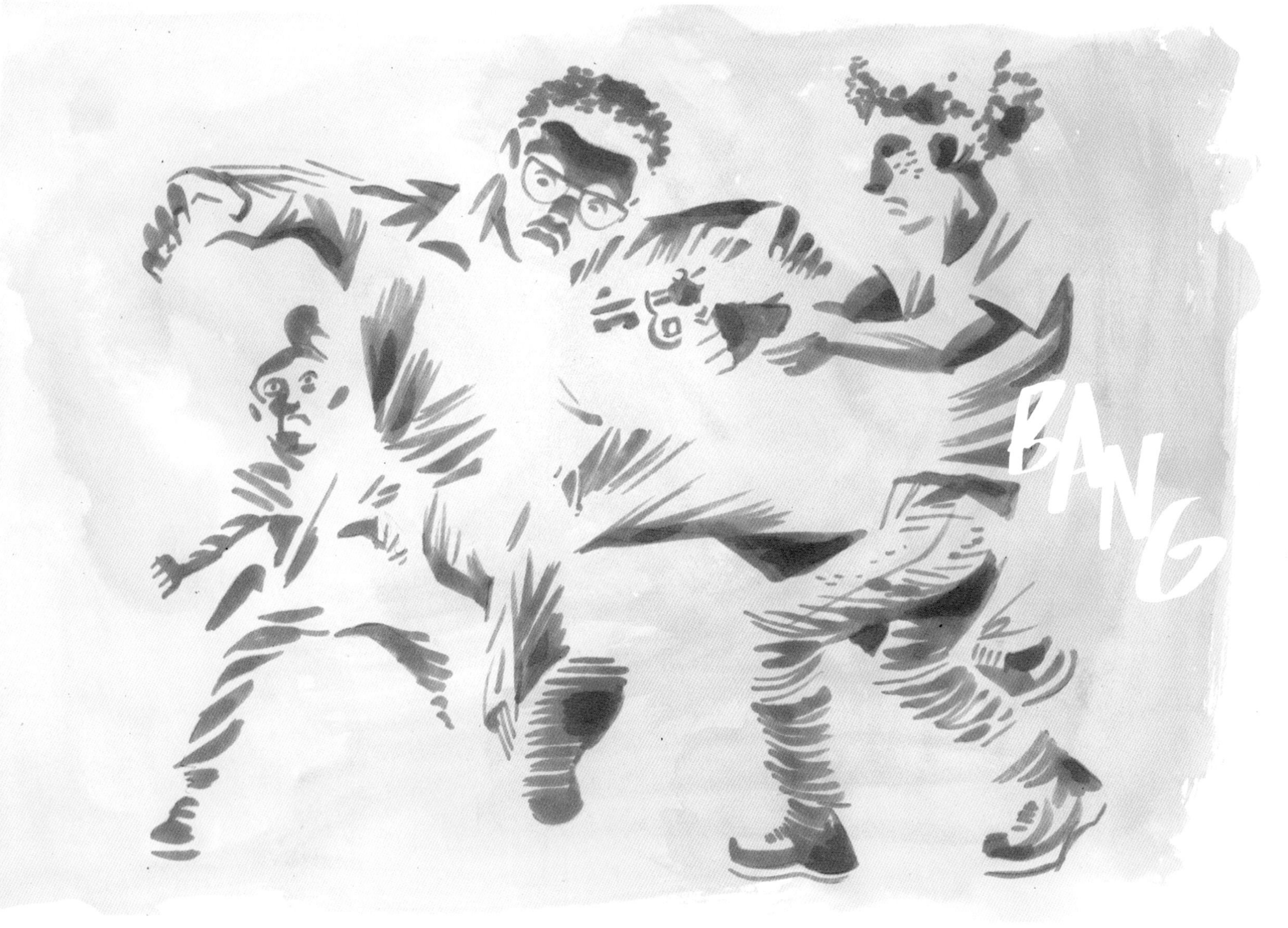
BANG

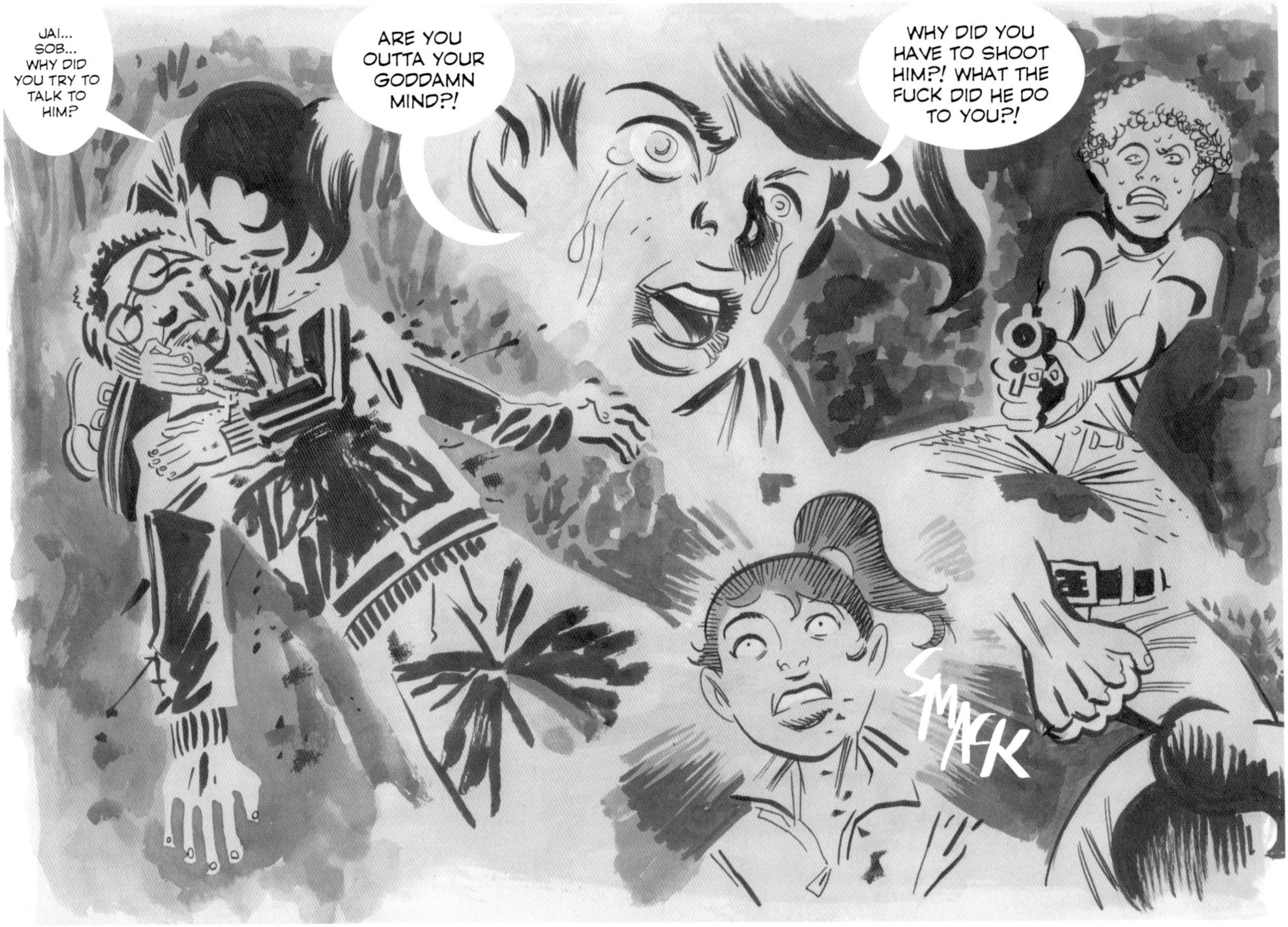
JAI... SOB... WHY DID YOU TRY TO TALK TO HIM?
ARE YOU OUTTA YOUR GODDAMN MIND?!
WHY DID YOU HAVE TO SHOOT HIM?! WHAT THE FUCK DID HE DO TO YOU?!
SMACK

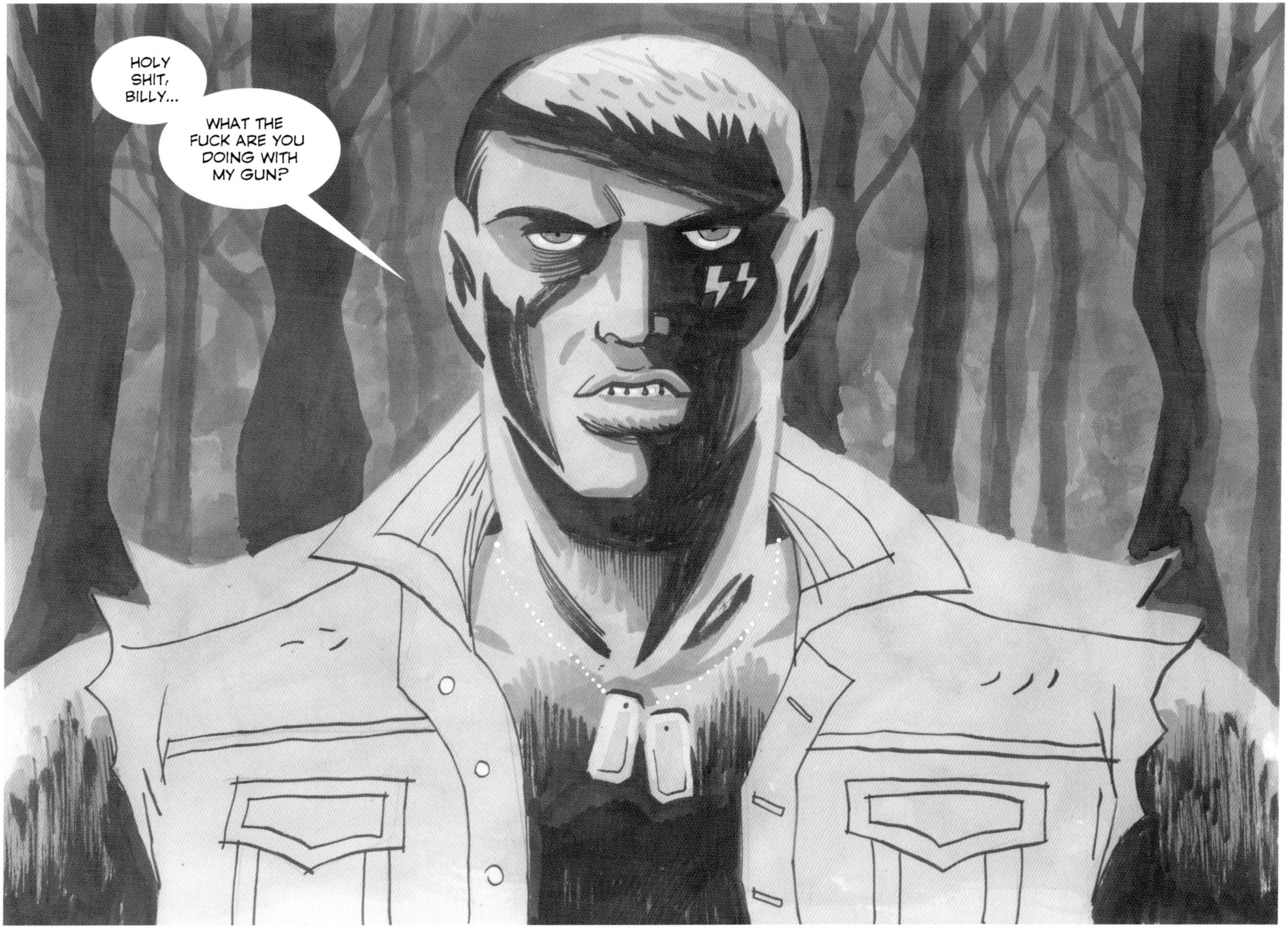
HOLY SHIT, BILLY...
WHAT THE FUCK ARE YOU DOING WITH MY GUN?

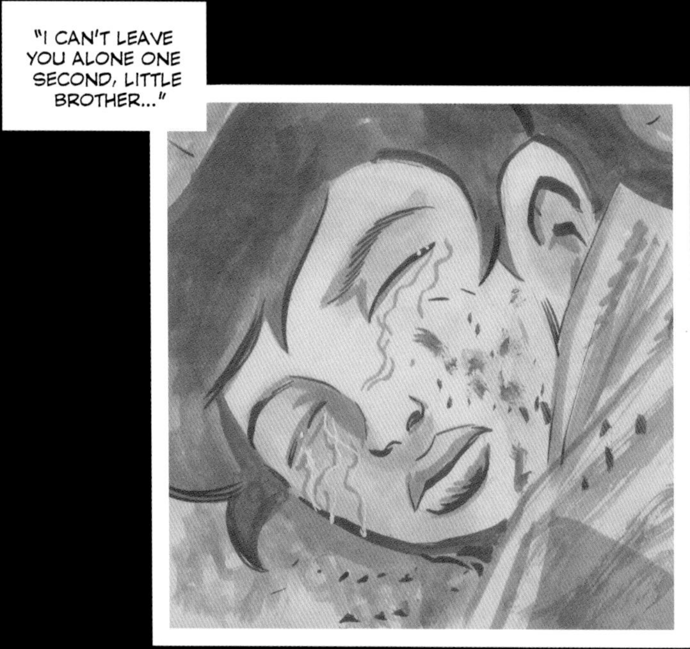
"I CAN'T LEAVE YOU ALONE ONE SECOND, LITTLE BROTHER..."

# CHAPTER 3

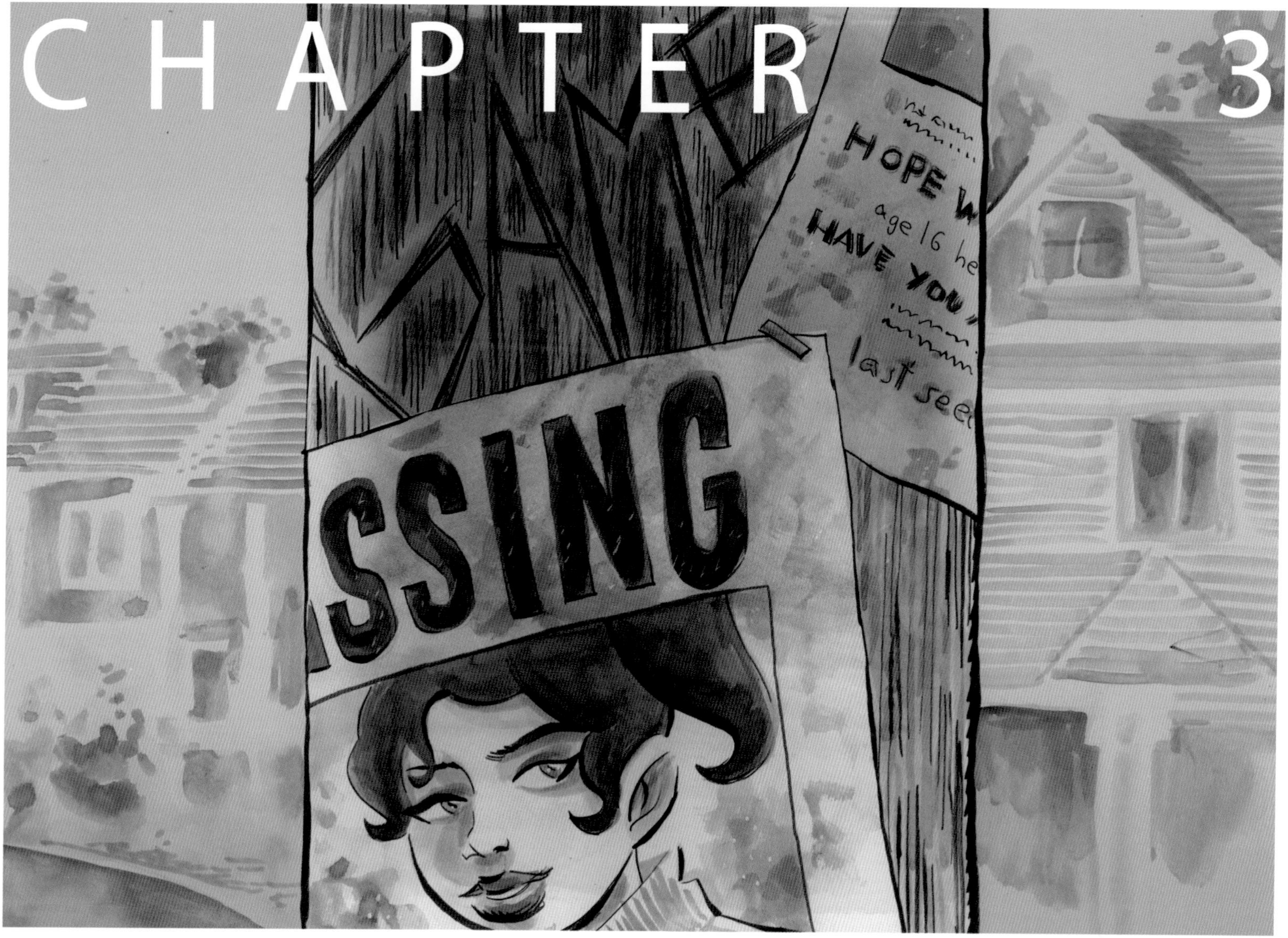
HOPE W
age 16 he
HAVE YOU
last see
SSING

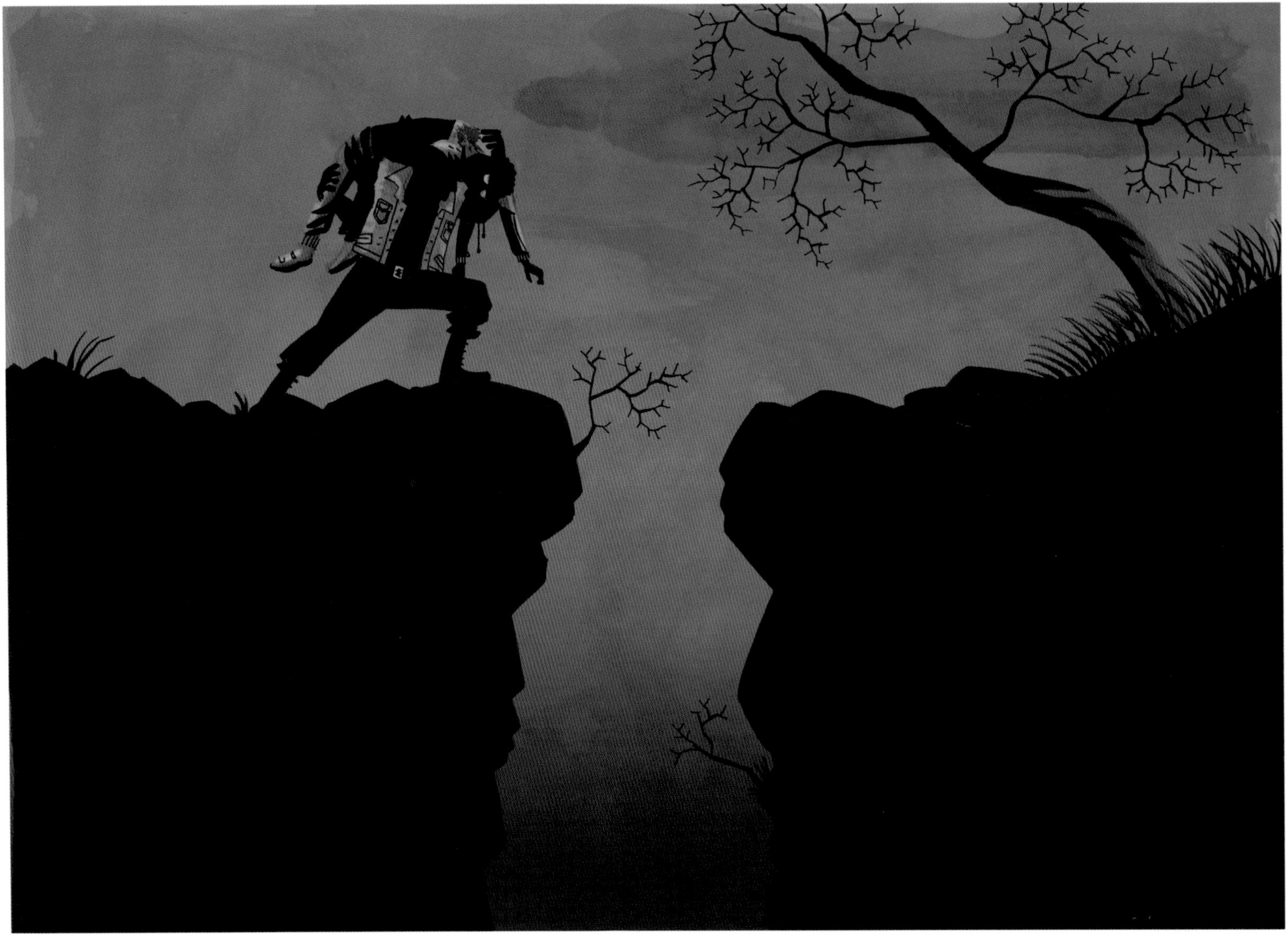

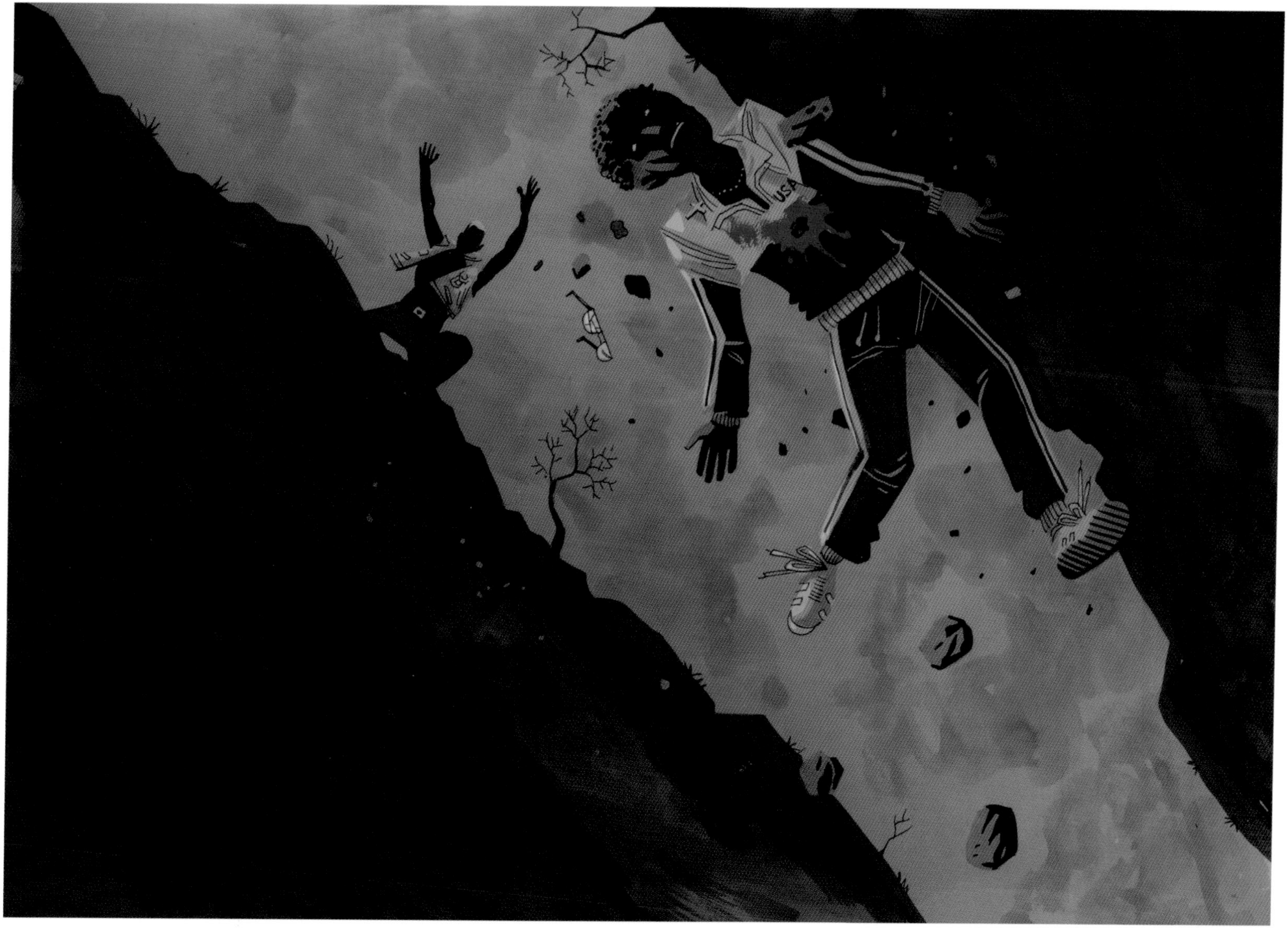
USA

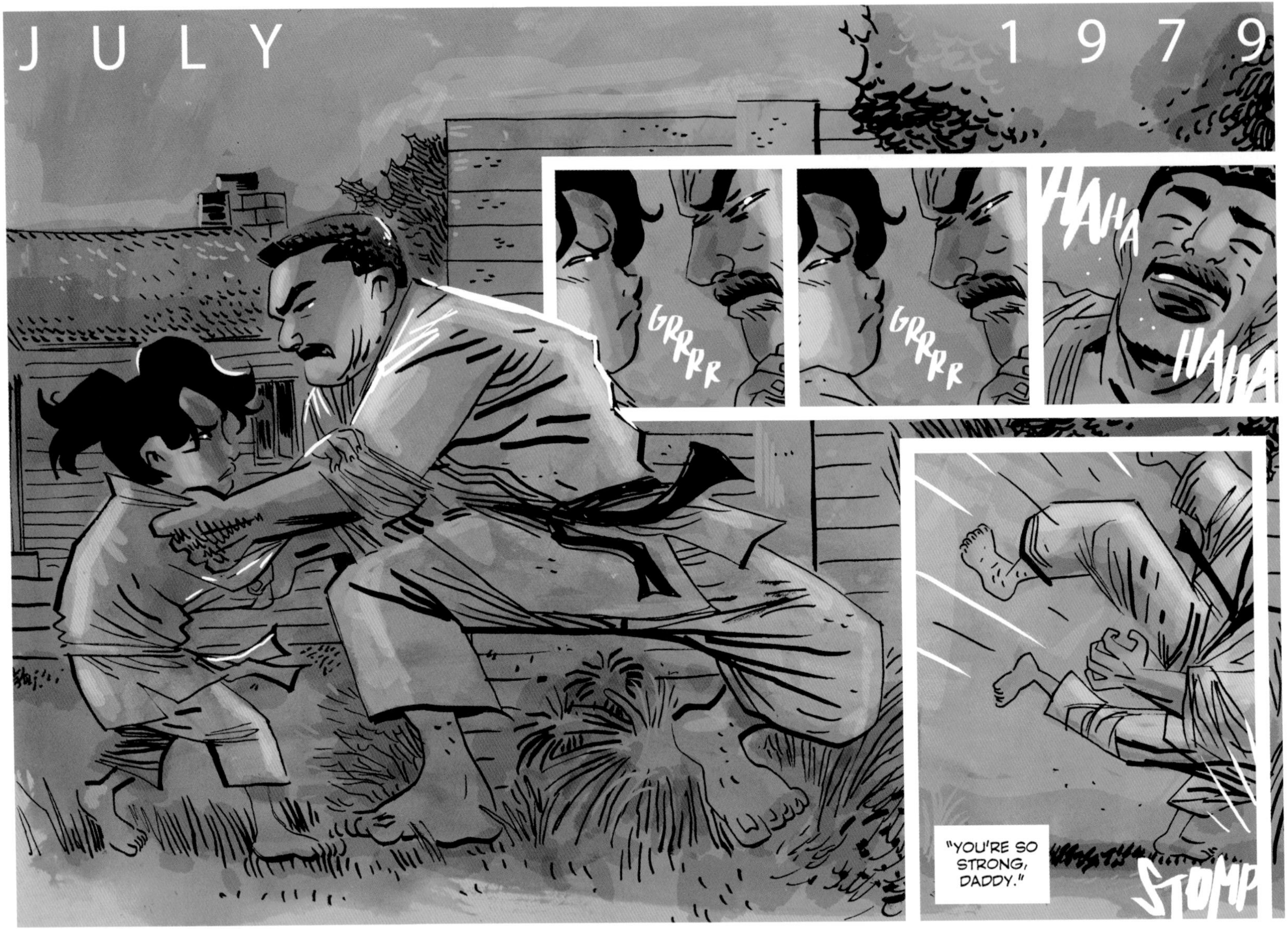
JULY 1979
GRRRR
GRRRR
HAHAHA
HAHAHA
"YOU'RE SO STRONG, DADDY."
STOMP

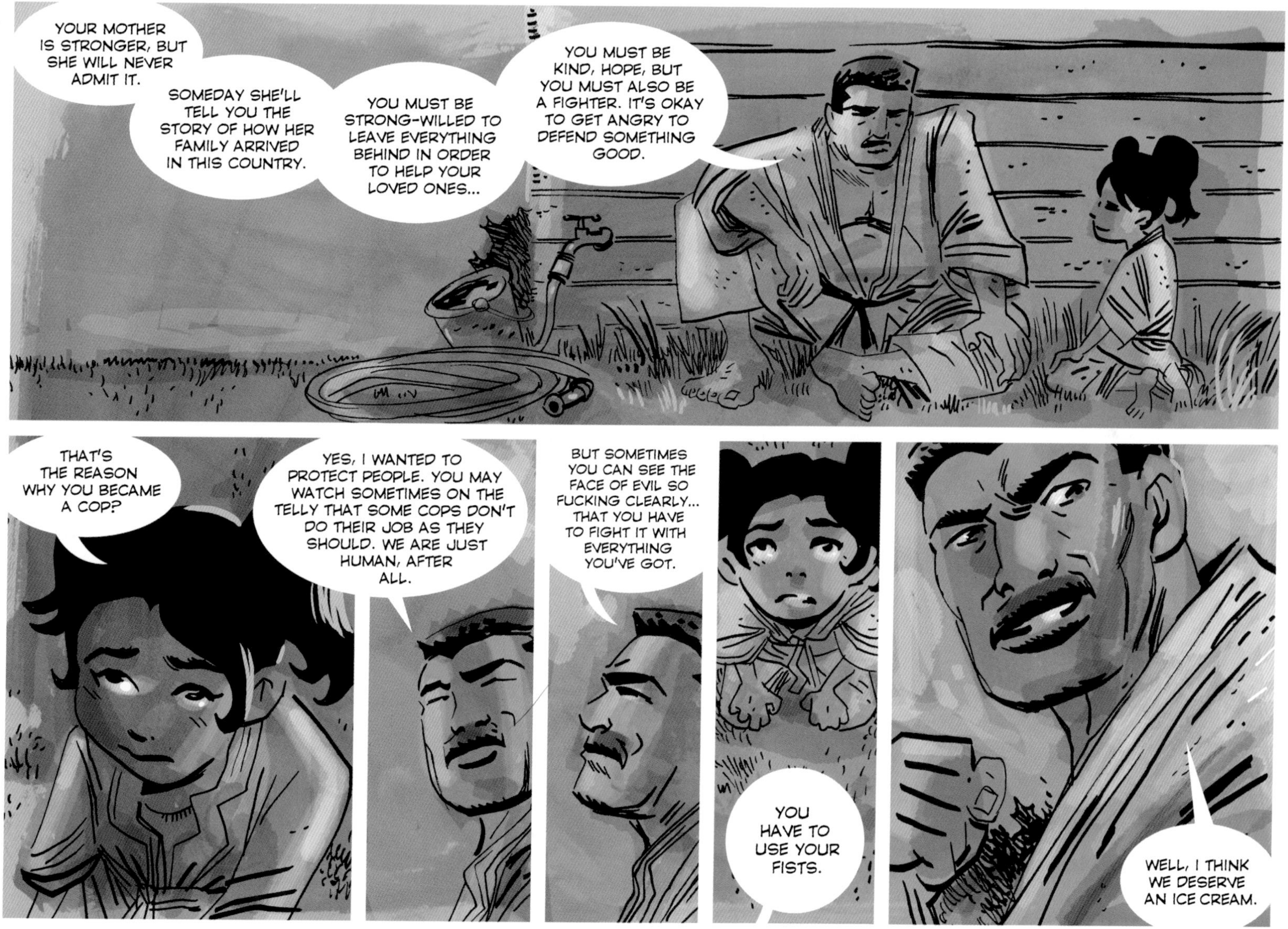
YOUR MOTHER IS STRONGER, BUT SHE WILL NEVER ADMIT IT.
SOMEDAY SHE'LL TELL YOU THE STORY OF HOW HER FAMILY ARRIVED IN THIS COUNTRY.
YOU MUST BE STRONG-WILLED TO LEAVE EVERYTHING BEHIND IN ORDER TO HELP YOUR LOVED ONES...
YOU MUST BE KIND, HOPE, BUT YOU MUST ALSO BE A FIGHTER. IT'S OKAY TO GET ANGRY TO DEFEND SOMETHING GOOD.
THAT'S THE REASON WHY YOU BECAME A COP?
YES, I WANTED TO PROTECT PEOPLE. YOU MAY WATCH SOMETIMES ON THE TELLY THAT SOME COPS DON'T DO THEIR JOB AS THEY SHOULD. WE ARE JUST HUMAN, AFTER ALL.
BUT SOMETIMES YOU CAN SEE THE FACE OF EVIL SO FUCKING CLEARLY... THAT YOU HAVE TO FIGHT IT WITH EVERYTHING YOU'VE GOT.
YOU HAVE TO USE YOUR FISTS.
WELL, I THINK WE DESERVE AN ICE CREAM.

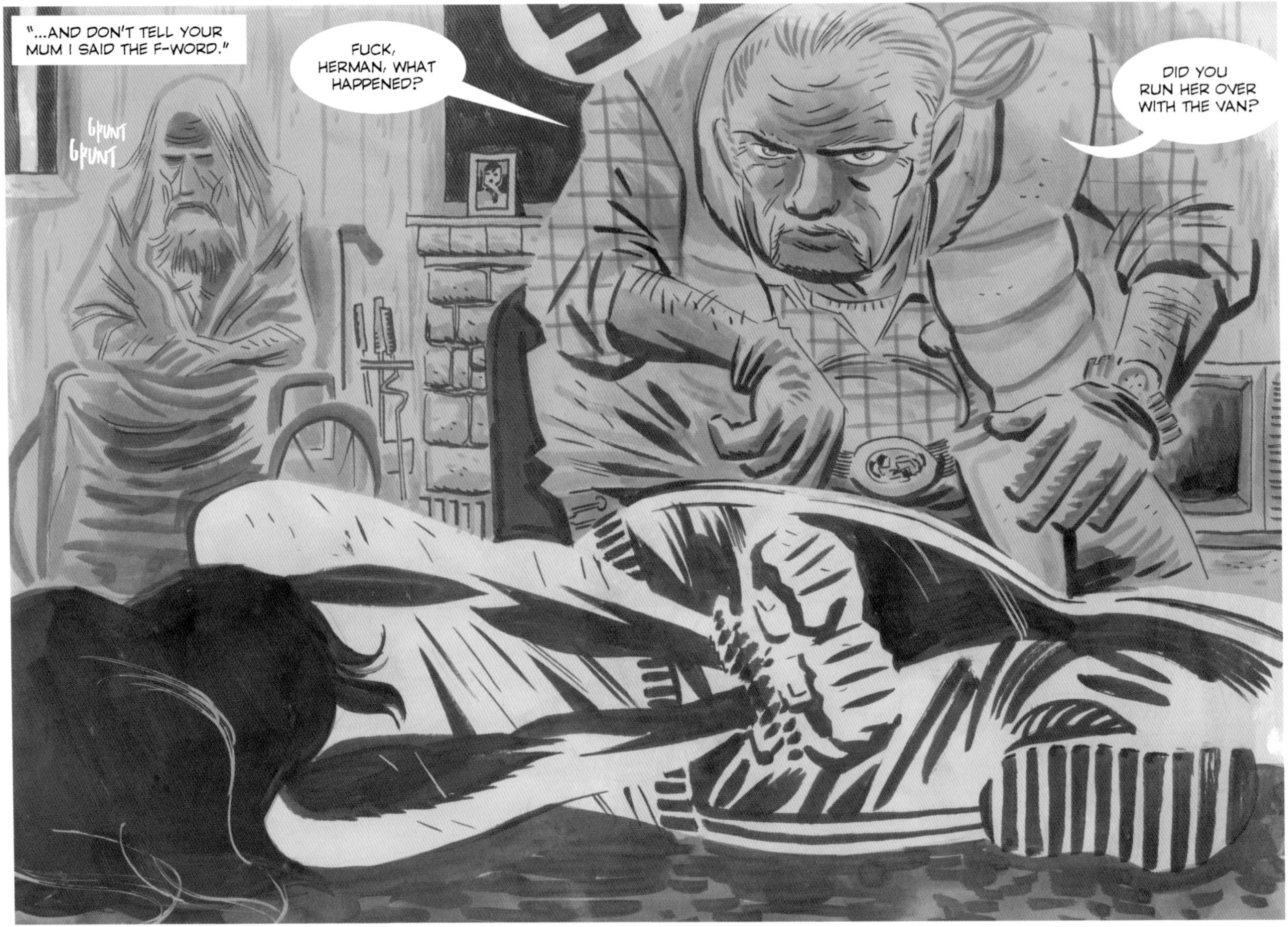
"...AND DON'T TELL YOUR MUM I SAID THE F-WORD."
GRUNT GRUNT
FUCK, HERMAN, WHAT HAPPENED?
DID YOU RUN HER OVER WITH THE VAN?

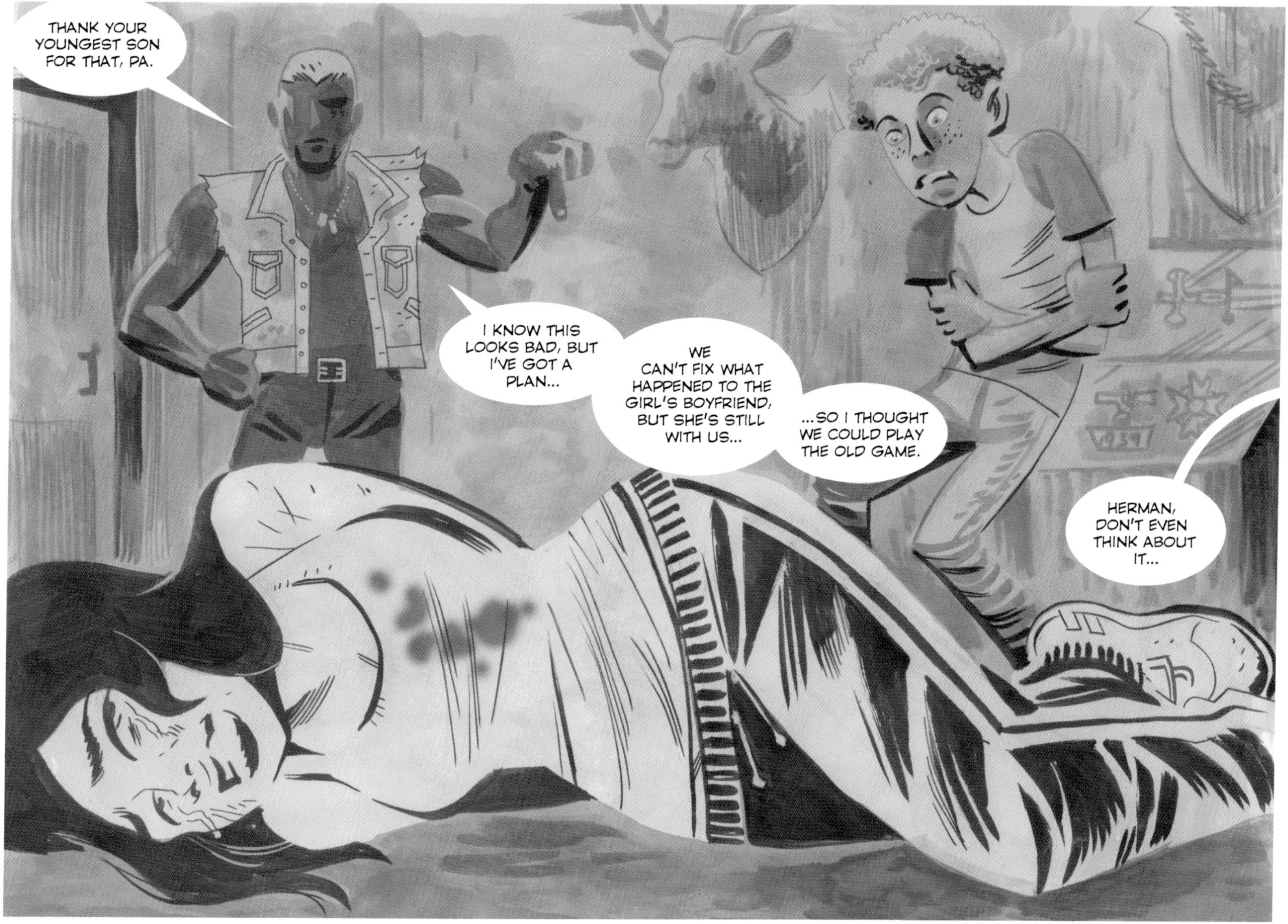
THANK YOUR YOUNGEST SON FOR THAT, PA.
I KNOW THIS LOOKS BAD, BUT I'VE GOT A PLAN...
WE CAN'T FIX WHAT HAPPENED TO THE GIRL'S BOYFRIEND, BUT SHE'S STILL WITH US...
...SO I THOUGHT WE COULD PLAY THE OLD GAME.
HERMAN, DON'T EVEN THINK ABOUT IT...

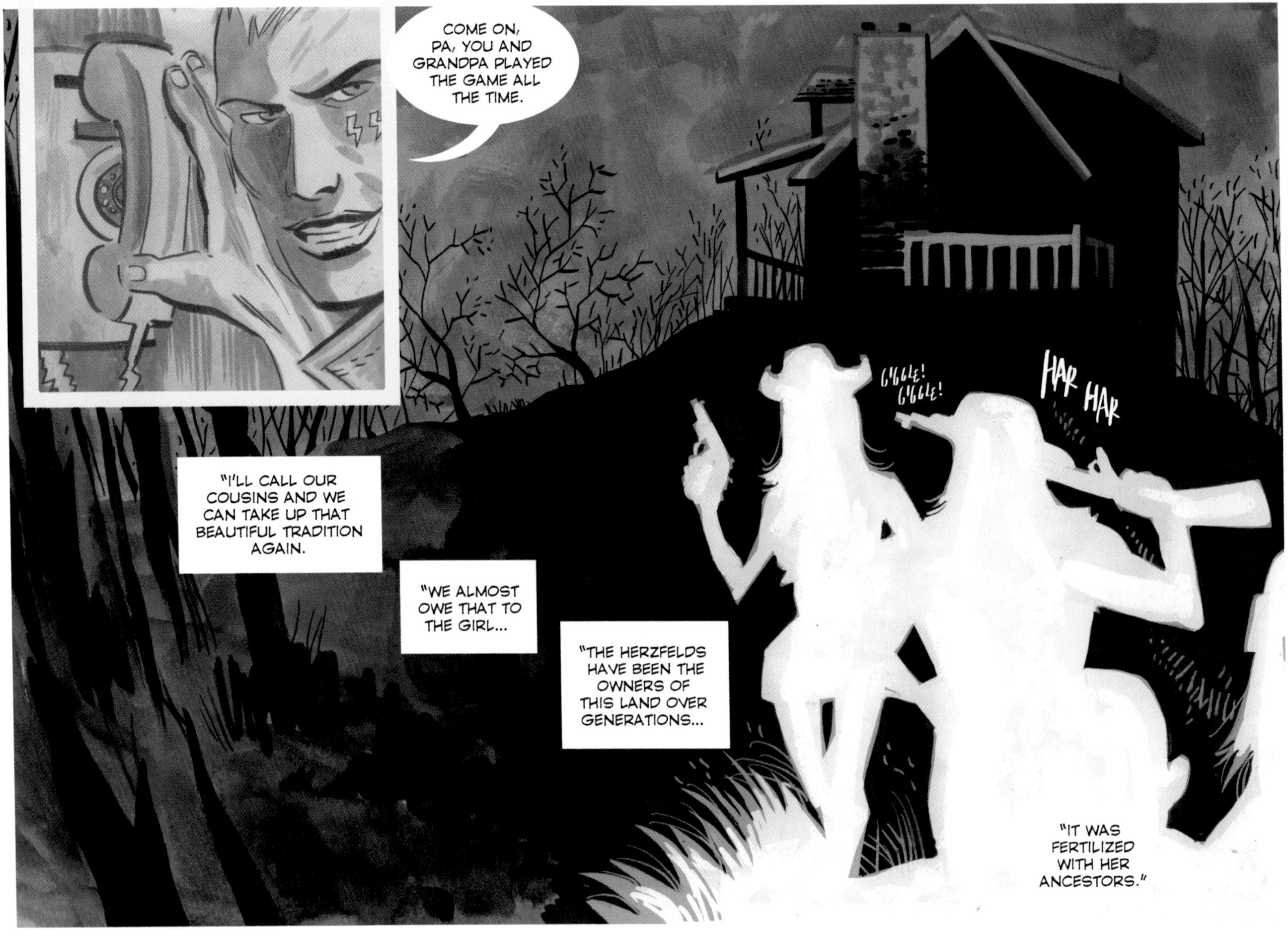
COME ON, PA, YOU AND GRANDPA PLAYED THE GAME ALL THE TIME.
"I'LL CALL OUR COUSINS AND WE CAN TAKE UP THAT BEAUTIFUL TRADITION AGAIN.
"WE ALMOST OWE THAT TO THE GIRL...
"THE HERZFELDS HAVE BEEN THE OWNERS OF THIS LAND OVER GENERATIONS...
GIGGLE! GIGGLE!
HAR HAR
"IT WAS FERTILIZED WITH HER ANCESTORS."

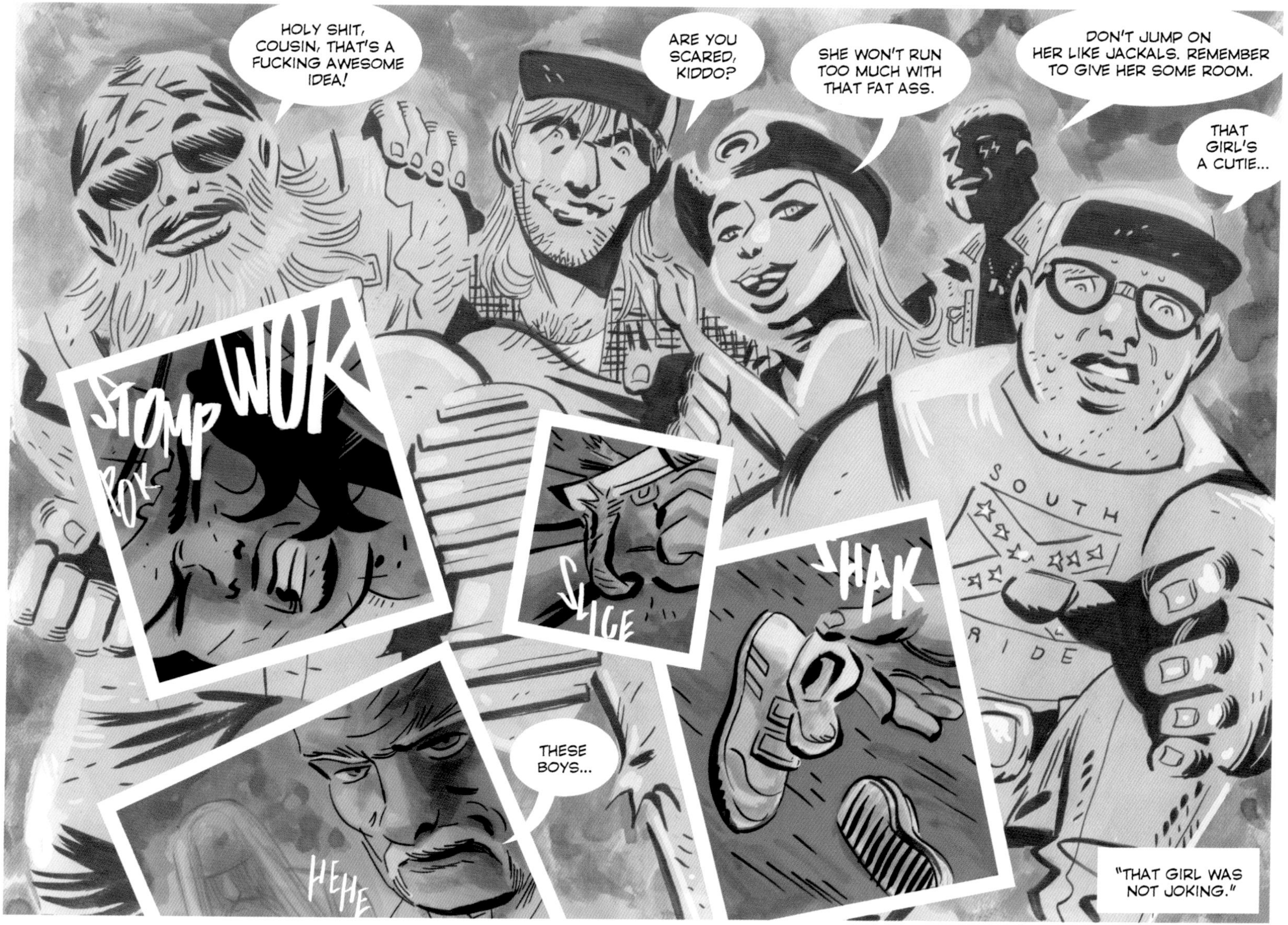
HOLY SHIT, COUSIN, THAT'S A FUCKING AWESOME IDEA!
ARE YOU SCARED, KIDDO?
SHE WON'T RUN TOO MUCH WITH THAT FAT ASS.
DON'T JUMP ON HER LIKE JACKALS. REMEMBER TO GIVE HER SOME ROOM.
THAT GIRL'S A CUTIE...
SOUTH
RIDE
STOMP
WOK
POK
SLICE
SHAK
THESE BOYS...
HEHE
"THAT GIRL WAS NOT JOKING."

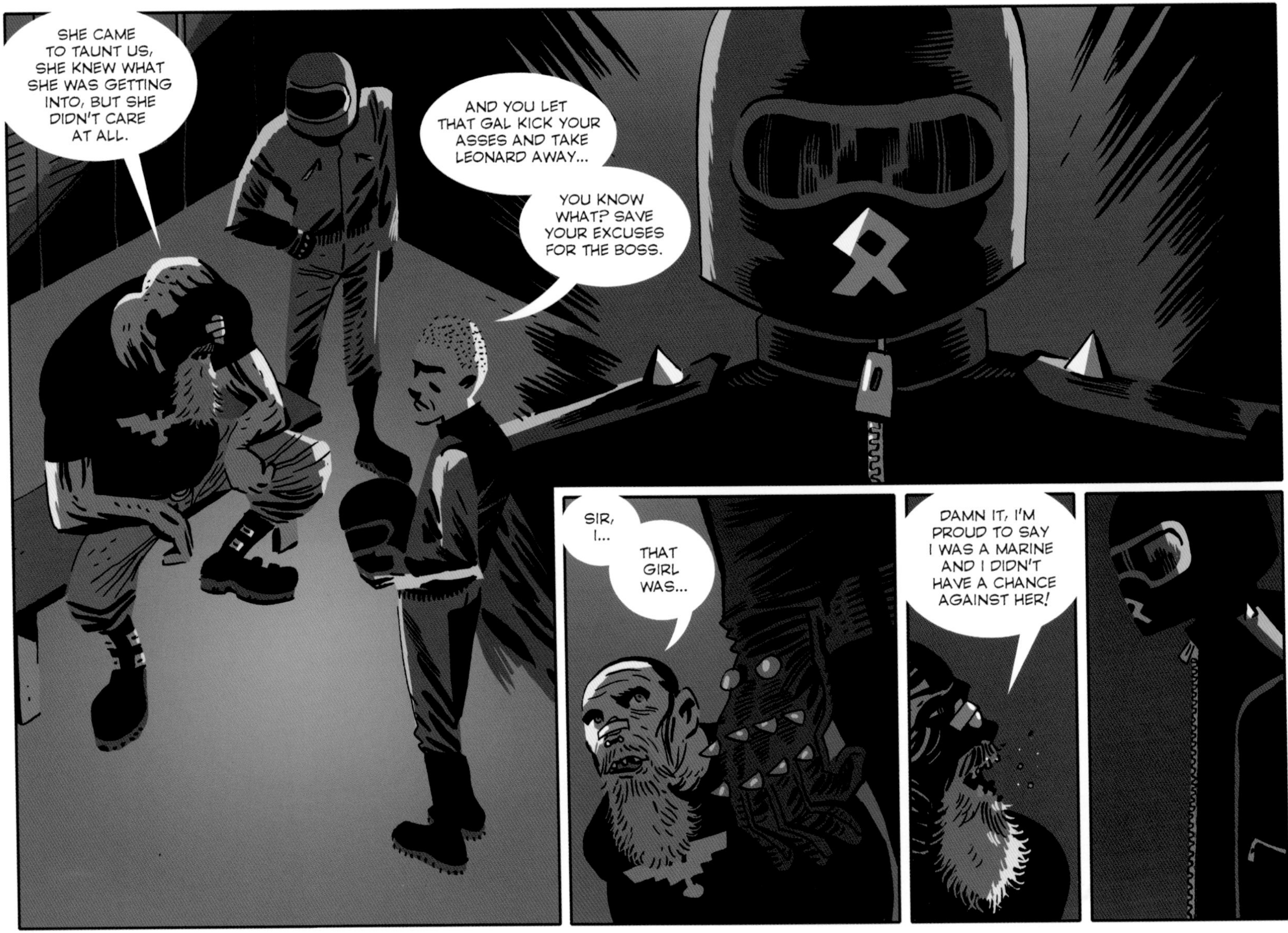
SHE CAME TO TAUNT US, SHE KNEW WHAT SHE WAS GETTING INTO, BUT SHE DIDN'T CARE AT ALL.
AND YOU LET THAT GAL KICK YOUR ASSES AND TAKE LEONARD AWAY...
YOU KNOW WHAT? SAVE YOUR EXCUSES FOR THE BOSS.
SIR, I...
THAT GIRL WAS...
DAMN IT, I'M PROUD TO SAY I WAS A MARINE AND I DIDN'T HAVE A CHANCE AGAINST HER!

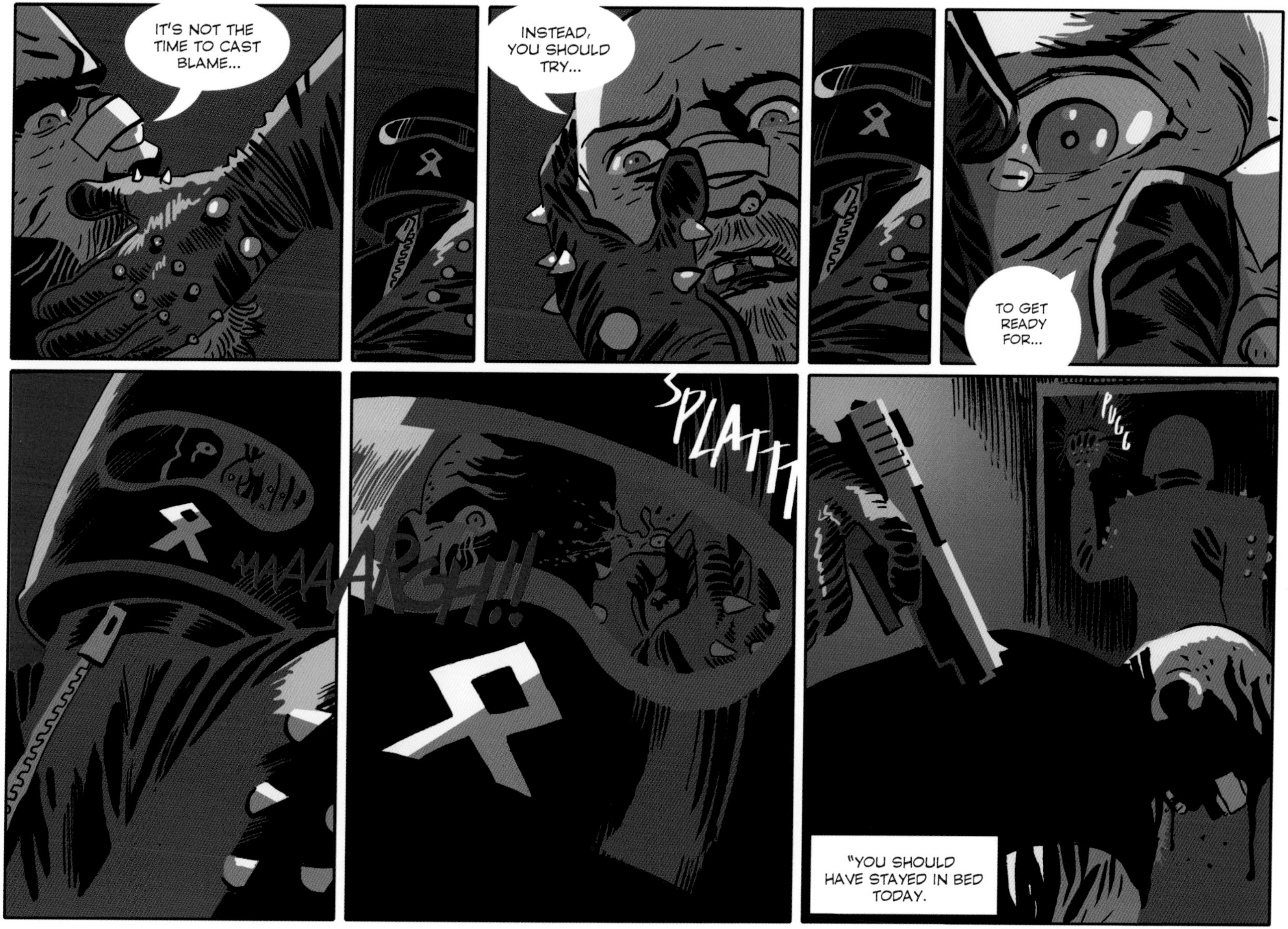
IT'S NOT THE TIME TO CAST BLAME...
INSTEAD, YOU SHOULD TRY...
TO GET READY FOR...
MAAAARGH!!
SPLATTT
PLUG
"YOU SHOULD HAVE STAYED IN BED TODAY.

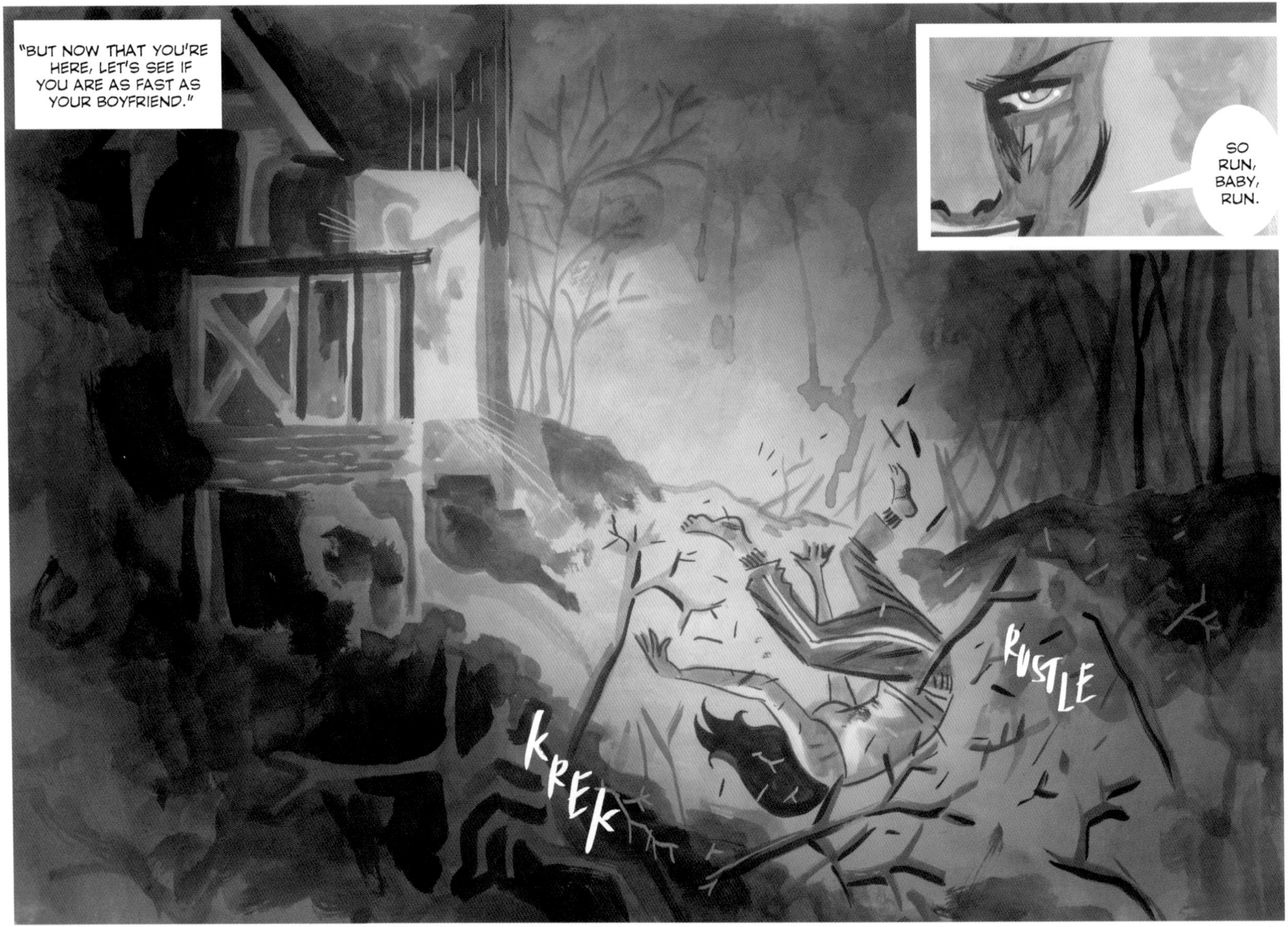
"BUT NOW THAT YOU'RE HERE, LET'S SEE IF YOU ARE AS FAST AS YOUR BOYFRIEND."
SO RUN, BABY, RUN.
KREEK
RUSTLE

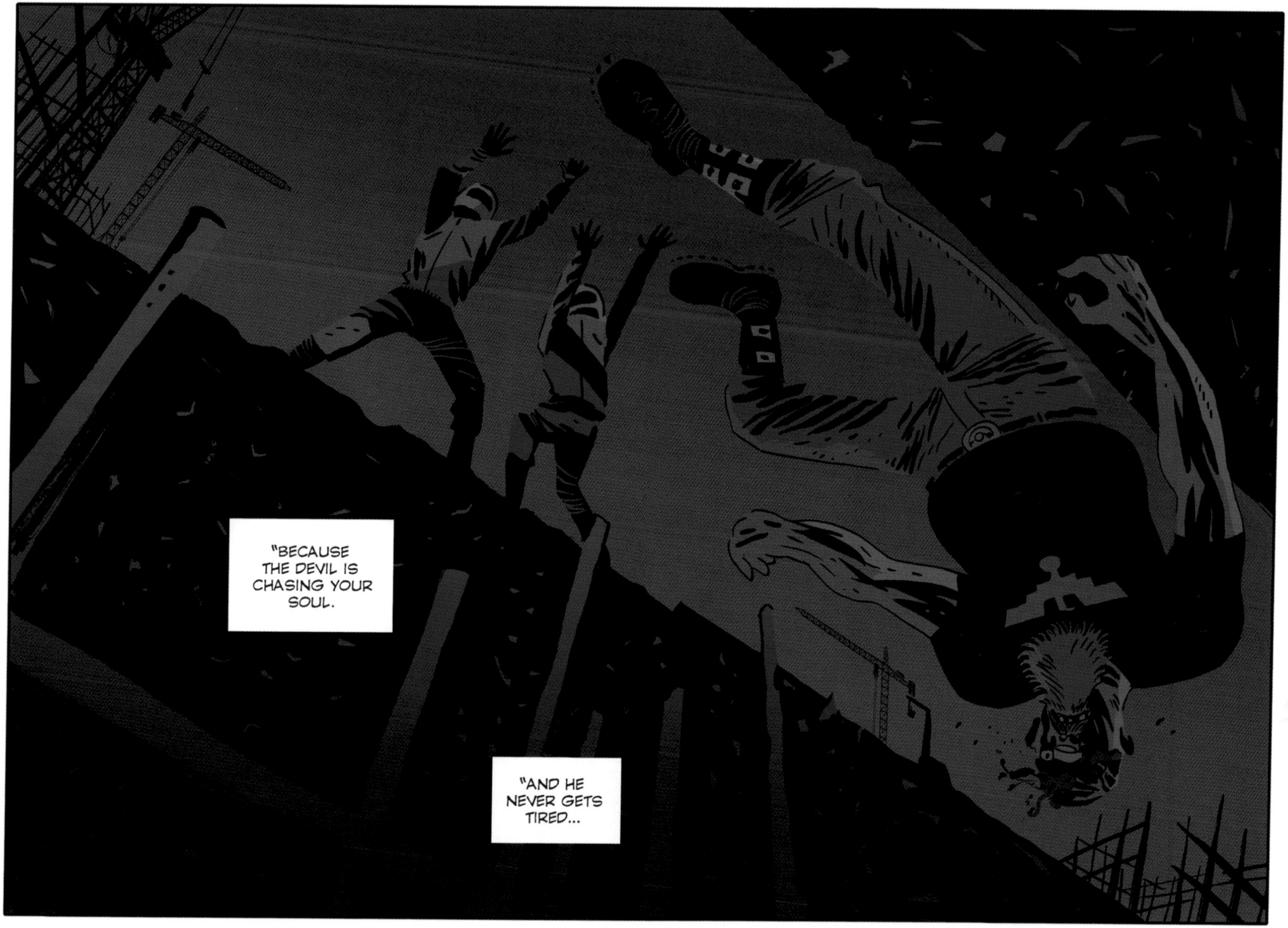
"BECAUSE THE DEVIL IS CHASING YOUR SOUL.
"AND HE NEVER GETS TIRED...

"...OF WELCOMING DAMNED SOULS INTO HELL."

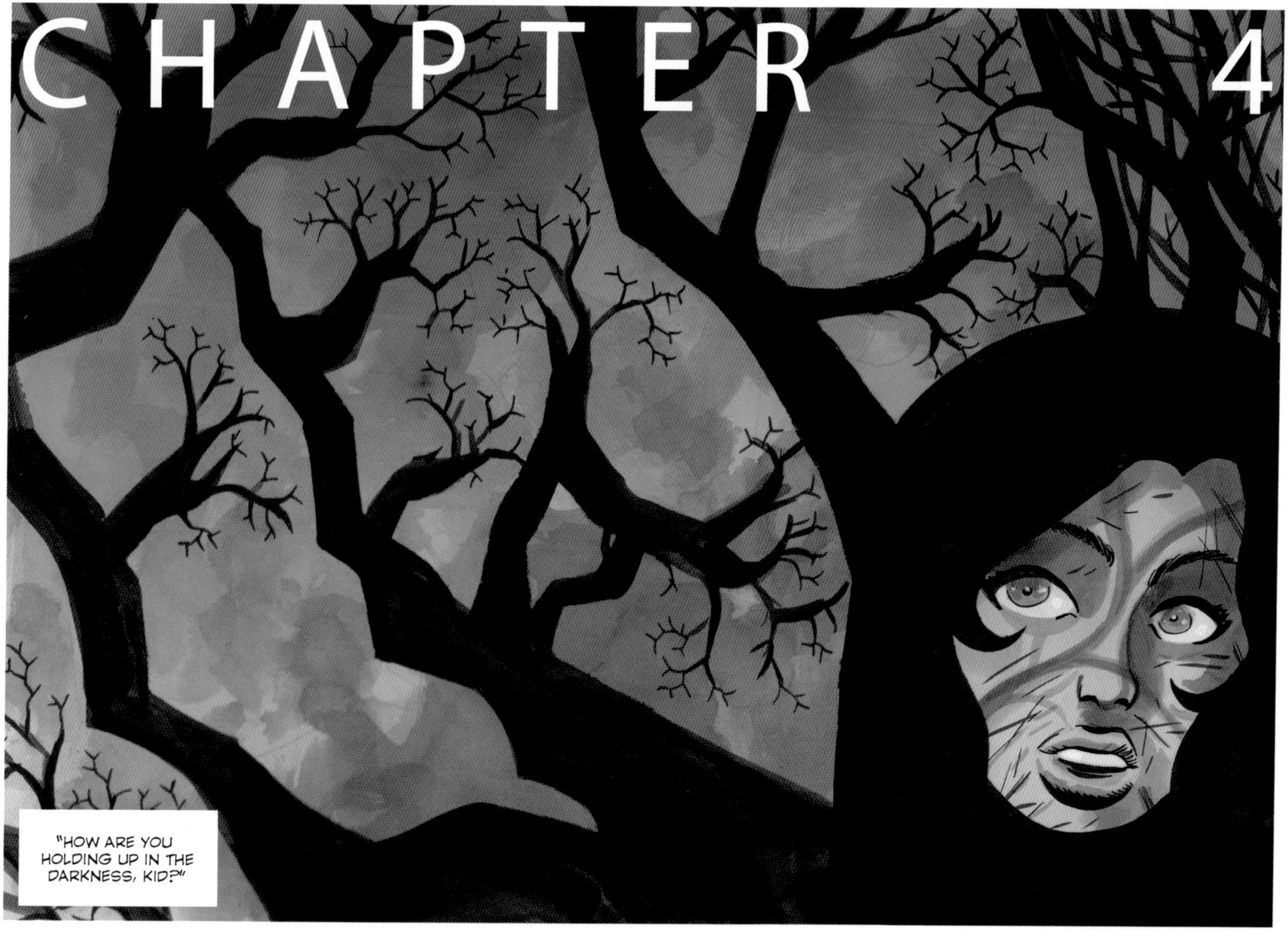
CHAPTER 4
"HOW ARE YOU HOLDING UP IN THE DARKNESS, KID?"

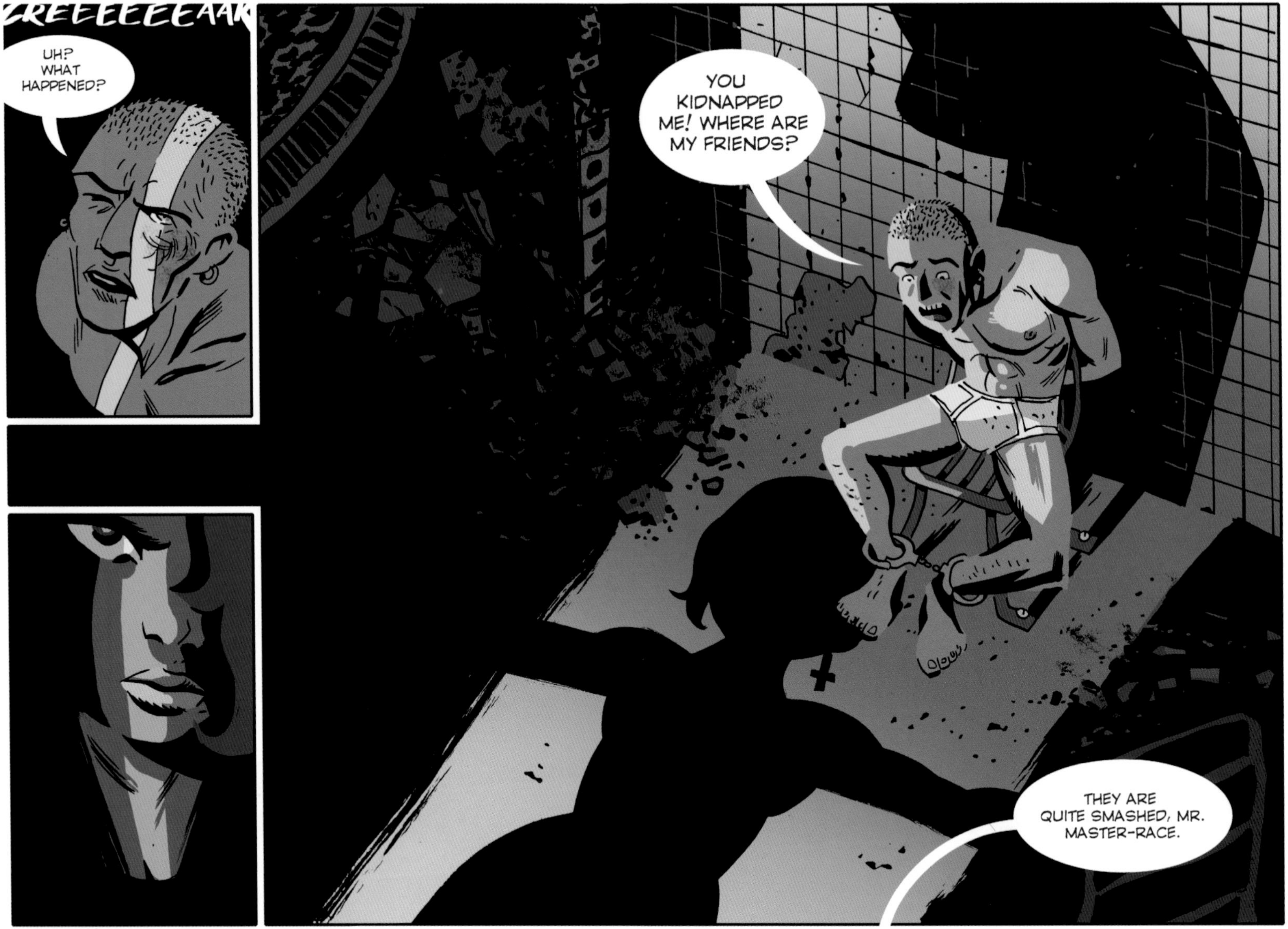
CREEEEEEEAAK
UH? WHAT HAPPENED?
YOU KIDNAPPED ME! WHERE ARE MY FRIENDS?
THEY ARE QUITE SMASHED, MR. MASTER-RACE.

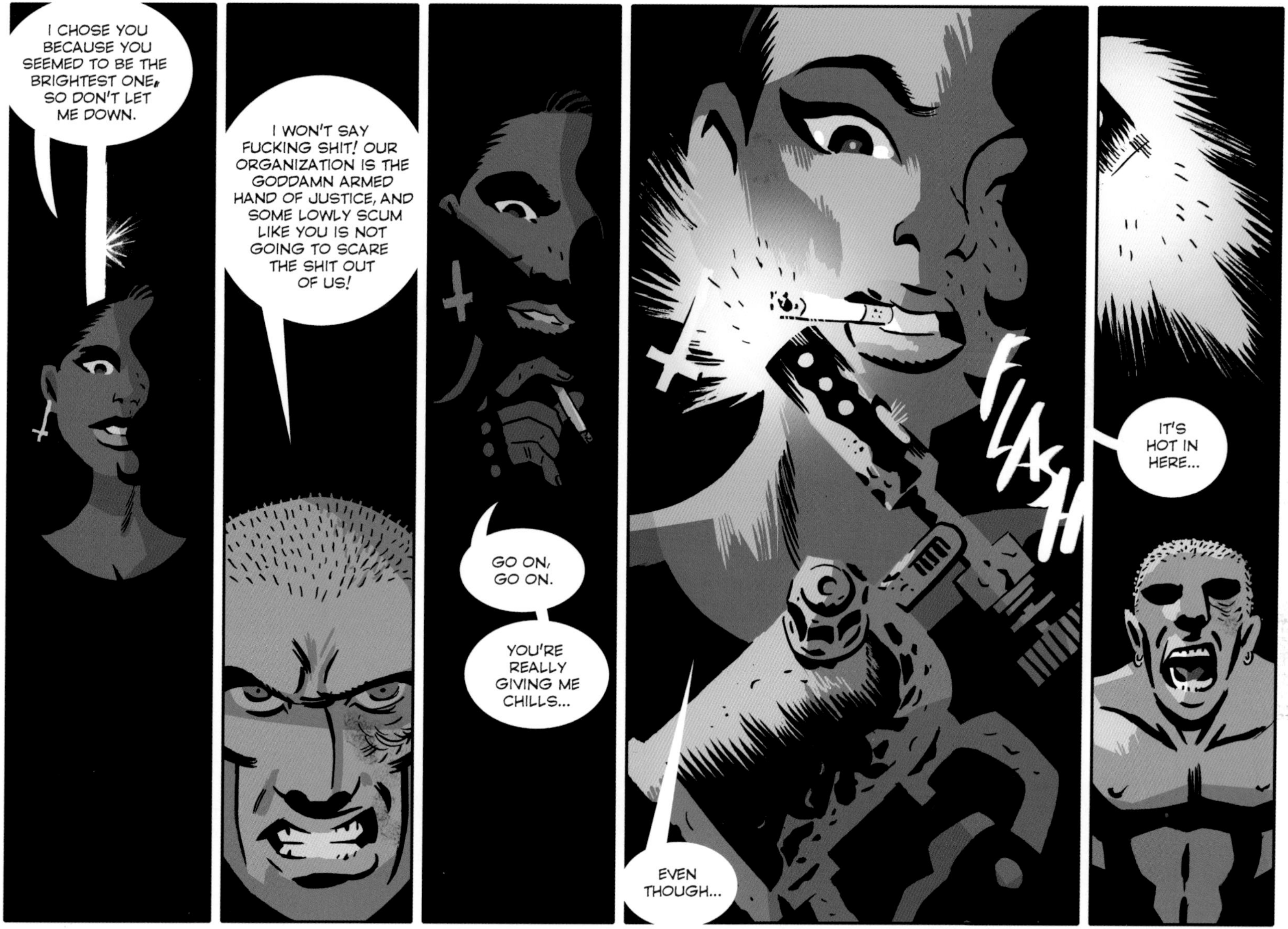
I CHOSE YOU BECAUSE YOU SEEMED TO BE THE BRIGHTEST ONE, SO DON'T LET ME DOWN.
I WON'T SAY FUCKING SHIT! OUR ORGANIZATION IS THE GODDAMN ARMED HAND OF JUSTICE, AND SOME LOWLY SCUM LIKE YOU IS NOT GOING TO SCARE THE SHIT OUT OF US!
GO ON, GO ON.
YOU'RE REALLY GIVING ME CHILLS...
FLASH
EVEN THOUGH...
IT'S HOT IN HERE...

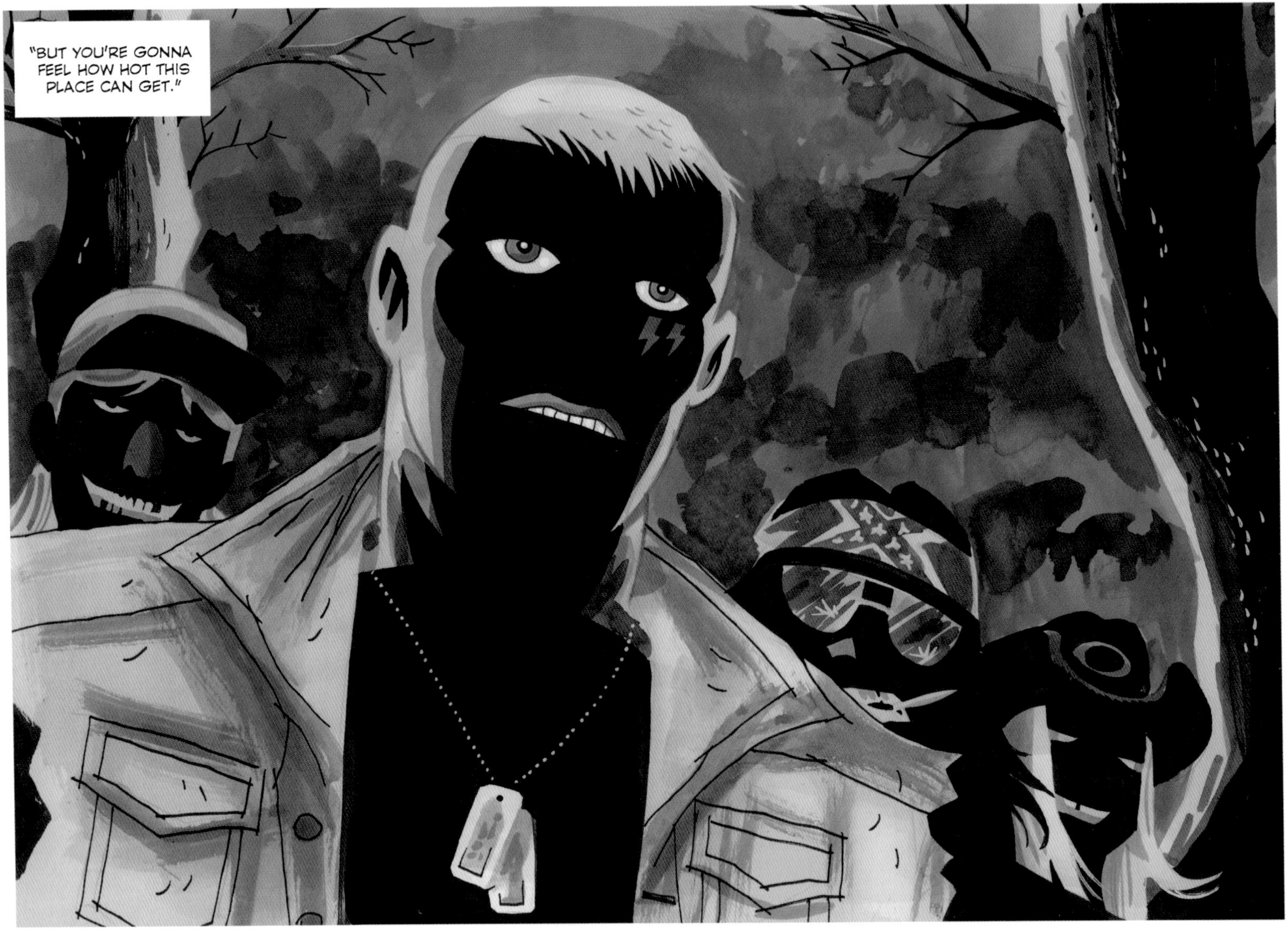
"BUT YOU'RE GONNA FEEL HOW HOT THIS PLACE CAN GET."

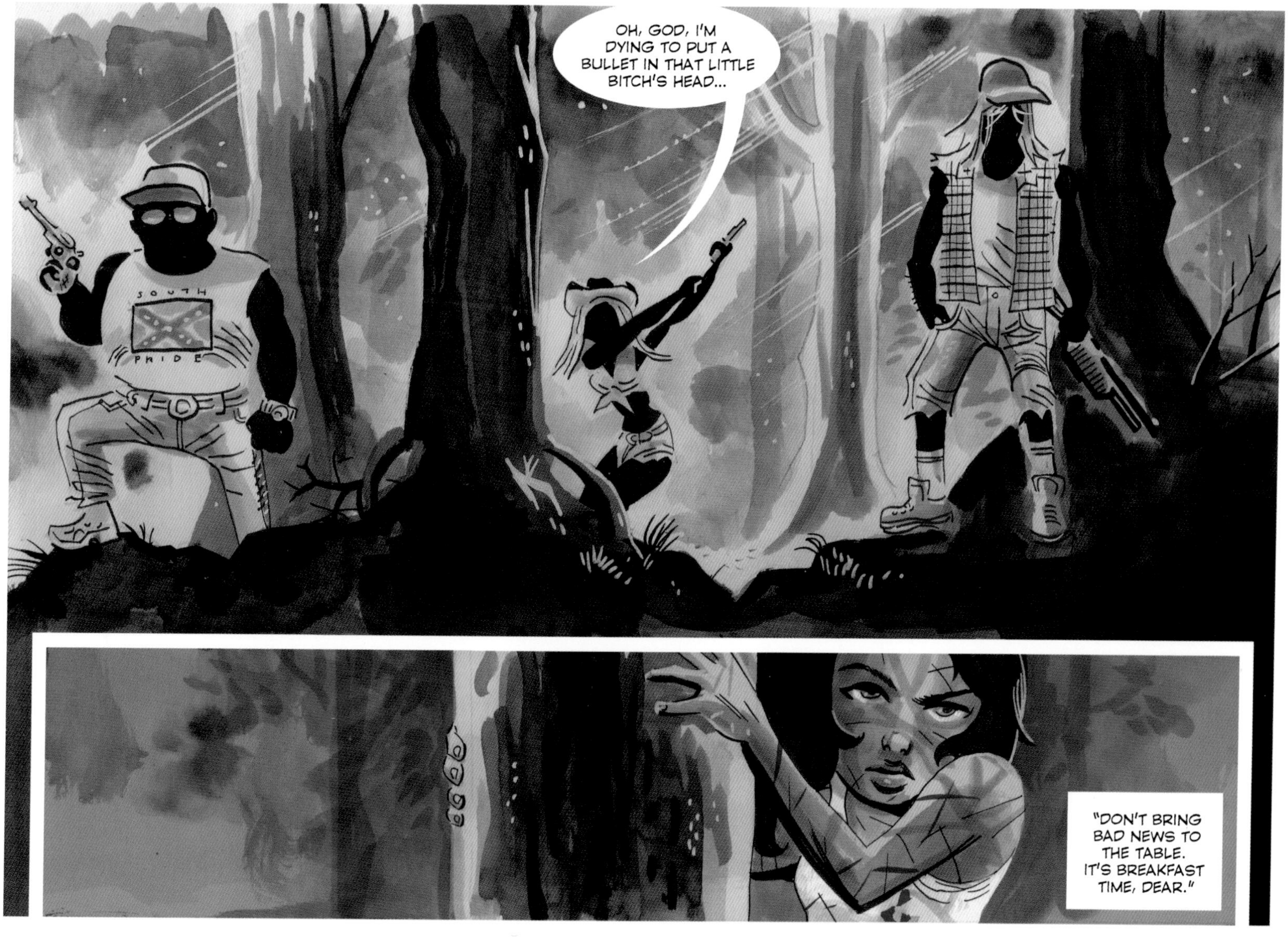
OH, GOD, I'M DYING TO PUT A BULLET IN THAT LITTLE BITCH'S HEAD...
SOUTH PRIDE
"DON'T BRING BAD NEWS TO THE TABLE. IT'S BREAKFAST TIME, DEAR."

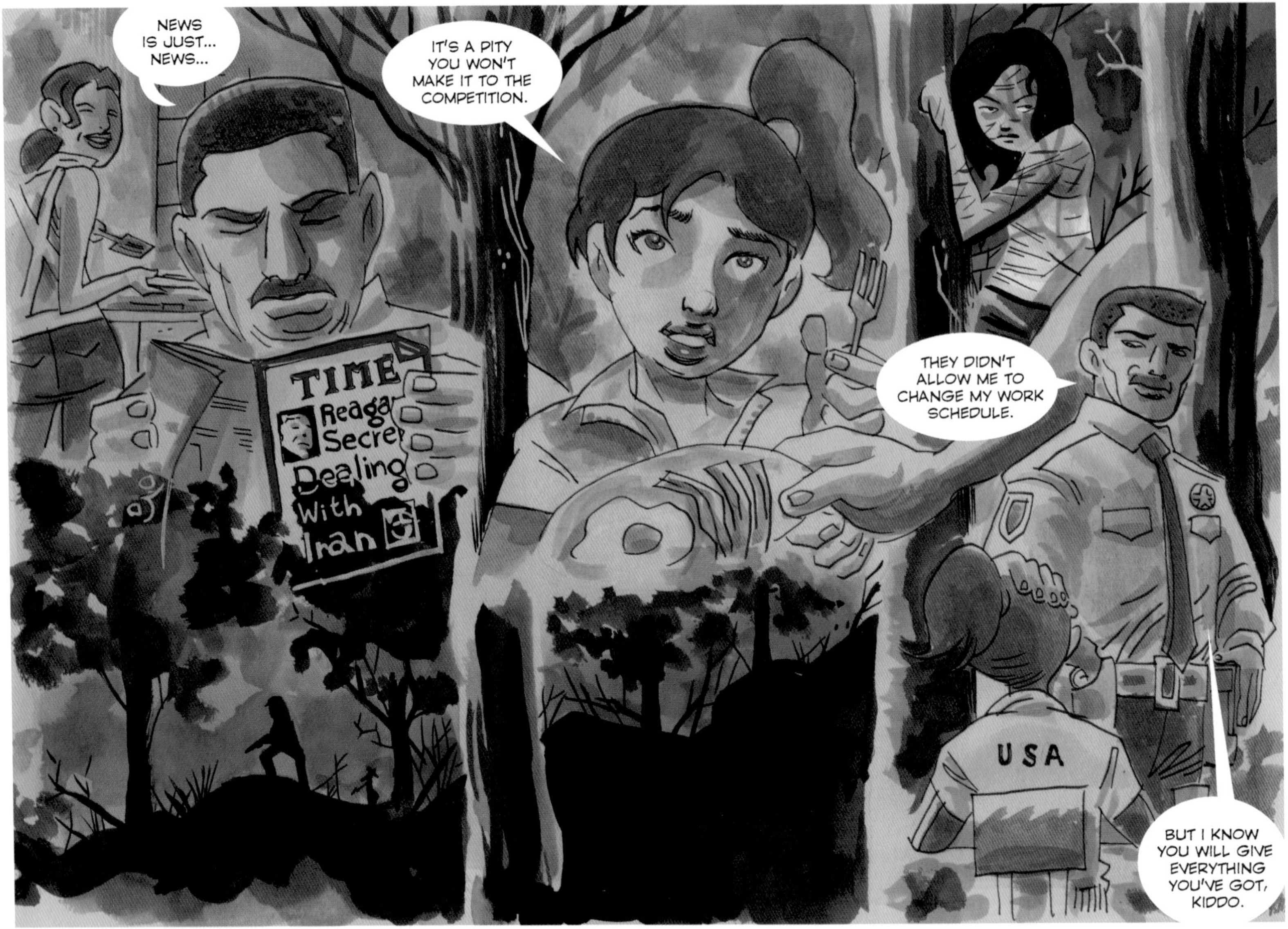
NEWS IS JUST... NEWS...
TIME
Reaga
Secre
Dealing
With
Iran
IT'S A PITY YOU WON'T MAKE IT TO THE COMPETITION.
THEY DIDN'T ALLOW ME TO CHANGE MY WORK SCHEDULE.
USA
BUT I KNOW YOU WILL GIVE EVERYTHING YOU'VE GOT, KIDDO.

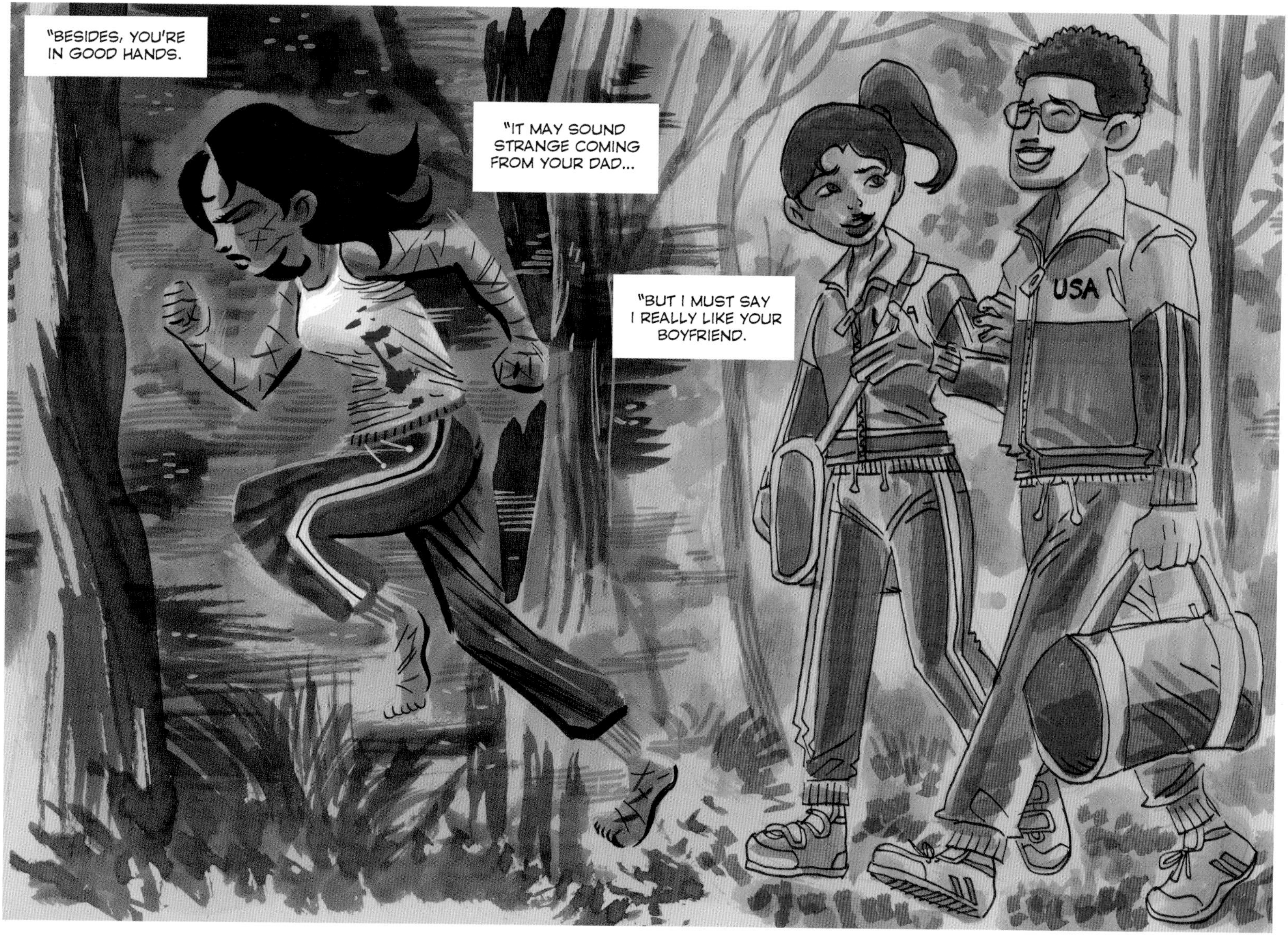
"BESIDES, YOU'RE IN GOOD HANDS.
"IT MAY SOUND STRANGE COMING FROM YOUR DAD...
"BUT I MUST SAY I REALLY LIKE YOUR BOYFRIEND.
USA

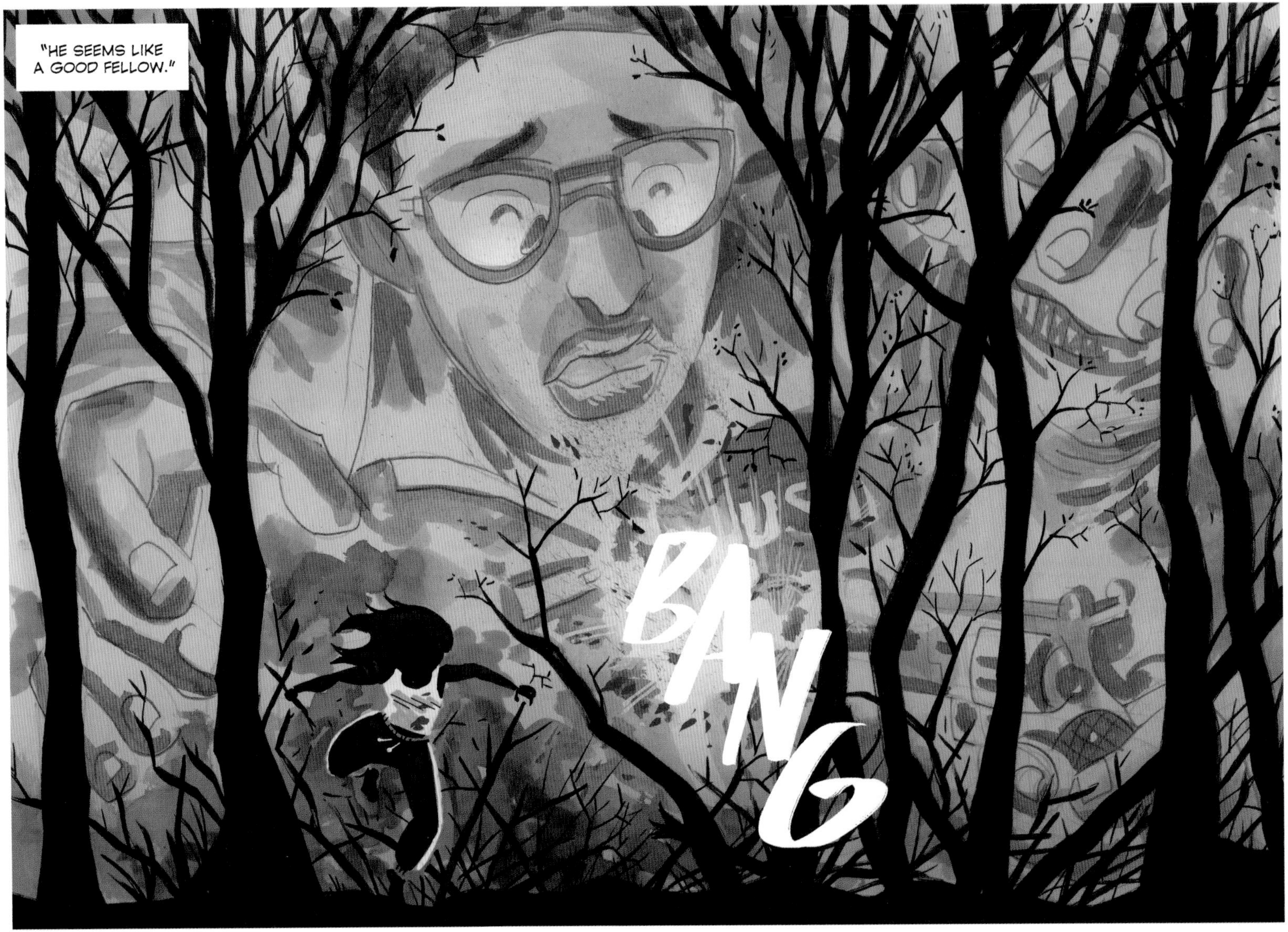
"HE SEEMS LIKE A GOOD FELLOW."
BANG

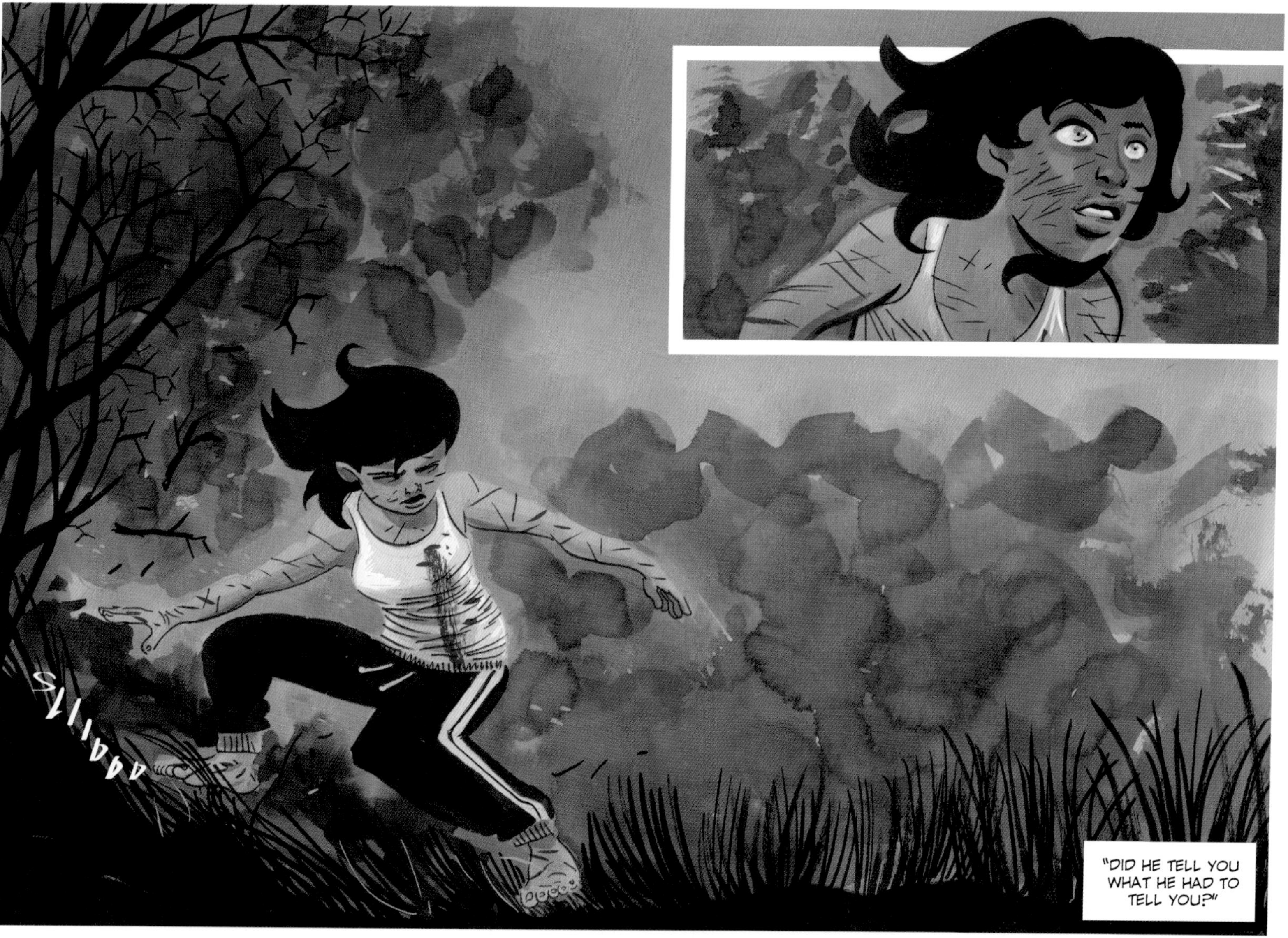
SLIIDDD
"DID HE TELL YOU WHAT HE HAD TO TELL YOU?"

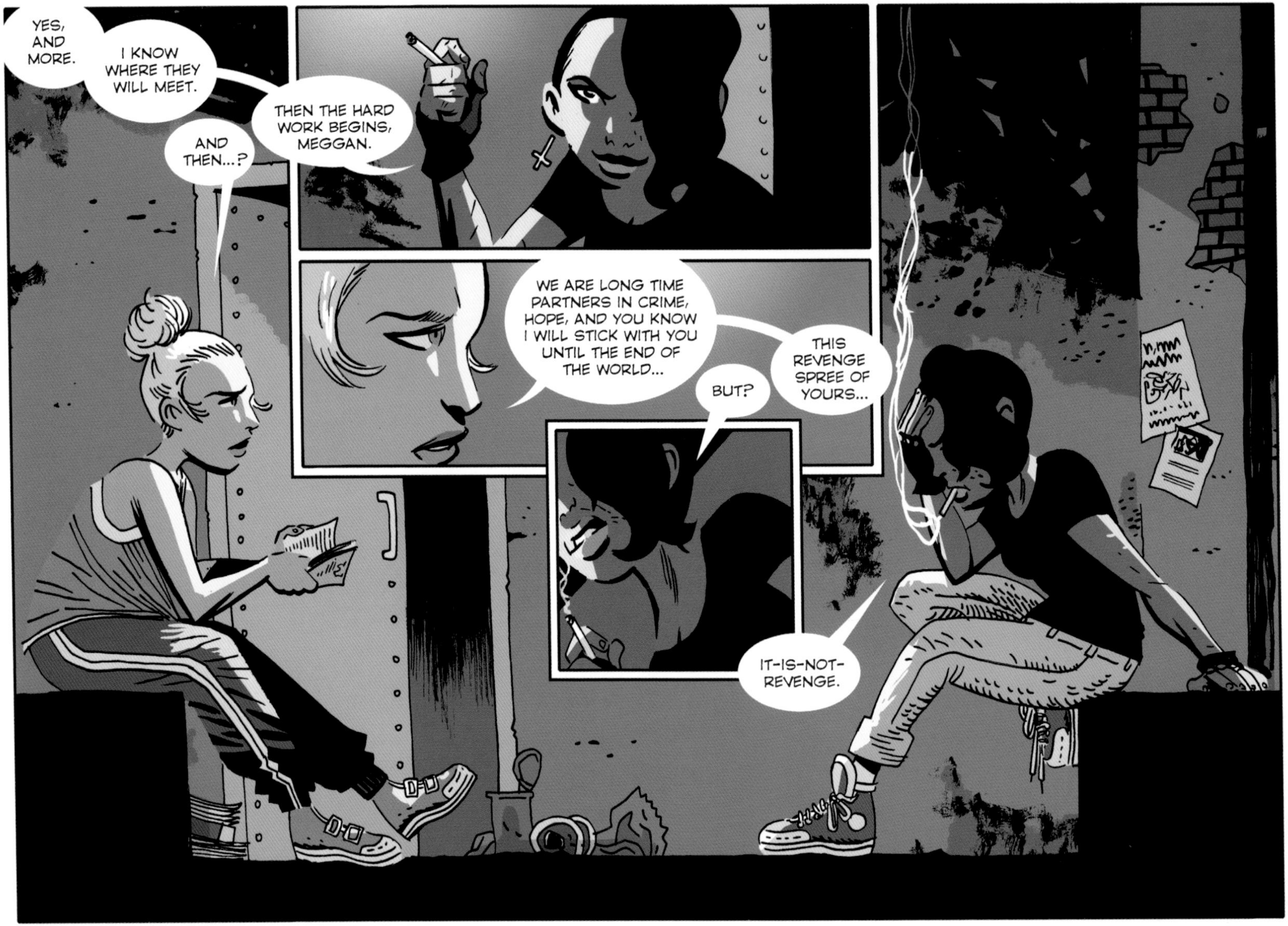
YES, AND MORE.
I KNOW WHERE THEY WILL MEET.
AND THEN...?
THEN THE HARD WORK BEGINS, MEGGAN.
WE ARE LONG TIME PARTNERS IN CRIME, HOPE, AND YOU KNOW I WILL STICK WITH YOU UNTIL THE END OF THE WORLD...
THIS REVENGE SPREE OF YOURS...
BUT?
IT-IS-NOT-REVENGE.

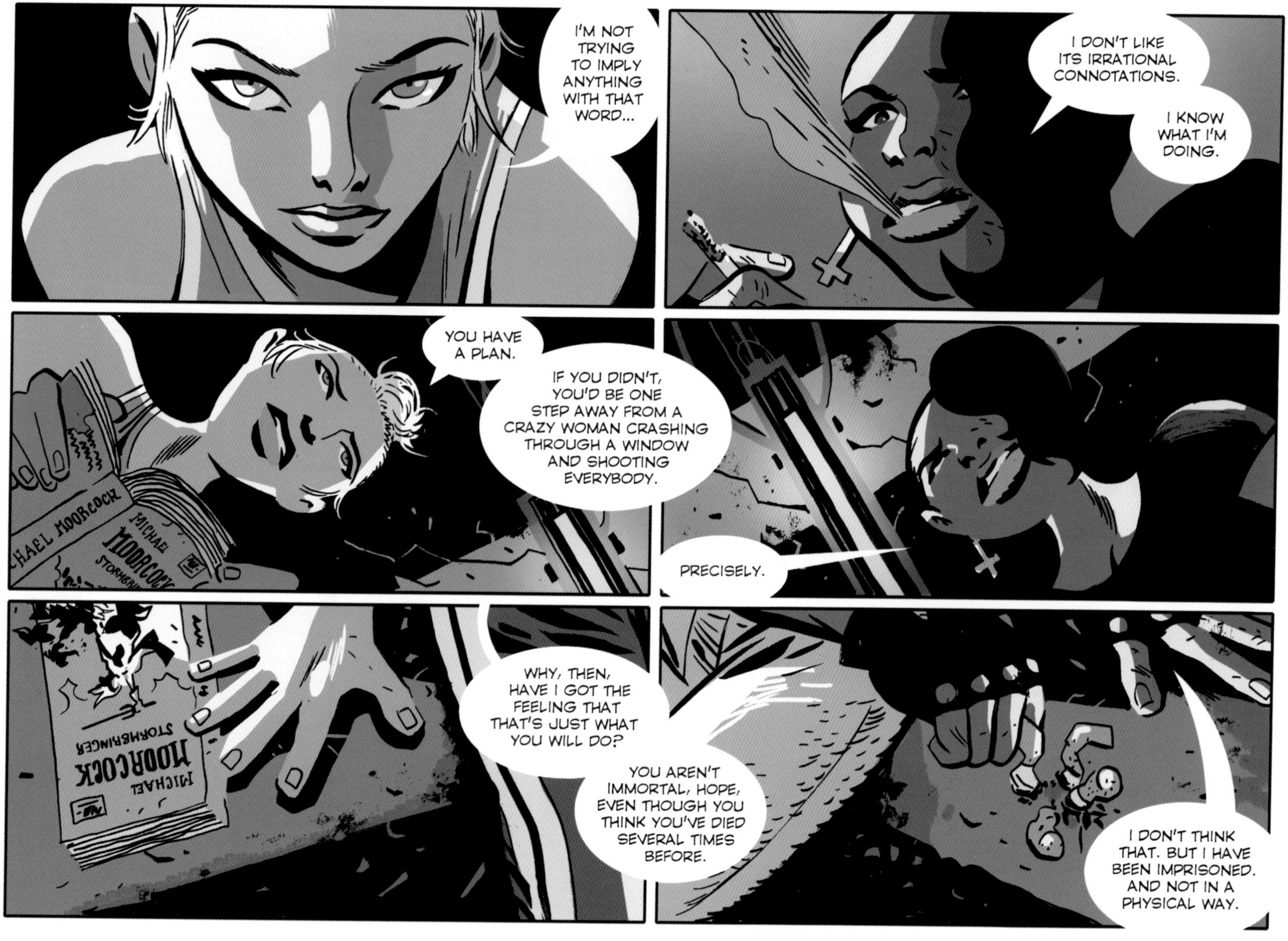
I'M NOT TRYING TO IMPLY ANYTHING WITH THAT WORD...
I DON'T LIKE ITS IRRATIONAL CONNOTATIONS.
I KNOW WHAT I'M DOING.
YOU HAVE A PLAN.
IF YOU DIDN'T, YOU'D BE ONE STEP AWAY FROM A CRAZY WOMAN CRASHING THROUGH A WINDOW AND SHOOTING EVERYBODY.
PRECISELY.
MICHAEL MOORCOCK
STORMBRINGER
WHY, THEN, HAVE I GOT THE FEELING THAT THAT'S JUST WHAT YOU WILL DO?
YOU AREN'T IMMORTAL, HOPE, EVEN THOUGH YOU THINK YOU'VE DIED SEVERAL TIMES BEFORE.
I DON'T THINK THAT. BUT I HAVE BEEN IMPRISONED. AND NOT IN A PHYSICAL WAY.

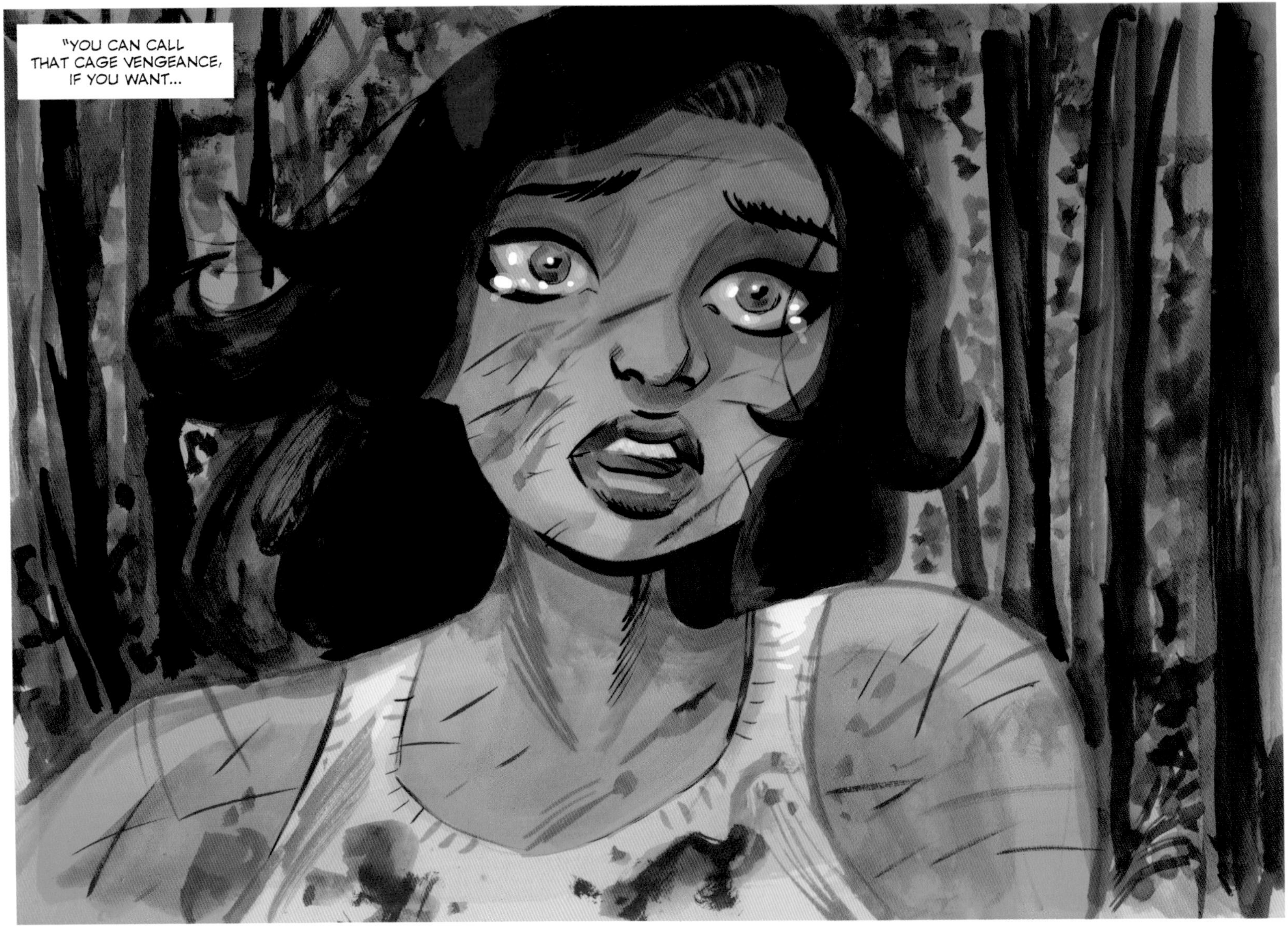
"YOU CAN CALL THAT CAGE VENGEANCE, IF YOU WANT...

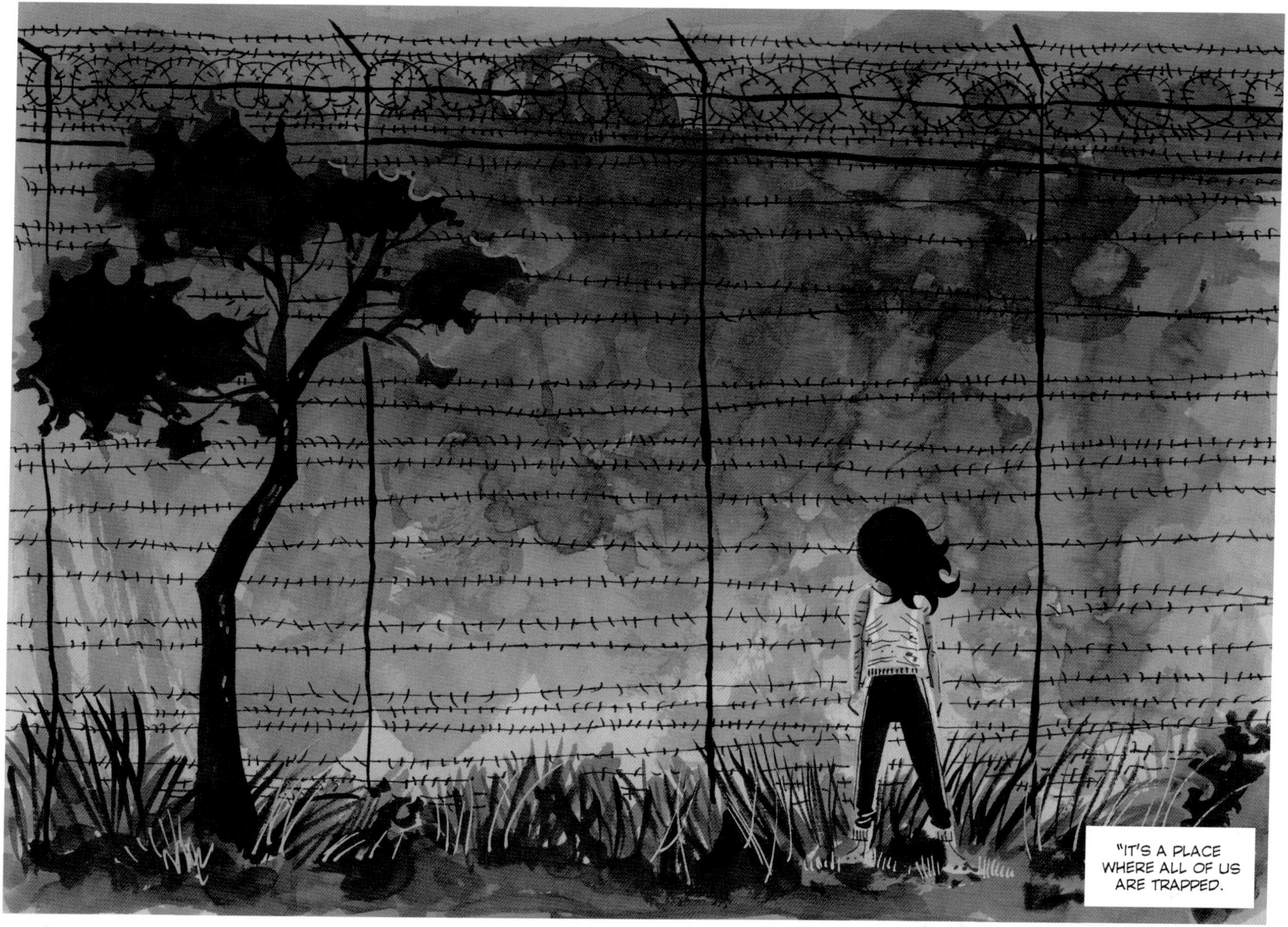
"IT'S A PLACE
WHERE ALL OF US
ARE TRAPPED.

"BUT I'M THE PRISON WARDEN THIS TIME."

# CHAPTER 5

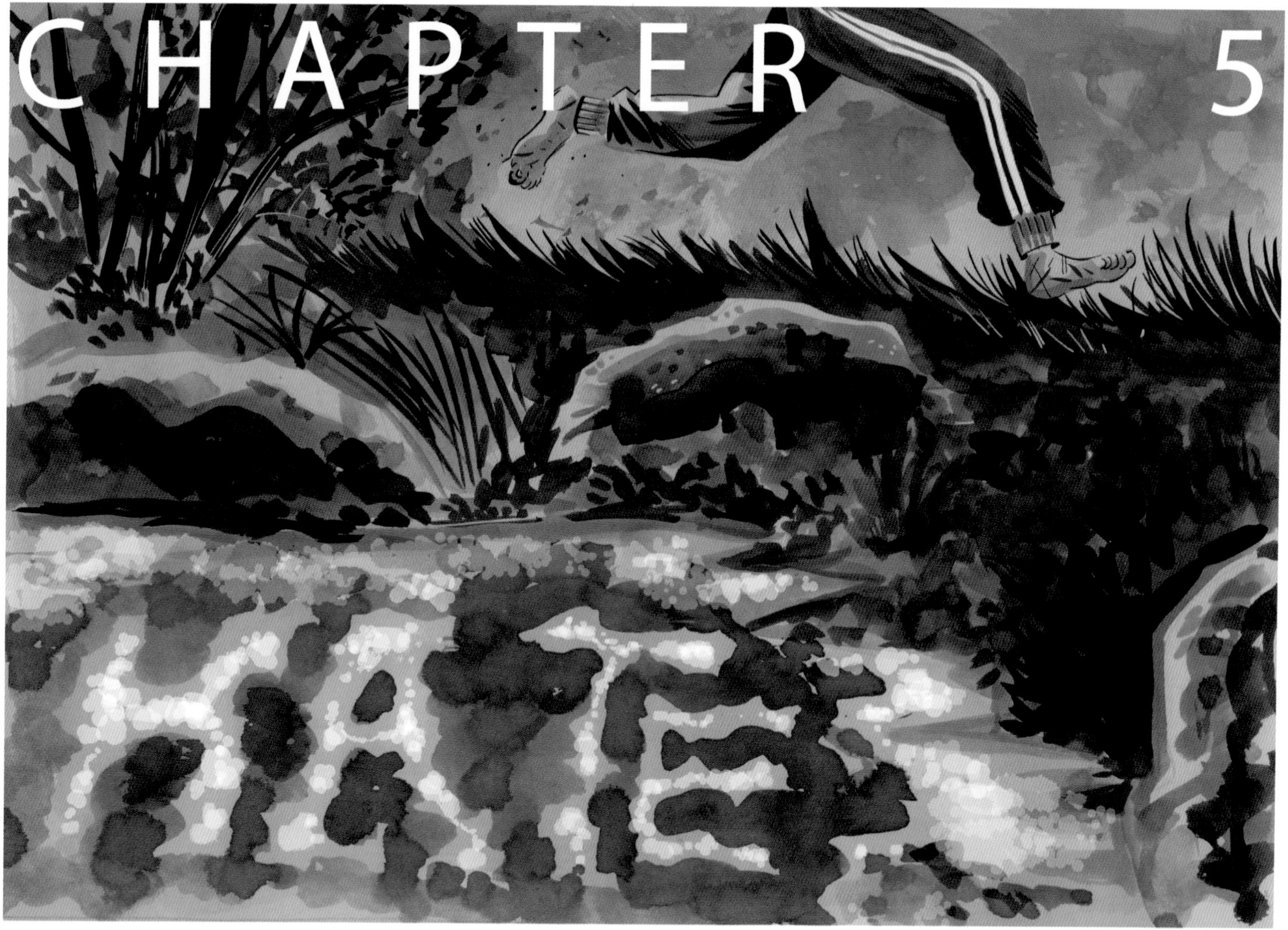

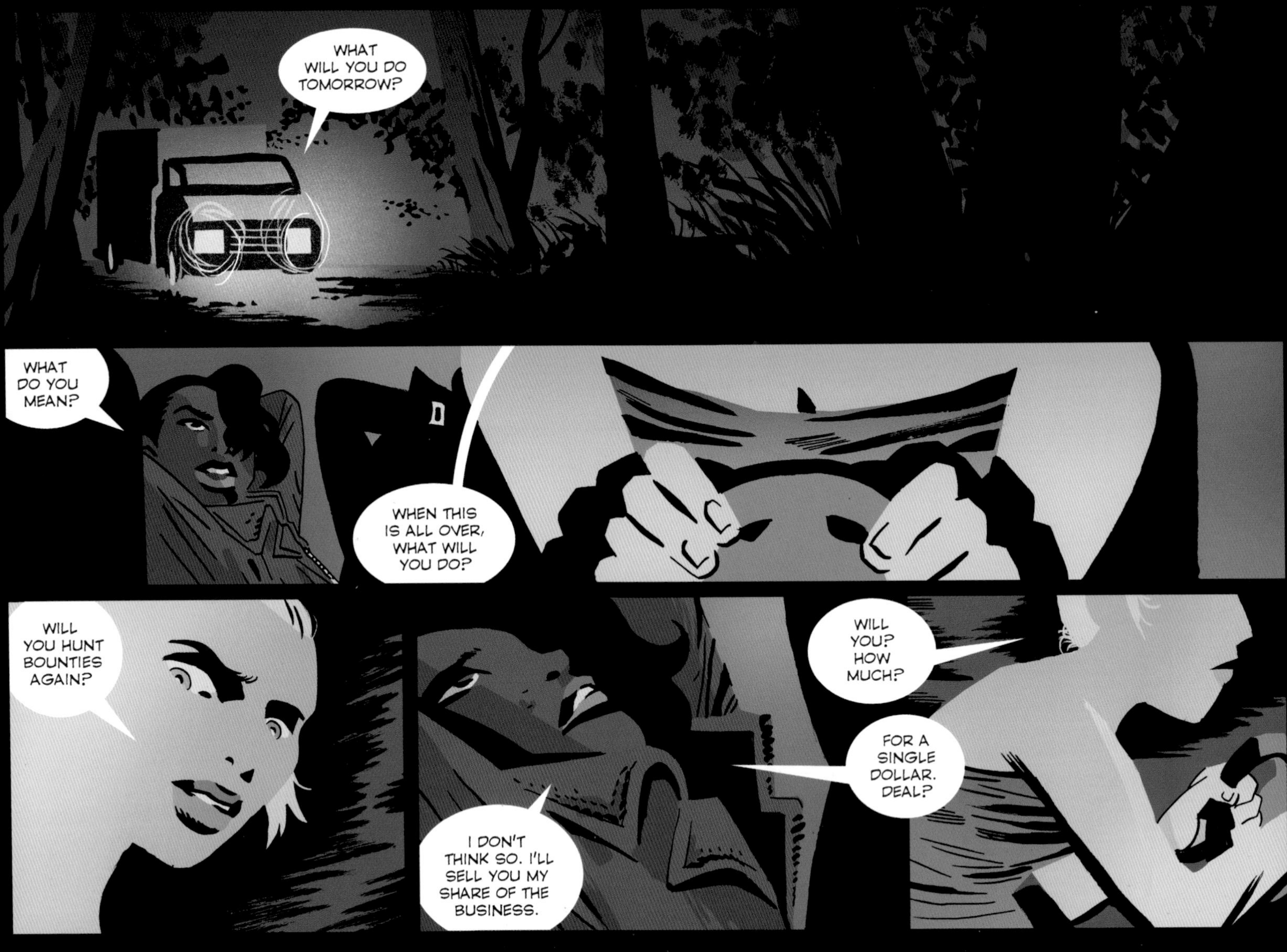
WHAT WILL YOU DO TOMORROW?
WHAT DO YOU MEAN?
WHEN THIS IS ALL OVER, WHAT WILL YOU DO?
WILL YOU HUNT BOUNTIES AGAIN?
I DON'T THINK SO. I'LL SELL YOU MY SHARE OF THE BUSINESS.
WILL YOU? HOW MUCH?
FOR A SINGLE DOLLAR. DEAL?

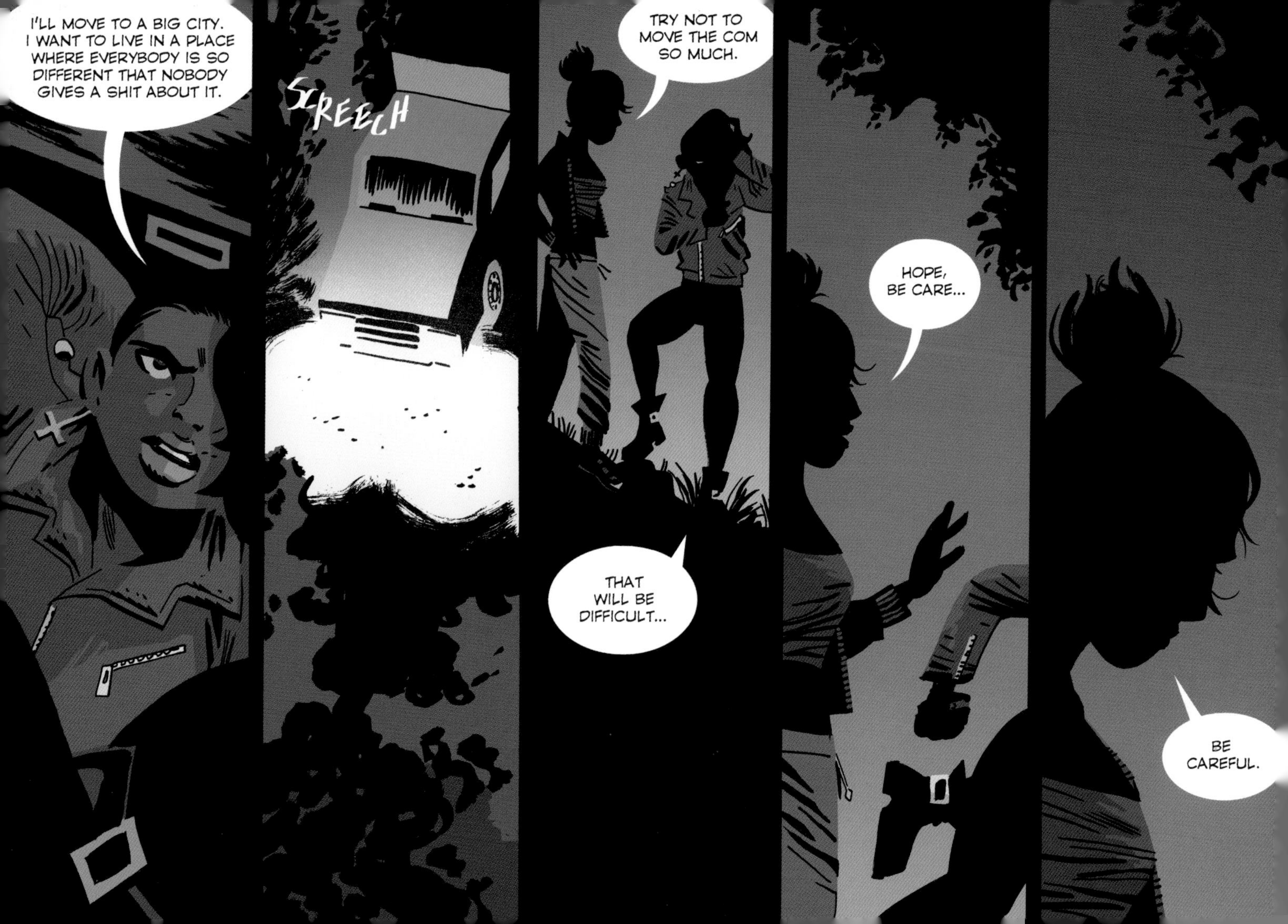
I'LL MOVE TO A BIG CITY. I WANT TO LIVE IN A PLACE WHERE EVERYBODY IS SO DIFFERENT THAT NOBODY GIVES A SHIT ABOUT IT.
SCREECH
TRY NOT TO MOVE THE COM SO MUCH.
THAT WILL BE DIFFICULT...
HOPE, BE CARE...
BE CAREFUL.

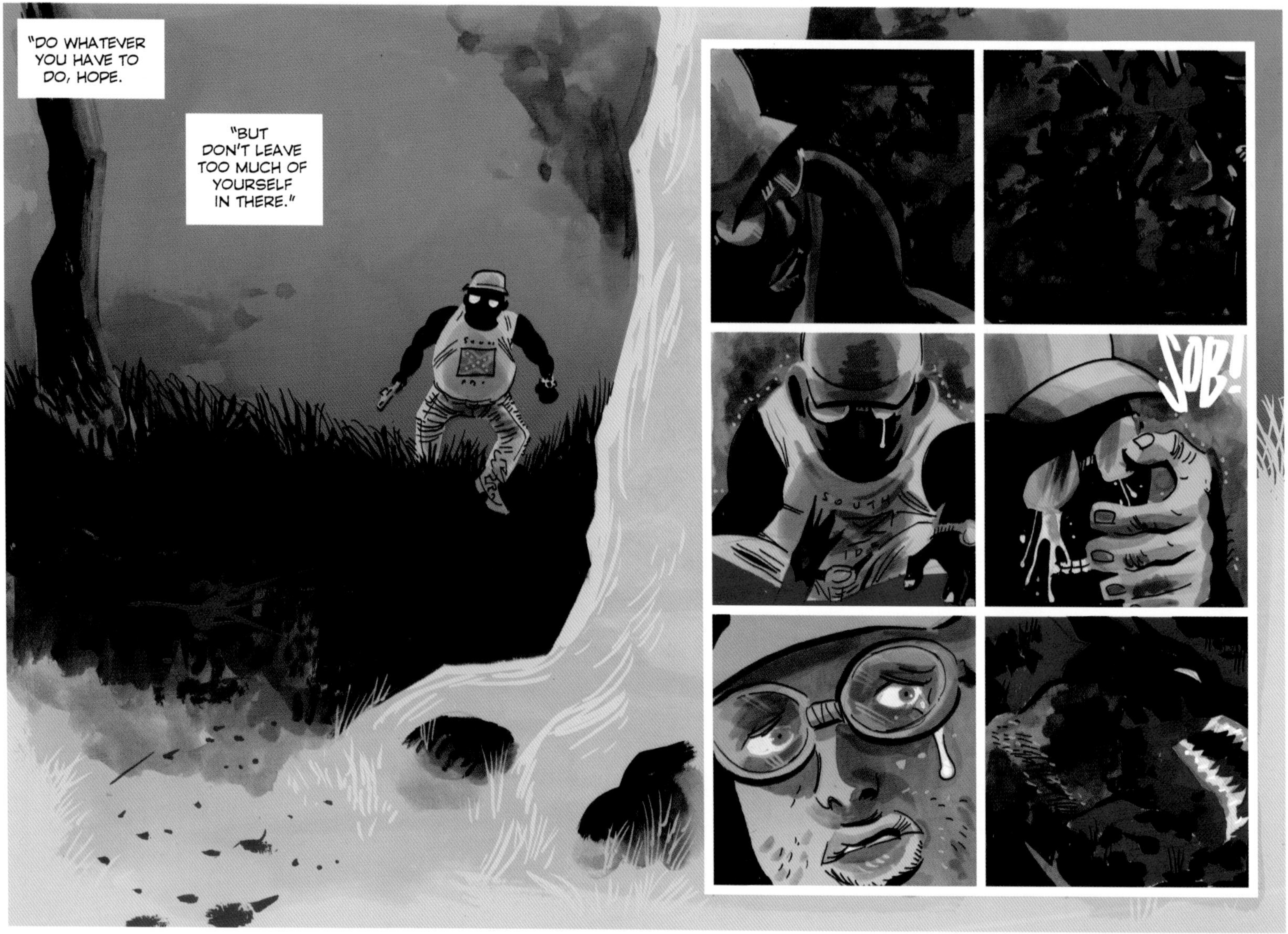
"DO WHATEVER YOU HAVE TO DO, HOPE.
"BUT DON'T LEAVE TOO MUCH OF YOURSELF IN THERE."
SOB!

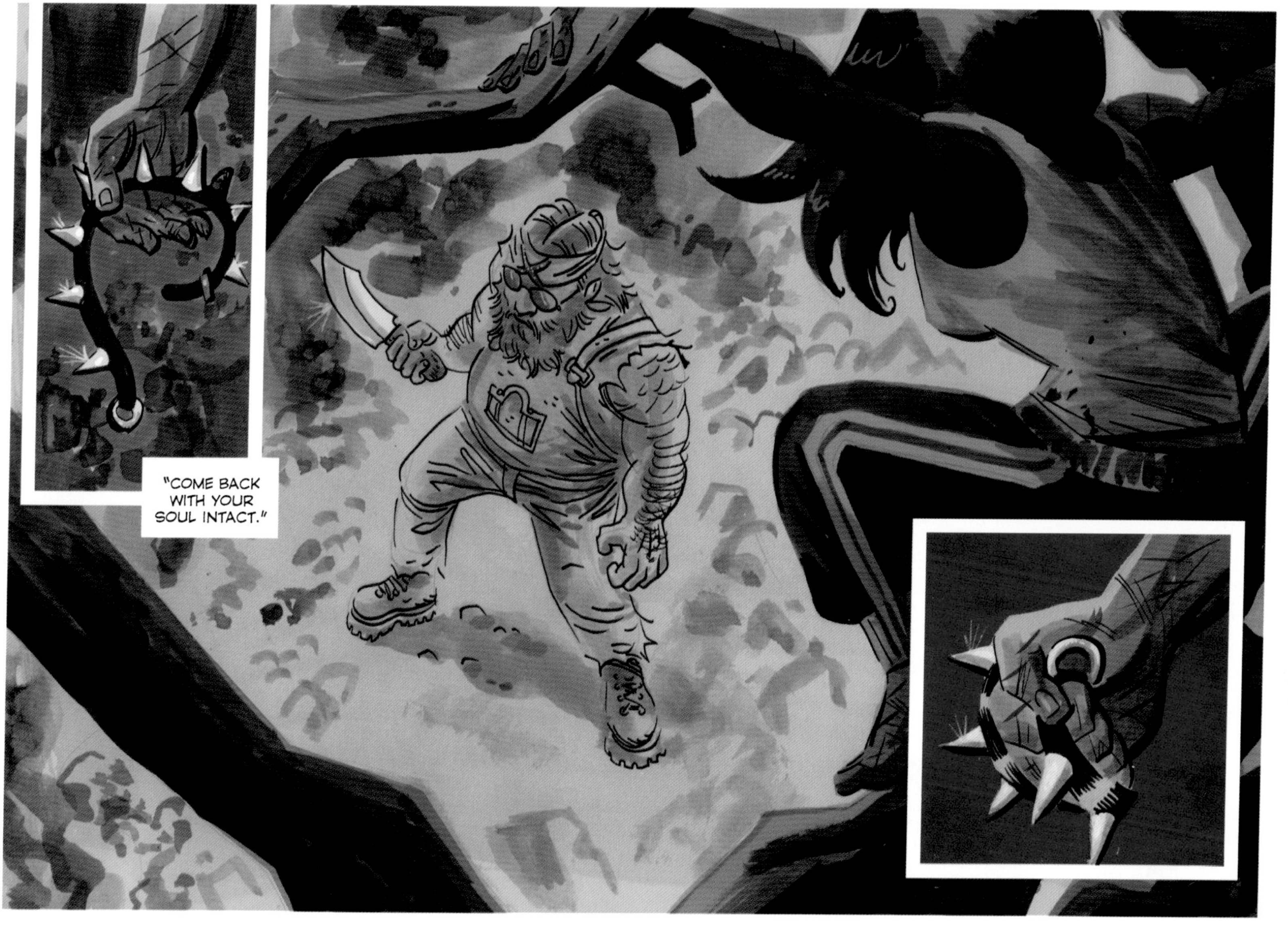
"COME BACK
WITH YOUR
SOUL INTACT."

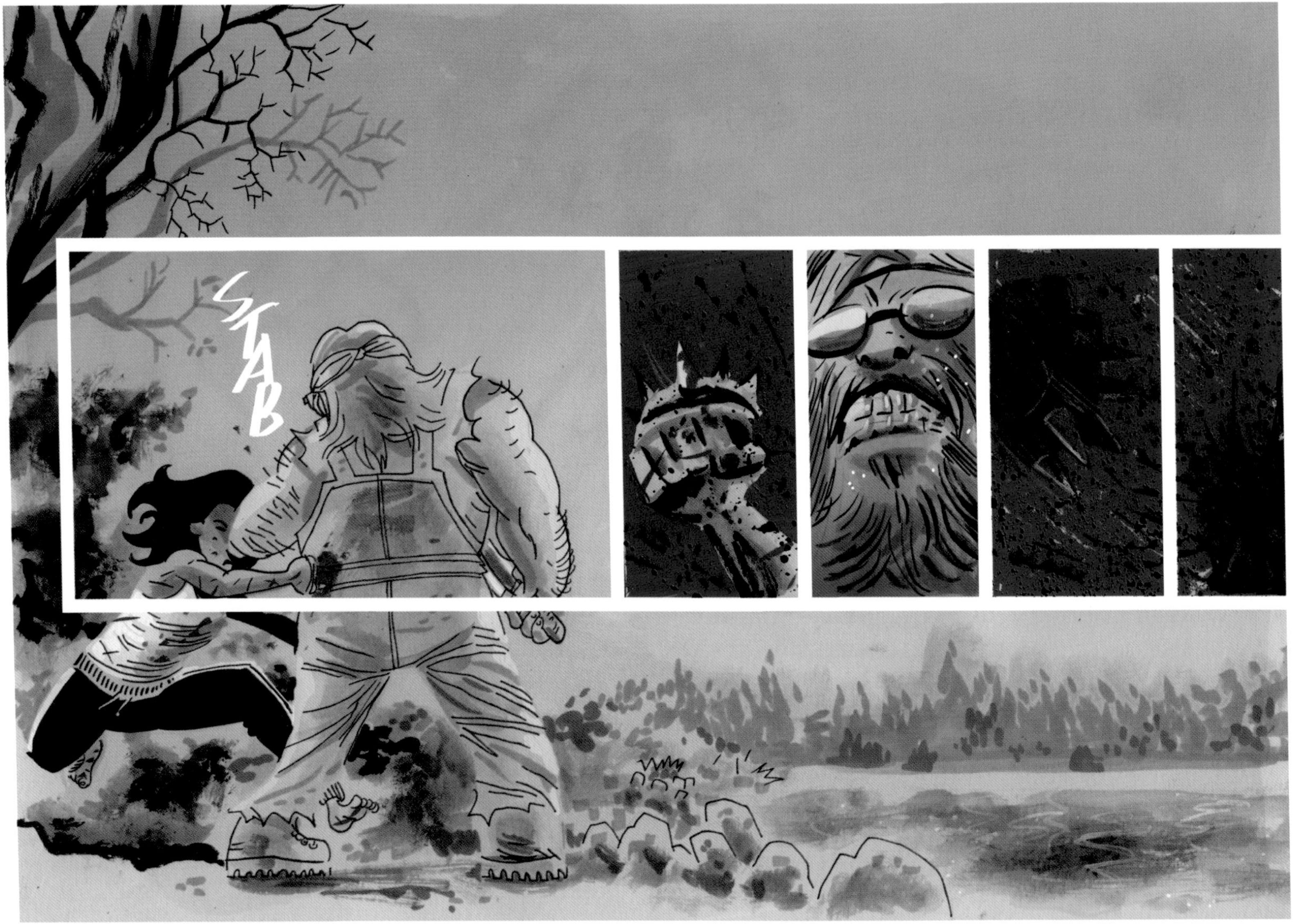
STAB

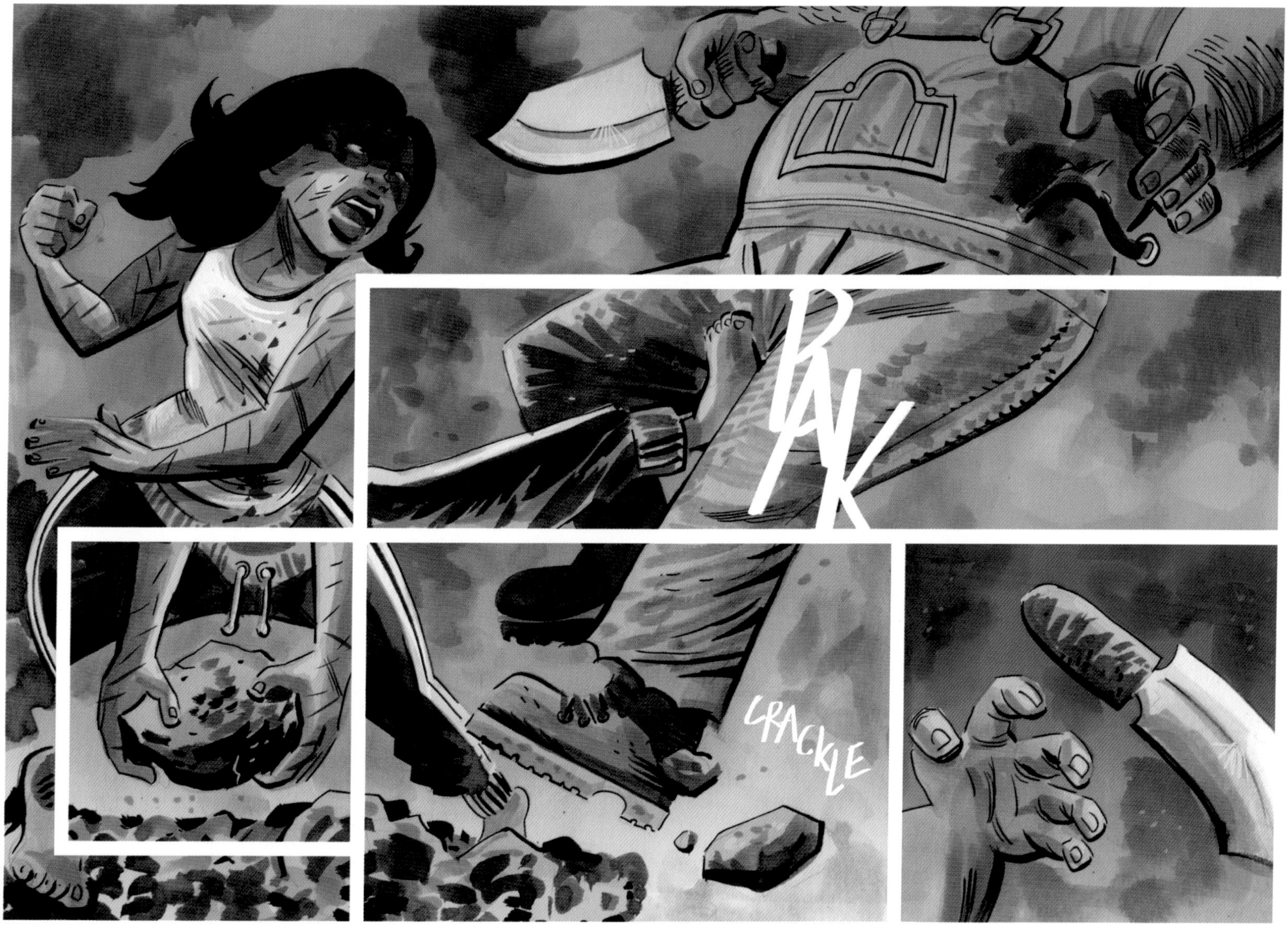
PLANK
CRACKLE

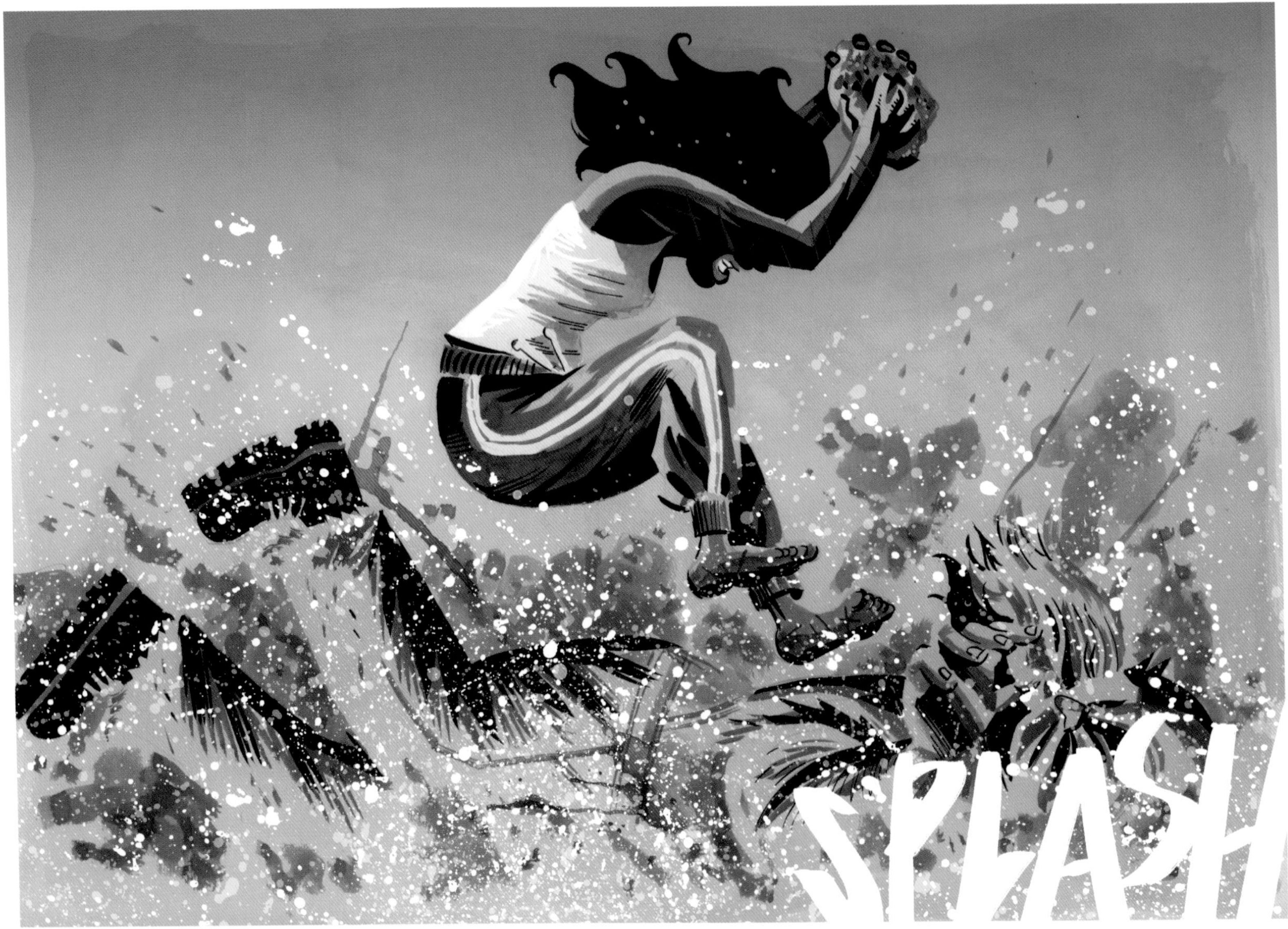
SPLASH

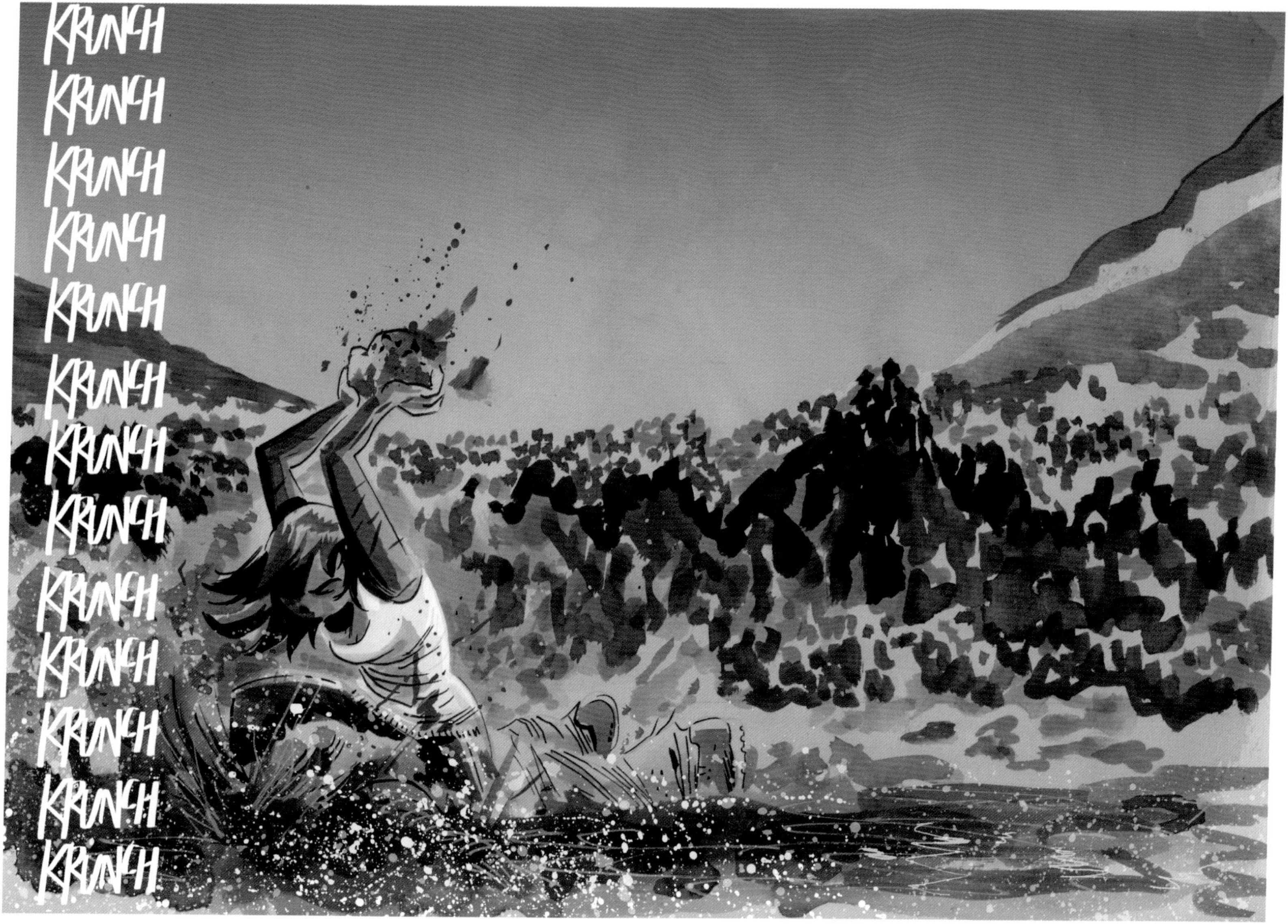
KRUNCH
KRUNCH
KRUNCH
KRUNCH
KRUNCH
KRUNCH
KRUNCH
KRUNCH
KRUNCH
KRUNCH
KRUNCH
KRUNCH
KRUNCH

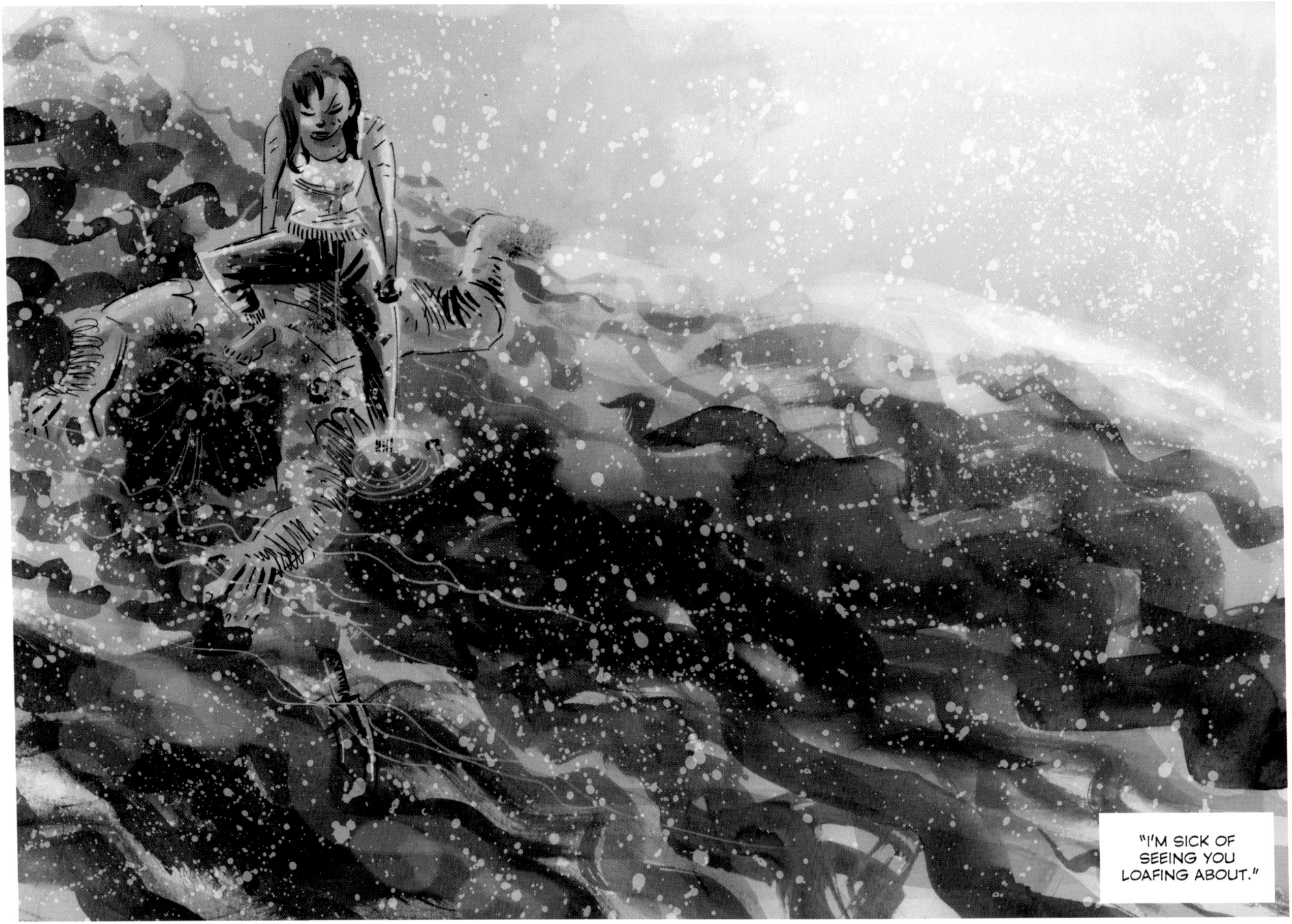
"I'M SICK OF SEEING YOU LOAFING ABOUT."

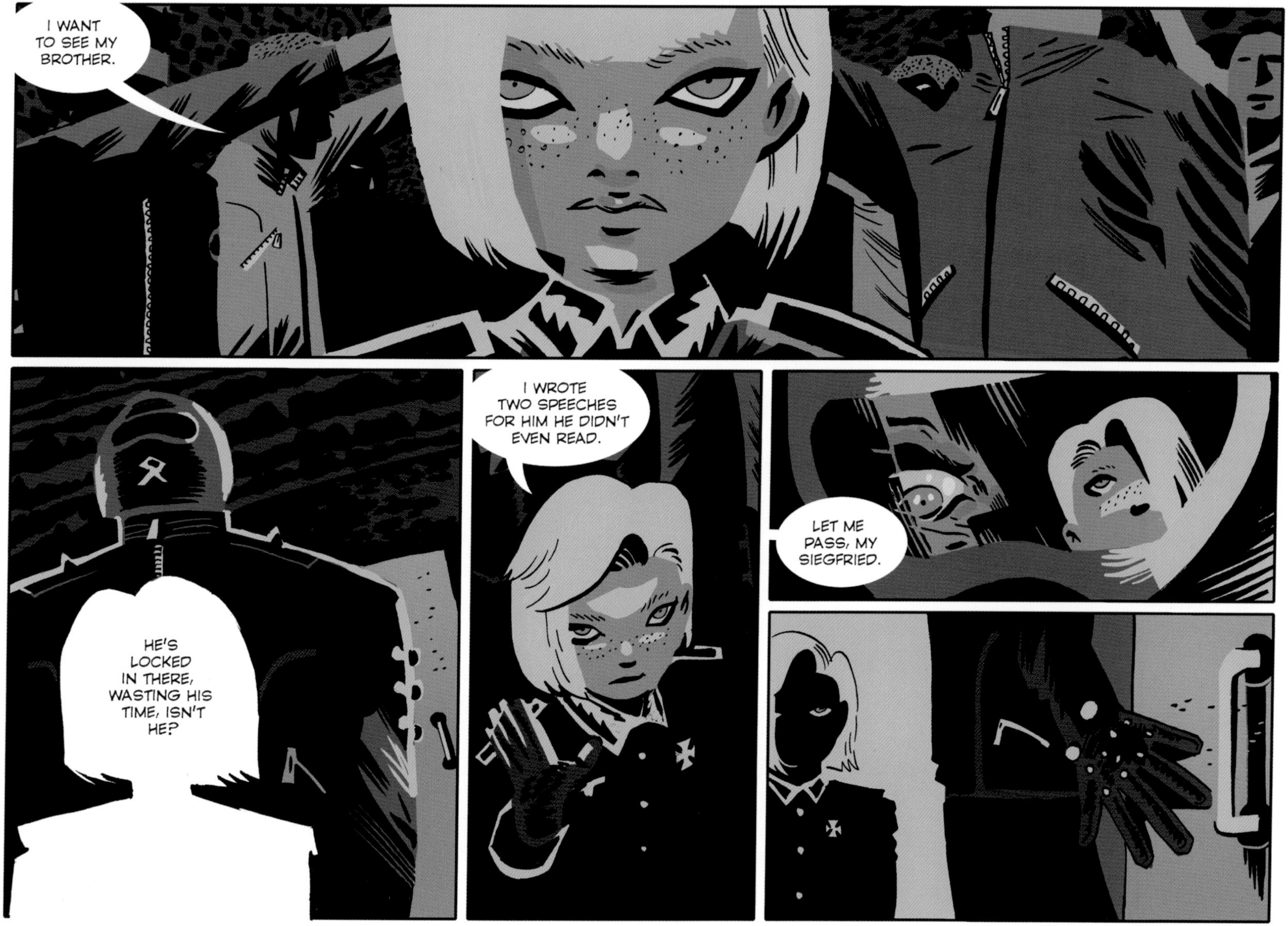
I WANT TO SEE MY BROTHER.
HE'S LOCKED IN THERE, WASTING HIS TIME, ISN'T HE?
I WROTE TWO SPEECHES FOR HIM HE DIDN'T EVEN READ.
LET ME PASS, MY SIEGFRIED.

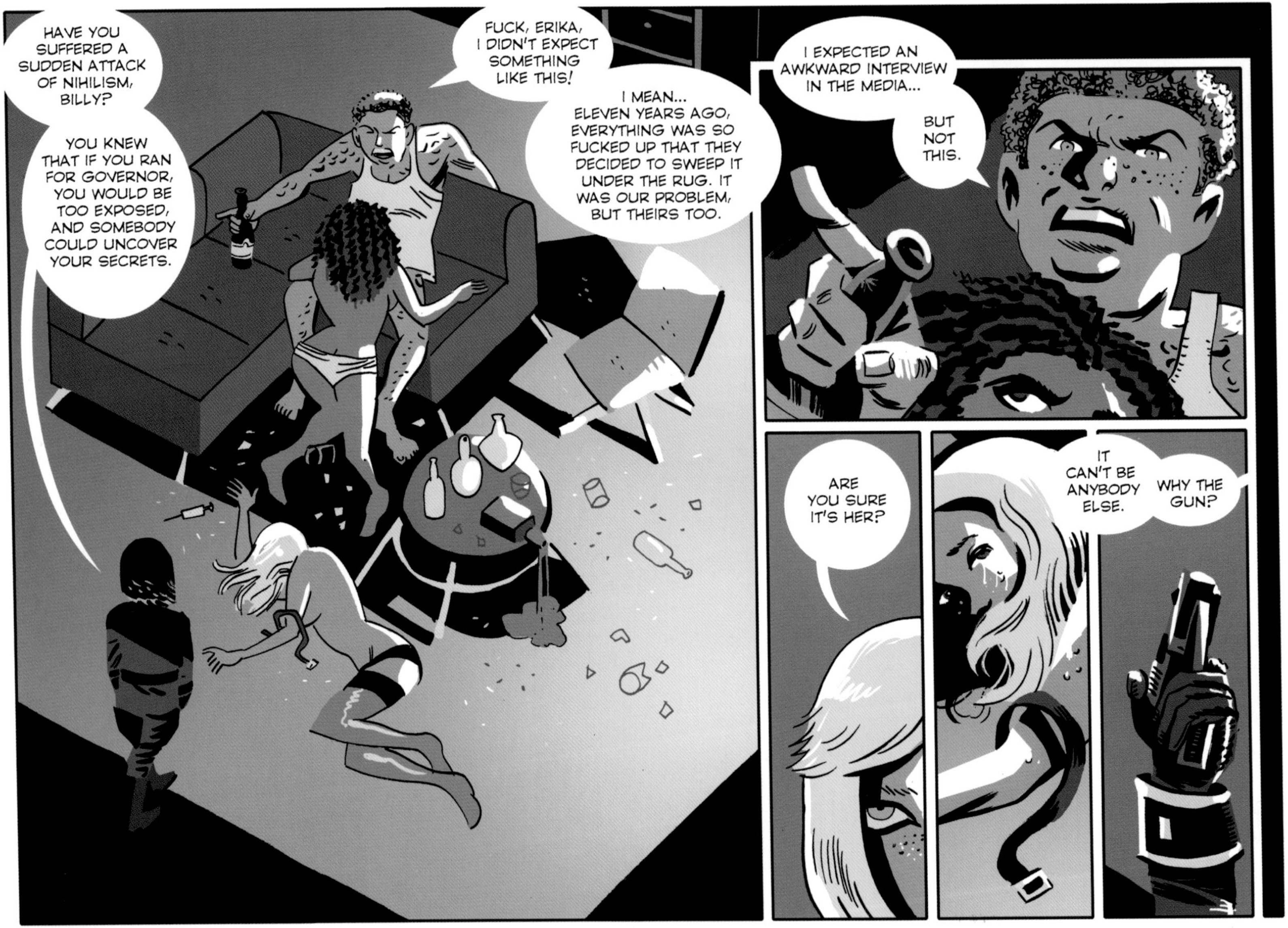
HAVE YOU SUFFERED A SUDDEN ATTACK OF NIHILISM, BILLY?
YOU KNEW THAT IF YOU RAN FOR GOVERNOR, YOU WOULD BE TOO EXPOSED, AND SOMEBODY COULD UNCOVER YOUR SECRETS.
FUCK, ERIKA, I DIDN'T EXPECT SOMETHING LIKE THIS!
I MEAN... ELEVEN YEARS AGO, EVERYTHING WAS SO FUCKED UP THAT THEY DECIDED TO SWEEP IT UNDER THE RUG. IT WAS OUR PROBLEM, BUT THEIRS TOO.
I EXPECTED AN AWKWARD INTERVIEW IN THE MEDIA...
BUT NOT THIS.
ARE YOU SURE IT'S HER?
IT CAN'T BE ANYBODY ELSE.
WHY THE GUN?

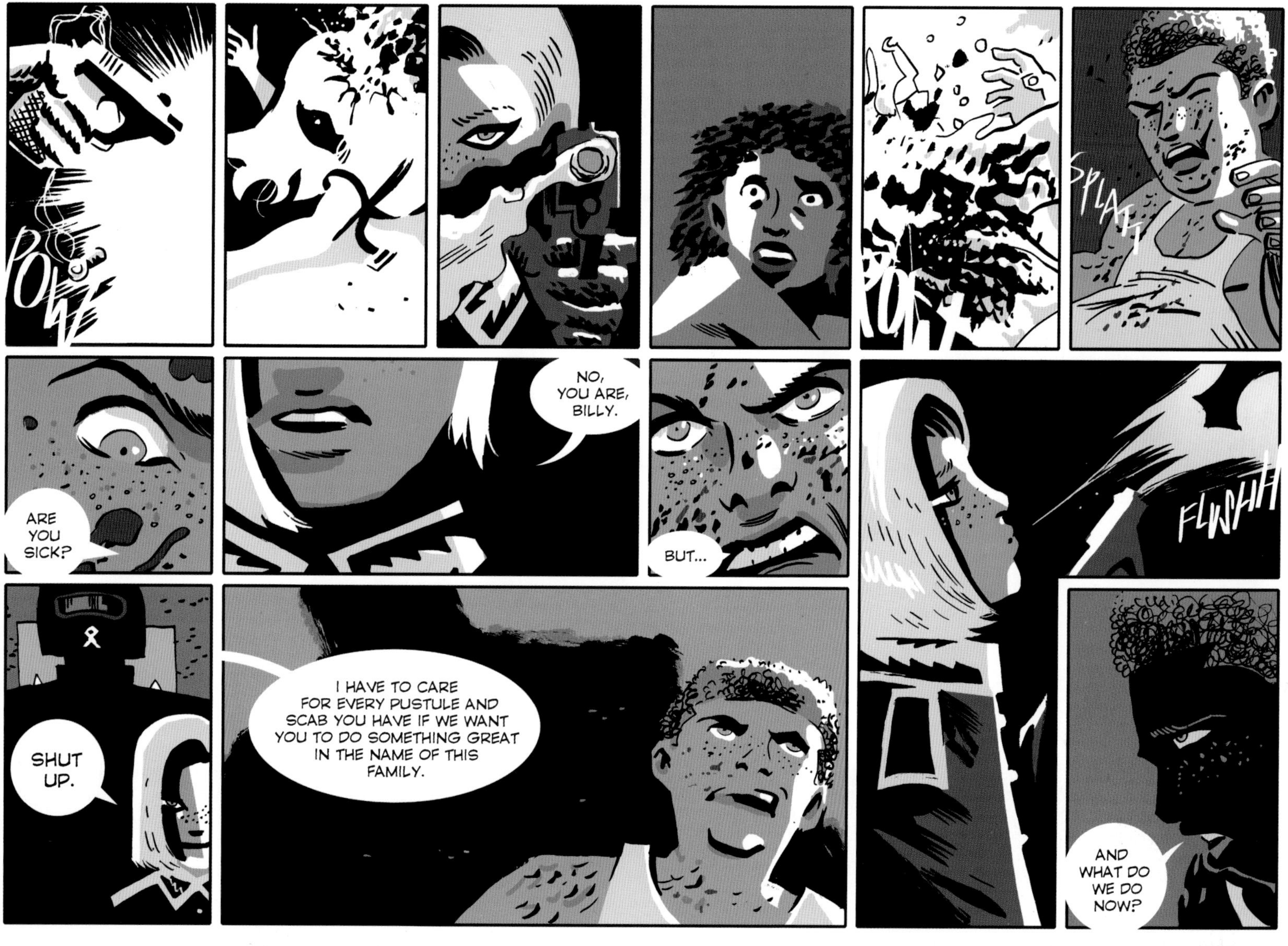
POW
SPLAT
POW
ARE YOU SICK?
NO, YOU ARE, BILLY.
BUT...
FLWSHH
SHUT UP.
I HAVE TO CARE FOR EVERY PUSTULE AND SCAB YOU HAVE IF WE WANT YOU TO DO SOMETHING GREAT IN THE NAME OF THIS FAMILY.
AND WHAT DO WE DO NOW?

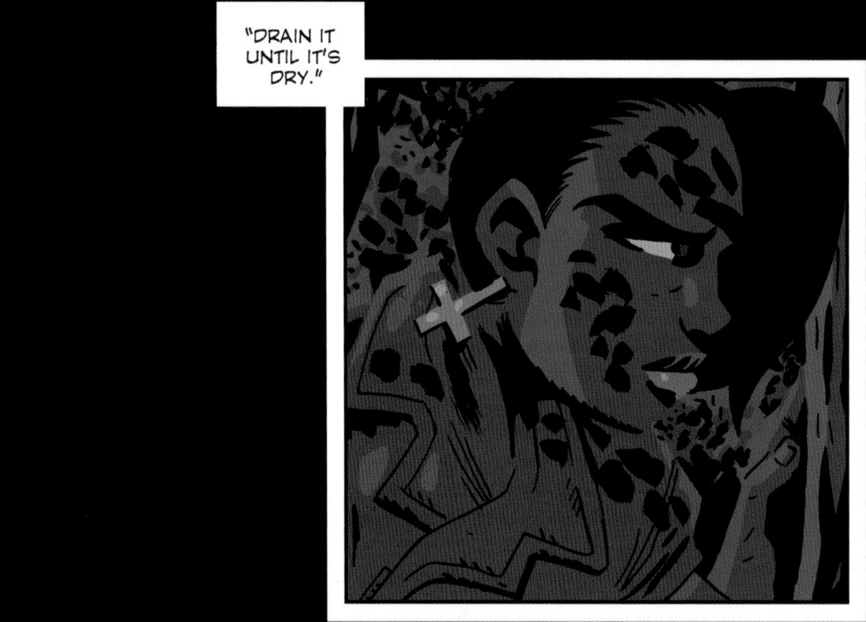
"DRAIN IT UNTIL IT'S DRY."

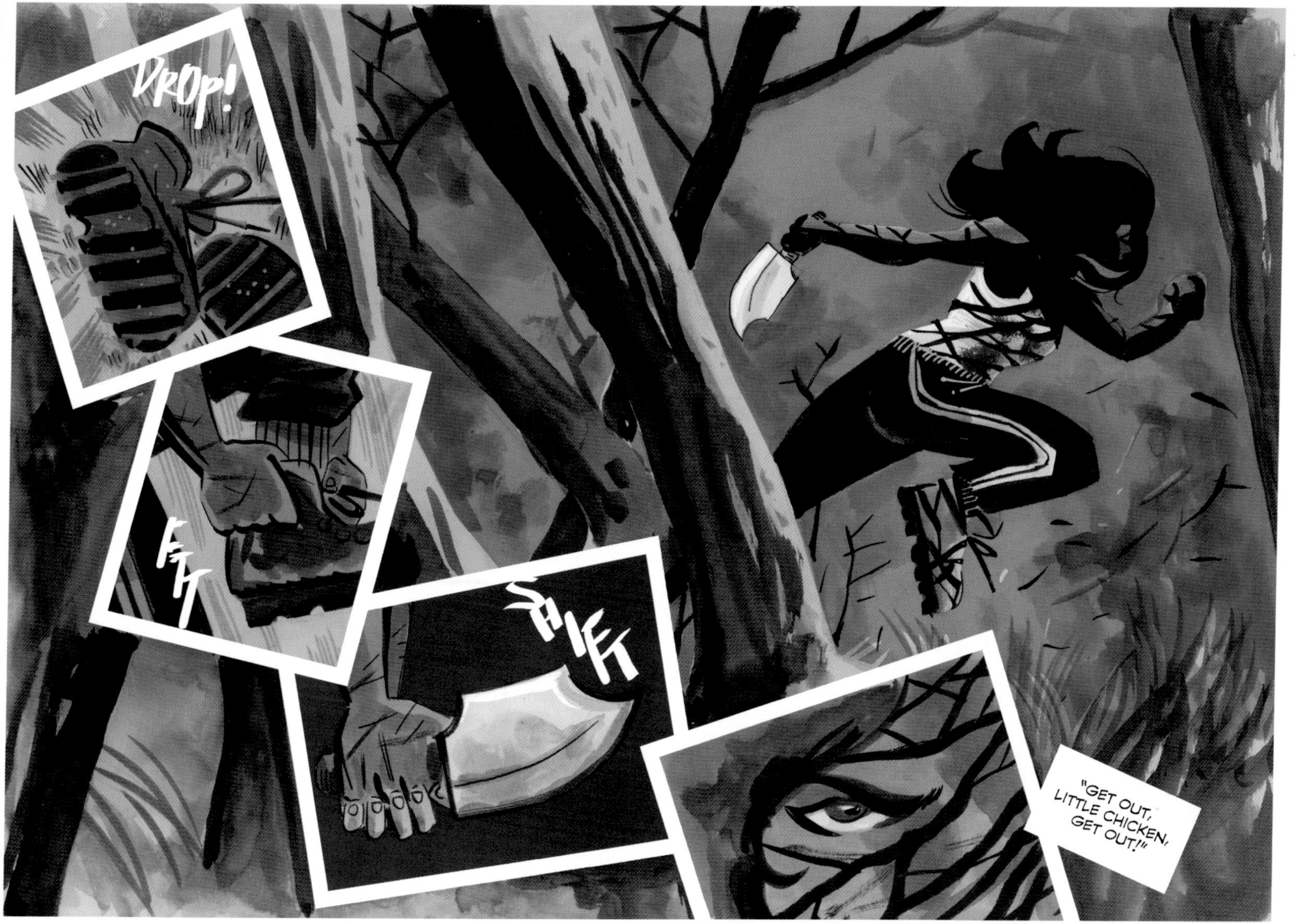
DROP!
FFT
SHIFT
"GET OUT, LITTLE CHICKEN, GET OUT!"

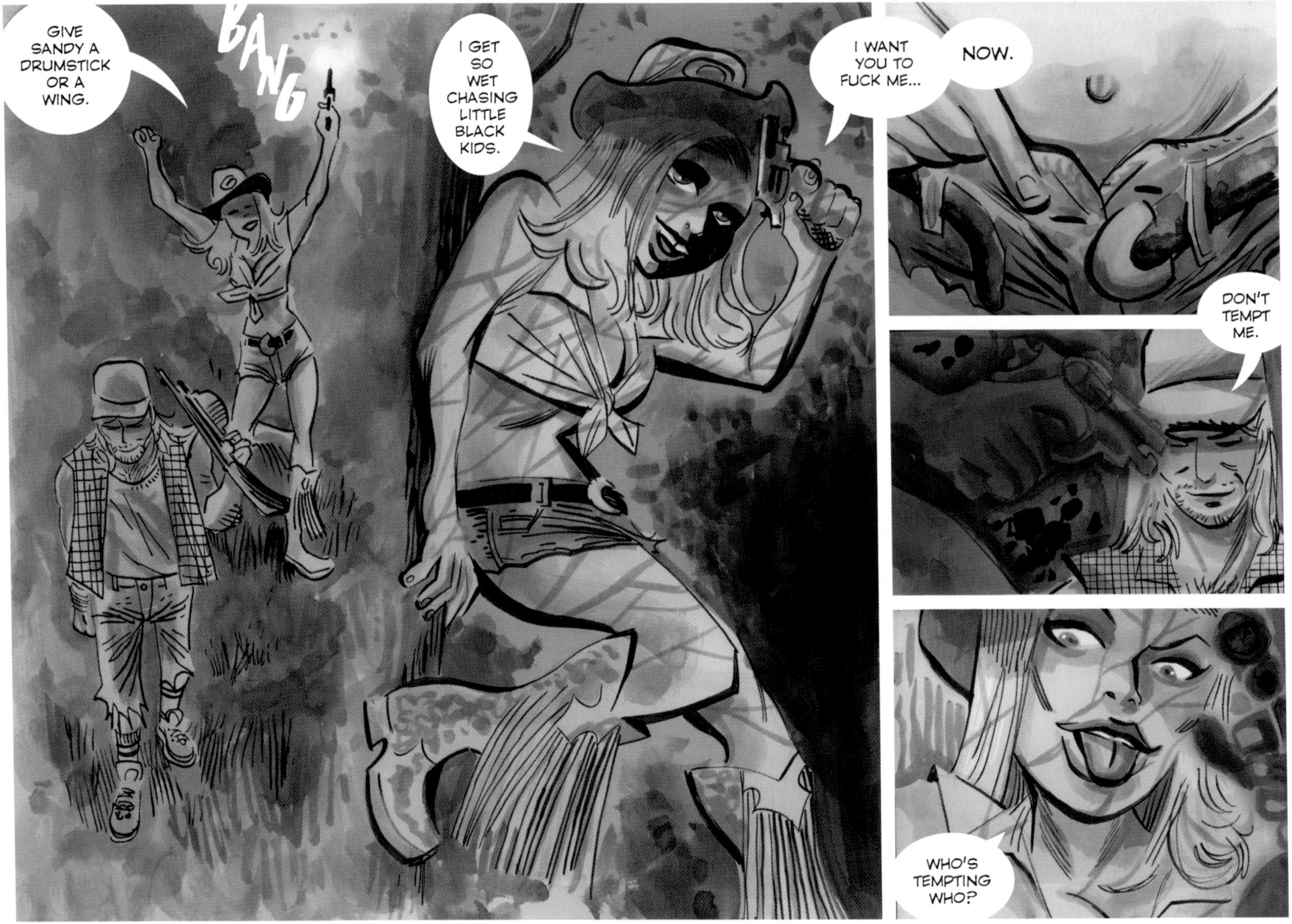
GIVE SANDY A DRUMSTICK OR A WING.
BANG
I GET SO WET CHASING LITTLE BLACK KIDS.
I WANT YOU TO FUCK ME...
NOW.
DON'T TEMPT ME.
WHO'S TEMPTING WHO?

# CHAPTER 6

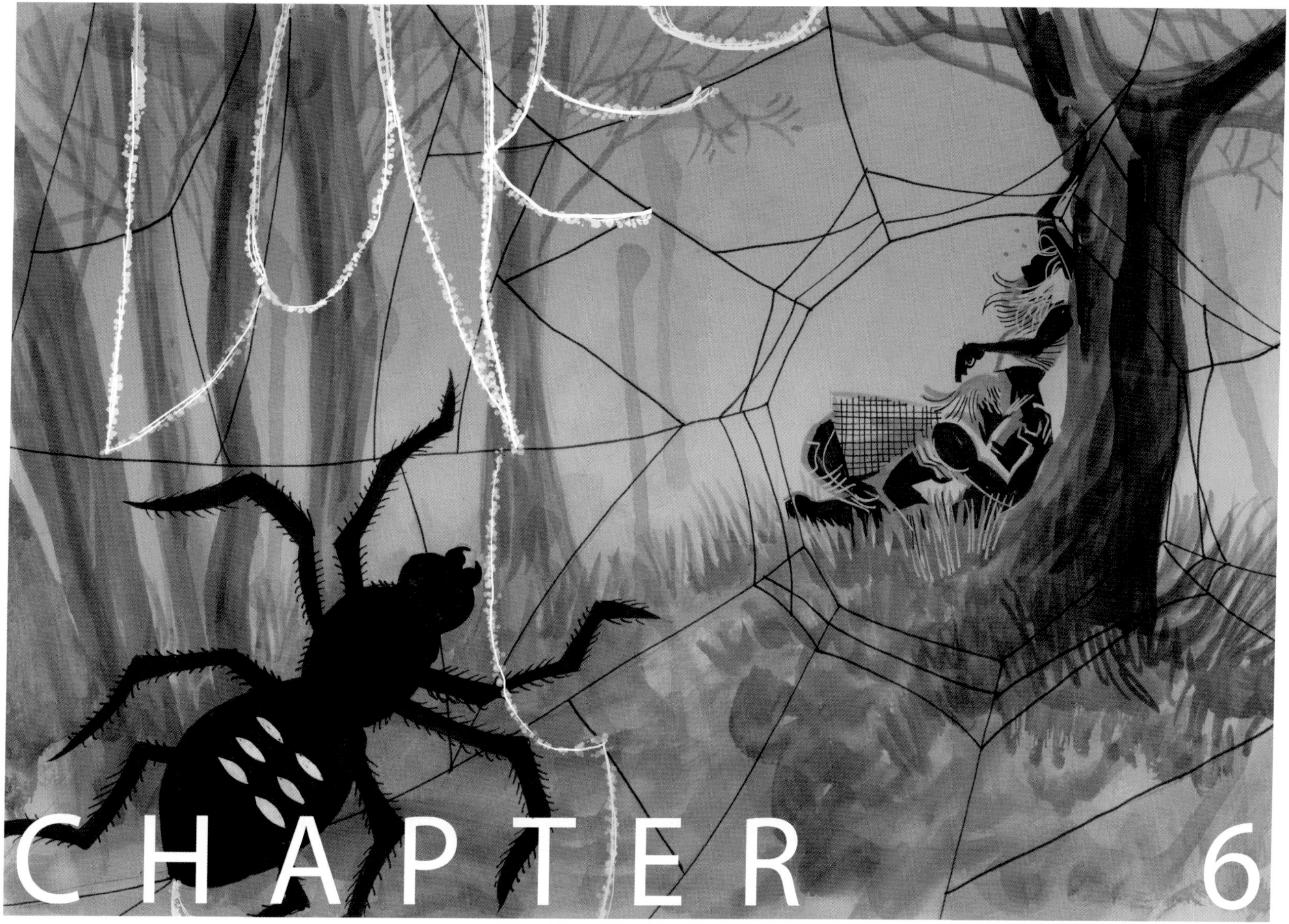

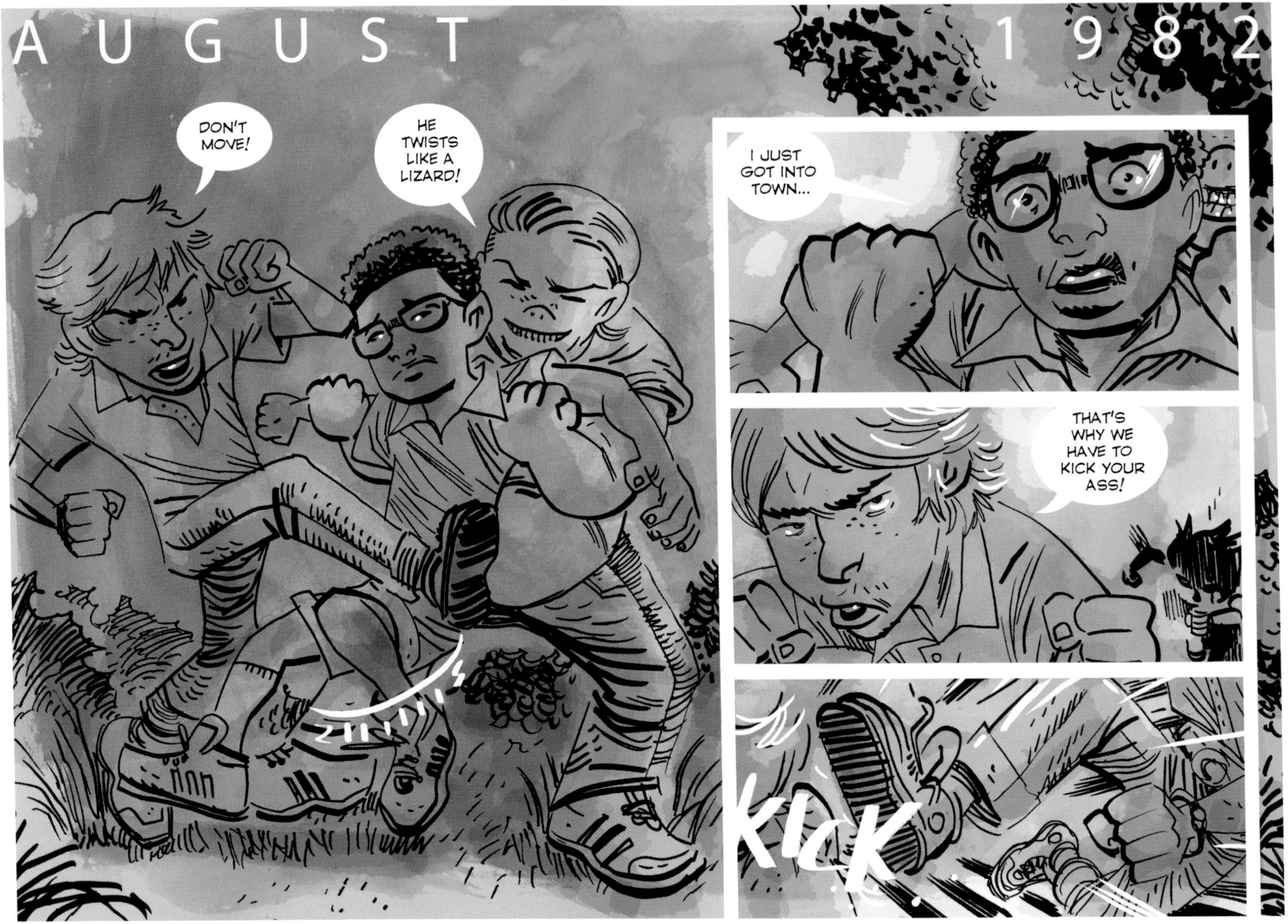
AUGUST 1982
DON'T MOVE!
HE TWISTS LIKE A LIZARD!
I JUST GOT INTO TOWN...
THAT'S WHY WE HAVE TO KICK YOUR ASS!
KICK

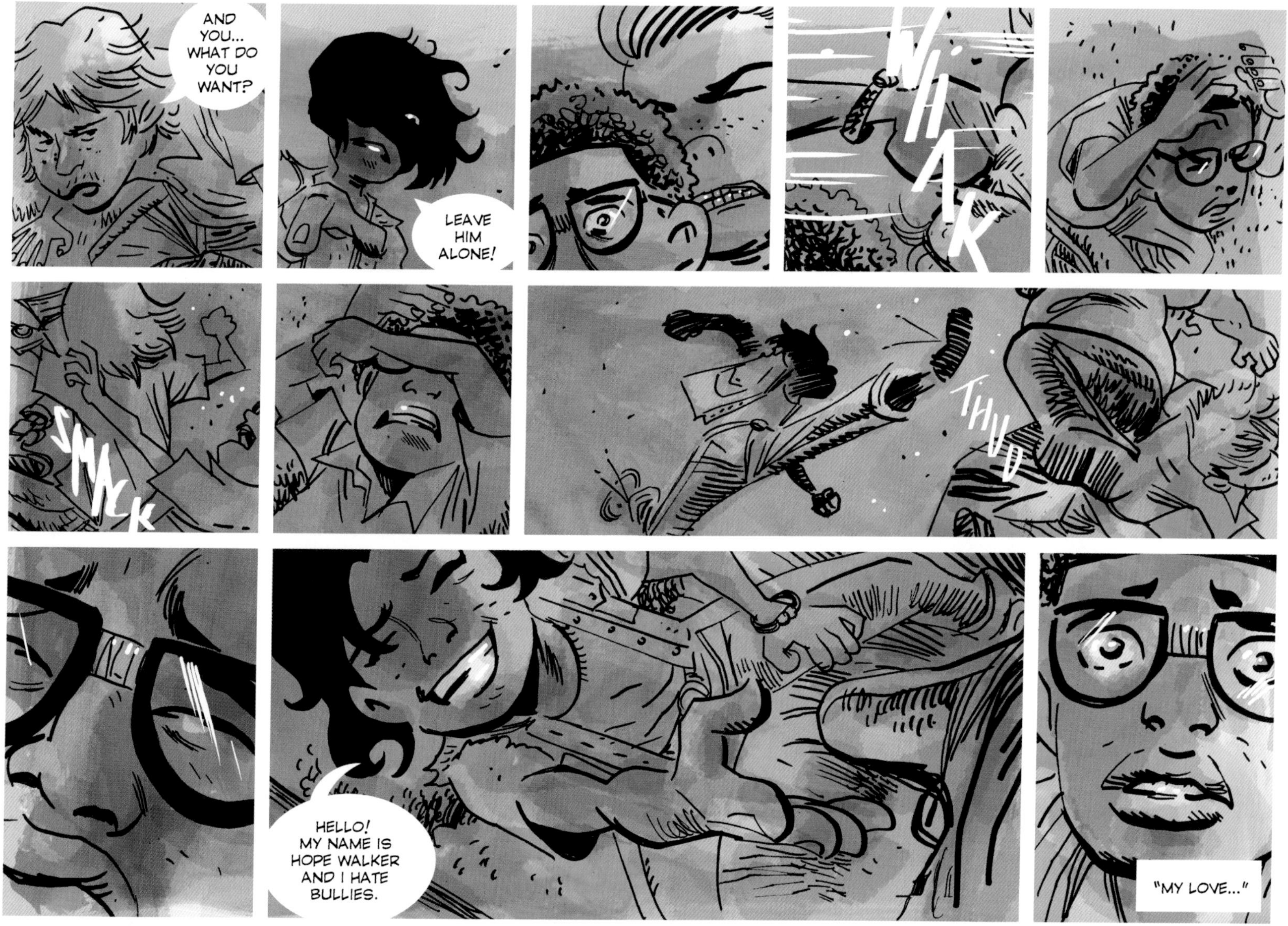
AND YOU... WHAT DO YOU WANT?
LEAVE HIM ALONE!
WHAK
SMACK
THUD
HELLO! MY NAME IS HOPE WALKER AND I HATE BULLIES.
"MY LOVE..."

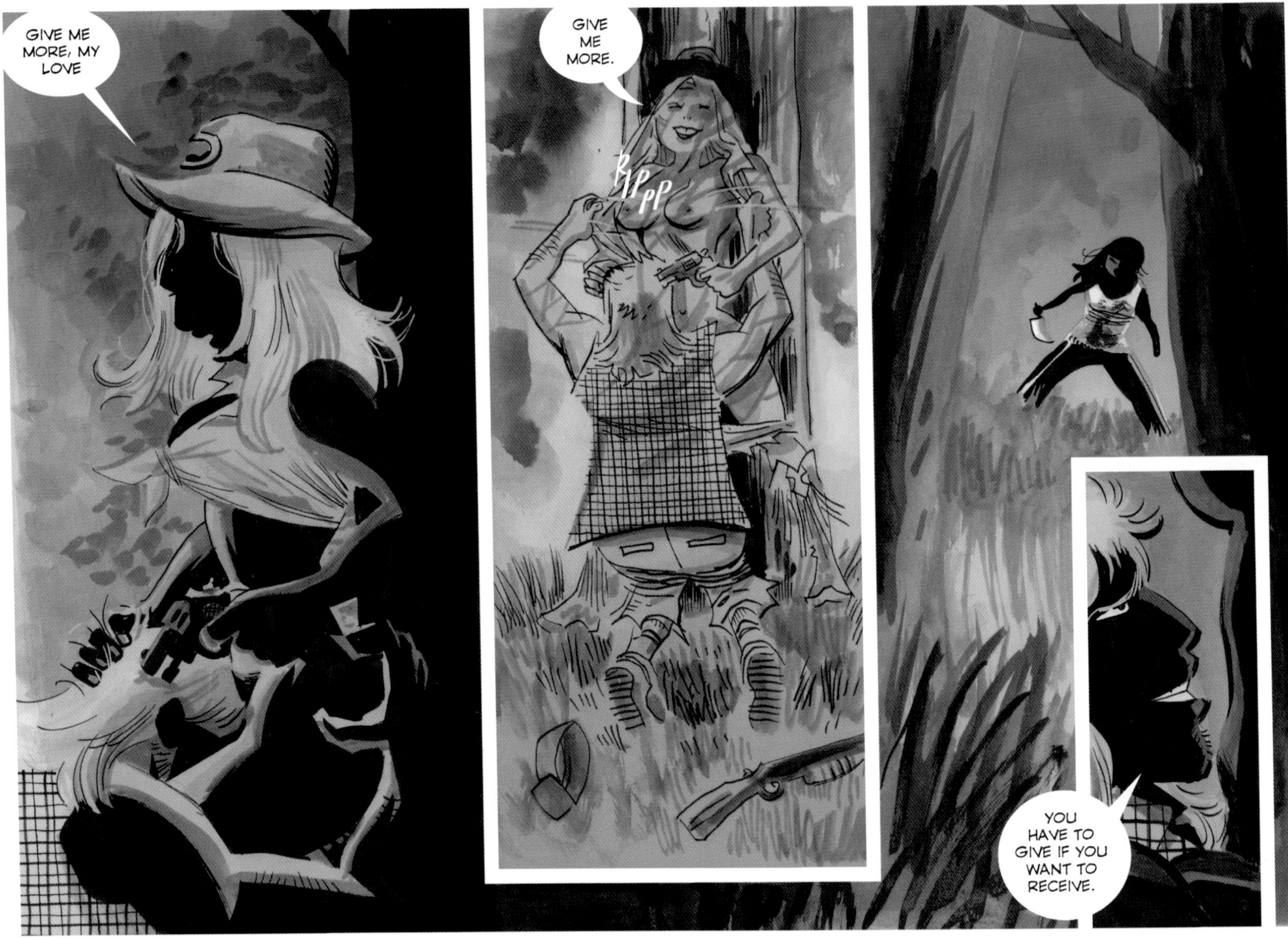
GIVE ME MORE, MY LOVE
GIVE ME MORE.
RIPPP
YOU HAVE TO GIVE IF YOU WANT TO RECEIVE.

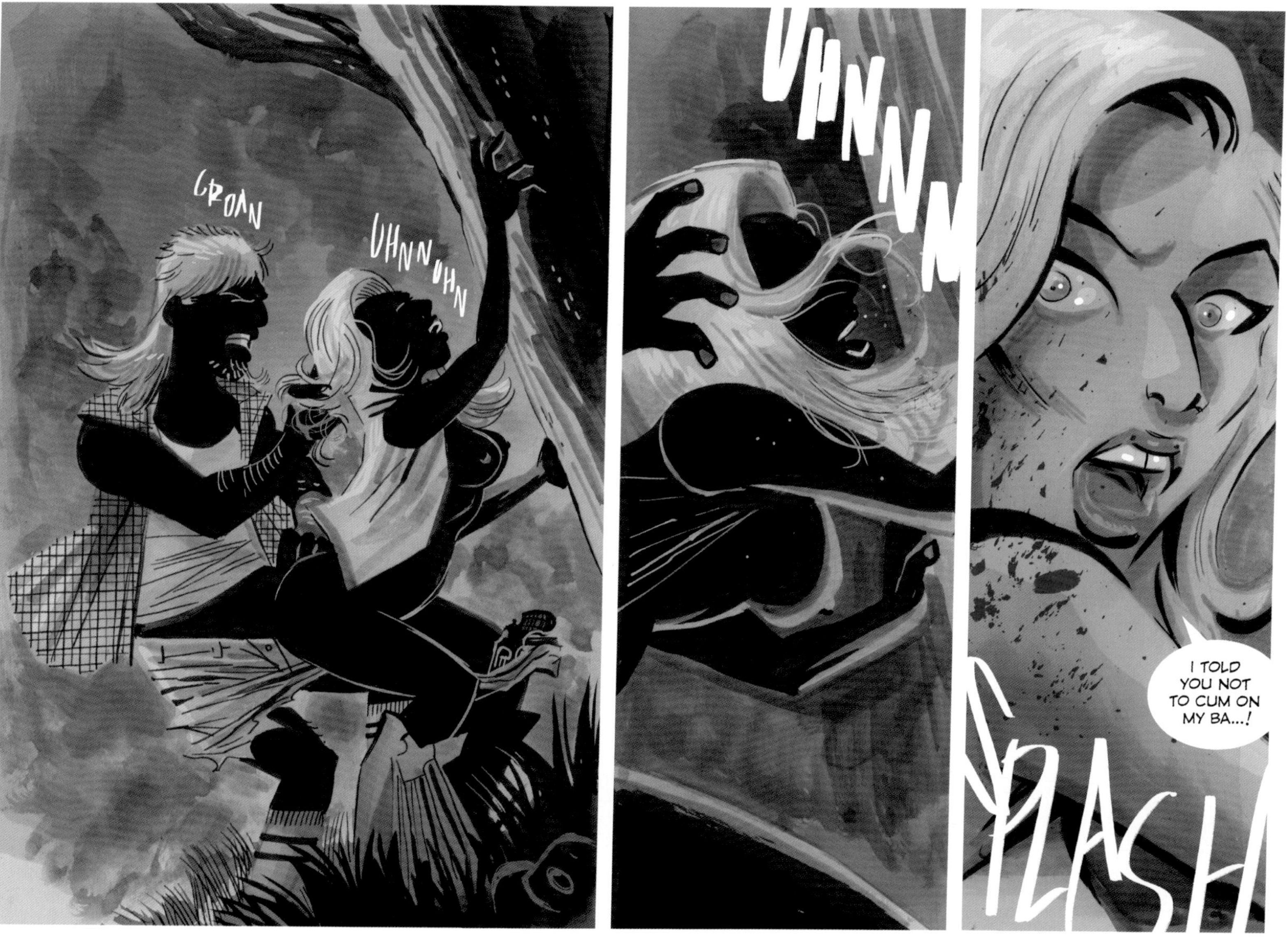
GROAN
UHNNUHN
UHNNNN
I TOLD YOU NOT TO CUM ON MY BA...!
SPLASH

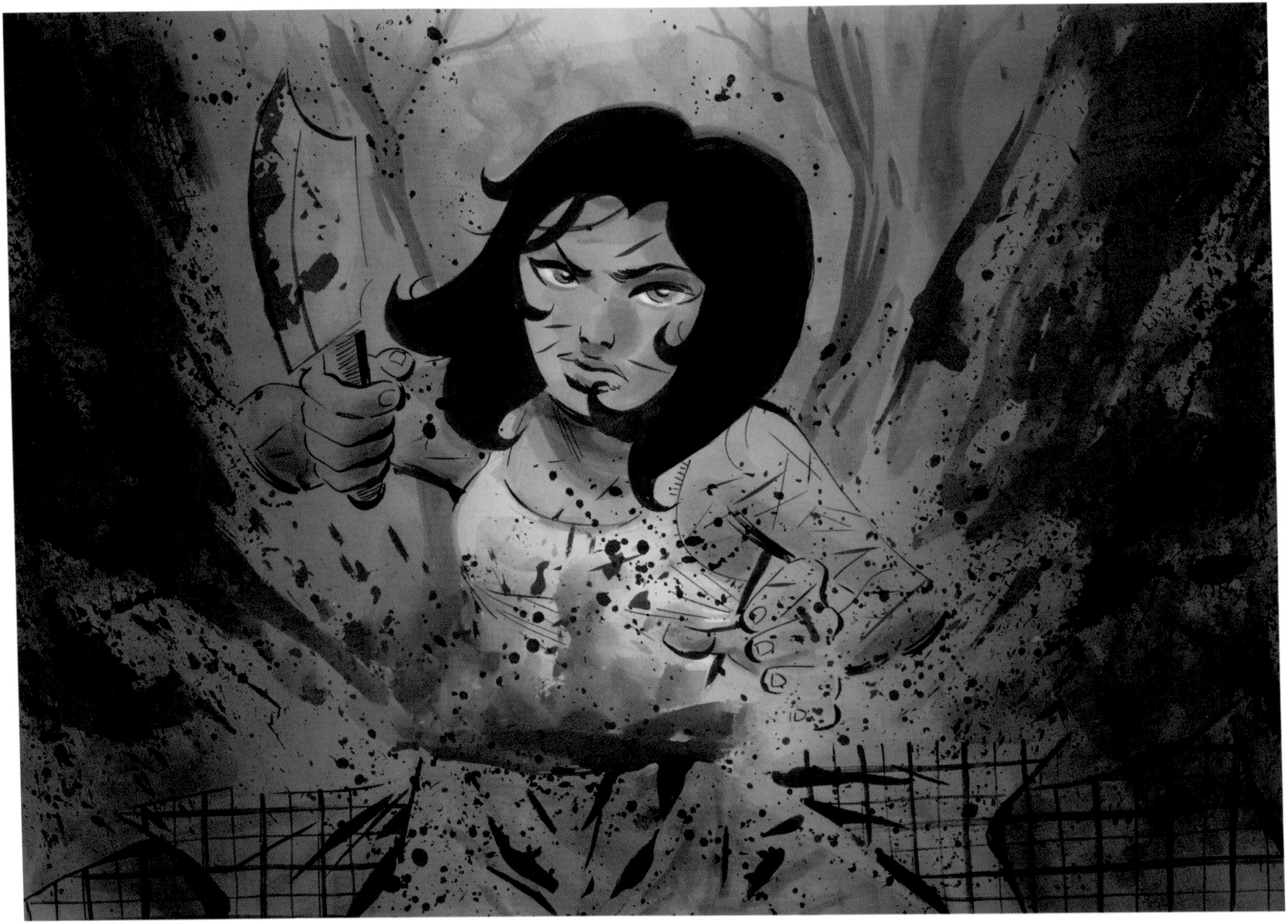

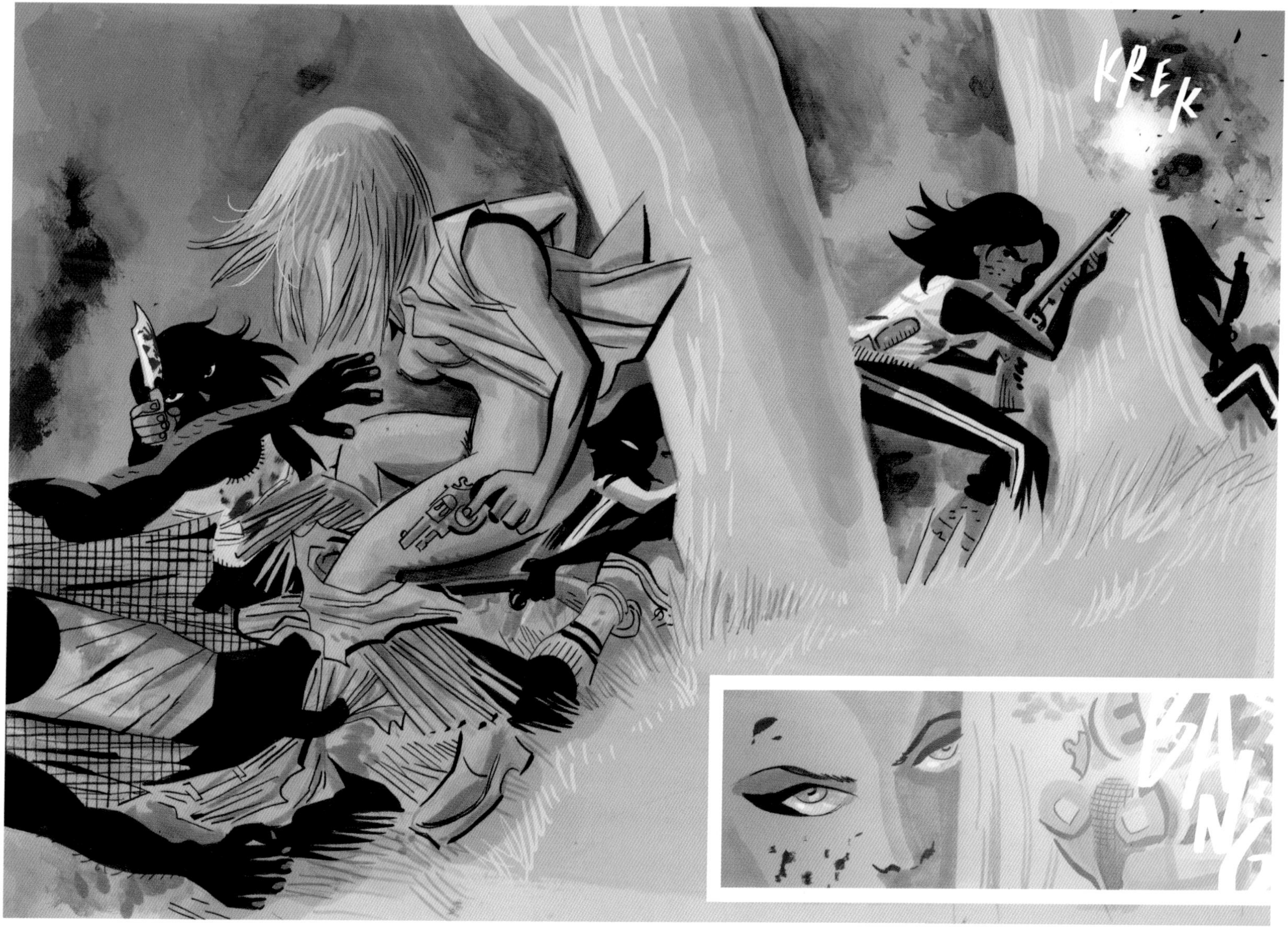
KREK

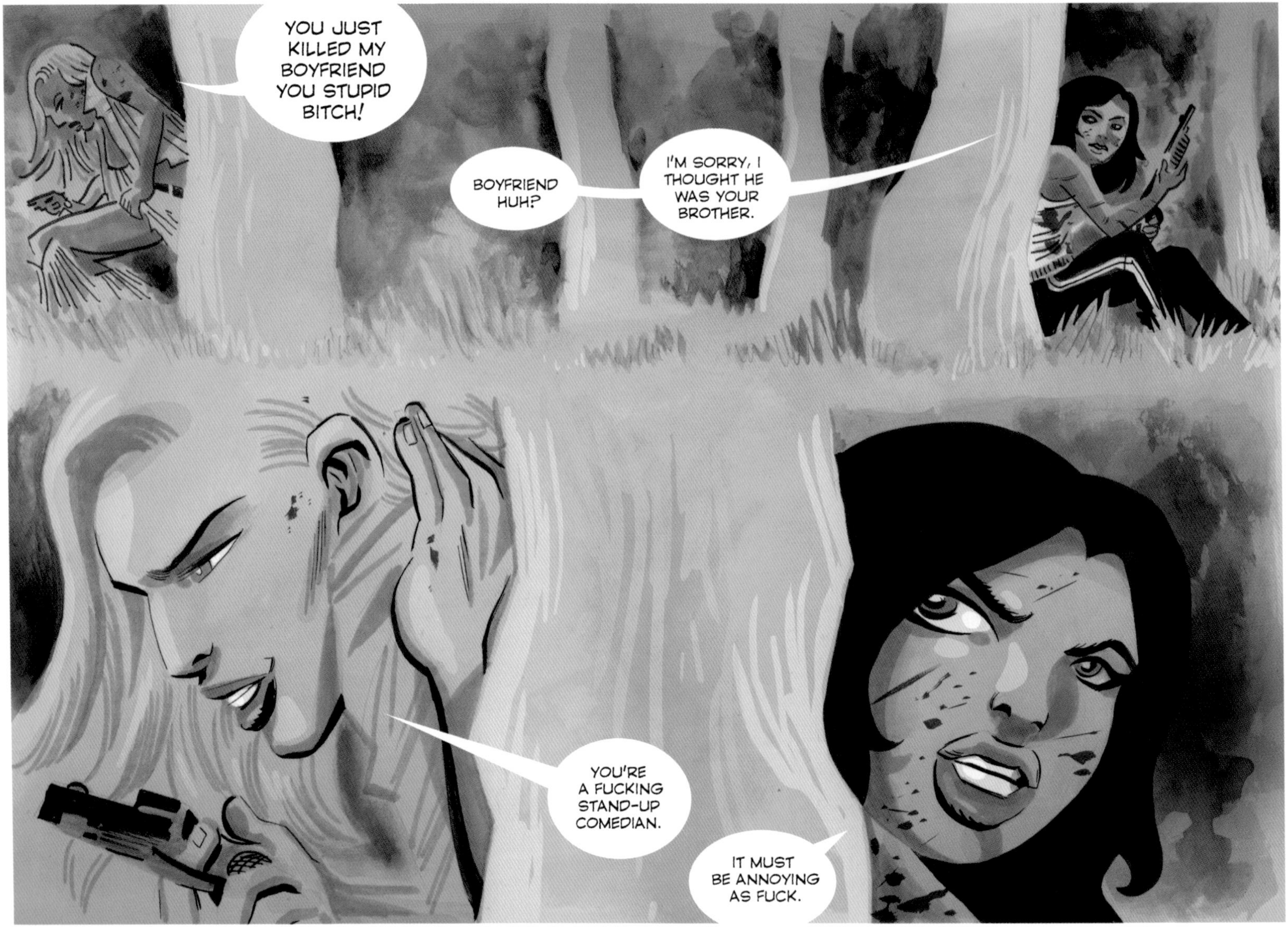
YOU JUST KILLED MY BOYFRIEND YOU STUPID BITCH!
I'M SORRY, I THOUGHT HE WAS YOUR BROTHER.
BOYFRIEND HUH?
YOU'RE A FUCKING STAND-UP COMEDIAN.
IT MUST BE ANNOYING AS FUCK.

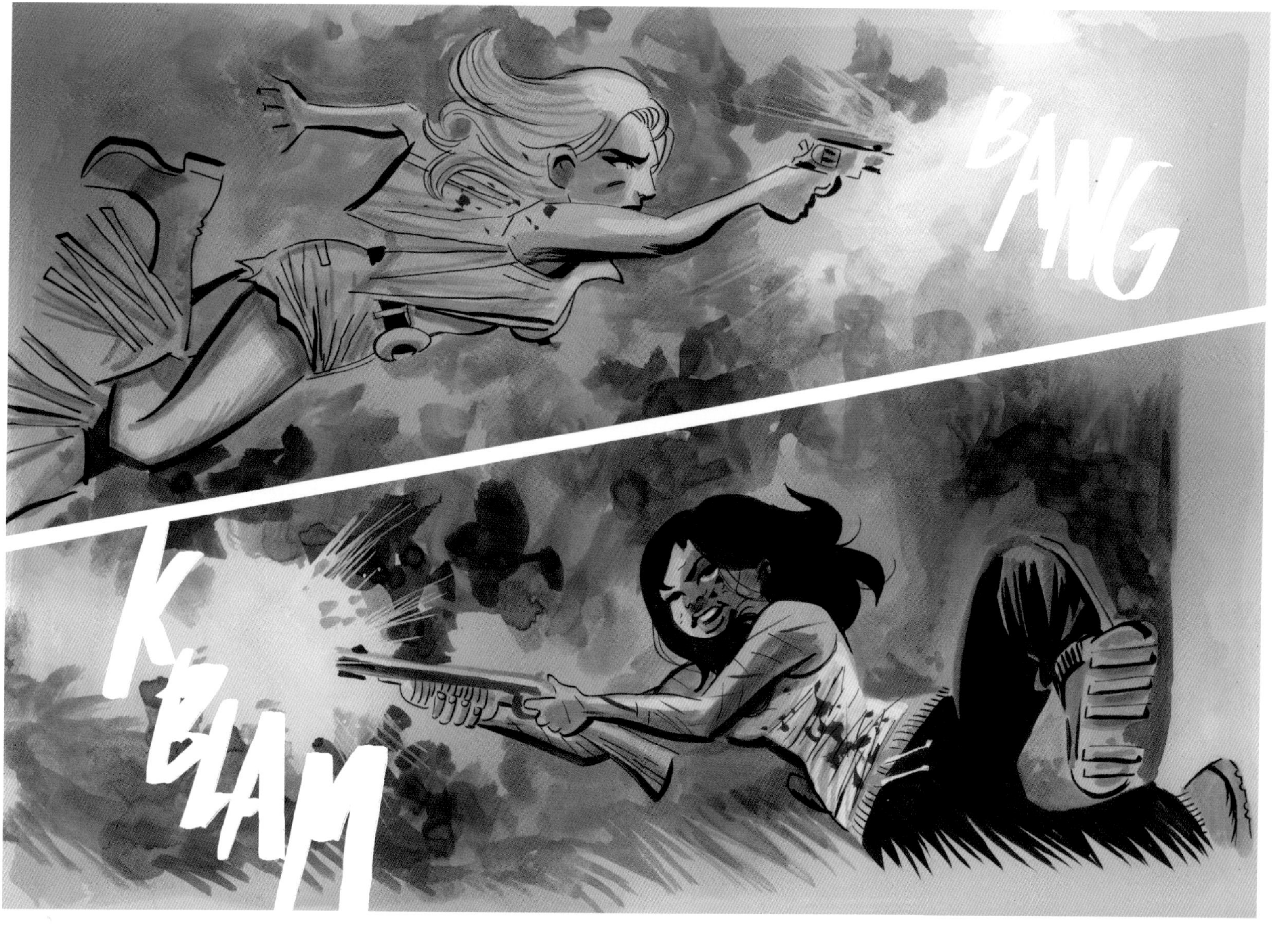
BANG
KBLAM

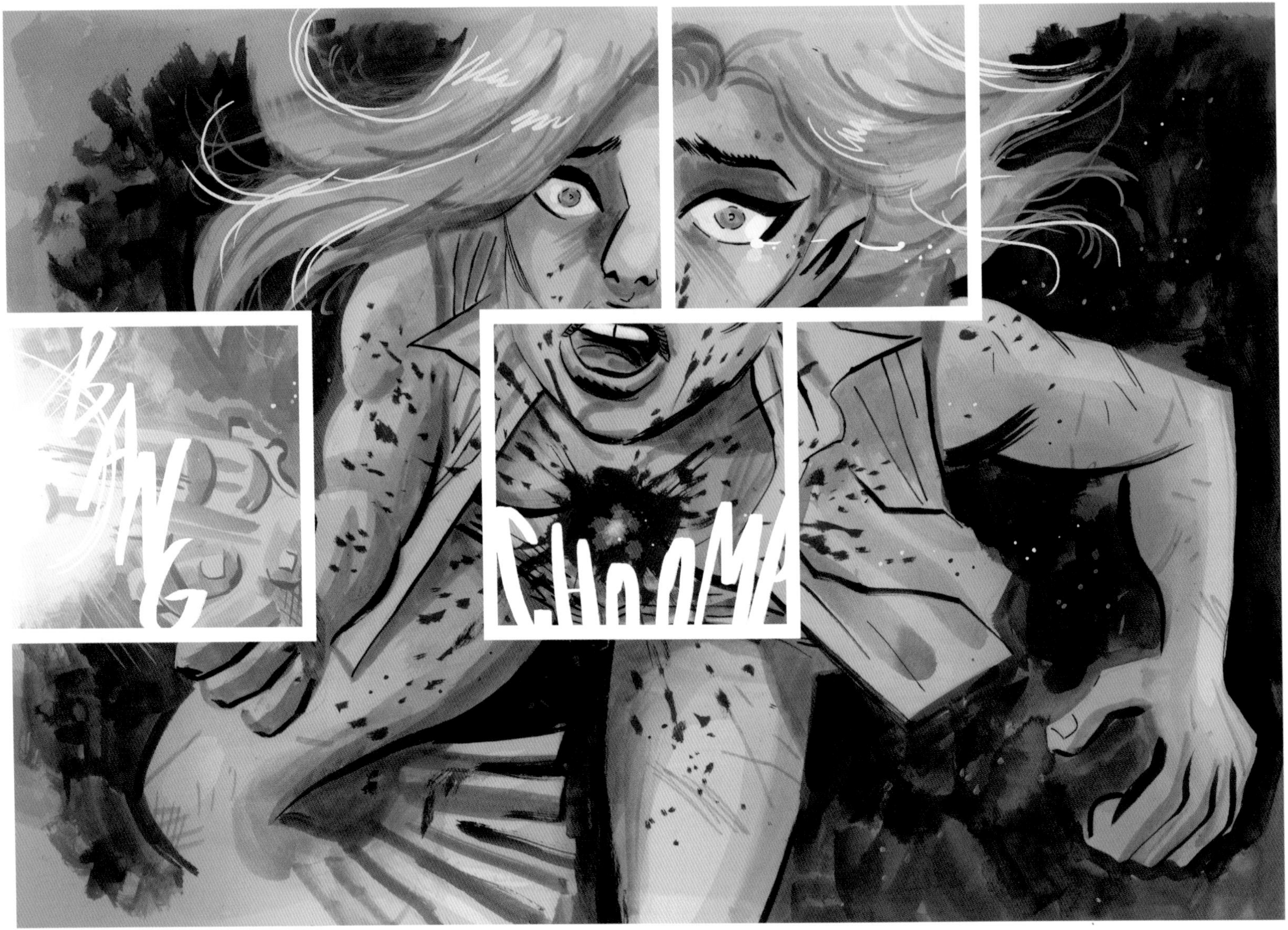
BANG
CHOOMA

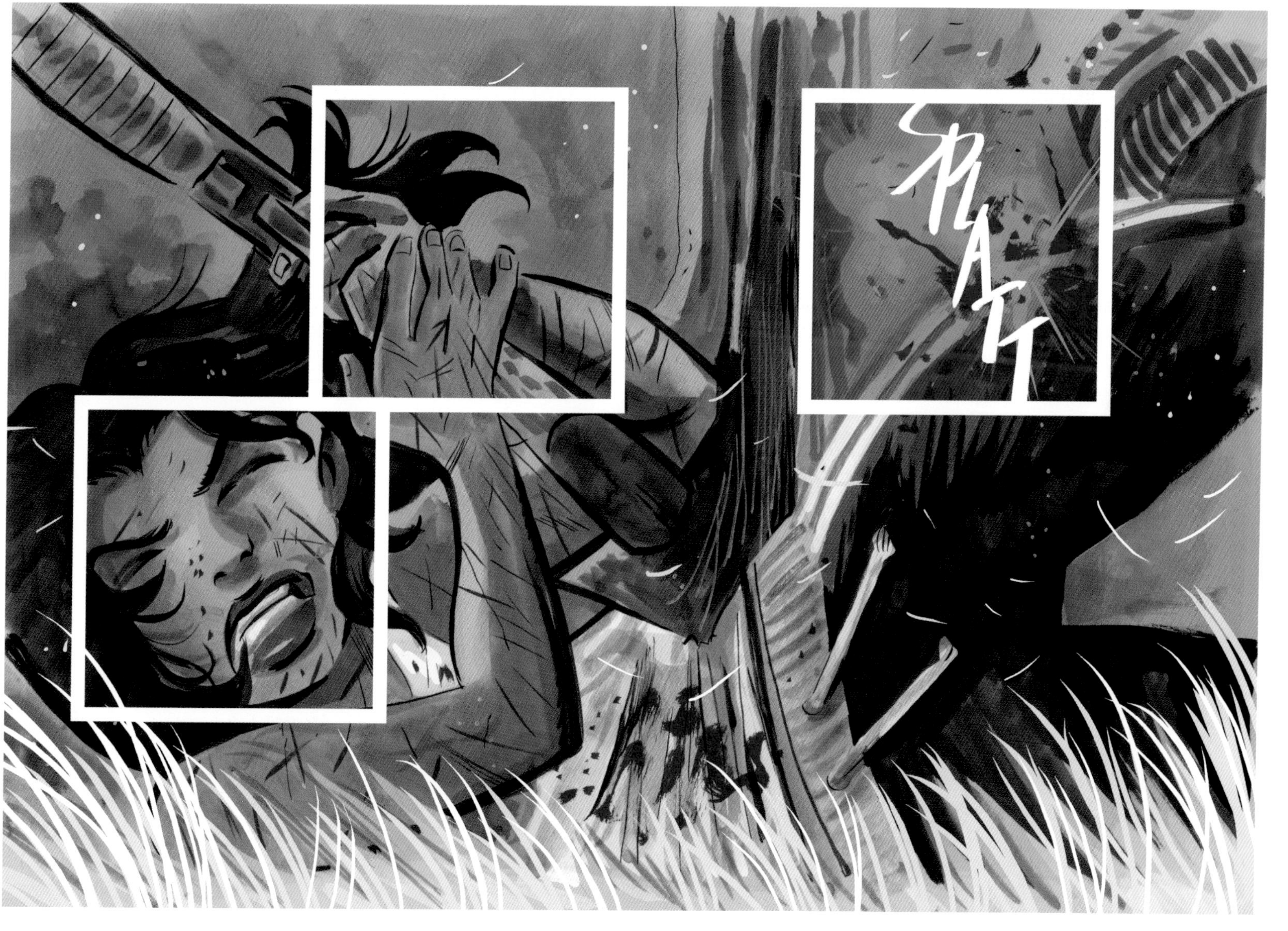
SPLATT

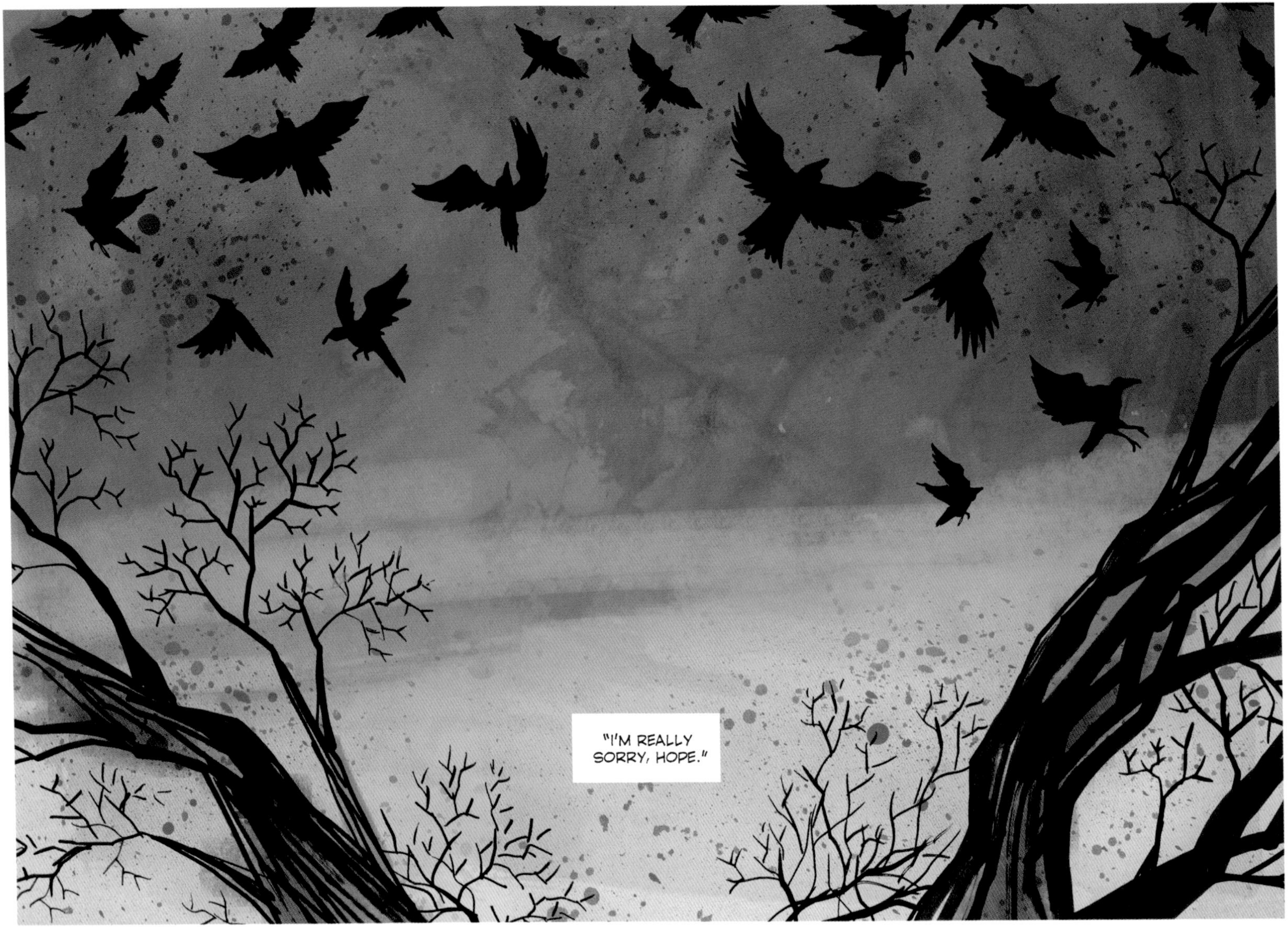
"I'M REALLY SORRY, HOPE."

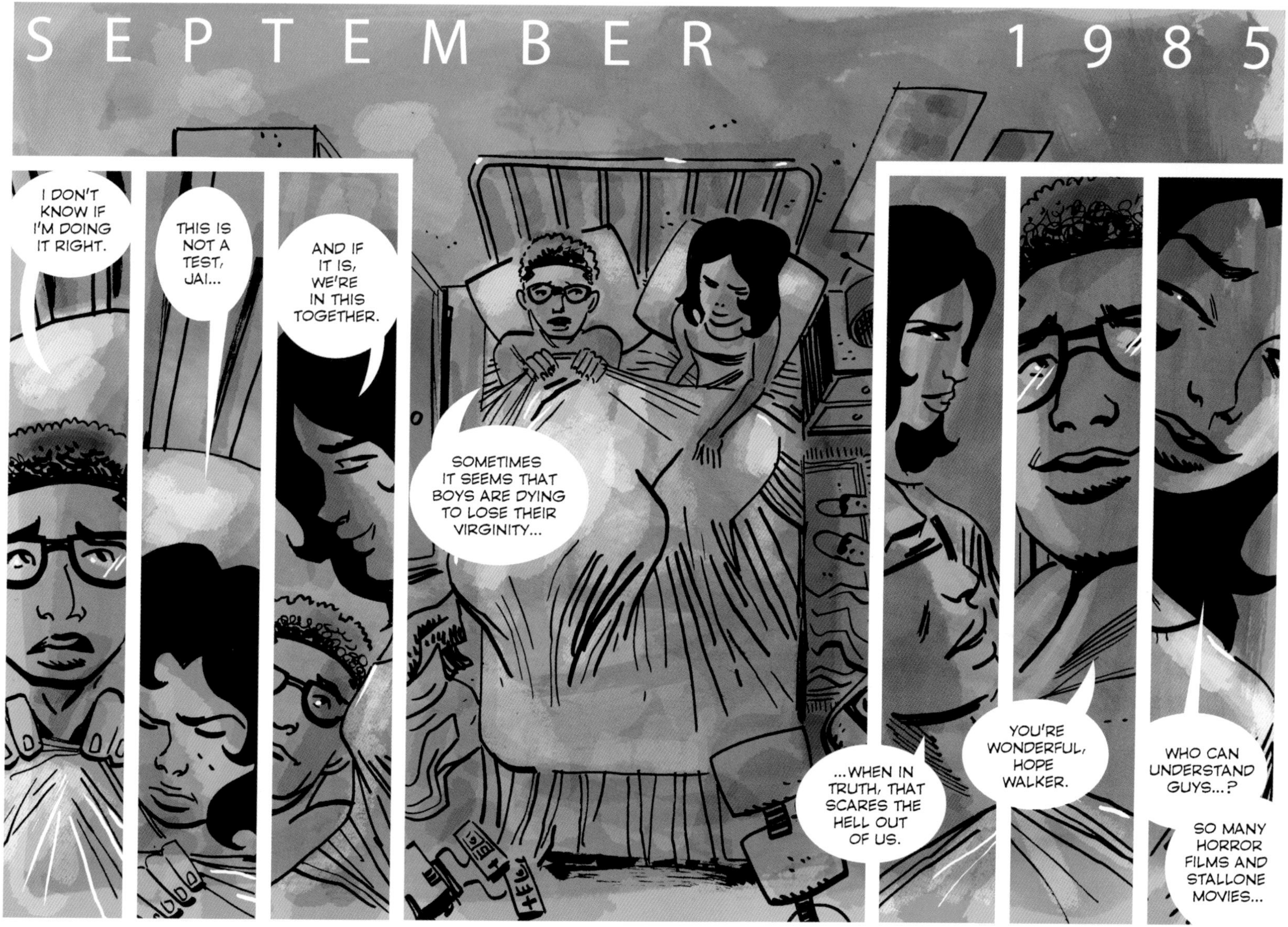
SEPTEMBER 1985
I DON'T KNOW IF I'M DOING IT RIGHT.
THIS IS NOT A TEST, JAI...
AND IF IT IS, WE'RE IN THIS TOGETHER.
SOMETIMES IT SEEMS THAT BOYS ARE DYING TO LOSE THEIR VIRGINITY...
...WHEN IN TRUTH, THAT SCARES THE HELL OUT OF US.
YOU'RE WONDERFUL, HOPE WALKER.
WHO CAN UNDERSTAND GUYS...?
SO MANY HORROR FILMS AND STALLONE MOVIES...

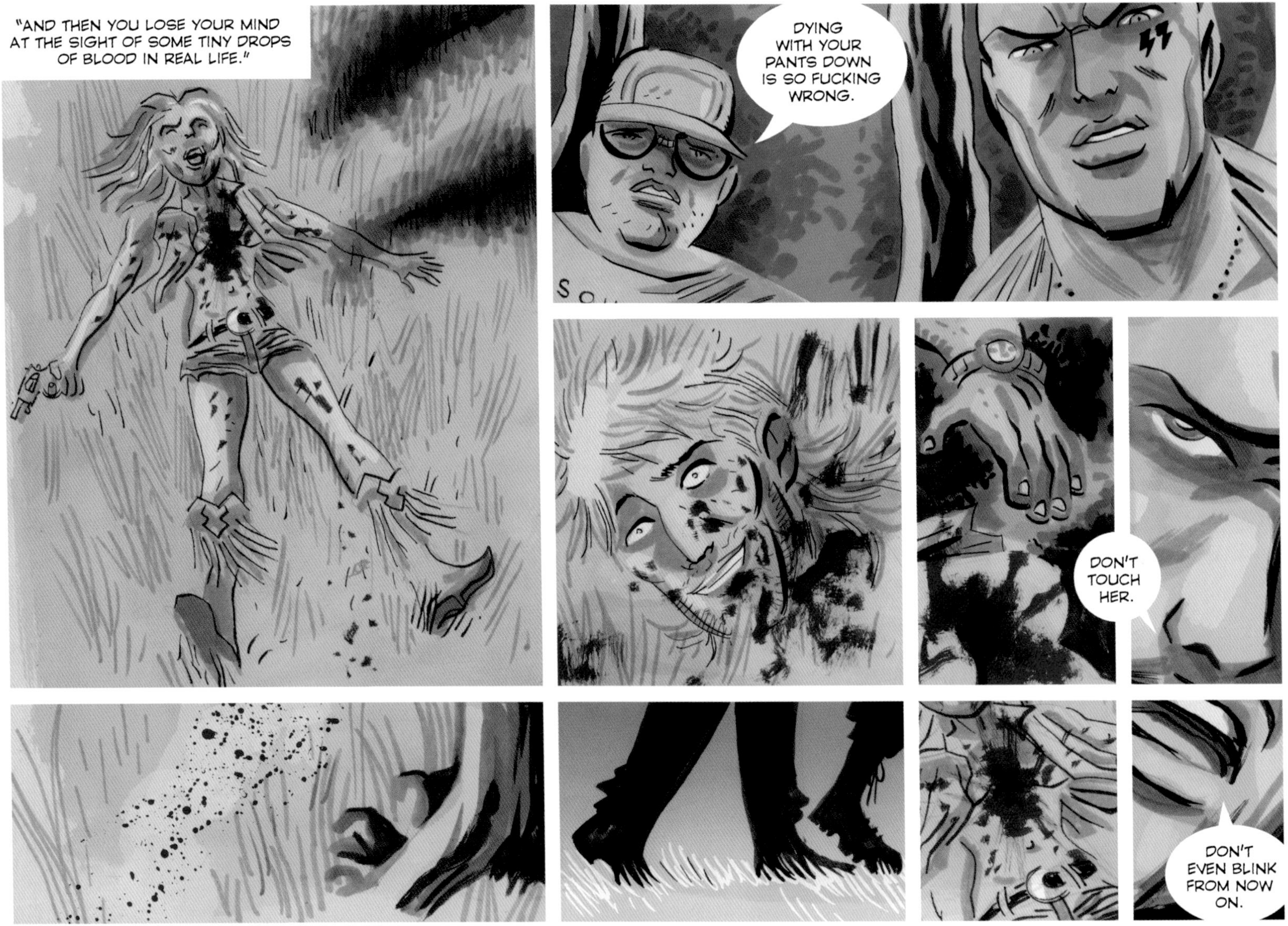
"AND THEN YOU LOSE YOUR MIND AT THE SIGHT OF SOME TINY DROPS OF BLOOD IN REAL LIFE."
DYING WITH YOUR PANTS DOWN IS SO FUCKING WRONG.
DON'T TOUCH HER.
DON'T EVEN BLINK FROM NOW ON.

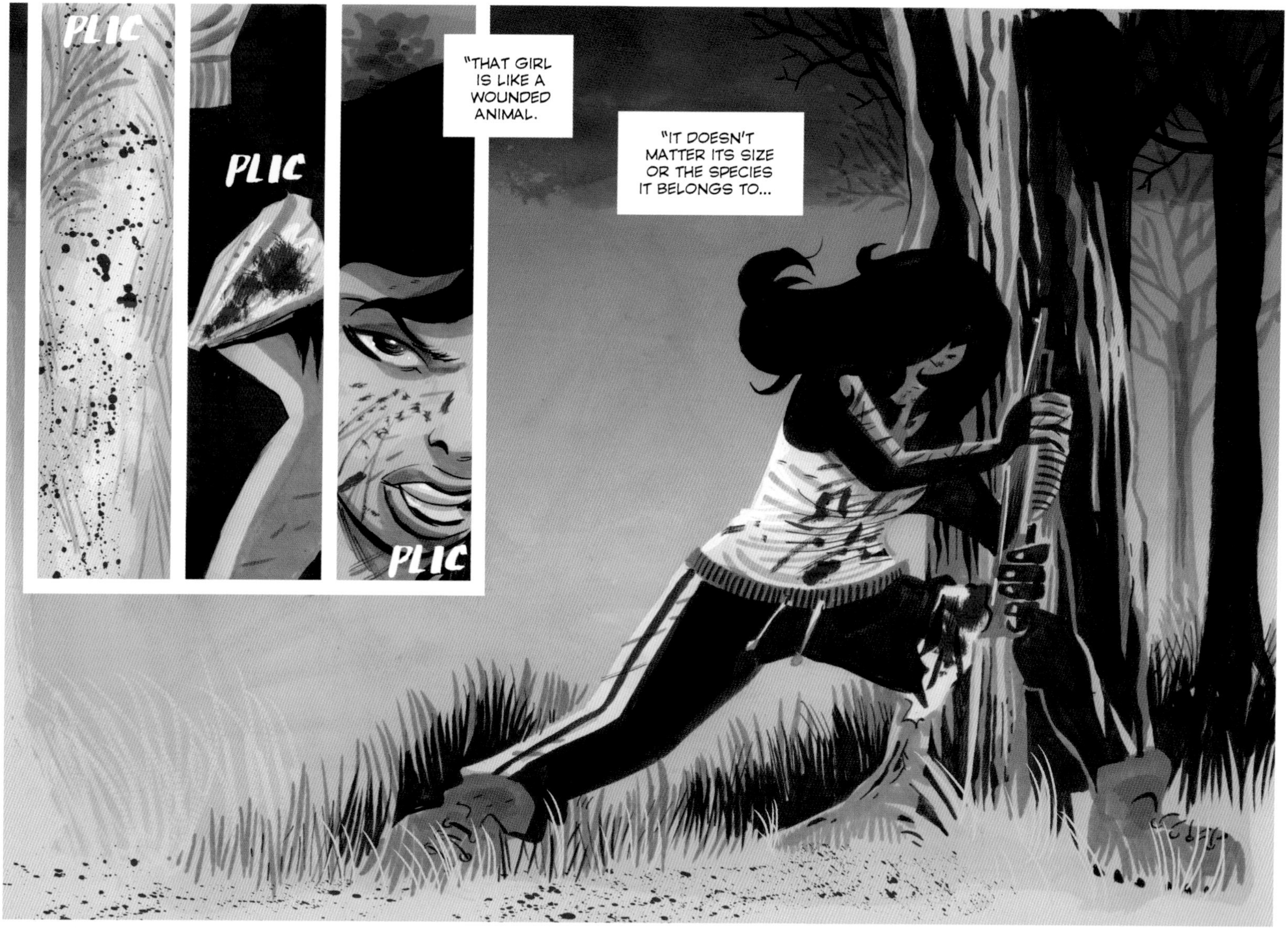
PLIC
PLIC
PLIC
"THAT GIRL IS LIKE A WOUNDED ANIMAL.
"IT DOESN'T MATTER ITS SIZE OR THE SPECIES IT BELONGS TO...

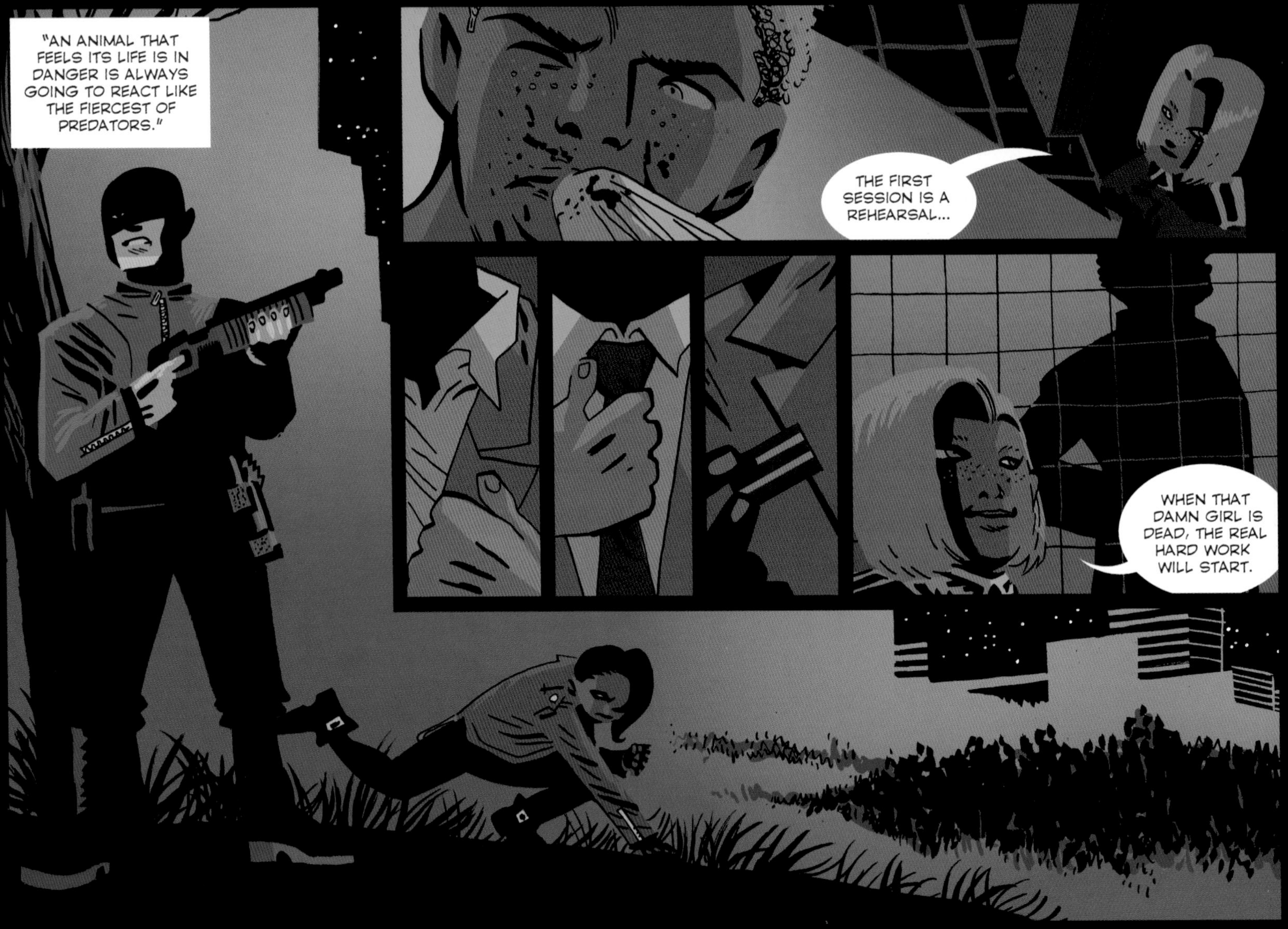

"AN ANIMAL THAT FEELS ITS LIFE IS IN DANGER IS ALWAYS GOING TO REACT LIKE THE FIERCEST OF PREDATORS."
THE FIRST SESSION IS A REHEARSAL...
WHEN THAT DAMN GIRL IS DEAD, THE REAL HARD WORK WILL START.

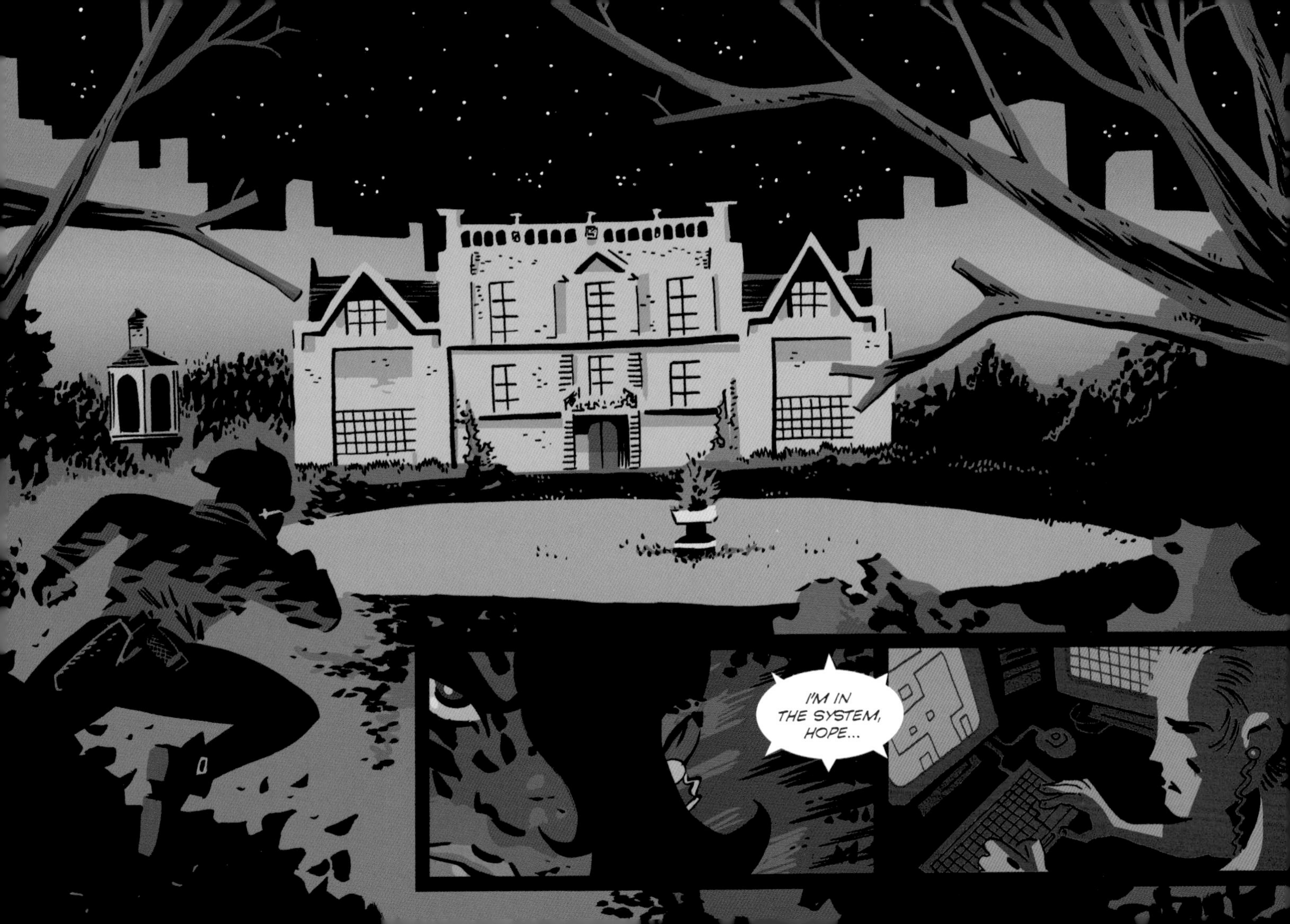
I'M IN THE SYSTEM, HOPE...

"BUT YOU'RE ALL ALONE FROM NOW ON."

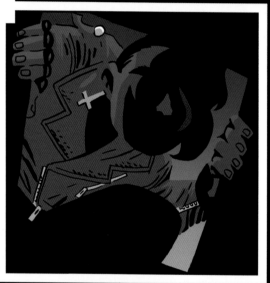

# CHAPTER 7

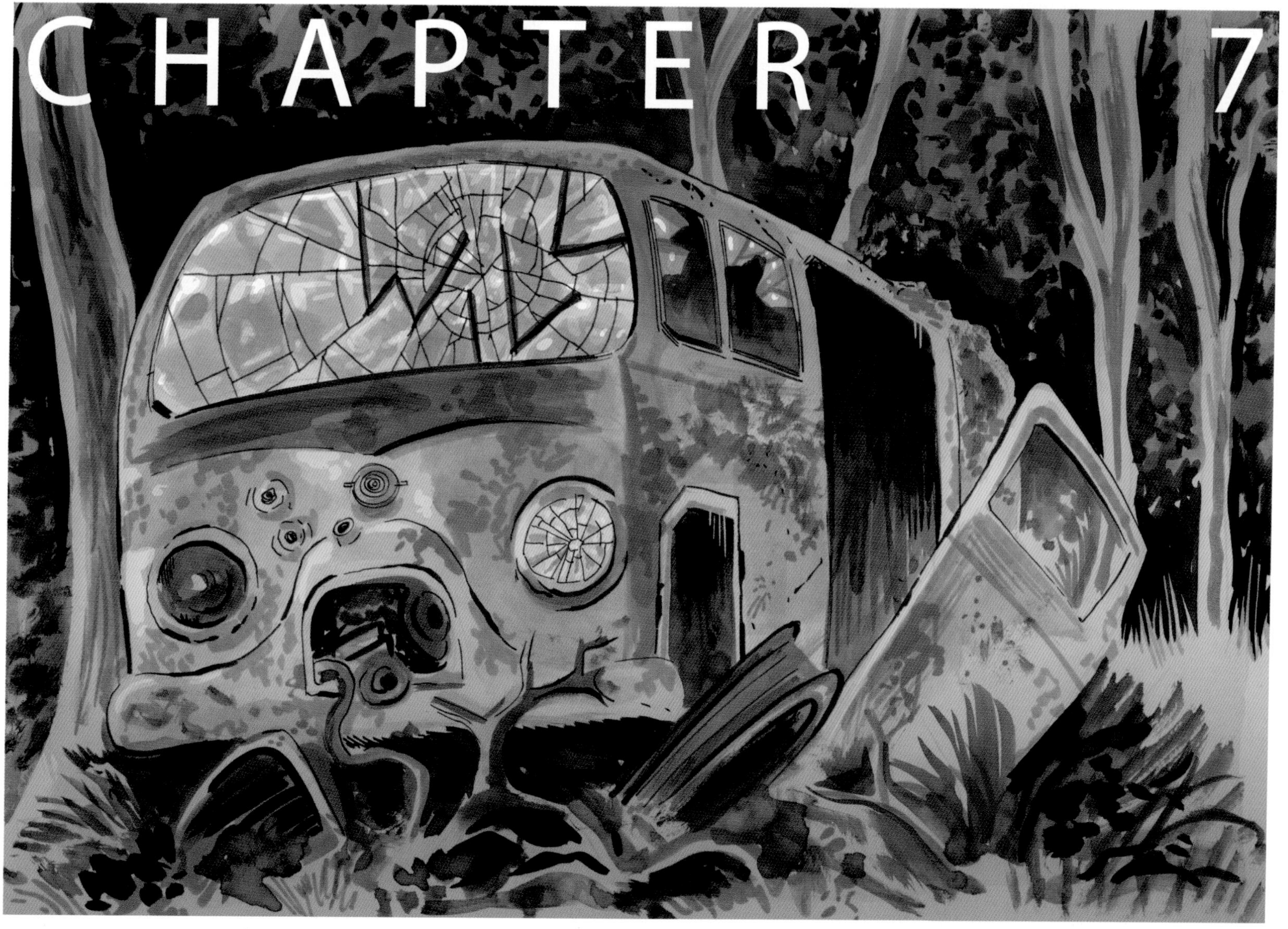
WILL

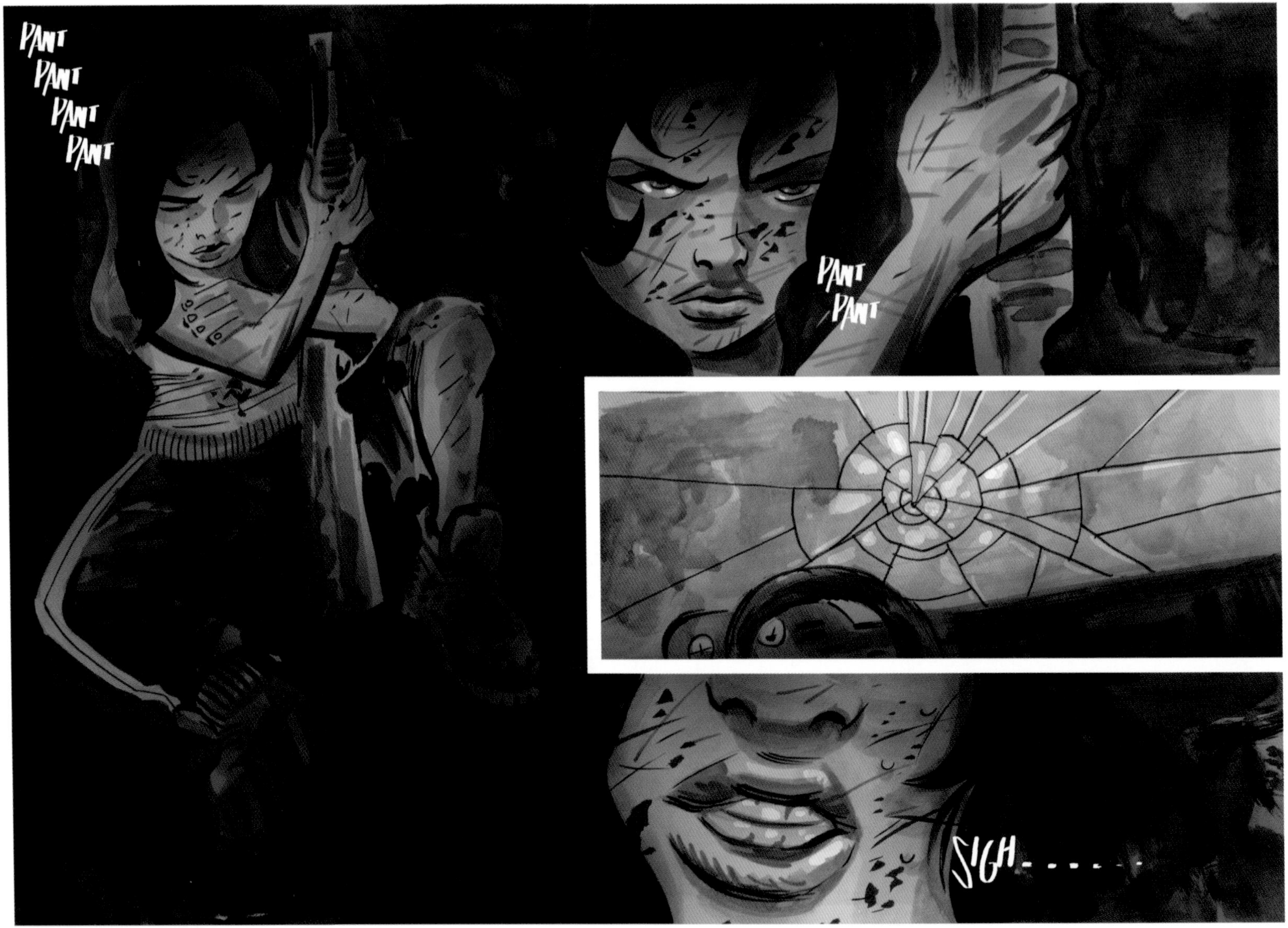
PANT
PANT
PANT
PANT
PANT
PANT
SIGH. . . . .

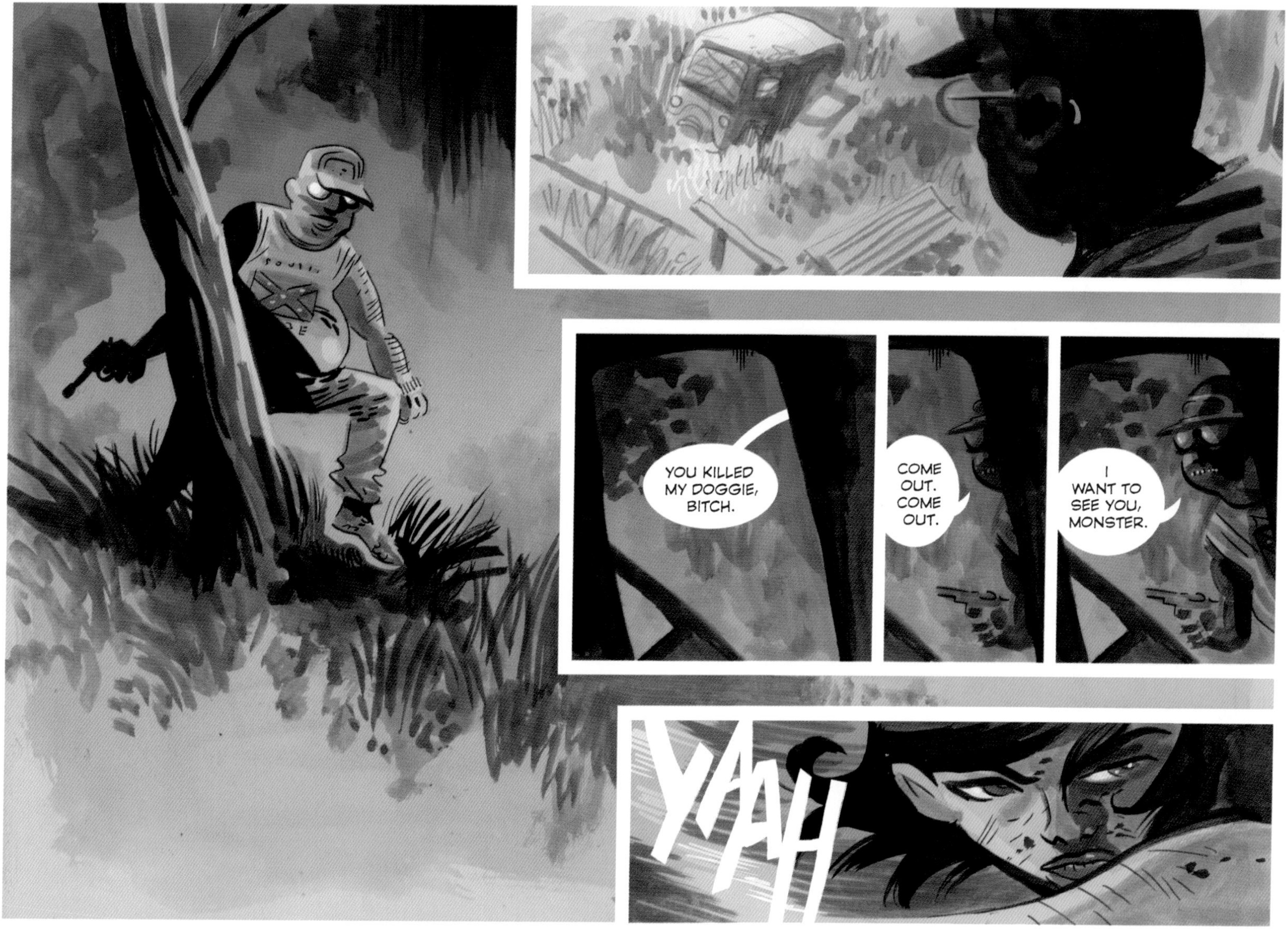
YOU KILLED MY DOGGIE, BITCH.
COME OUT. COME OUT.
I WANT TO SEE YOU, MONSTER.
YAAH

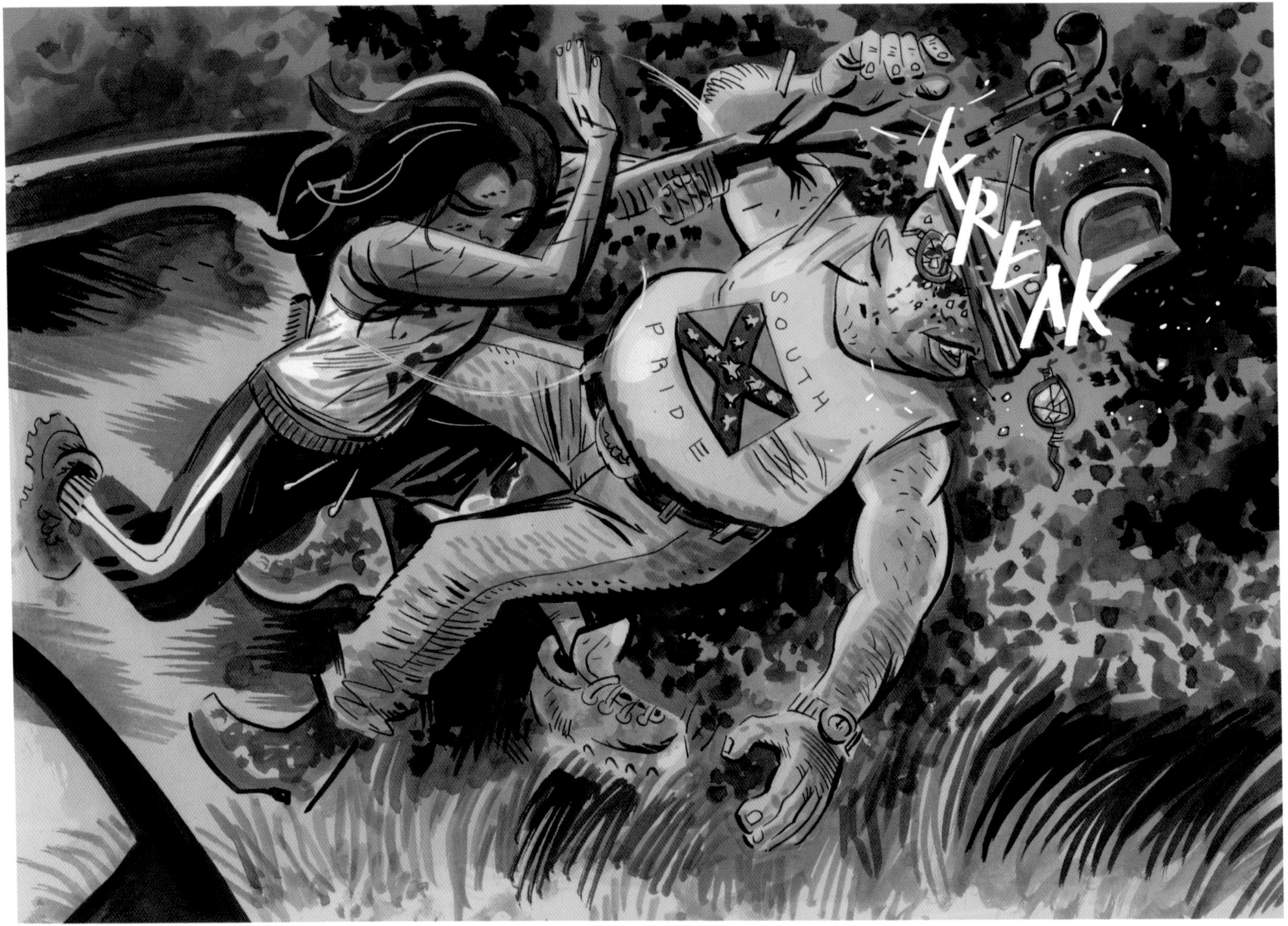
KREAK
SOUTH
PRIDE

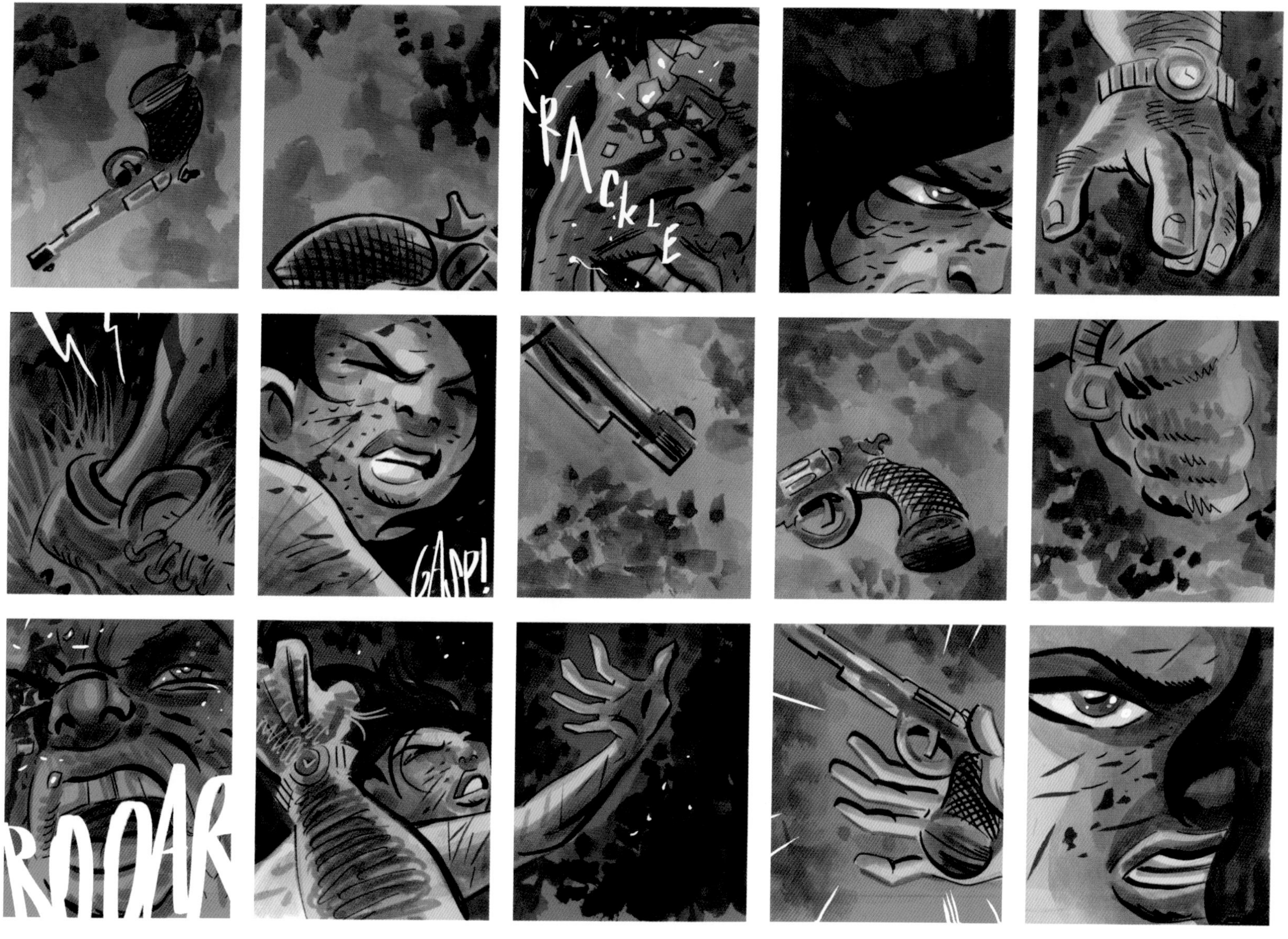
CRACKLE
GASP!
ROOAR

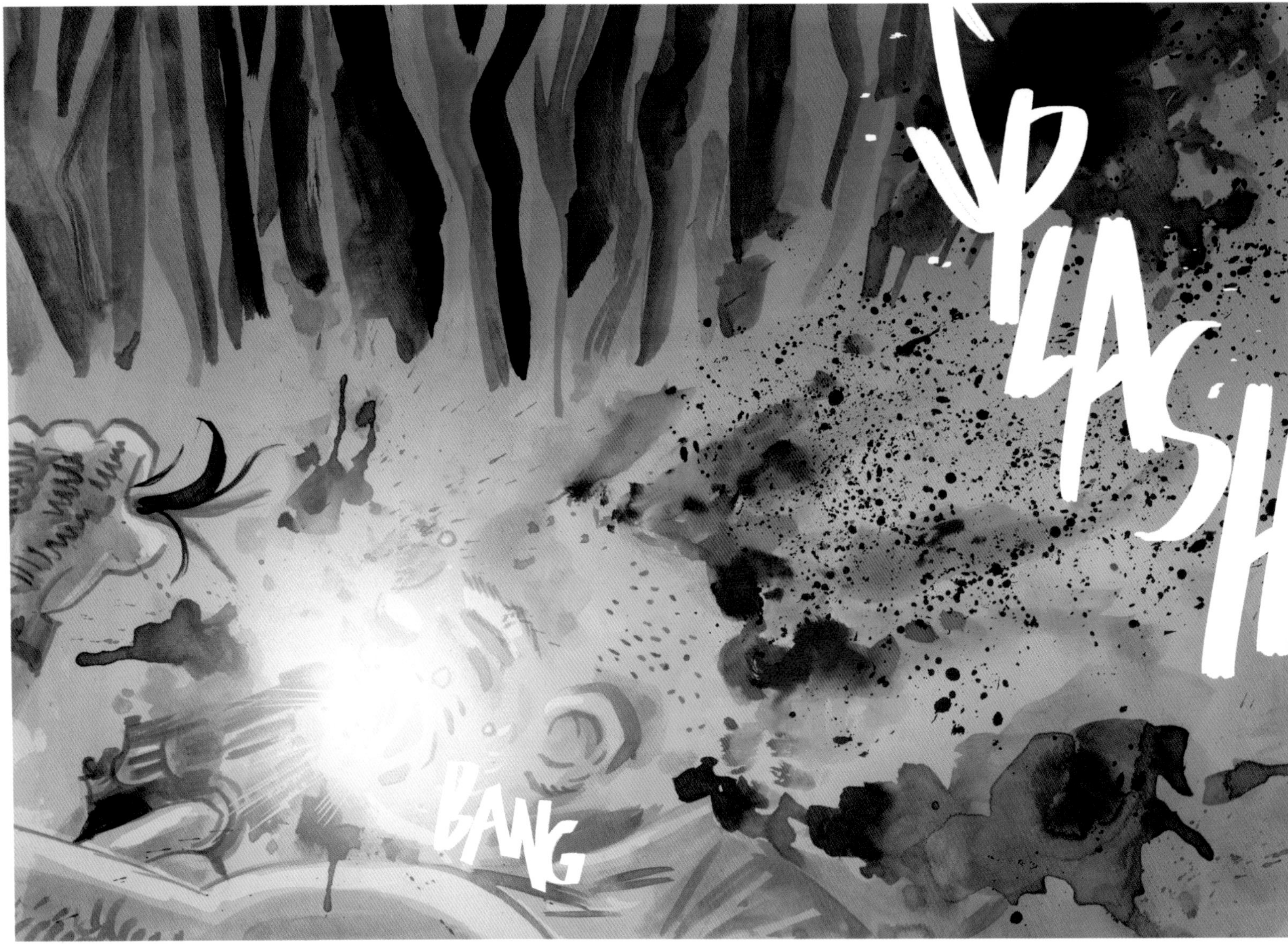
SPLASH
BANG

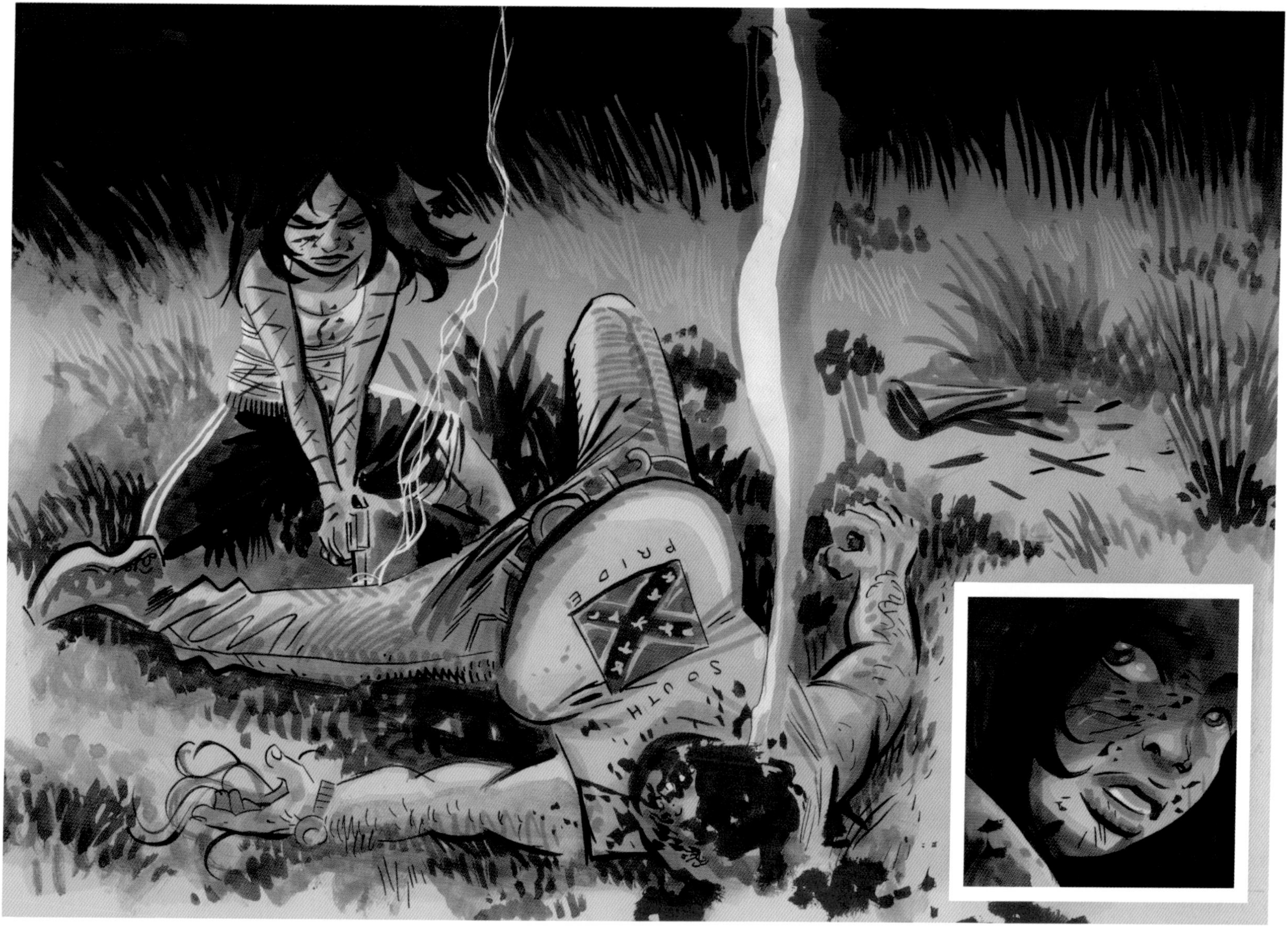
SOUTH
PRIDE

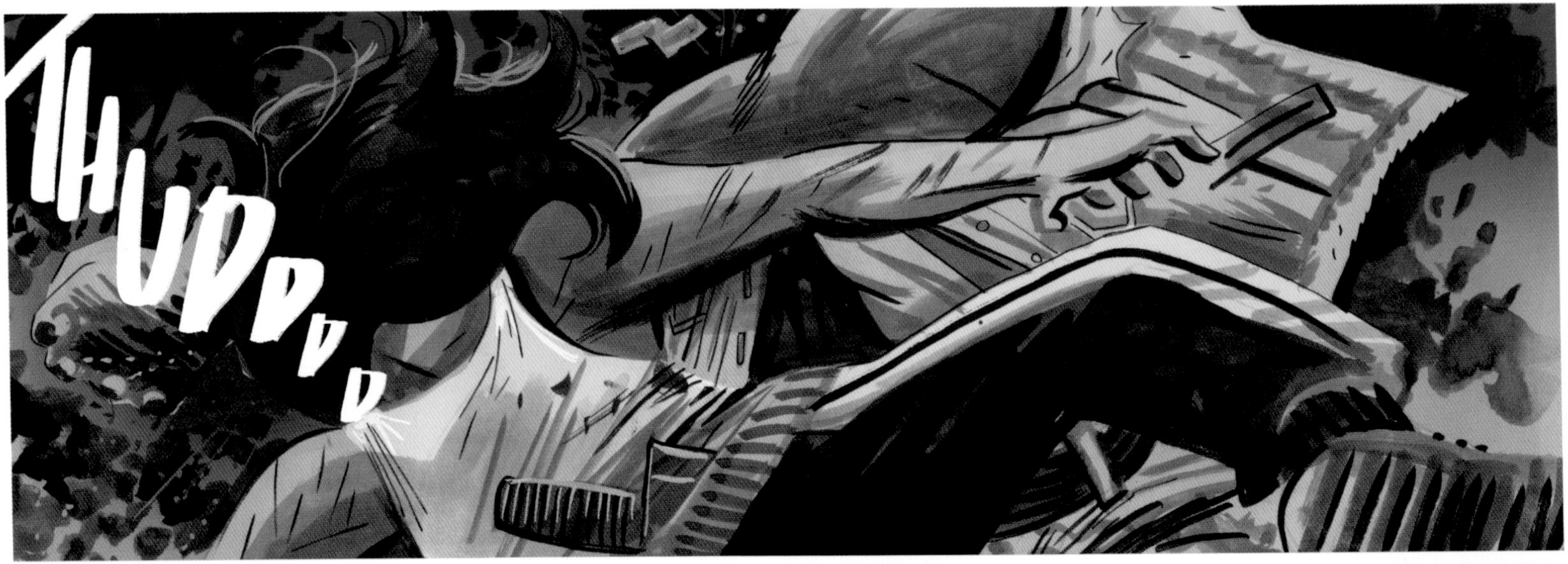
THUDDDDD
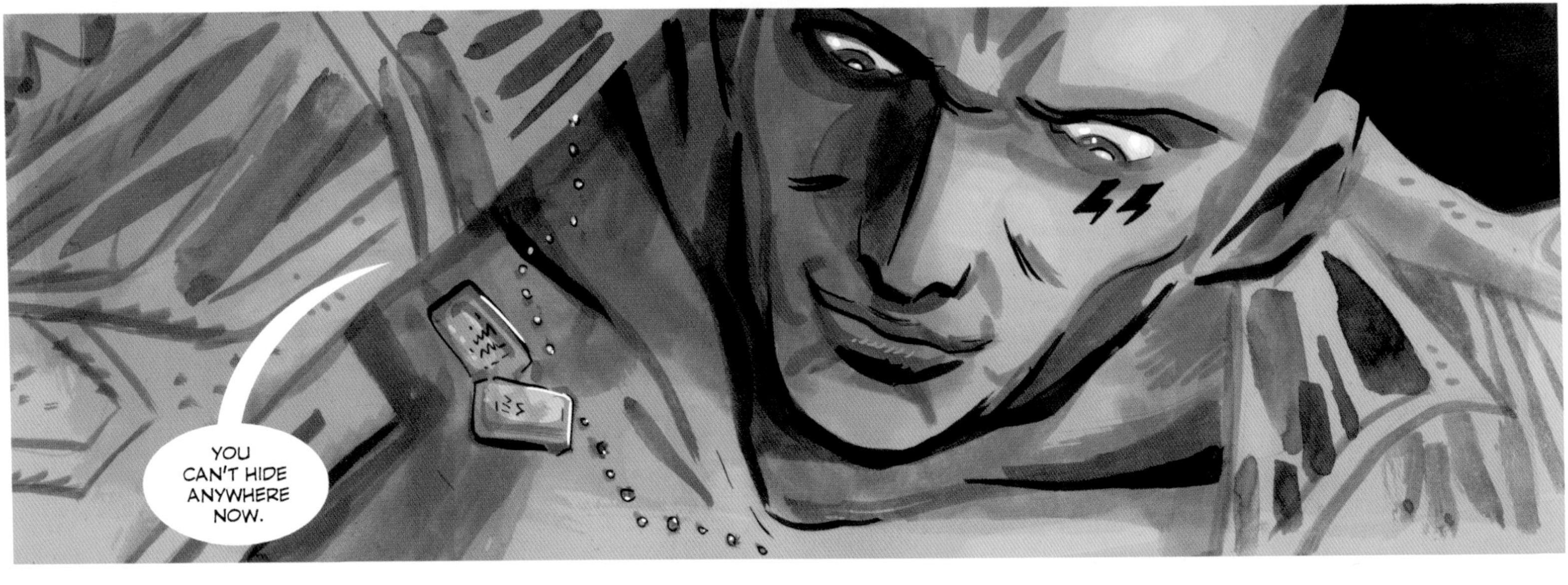
YOU CAN'T HIDE ANYWHERE NOW.

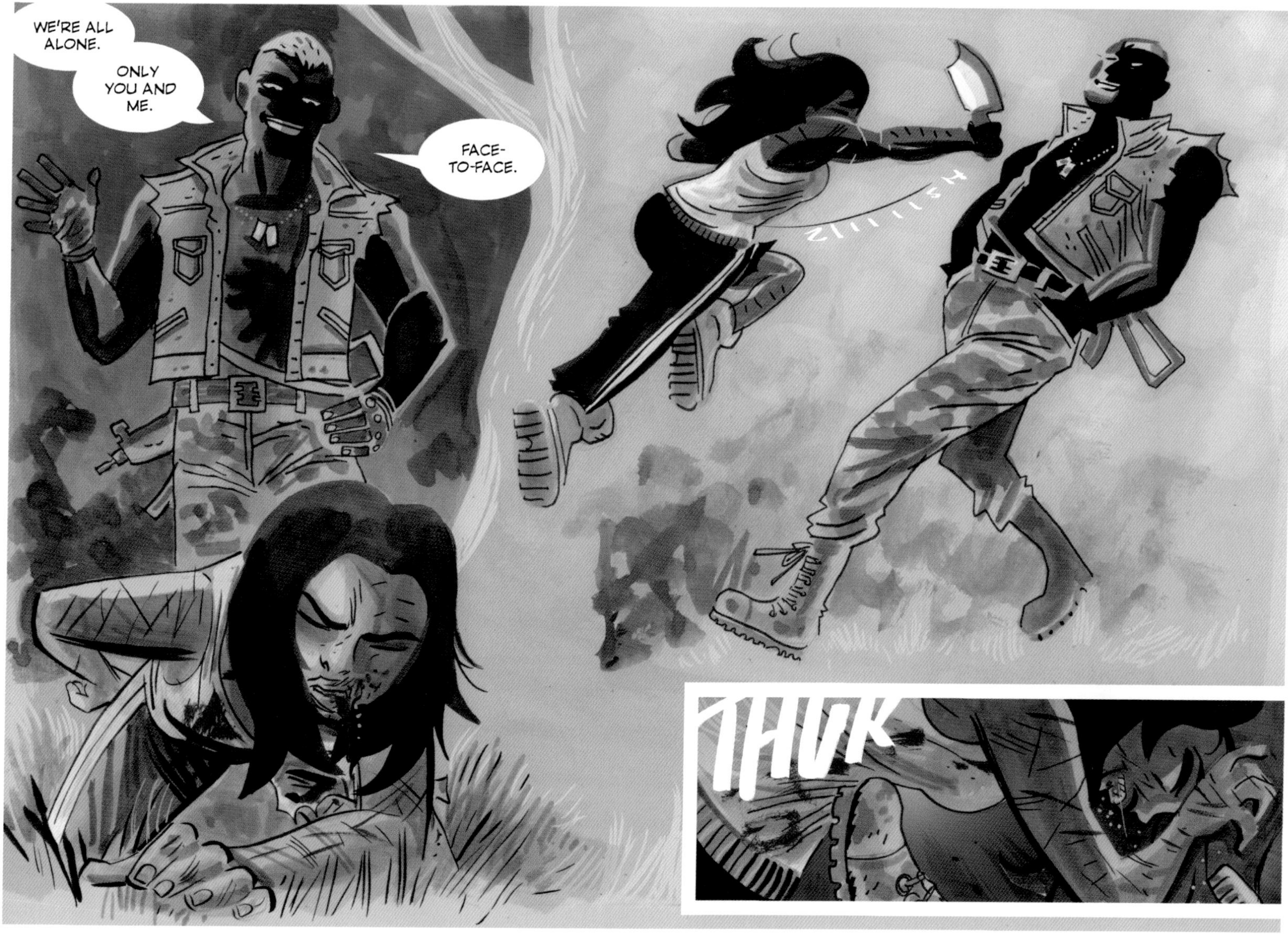
WE'RE ALL ALONE.
ONLY YOU AND ME.
FACE-TO-FACE.
ZIIIIISH
THUK

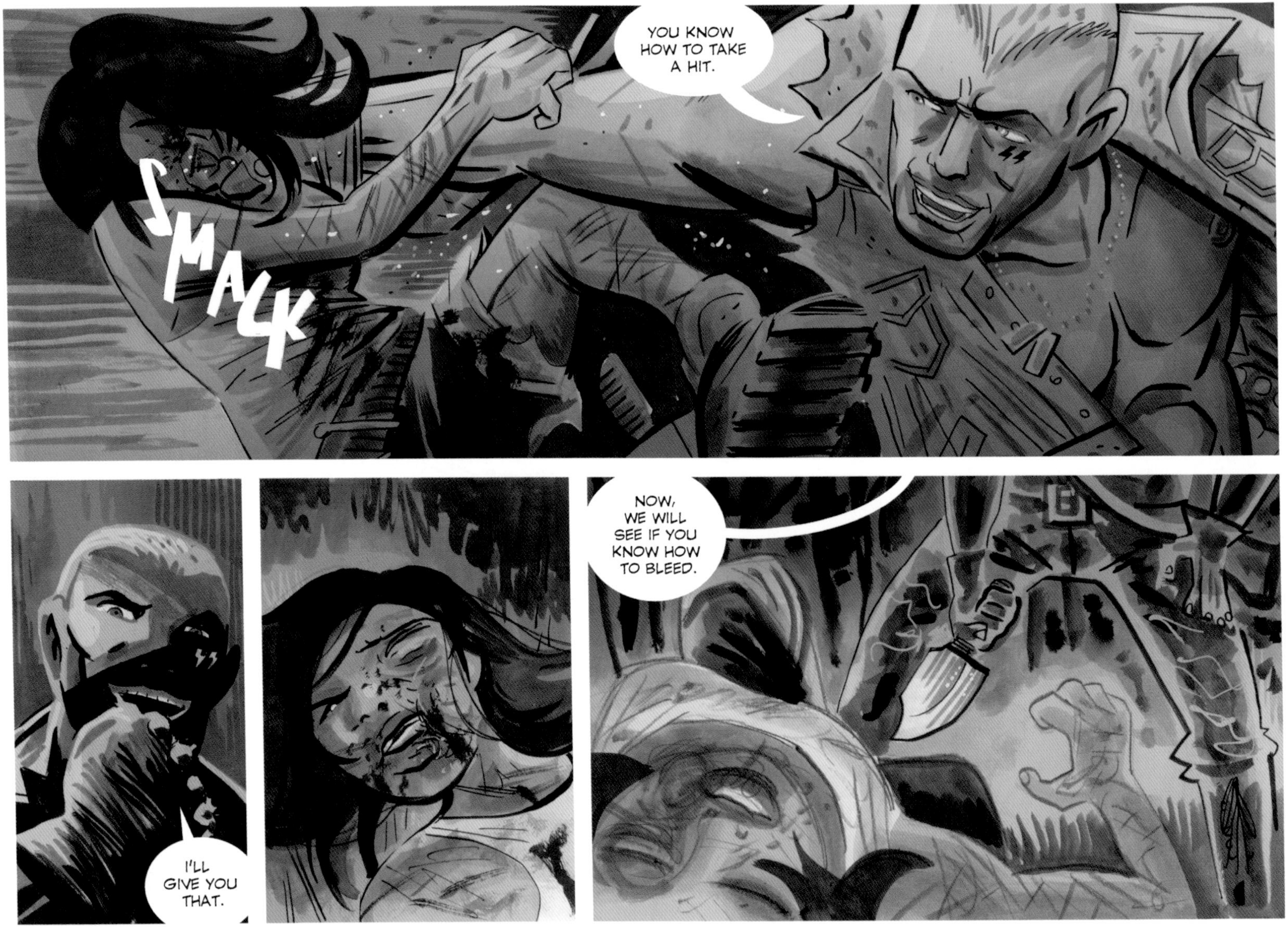
YOU KNOW HOW TO TAKE A HIT.
SMACK
I'LL GIVE YOU THAT.
NOW, WE WILL SEE IF YOU KNOW HOW TO BLEED.

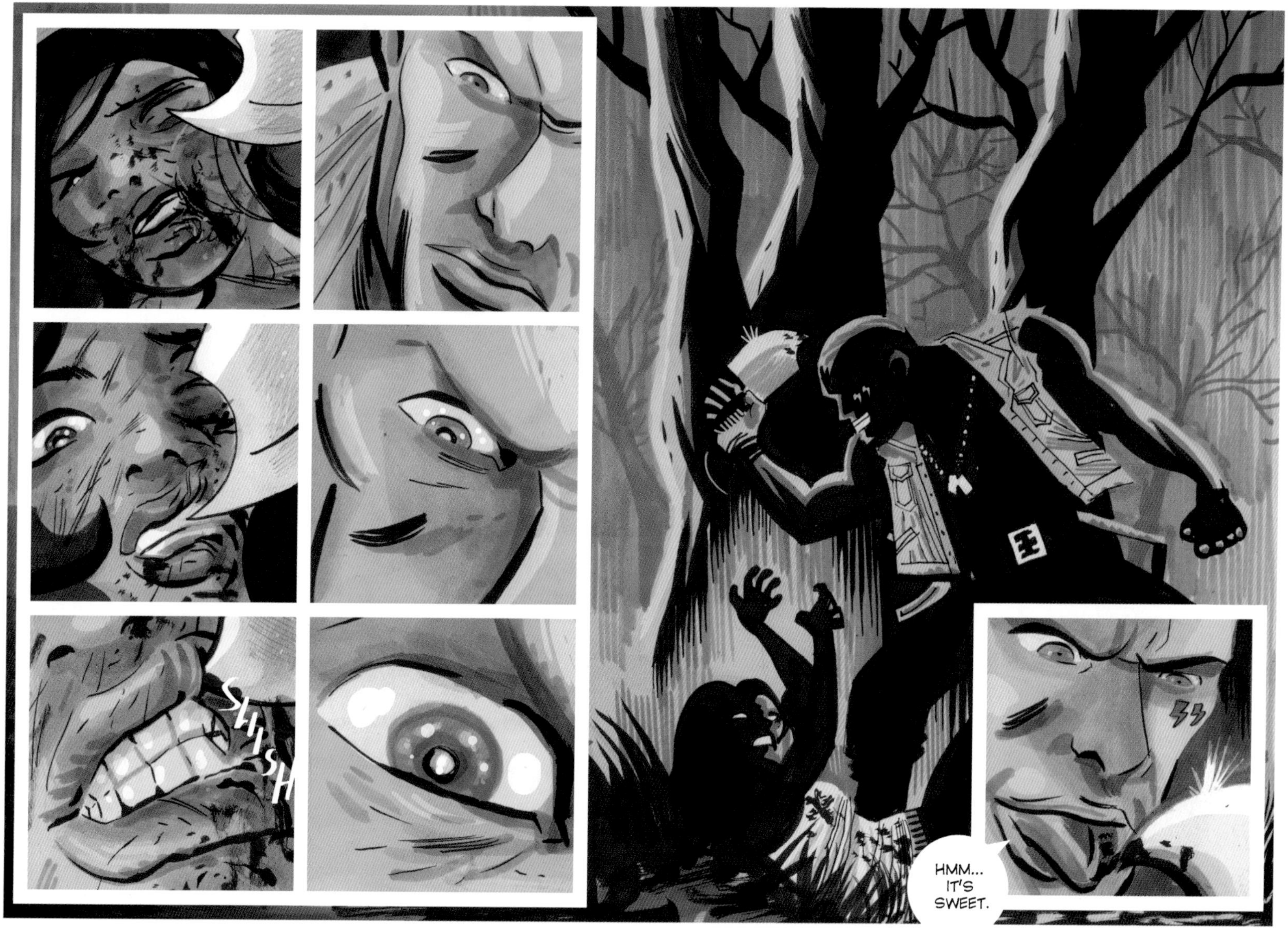
SHISH
HMM... IT'S SWEET.

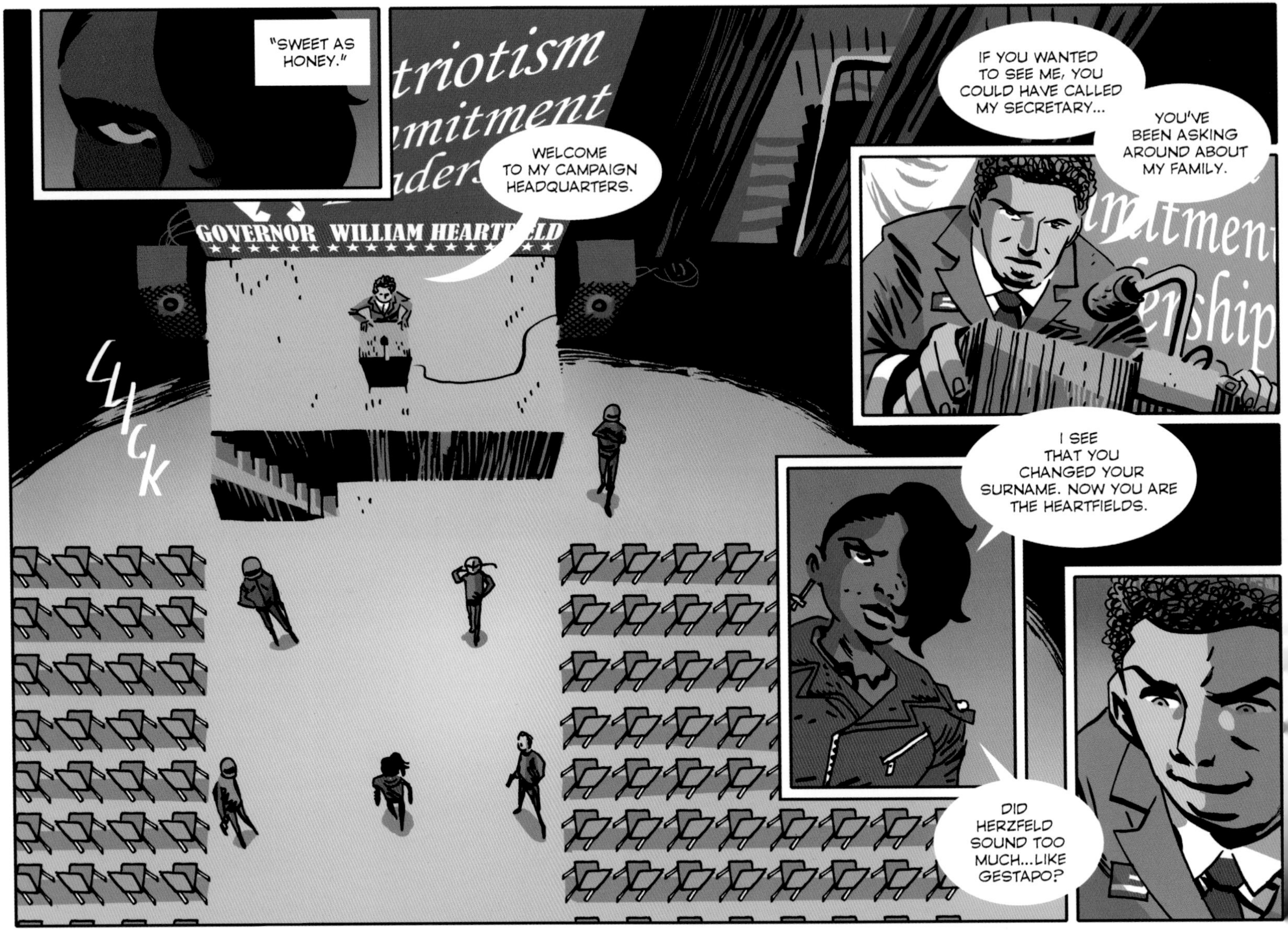
"SWEET AS HONEY."
WELCOME TO MY CAMPAIGN HEADQUARTERS.
GOVERNOR WILLIAM HEARTFIELD
CLICK
IF YOU WANTED TO SEE ME, YOU COULD HAVE CALLED MY SECRETARY...
YOU'VE BEEN ASKING AROUND ABOUT MY FAMILY.
I SEE THAT YOU CHANGED YOUR SURNAME. NOW YOU ARE THE HEARTFIELDS.
DID HERZFELD SOUND TOO MUCH...LIKE GESTAPO?

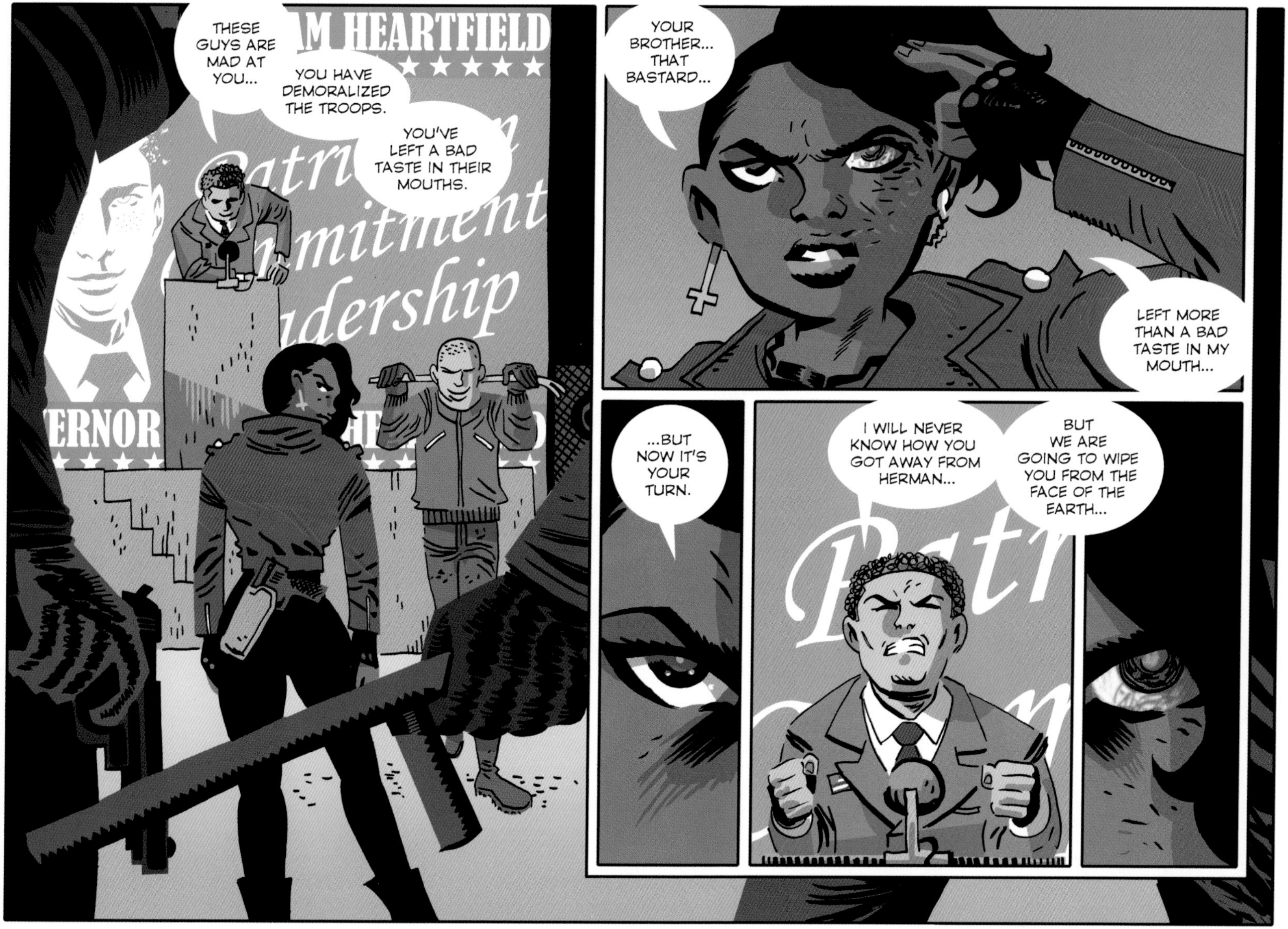
M HEARTFIELD
THESE GUYS ARE MAD AT YOU...
YOU HAVE DEMORALIZED THE TROOPS.
YOU'VE LEFT A BAD TASTE IN THEIR MOUTHS.
YOUR BROTHER... THAT BASTARD...
LEFT MORE THAN A BAD TASTE IN MY MOUTH...
...BUT NOW IT'S YOUR TURN.
I WILL NEVER KNOW HOW YOU GOT AWAY FROM HERMAN...
BUT WE ARE GOING TO WIPE YOU FROM THE FACE OF THE EARTH...

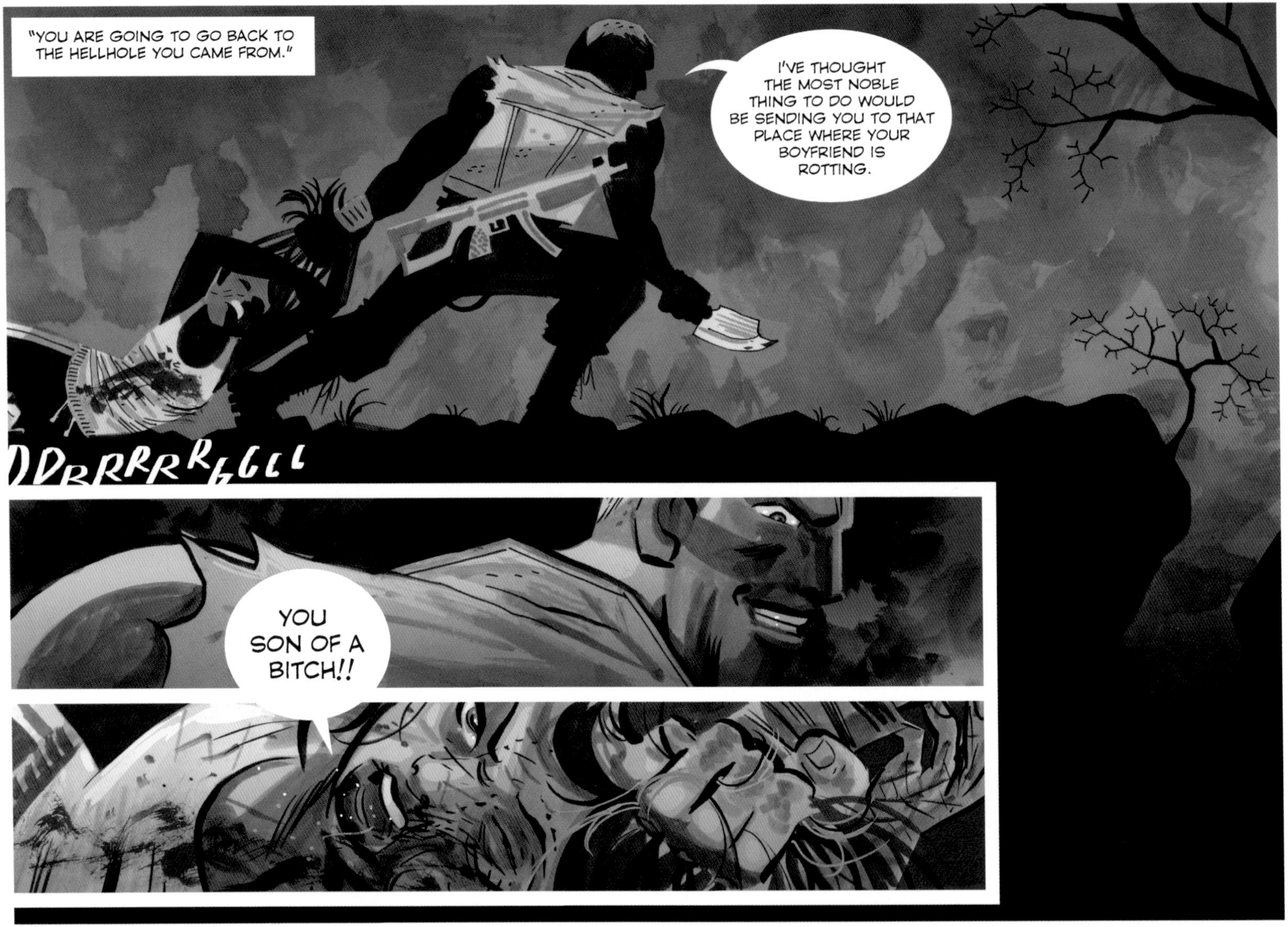
"YOU ARE GOING TO GO BACK TO THE HELLHOLE YOU CAME FROM."
I'VE THOUGHT THE MOST NOBLE THING TO DO WOULD BE SENDING YOU TO THAT PLACE WHERE YOUR BOYFRIEND IS ROTTING.
DDRRRRRRGGLL
YOU SON OF A BITCH!!

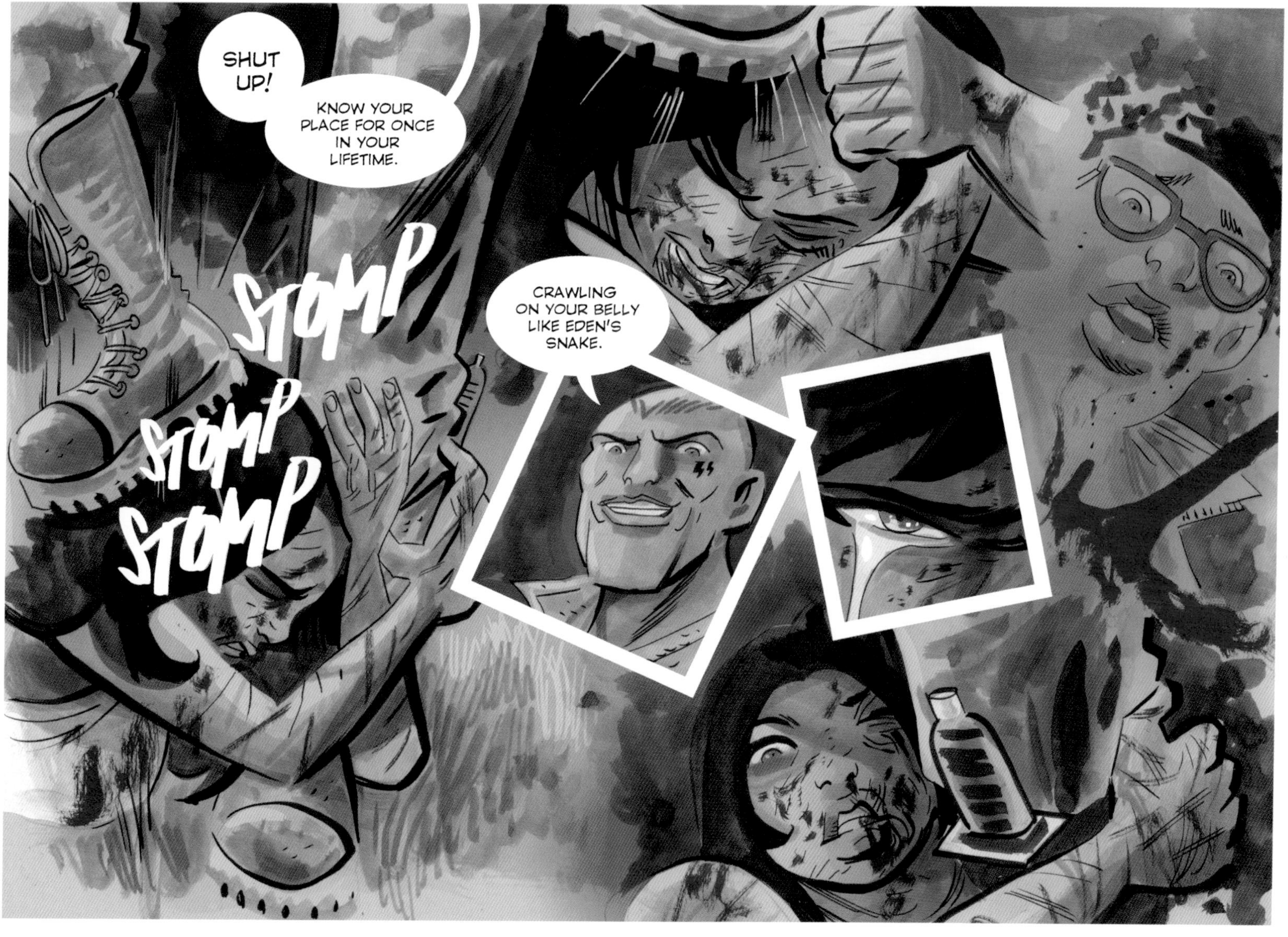
SHUT UP!
KNOW YOUR PLACE FOR ONCE IN YOUR LIFETIME.
STOMP
STOMP
STOMP
CRAWLING ON YOUR BELLY LIKE EDEN'S SNAKE.

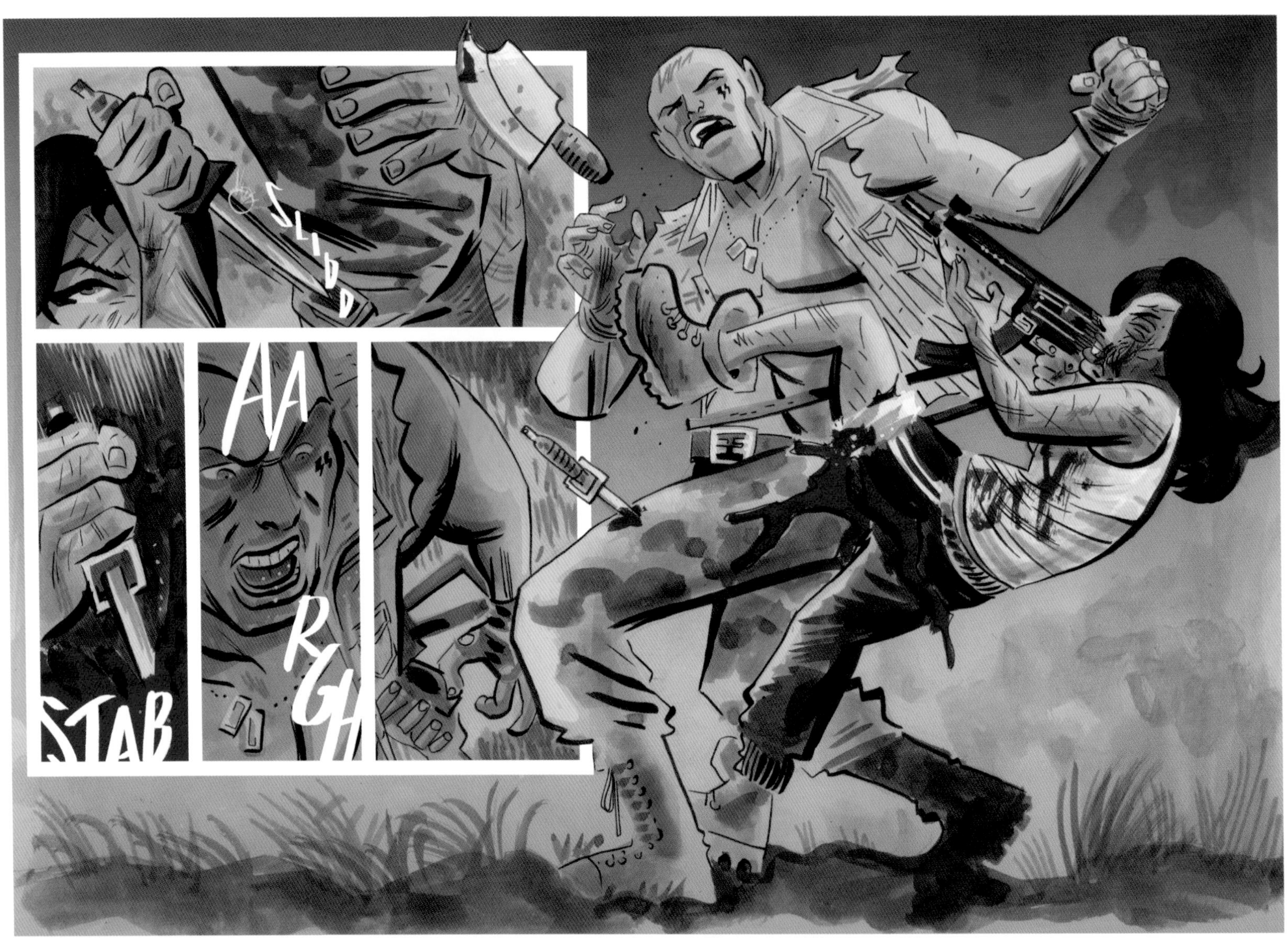
SLIDD
STAB
AARGH

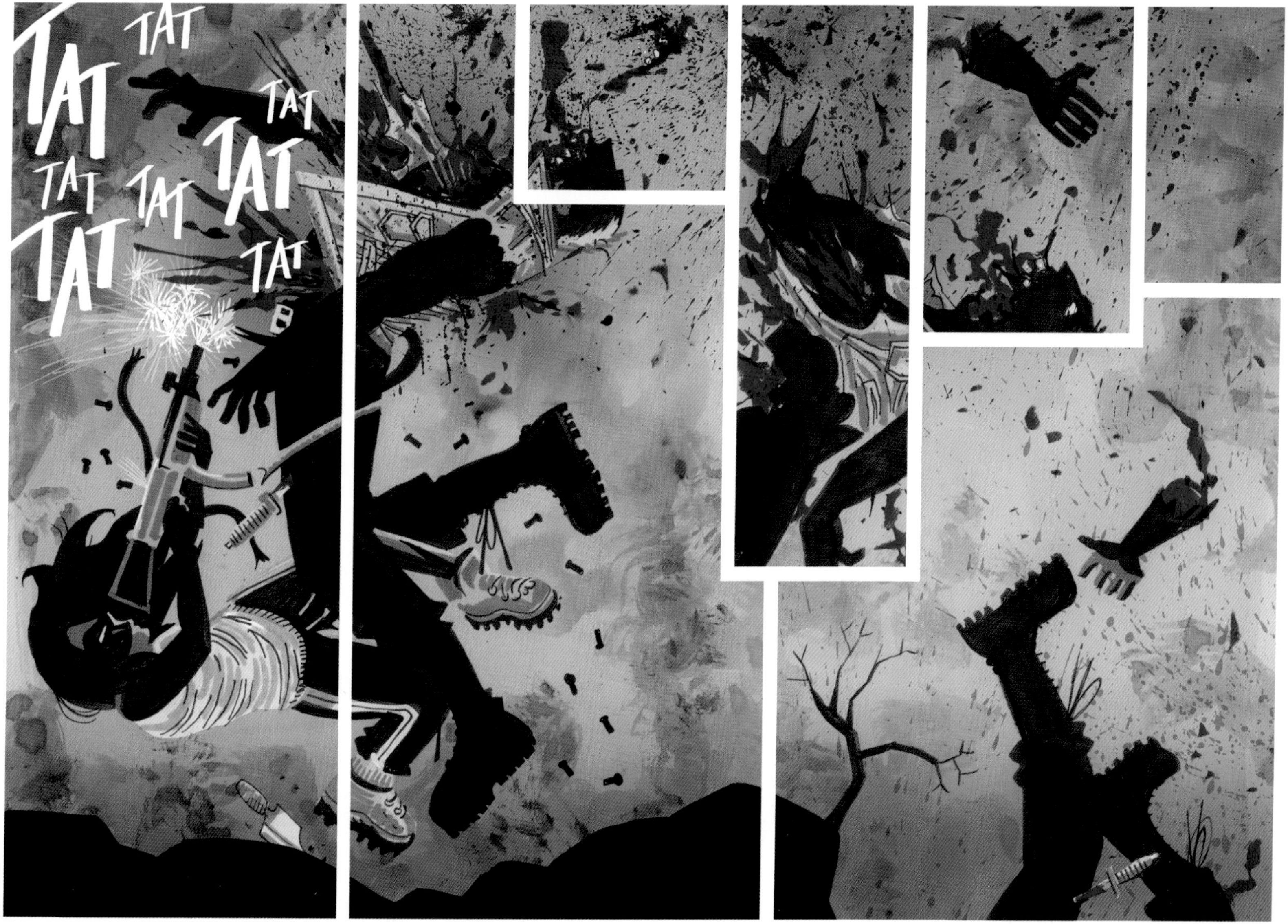
TAT
TAT
TAT
TAT
TAT
TAT
TAT
TAT

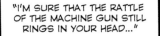

"I'M SURE THAT THE RATTLE OF THE MACHINE GUN STILL RINGS IN YOUR HEAD..."

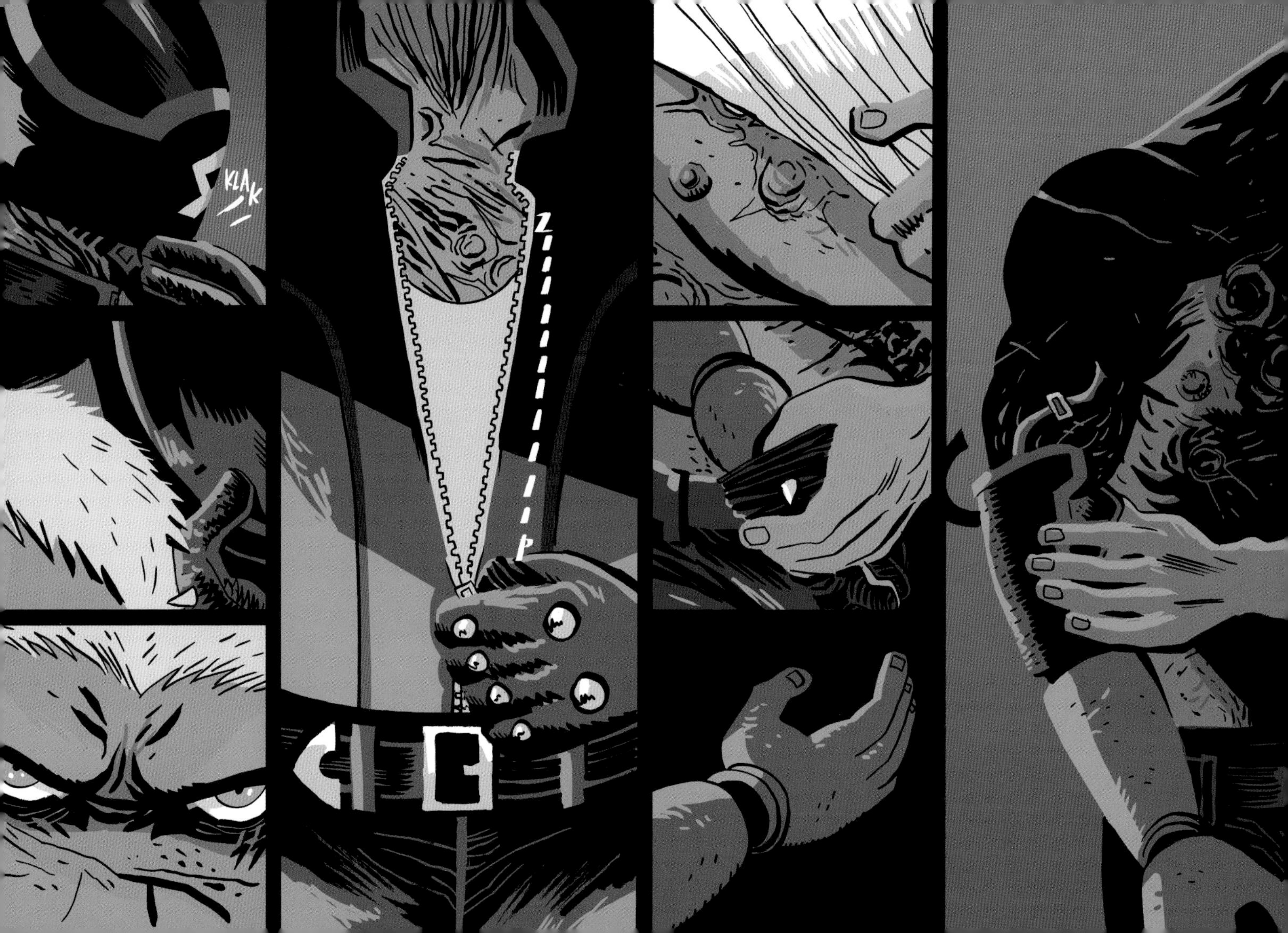
KLAK
ZIIIIIIIIIIP

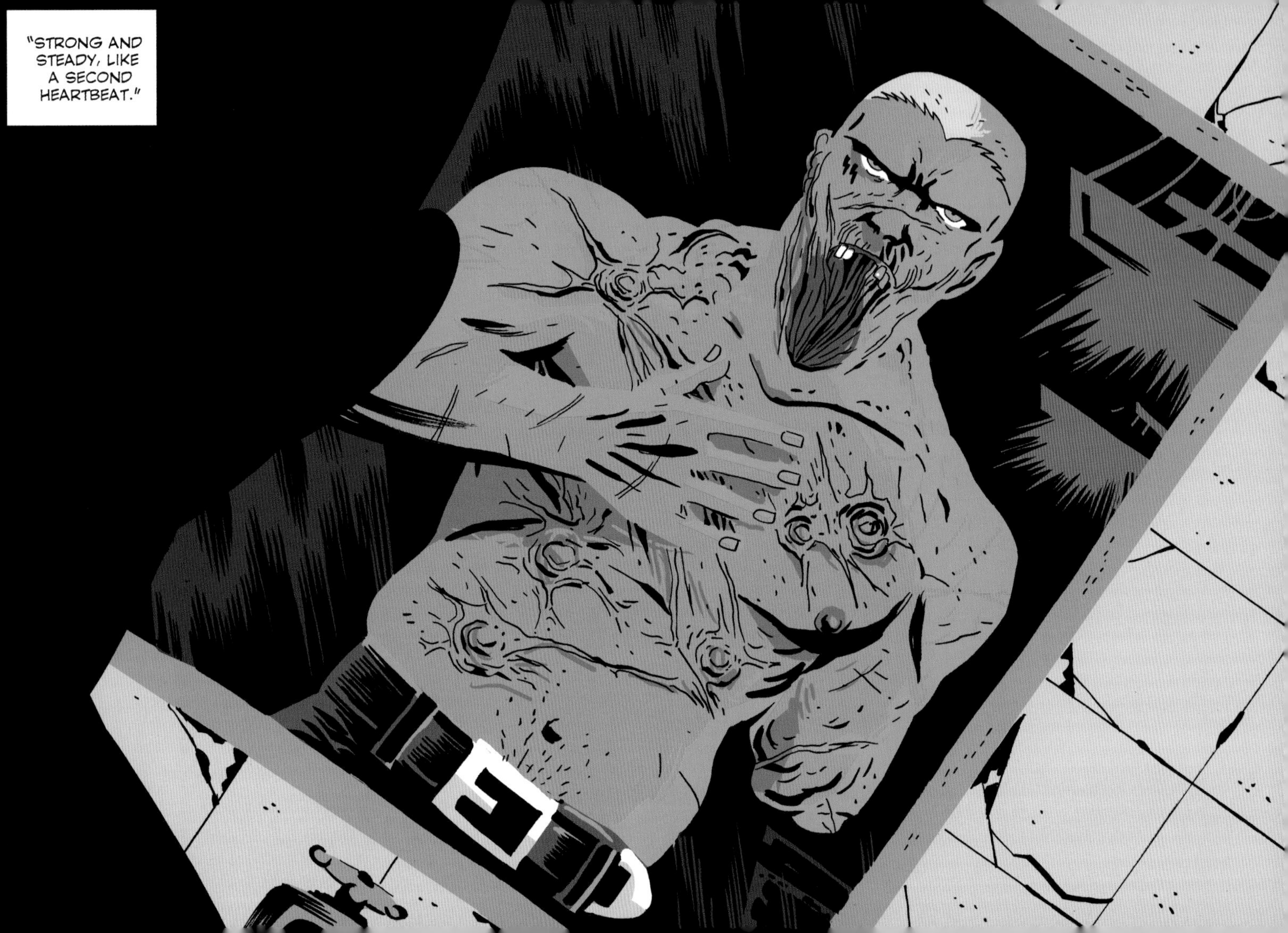
"STRONG AND STEADY, LIKE A SECOND HEARTBEAT."

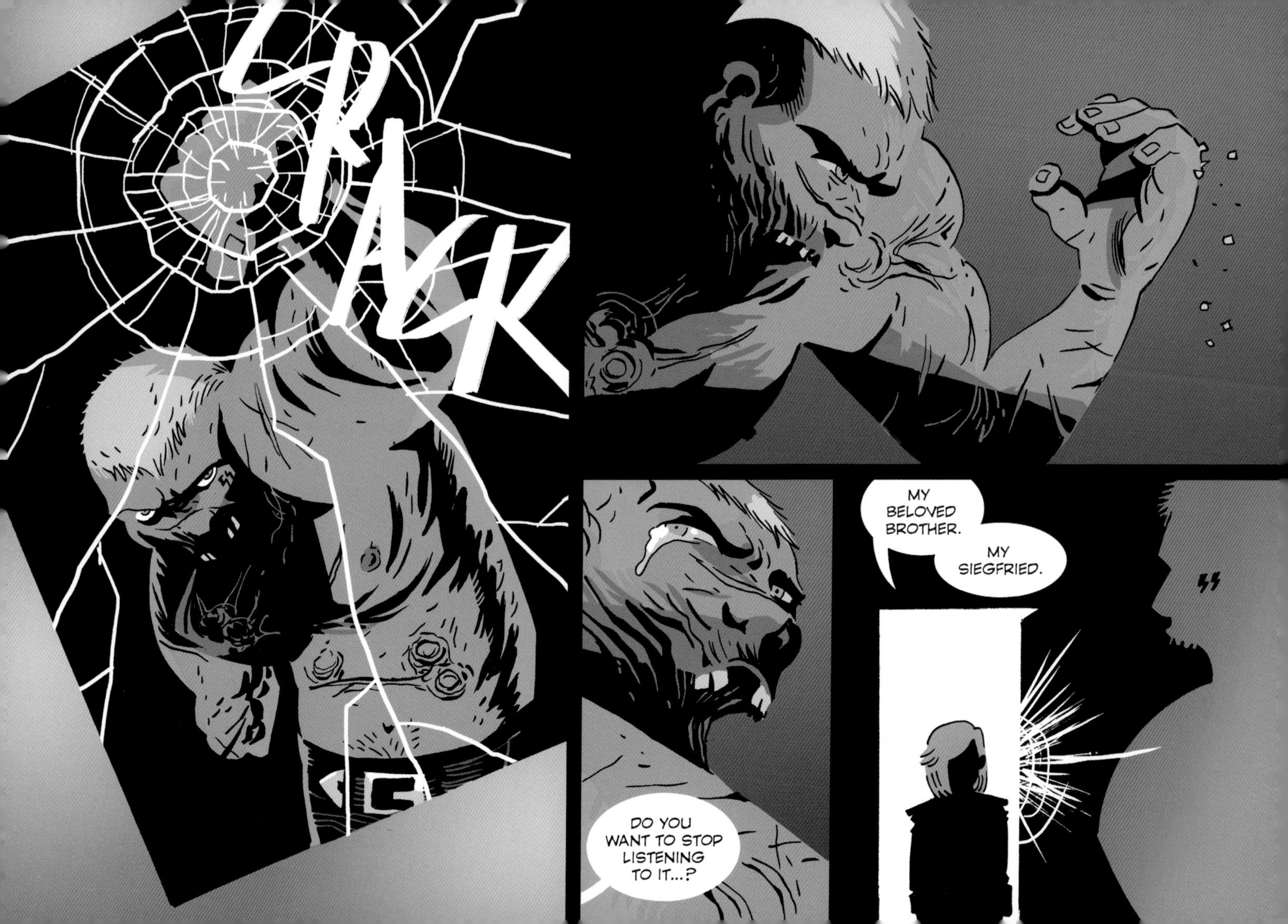
CRACK
DO YOU WANT TO STOP LISTENING TO IT...?
MY BELOVED BROTHER.
MY SIEGFRIED.

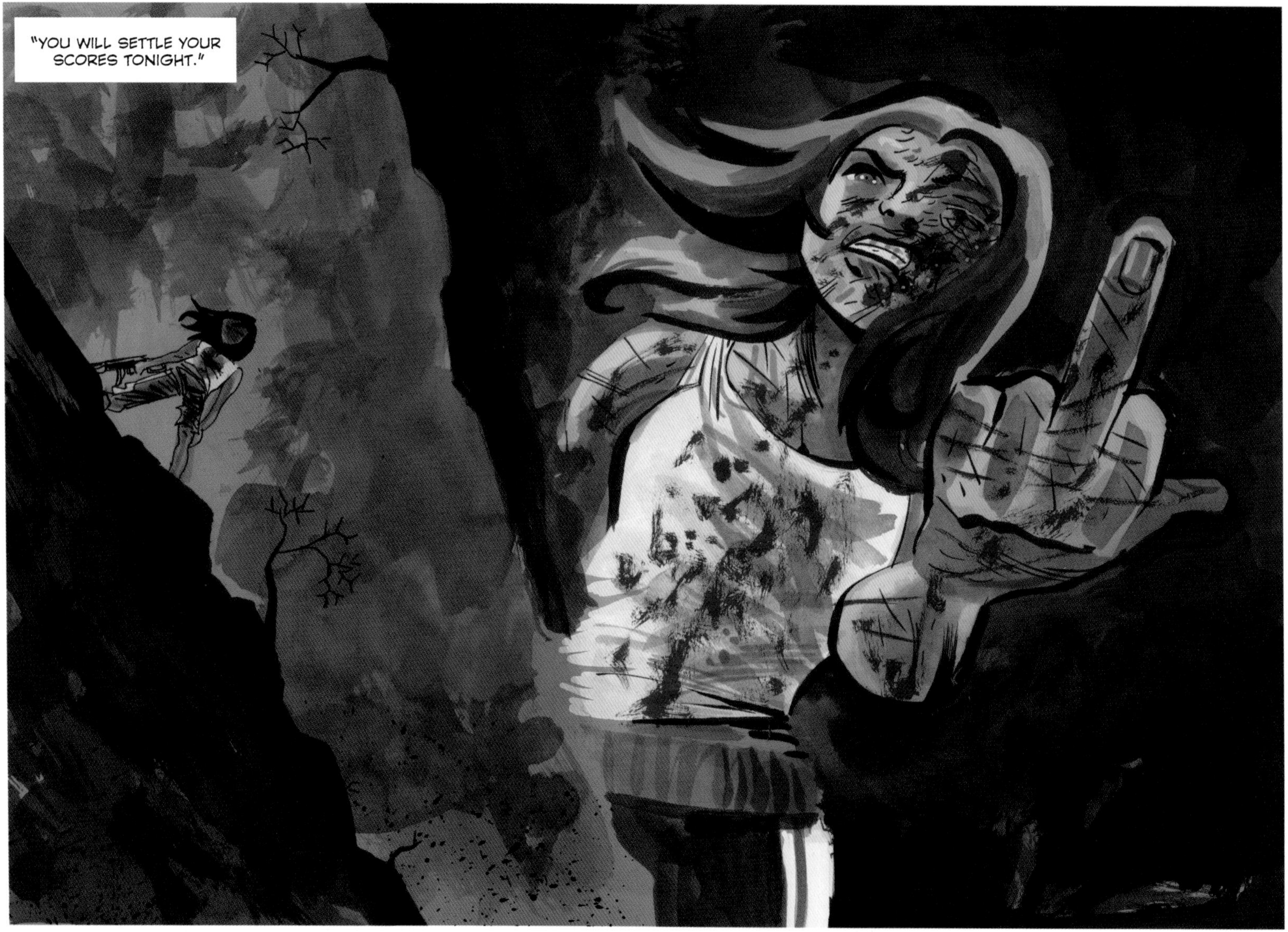
"YOU WILL SETTLE YOUR SCORES TONIGHT."

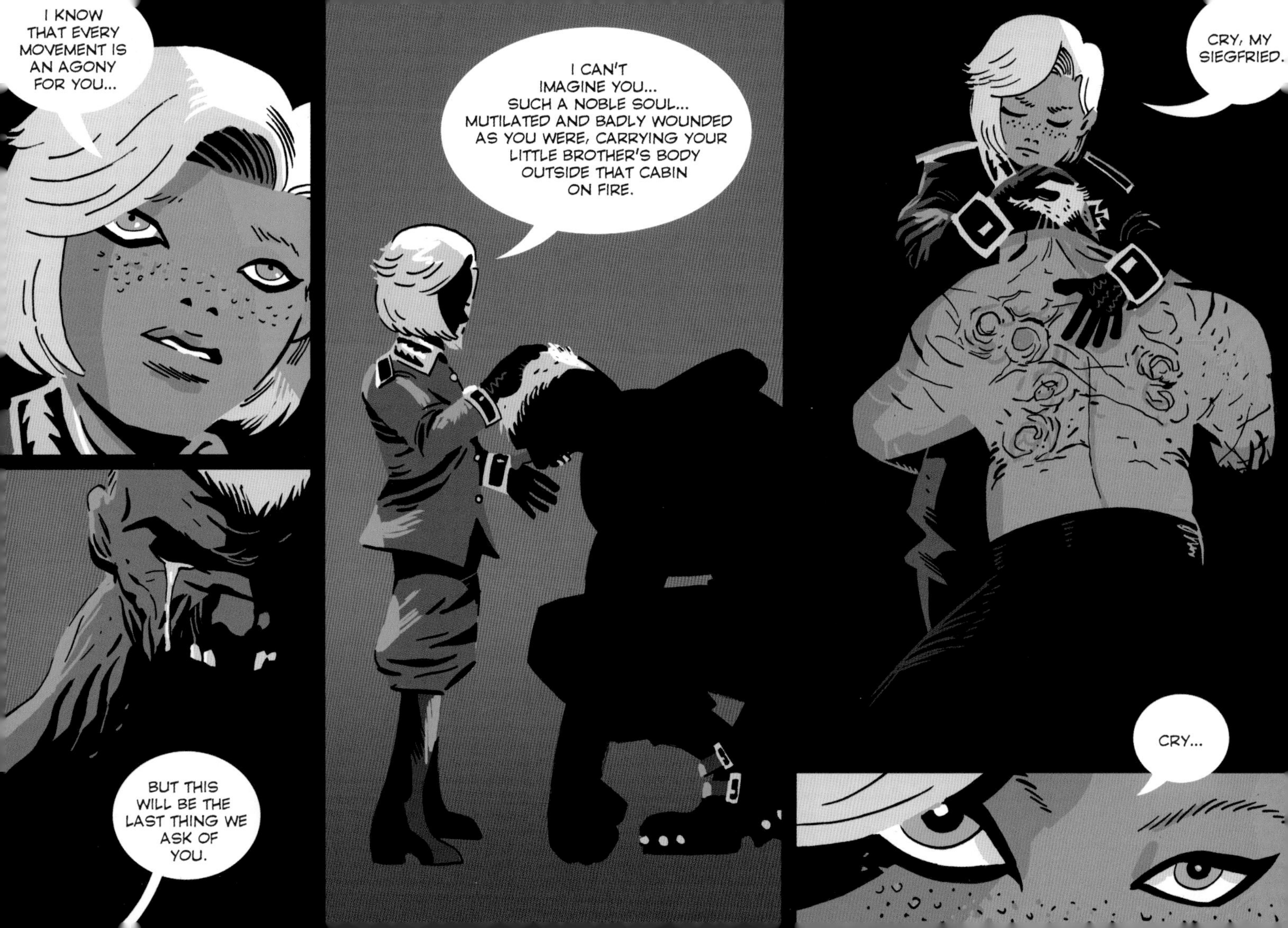
I KNOW THAT EVERY MOVEMENT IS AN AGONY FOR YOU...
BUT THIS WILL BE THE LAST THING WE ASK OF YOU.
I CAN'T IMAGINE YOU... SUCH A NOBLE SOUL... MUTILATED AND BADLY WOUNDED AS YOU WERE, CARRYING YOUR LITTLE BROTHER'S BODY OUTSIDE THAT CABIN ON FIRE.
CRY, MY SIEGFRIED.
CRY...

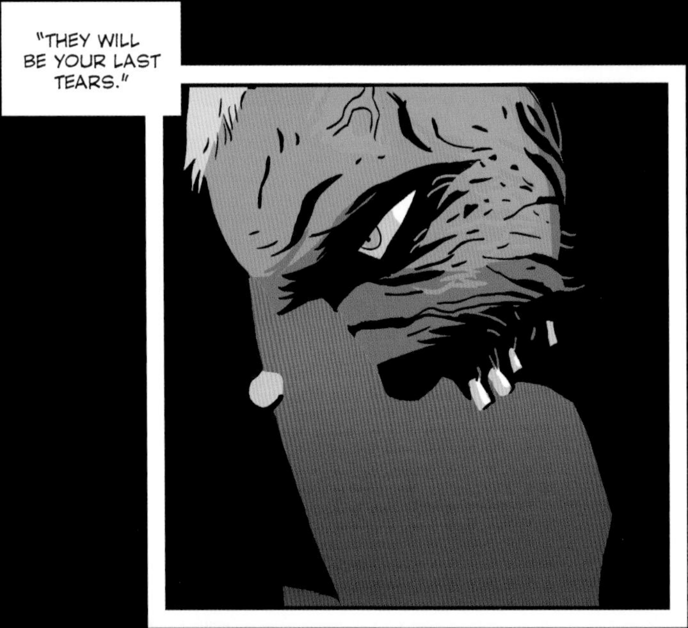
"THEY WILL BE YOUR LAST TEARS."

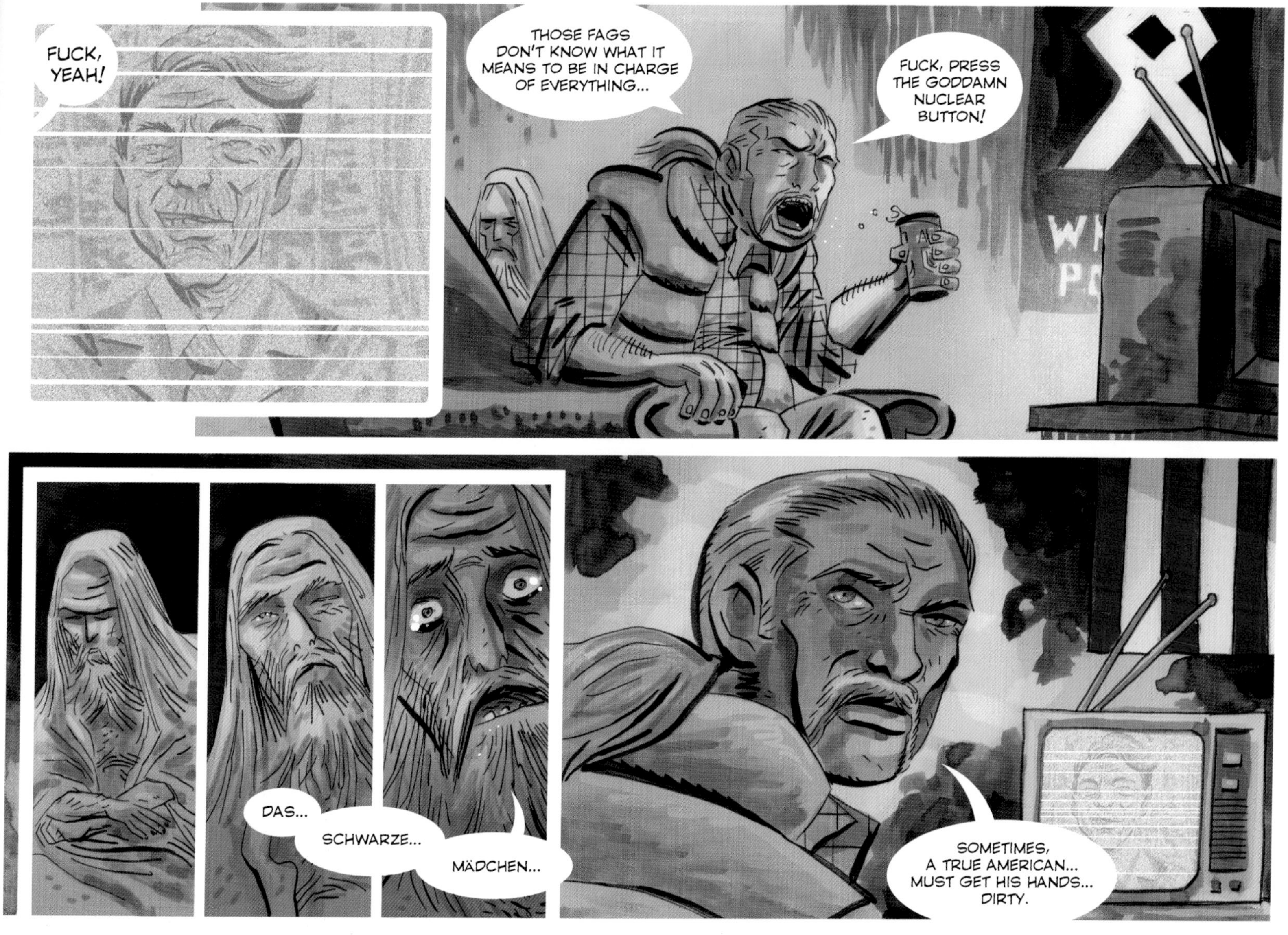
FUCK, YEAH!
THOSE FAGS DON'T KNOW WHAT IT MEANS TO BE IN CHARGE OF EVERYTHING...
FUCK, PRESS THE GODDAMN NUCLEAR BUTTON!
DAS...
SCHWARZE...
MÄDCHEN...
SOMETIMES, A TRUE AMERICAN... MUST GET HIS HANDS... DIRTY.

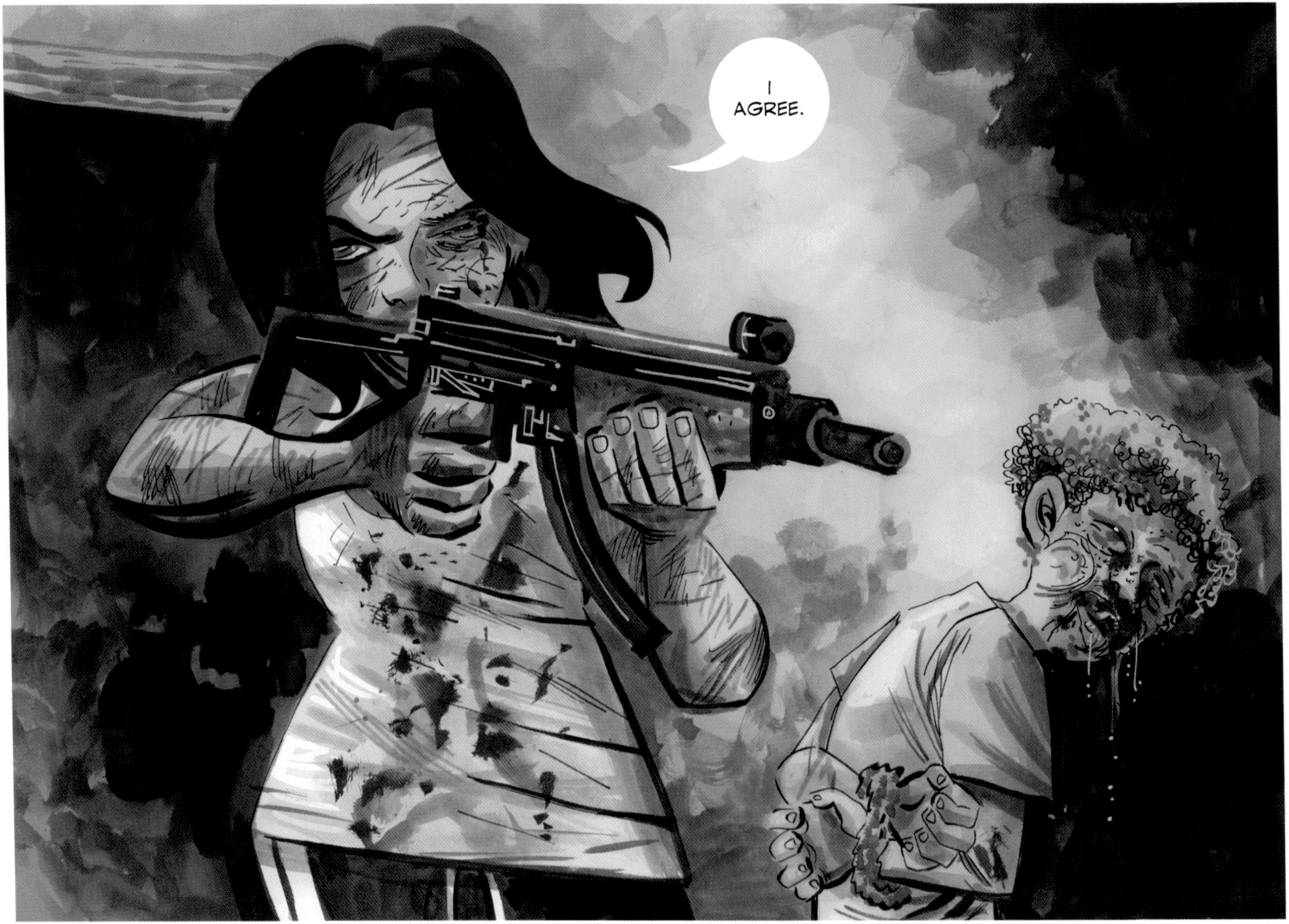
I AGREE.

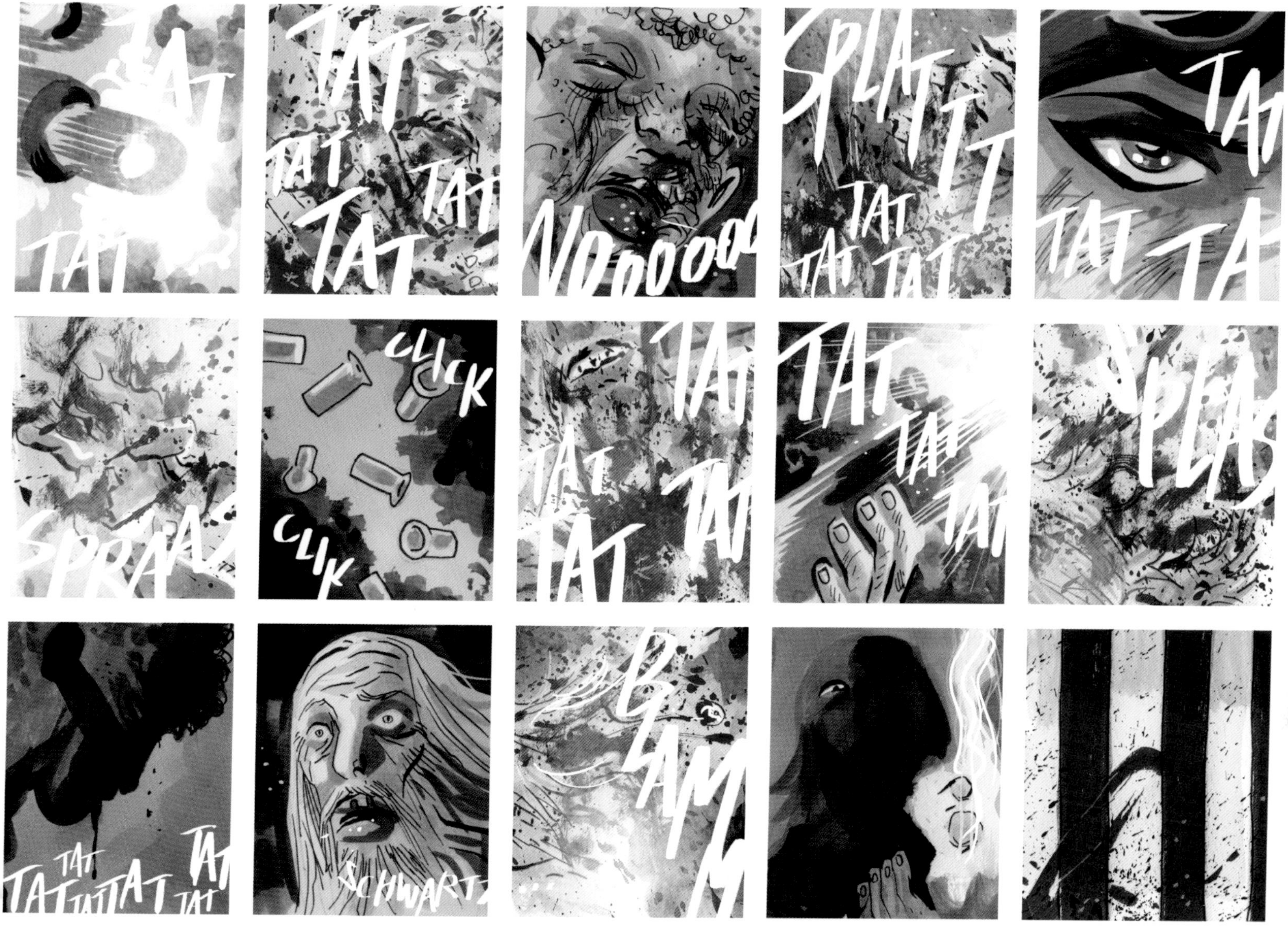
TAT
TAT
TAT
TAT
TAT
TAT
NOOOOO
SPLAT
TAT
TAT
TAT
TAT
TAT
TA
SPRAA
CLICK
CLIK
TAT
TAT
TAT
TAT
TAT
TAT
TAT
PLAS
TAT
TATTATTAT
TAT
TAT
SCHWARTZ
BLAM

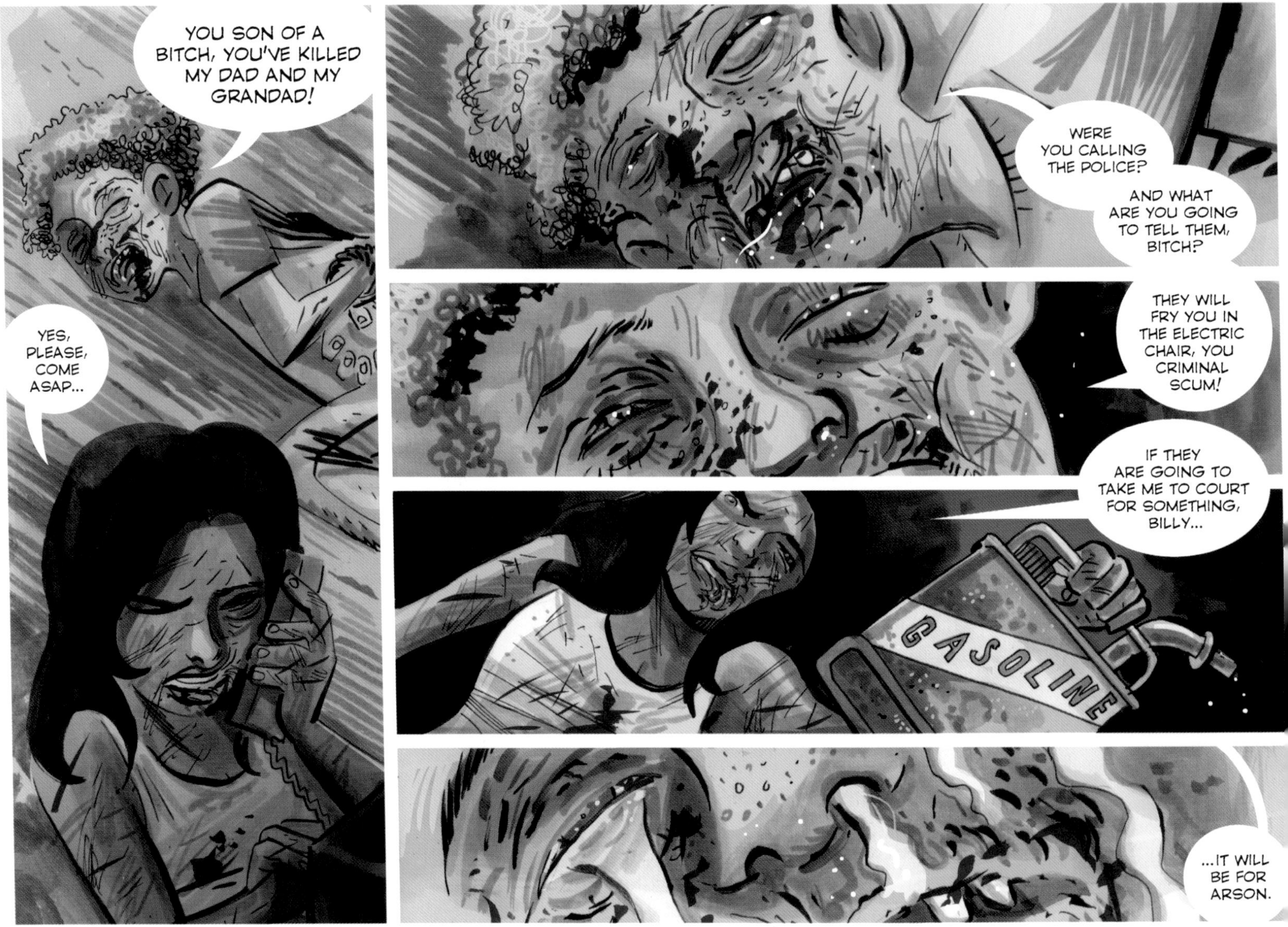
YOU SON OF A BITCH, YOU'VE KILLED MY DAD AND MY GRANDAD!
YES, PLEASE, COME ASAP...
WERE YOU CALLING THE POLICE?
AND WHAT ARE YOU GOING TO TELL THEM, BITCH?
THEY WILL FRY YOU IN THE ELECTRIC CHAIR, YOU CRIMINAL SCUM!
IF THEY ARE GOING TO TAKE ME TO COURT FOR SOMETHING, BILLY...
GASOLINE
...IT WILL BE FOR ARSON.

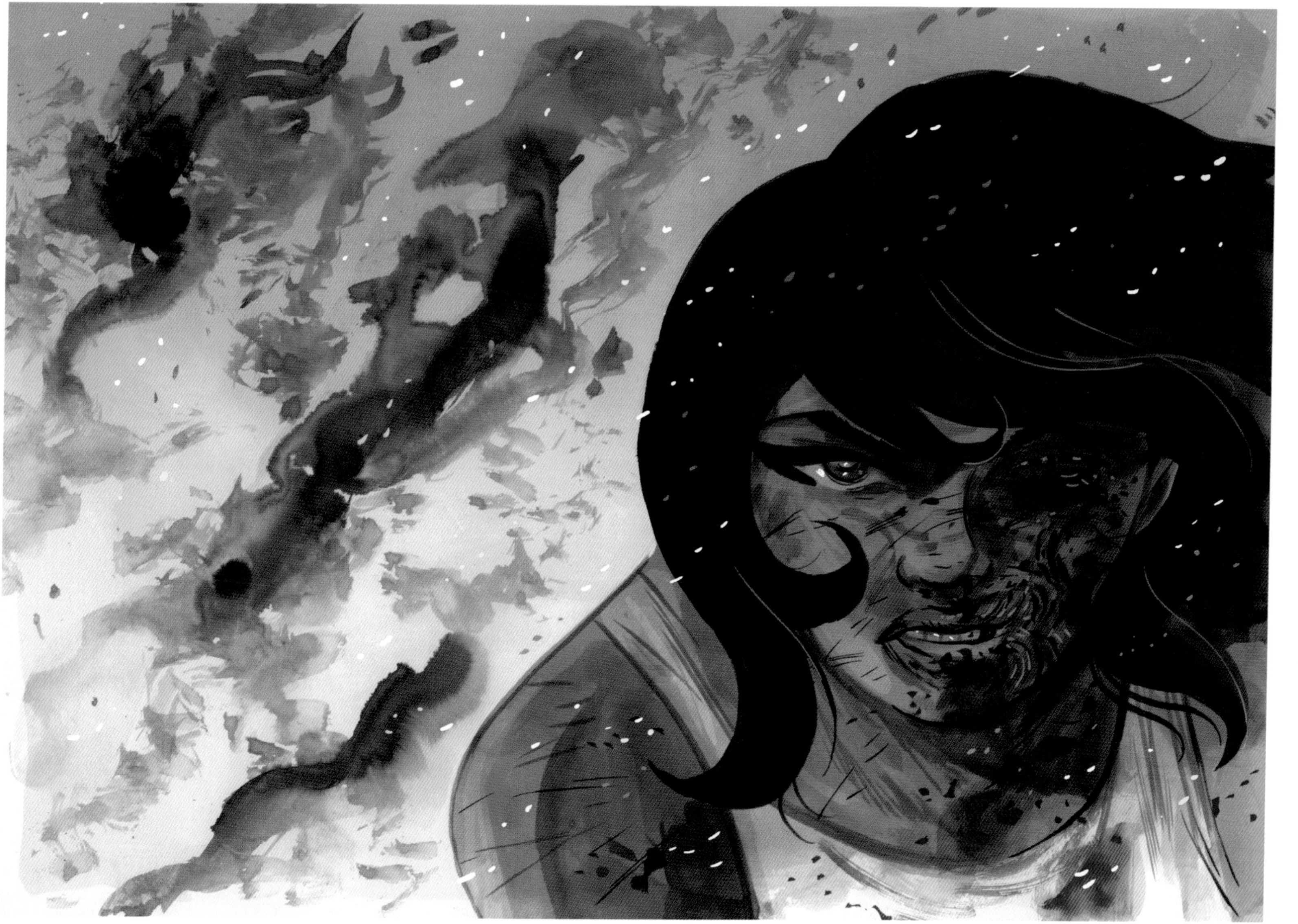

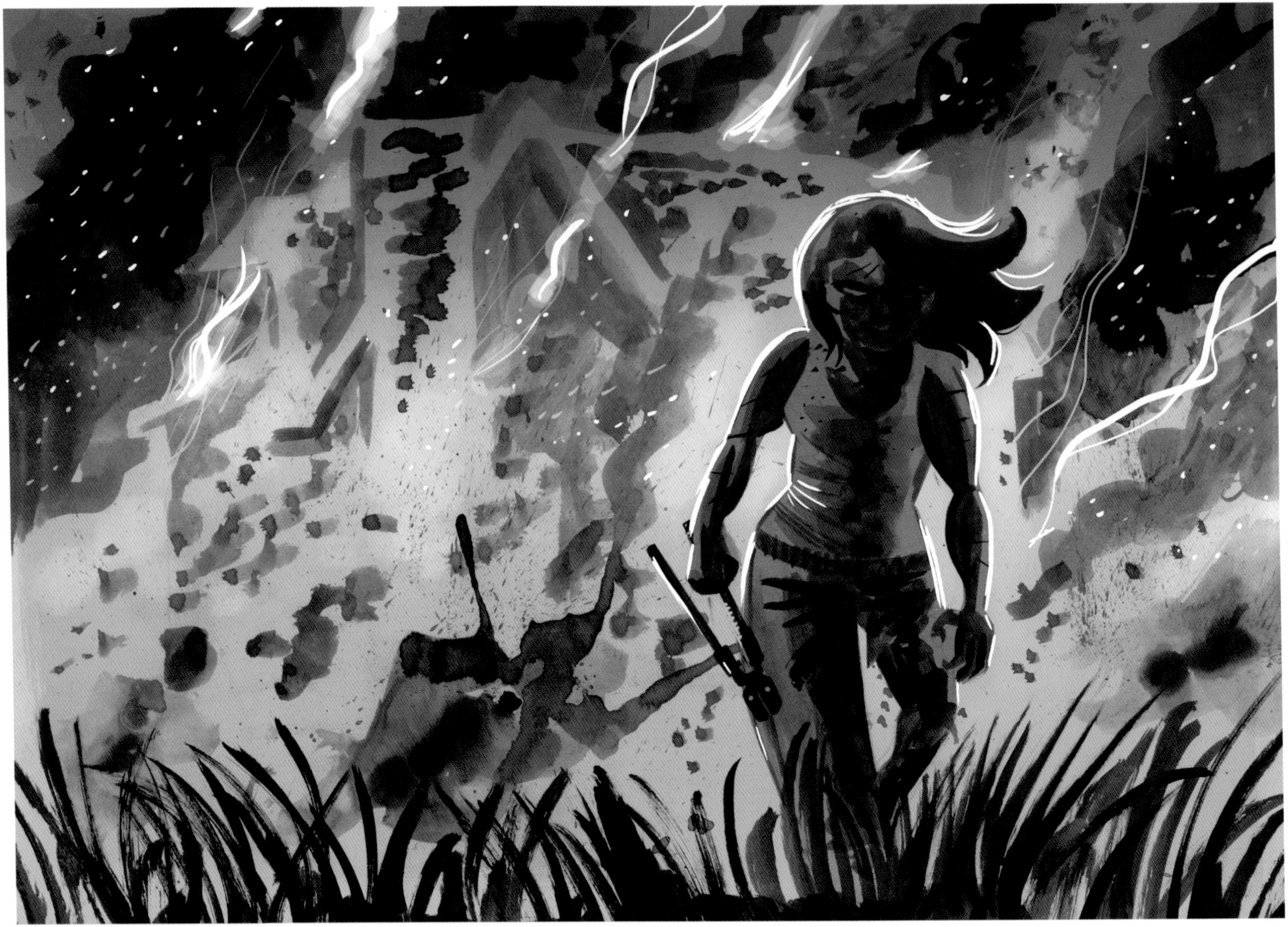

# CHAPTER 8

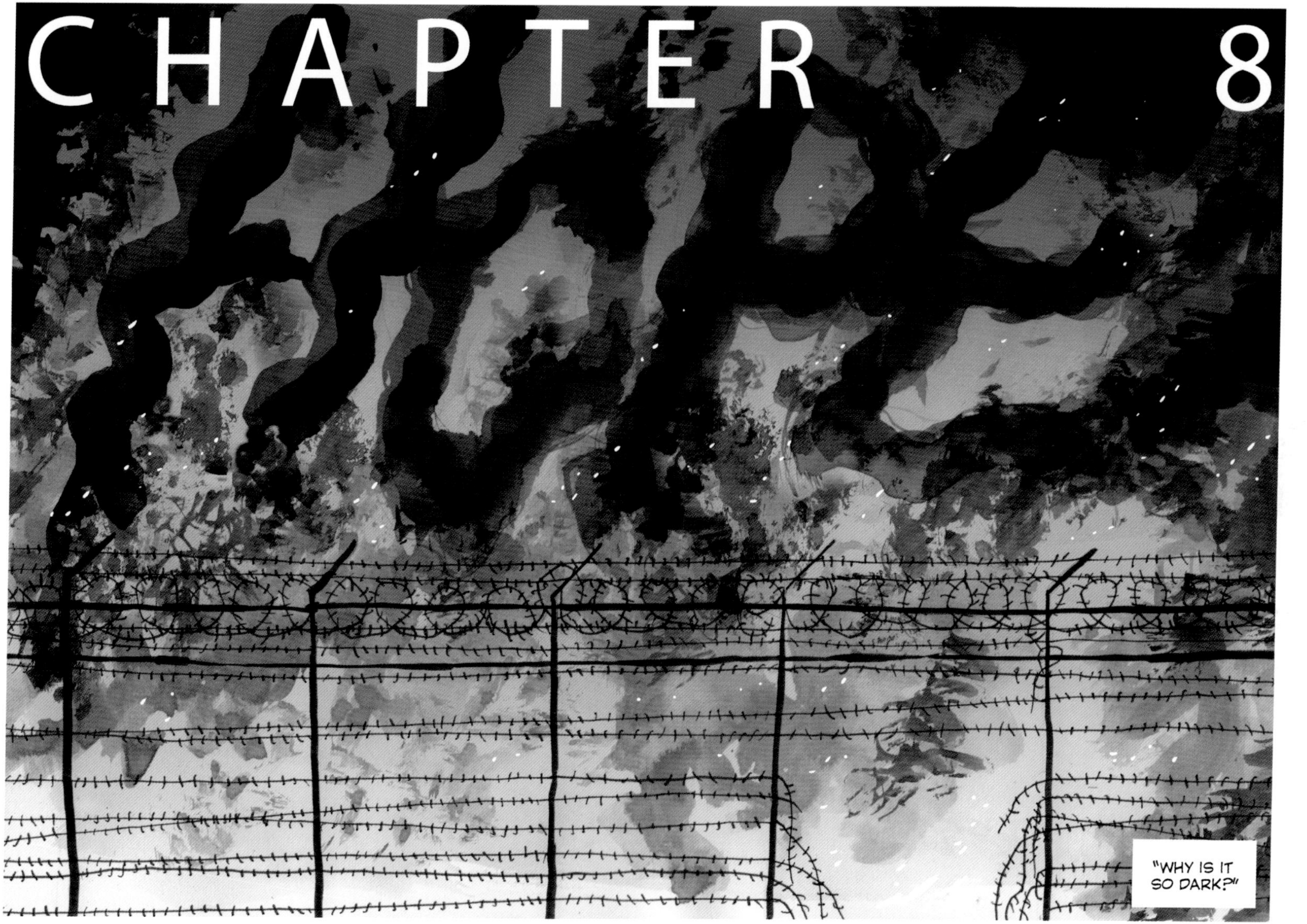
"WHY IS IT
SO DARK?"

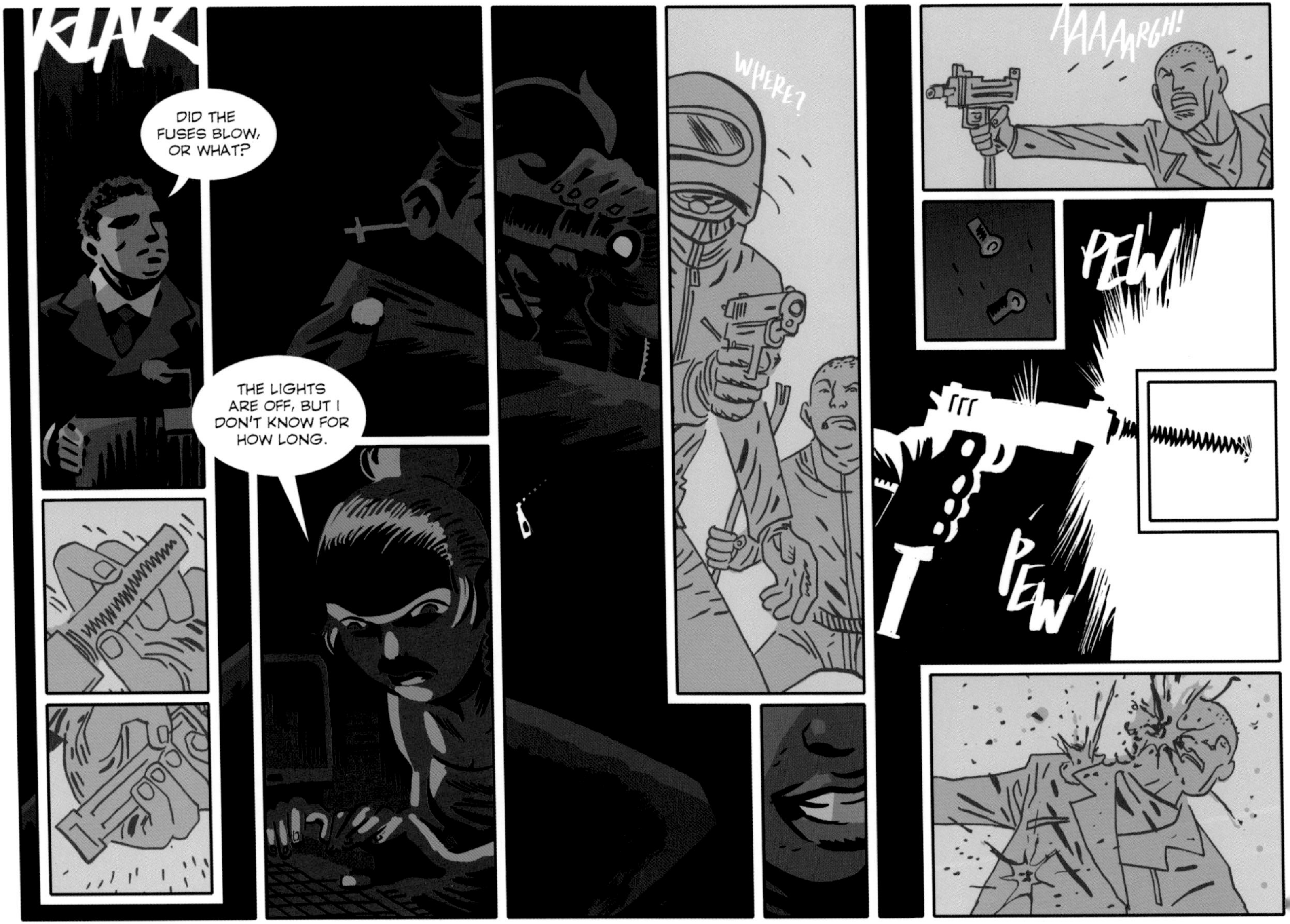
KLAK
DID THE FUSES BLOW, OR WHAT?
THE LIGHTS ARE OFF, BUT I DON'T KNOW FOR HOW LONG.
WHERE?
AAAAARGH!
PEW
PEW

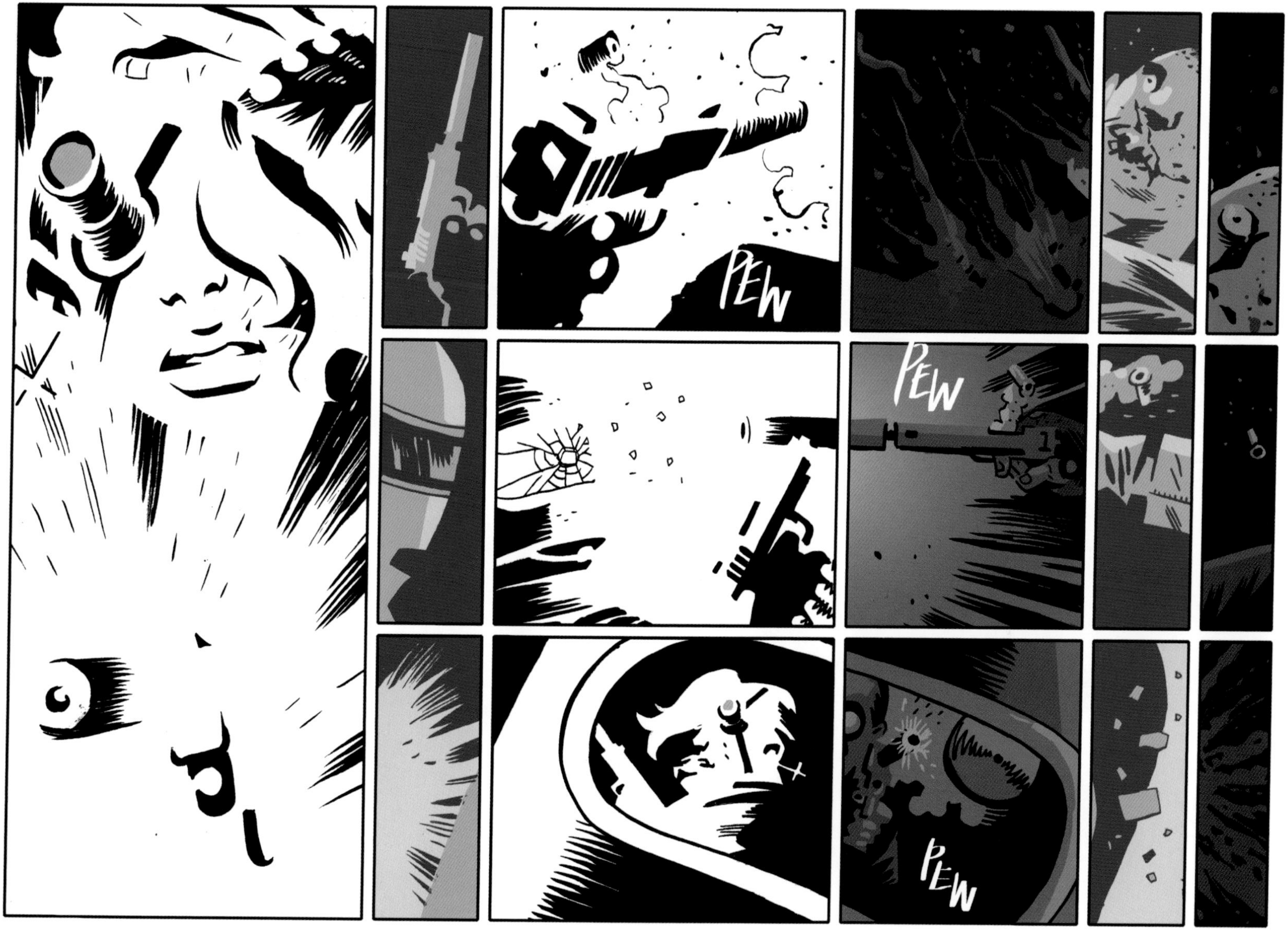
PEW
PEW
PEW

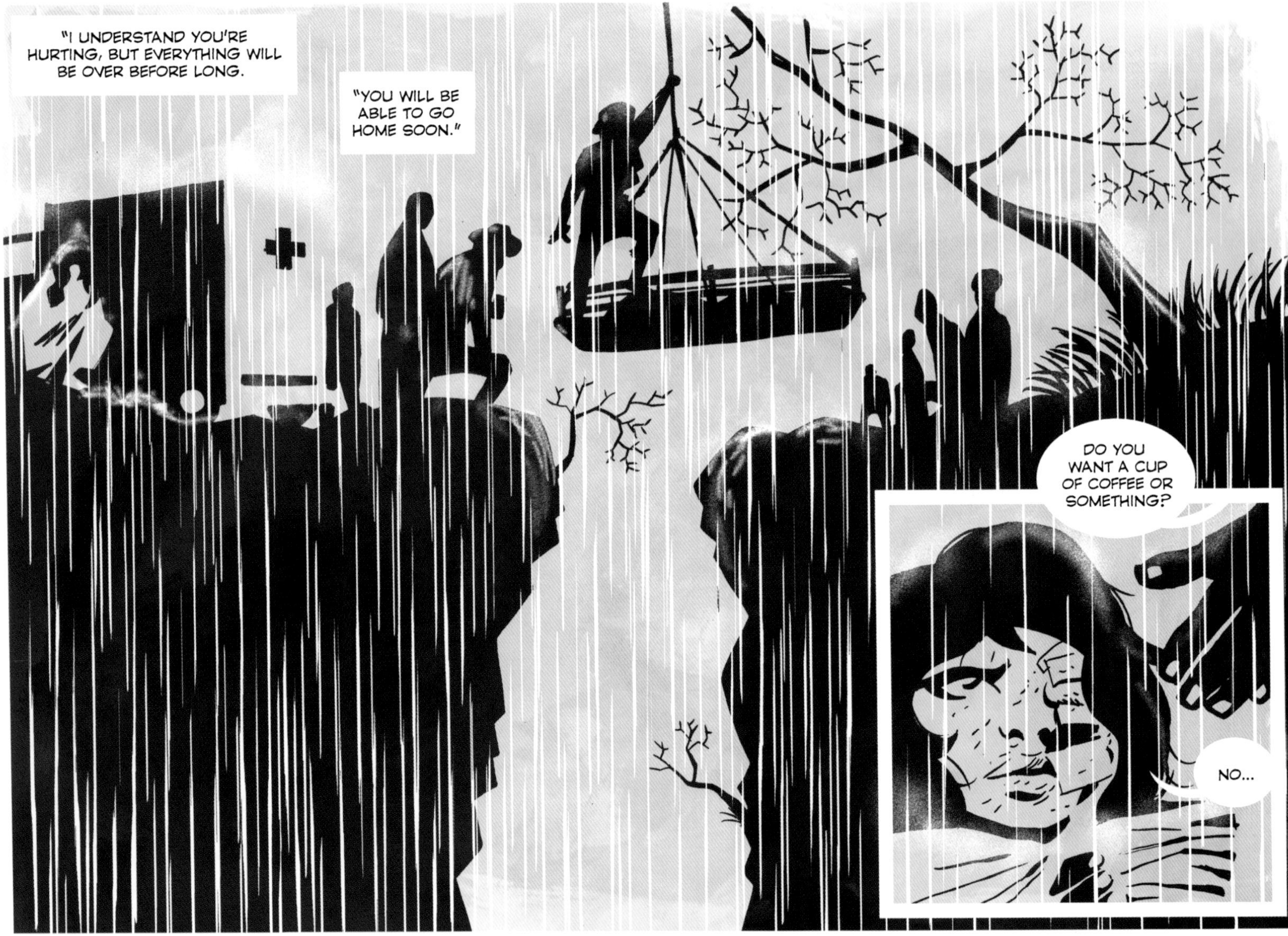
"I UNDERSTAND YOU'RE HURTING, BUT EVERYTHING WILL BE OVER BEFORE LONG.
"YOU WILL BE ABLE TO GO HOME SOON."
DO YOU WANT A CUP OF COFFEE OR SOMETHING?
NO...

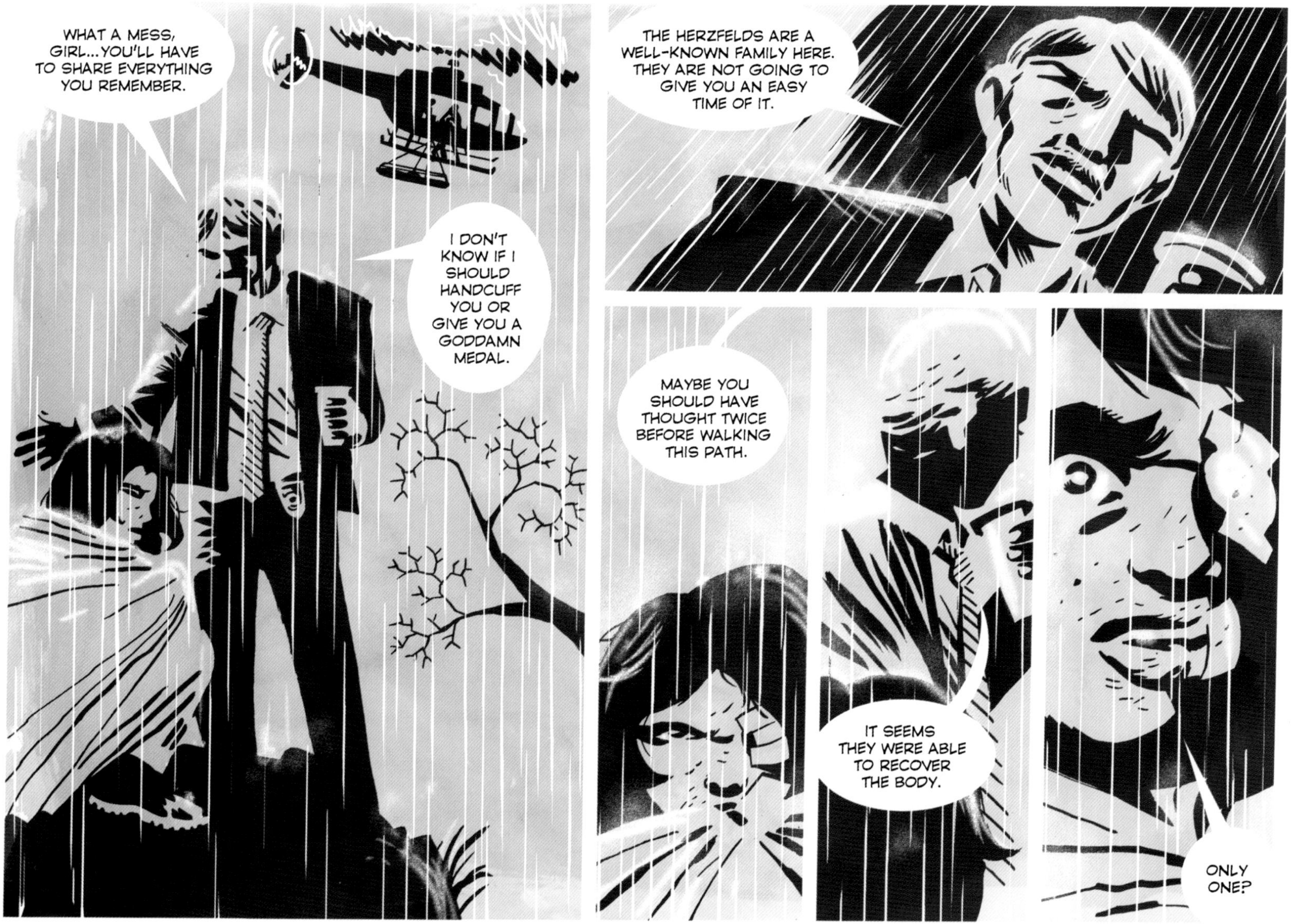
WHAT A MESS, GIRL...YOU'LL HAVE TO SHARE EVERYTHING YOU REMEMBER.
I DON'T KNOW IF I SHOULD HANDCUFF YOU OR GIVE YOU A GODDAMN MEDAL.
THE HERZFELDS ARE A WELL-KNOWN FAMILY HERE. THEY ARE NOT GOING TO GIVE YOU AN EASY TIME OF IT.
MAYBE YOU SHOULD HAVE THOUGHT TWICE BEFORE WALKING THIS PATH.
IT SEEMS THEY WERE ABLE TO RECOVER THE BODY.
ONLY ONE?

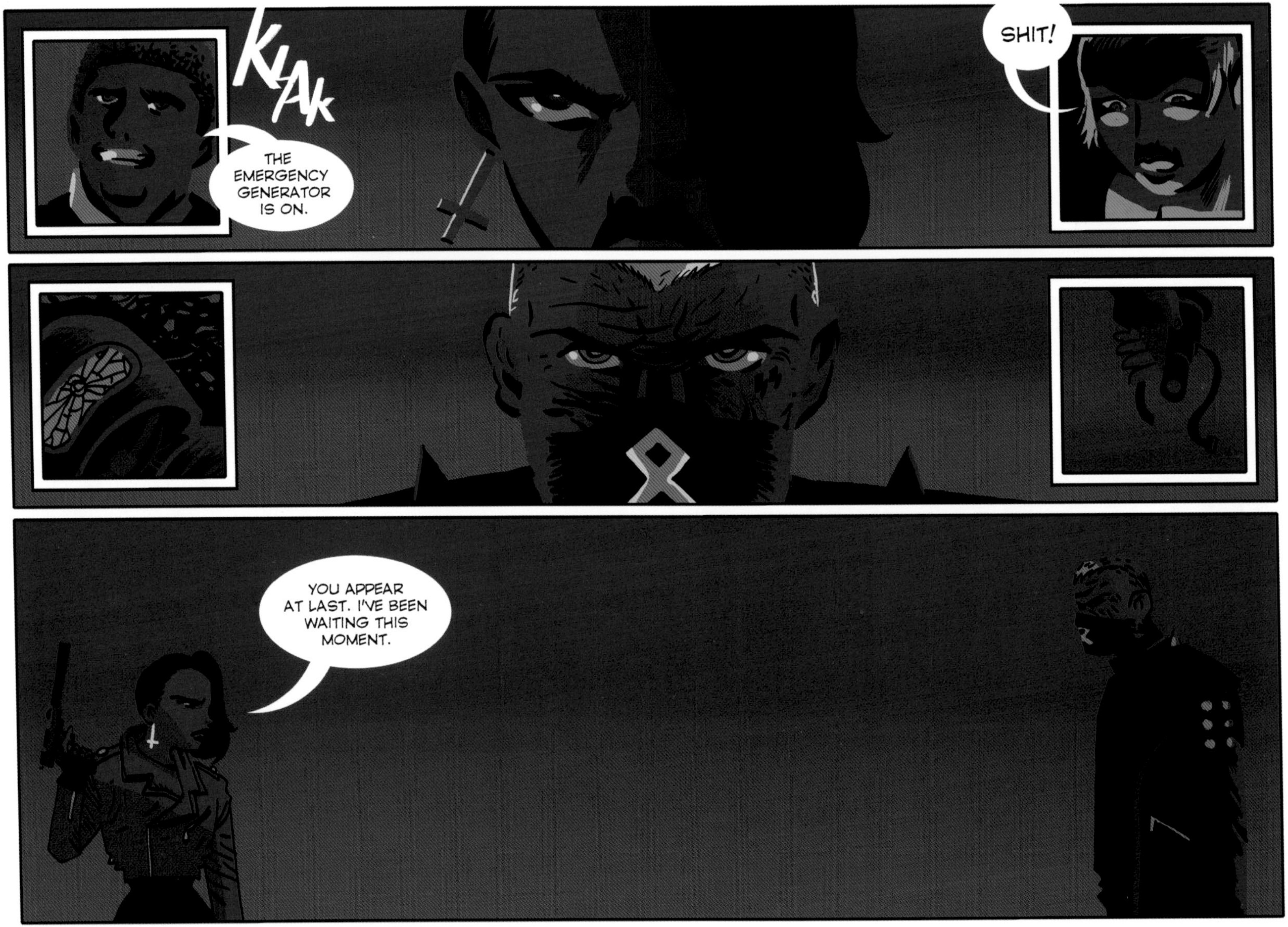
KLAK
THE EMERGENCY GENERATOR IS ON.
SHIT!
YOU APPEAR AT LAST. I'VE BEEN WAITING THIS MOMENT.

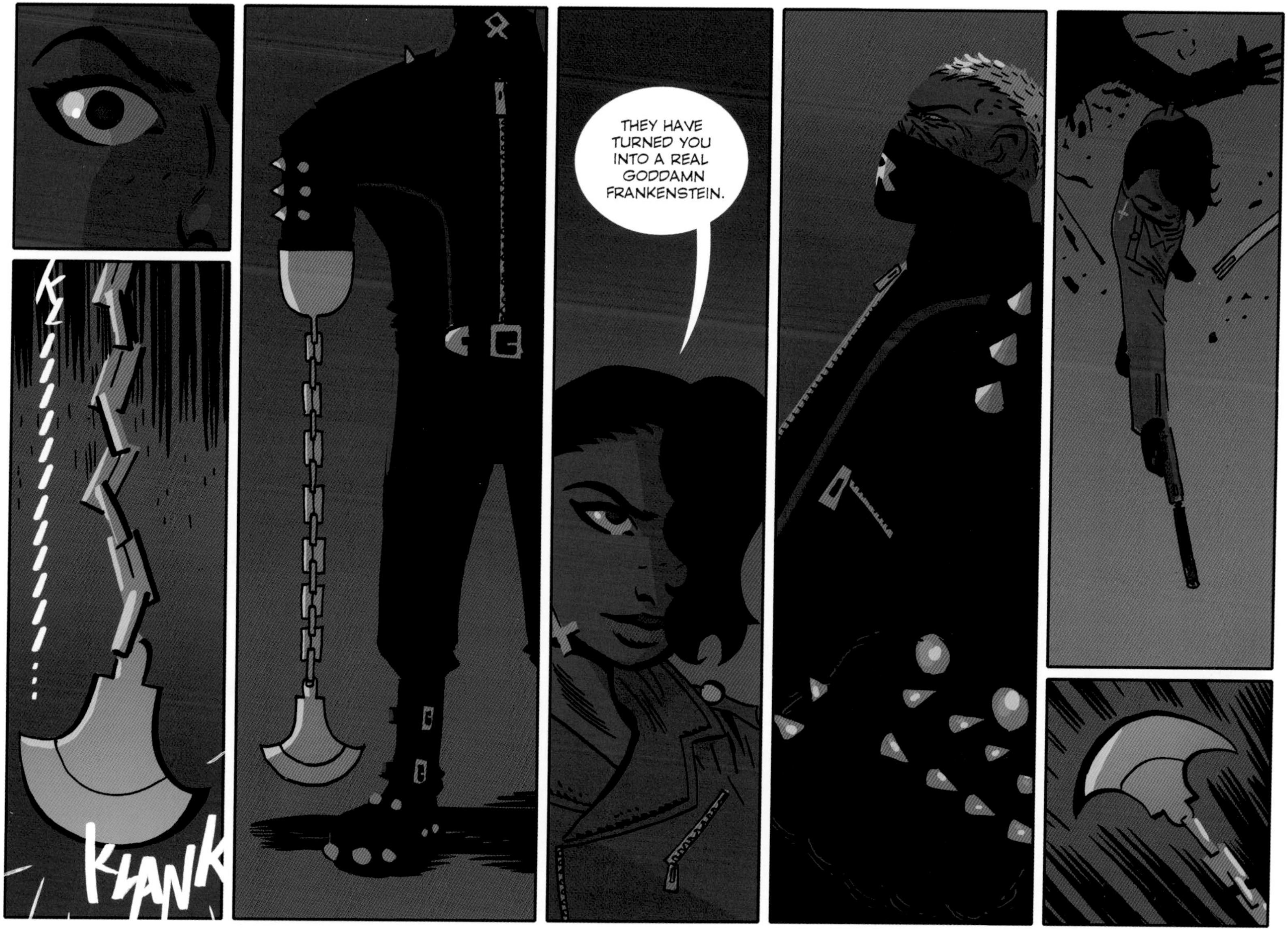
KLANK
THEY HAVE TURNED YOU INTO A REAL GODDAMN FRANKENSTEIN.

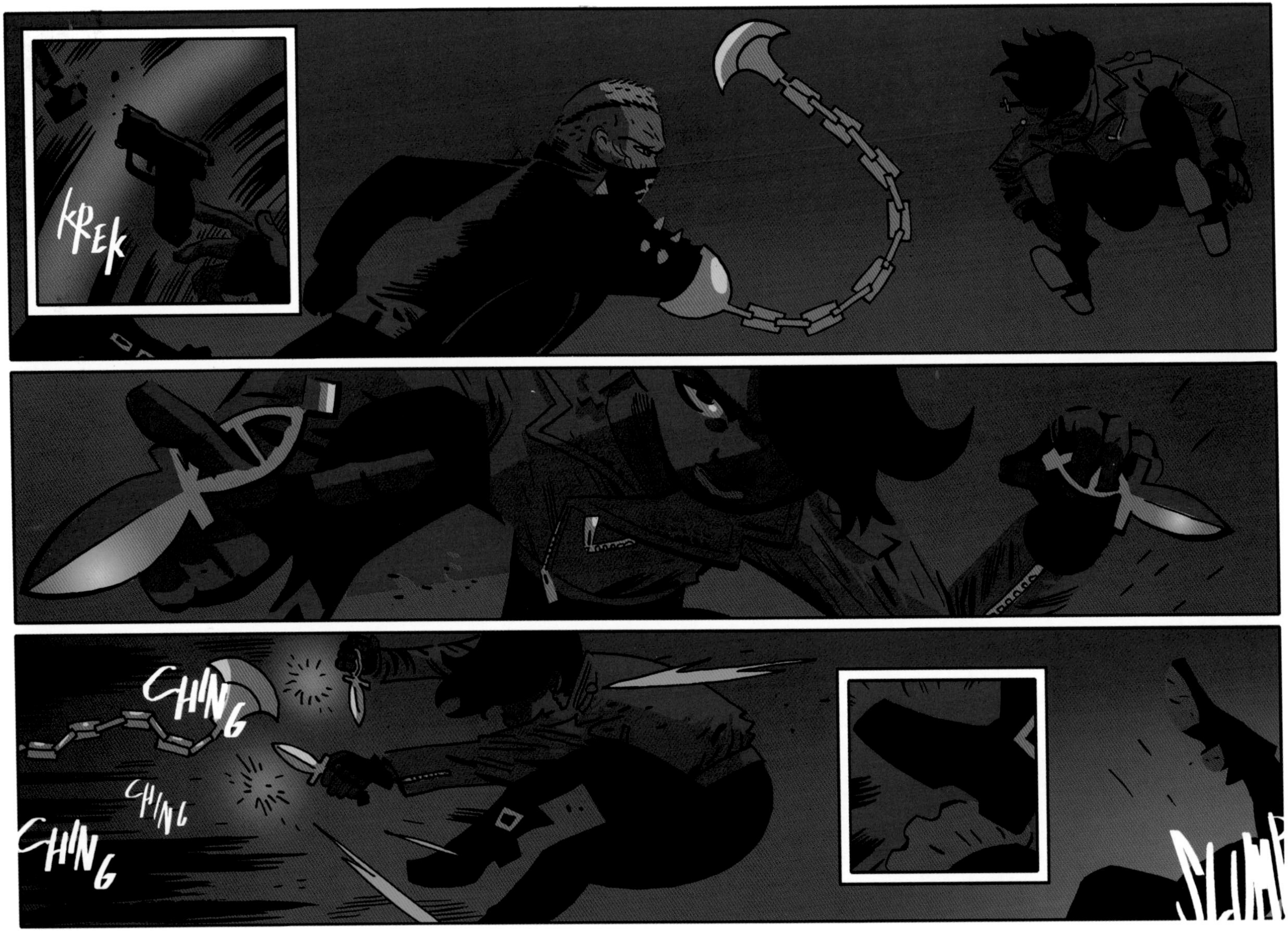
KREK
CHING
CHING
CHING
SLUMP

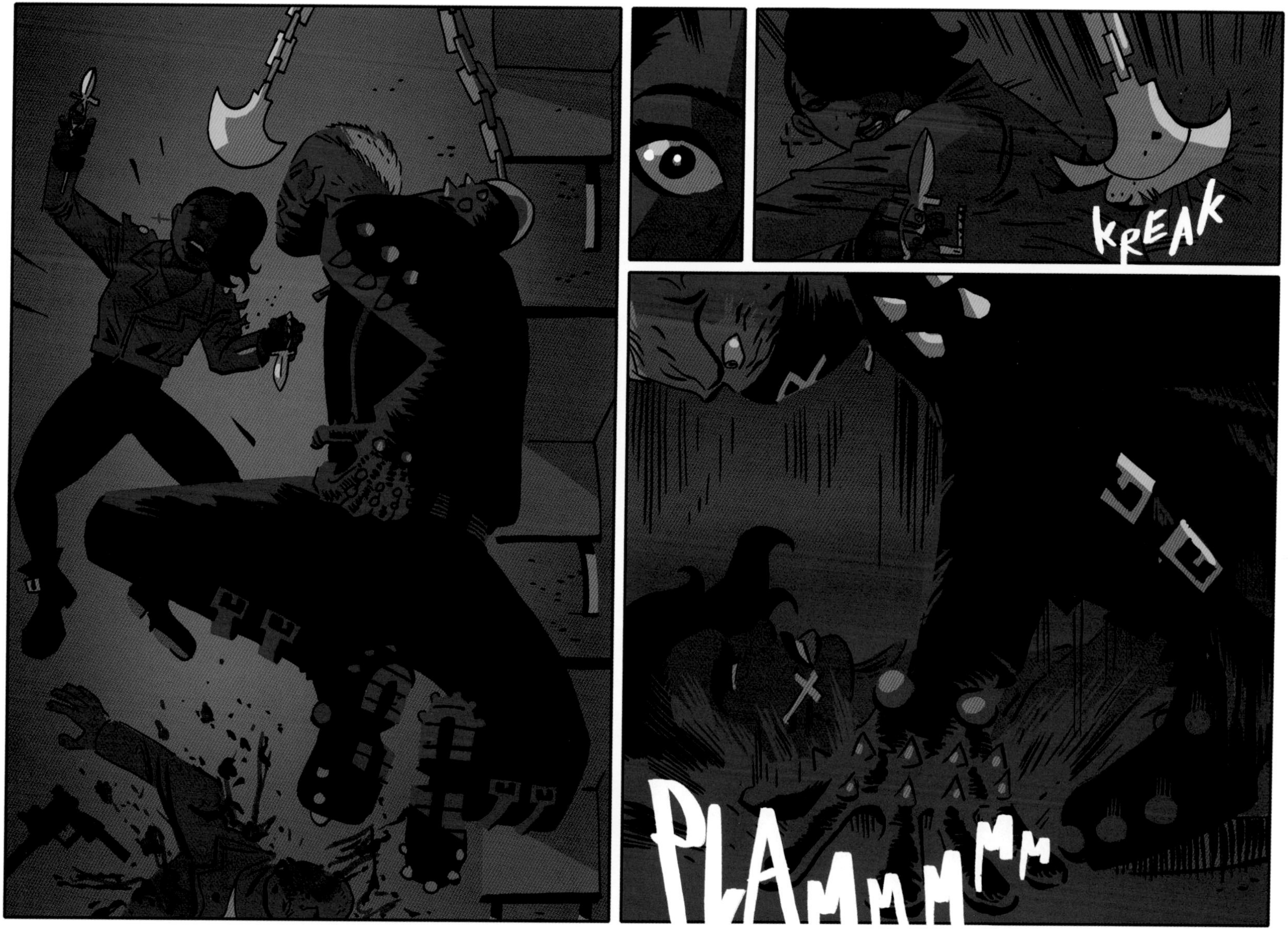
KREAK
PLAMMMMMM

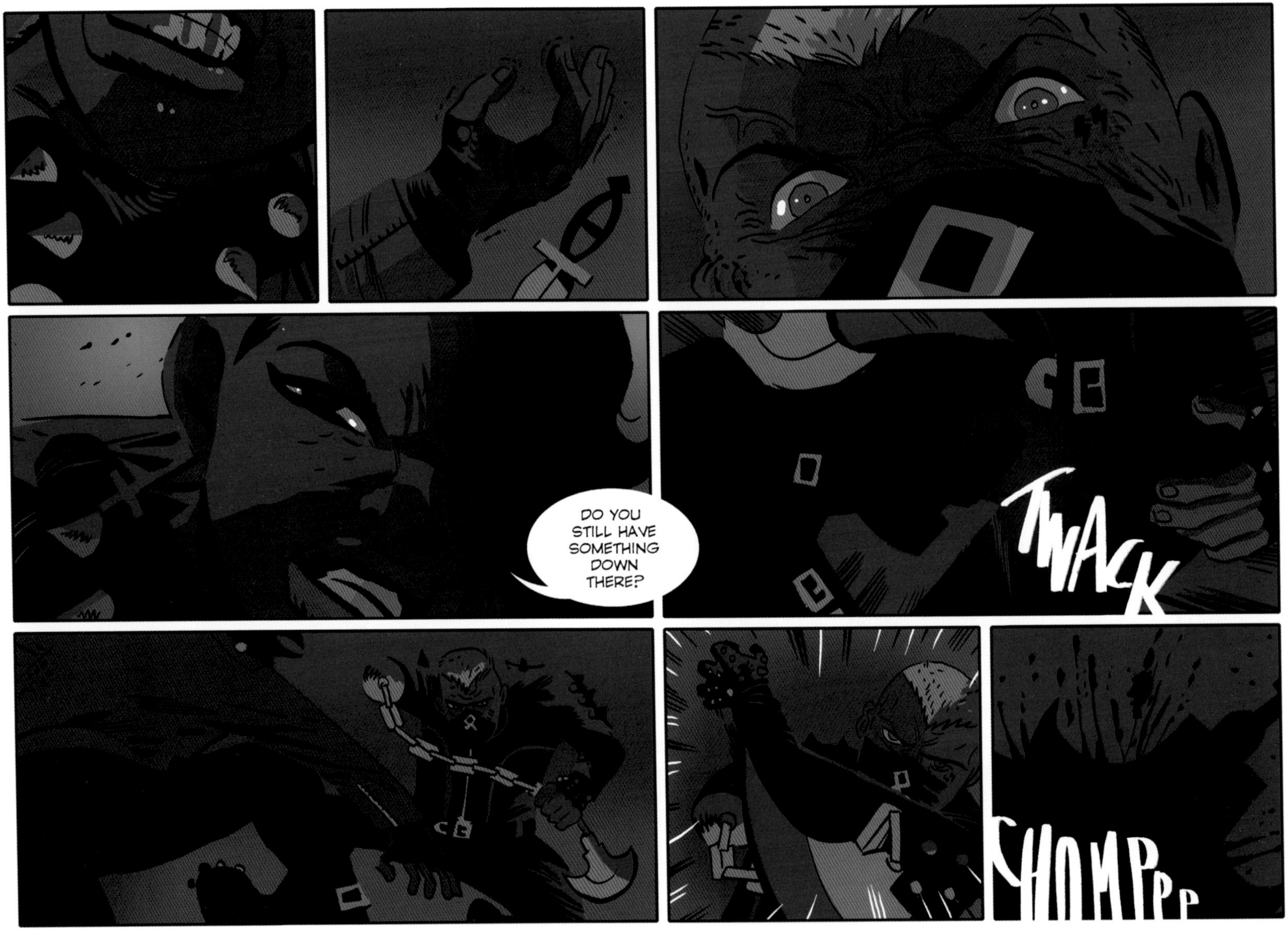
DO YOU STILL HAVE SOMETHING DOWN THERE?
TWACK
CHOMPPP

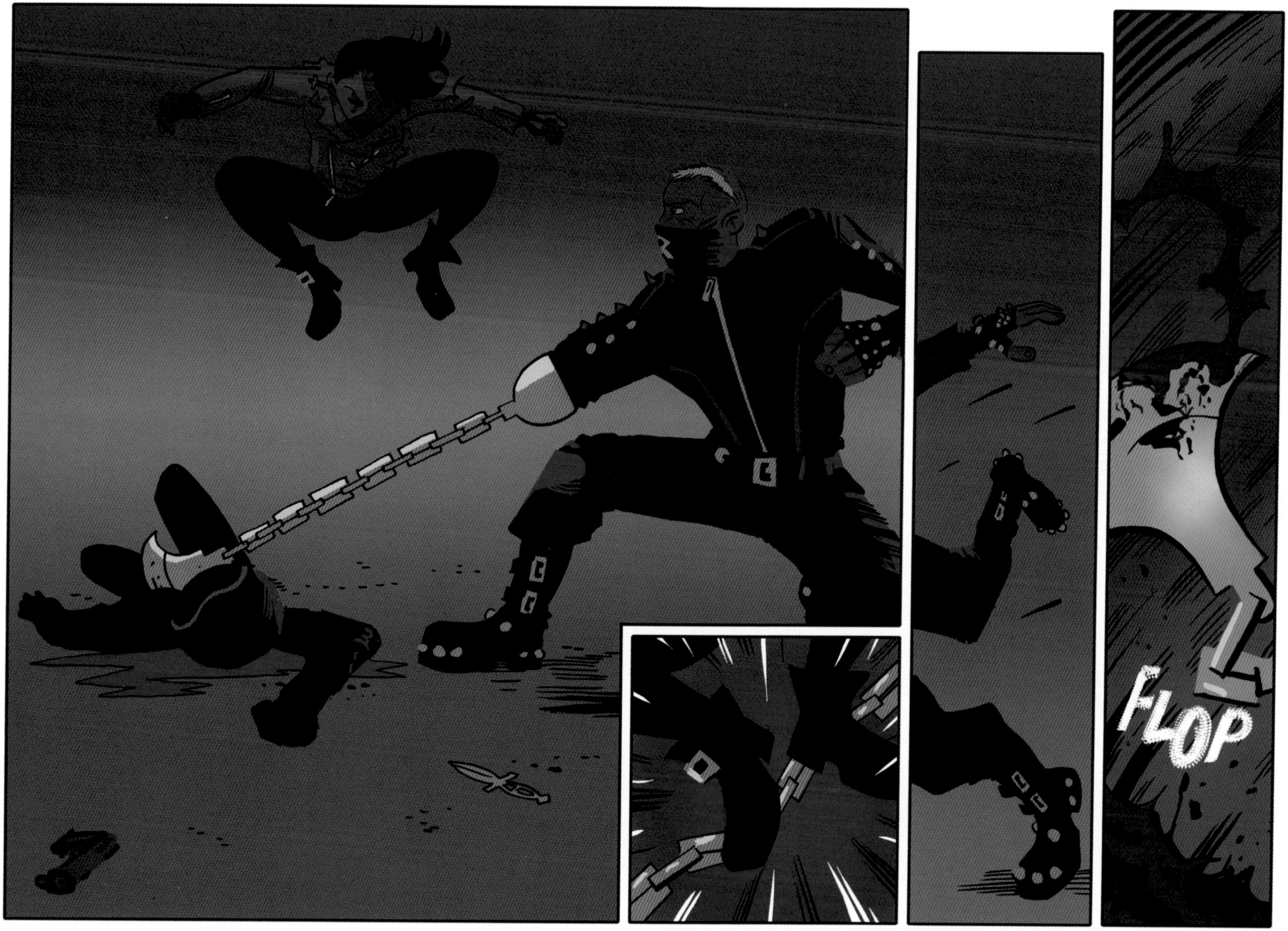
FLOP

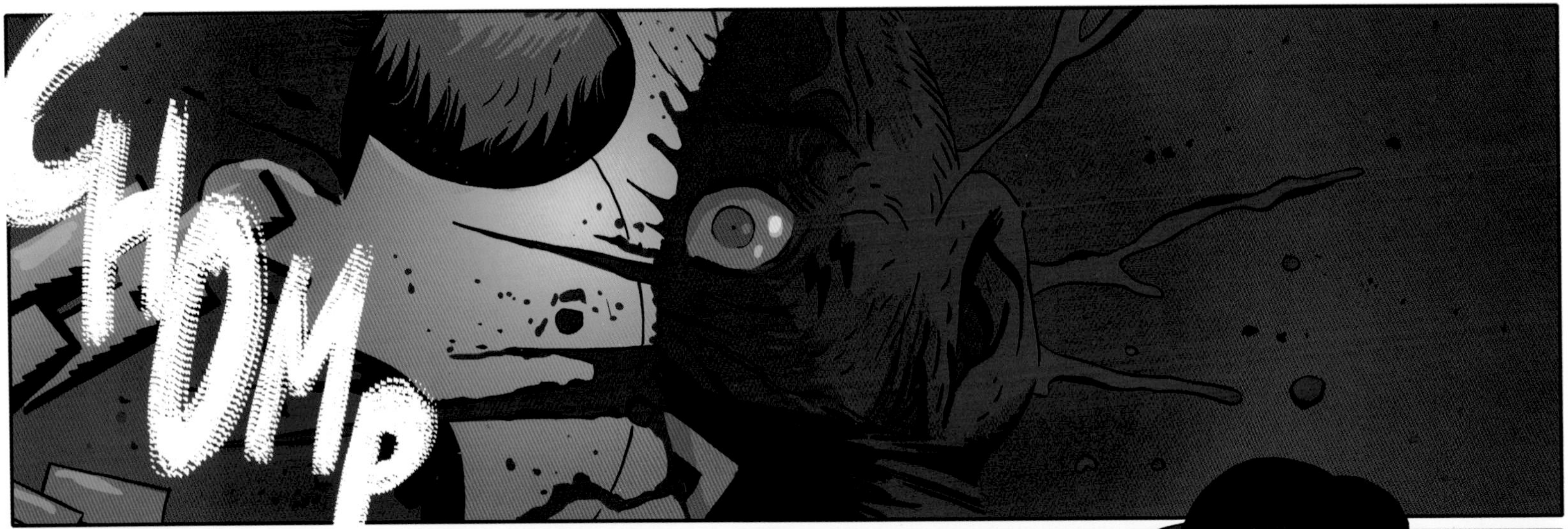
CHOMP

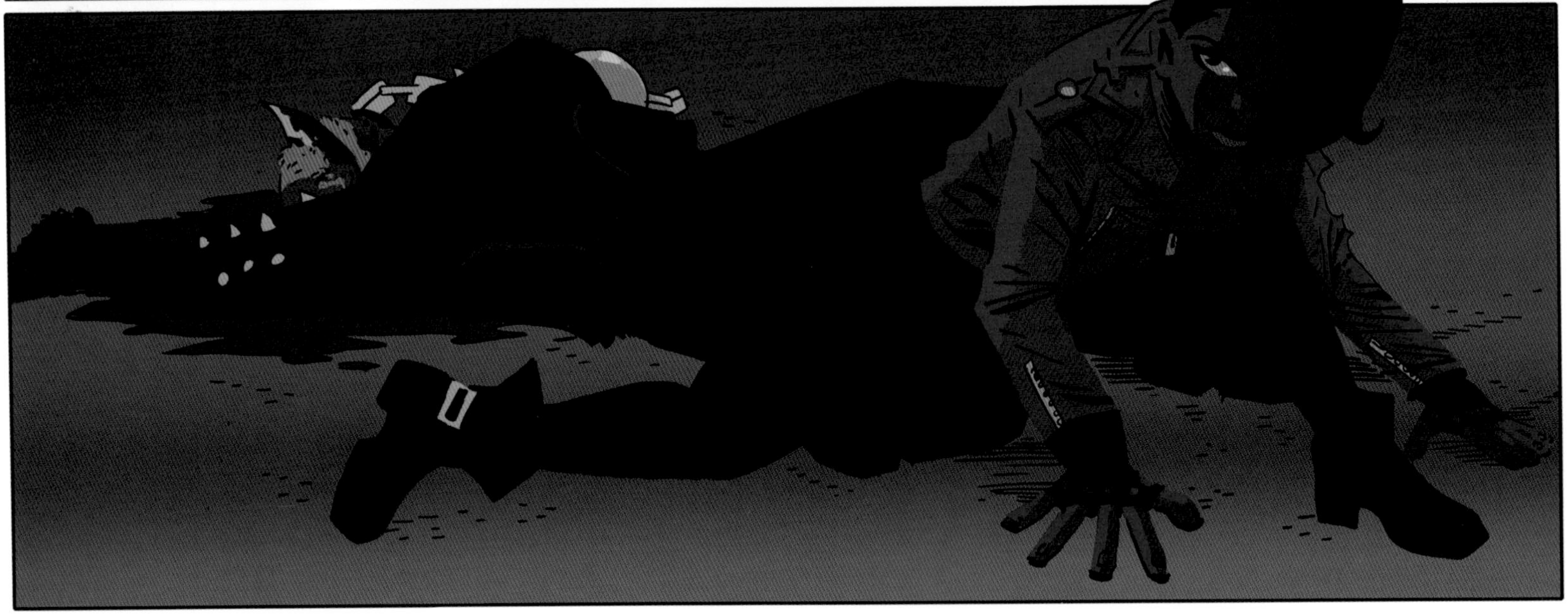

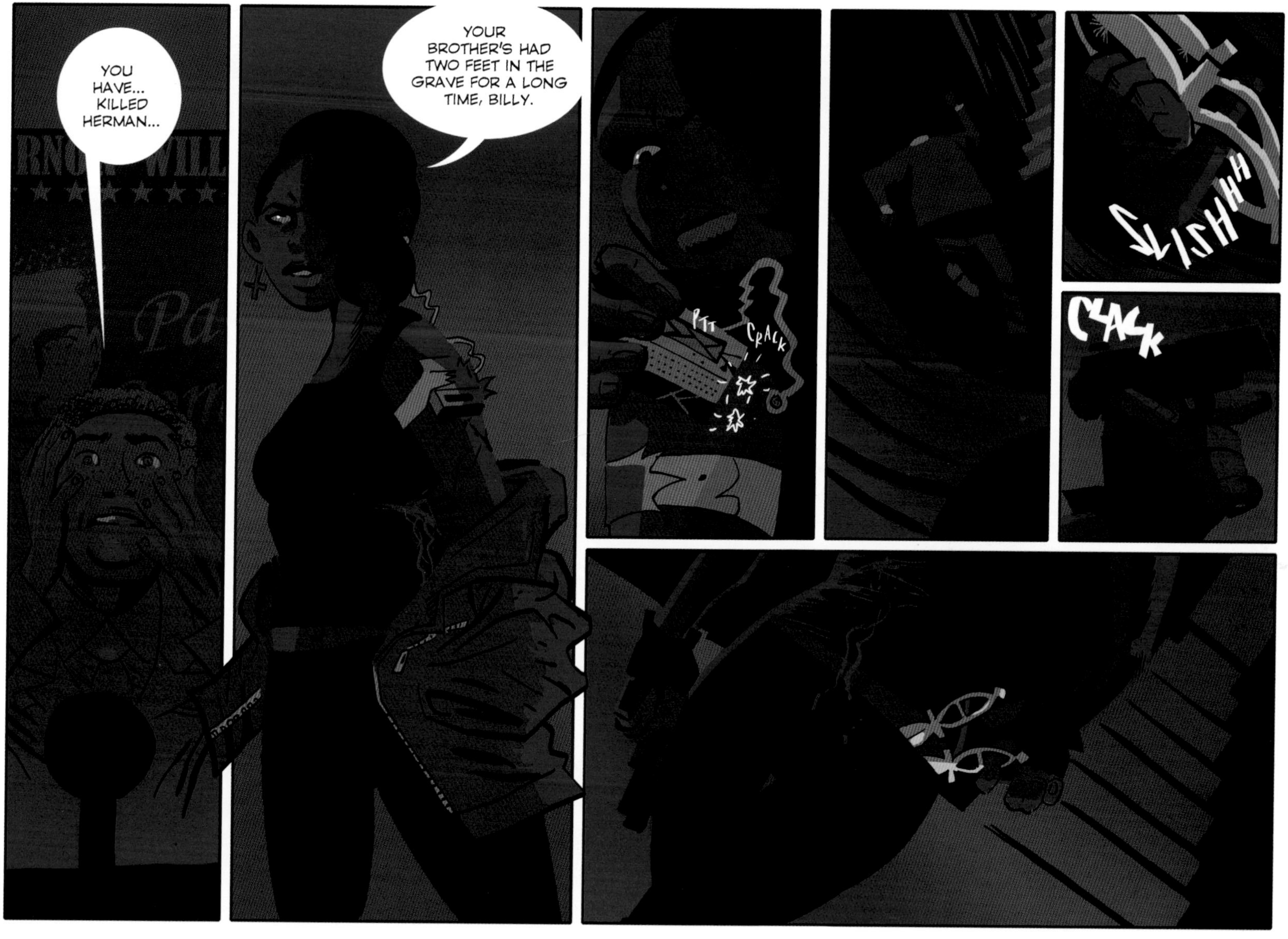
YOU HAVE... KILLED HERMAN...
YOUR BROTHER'S HAD TWO FEET IN THE GRAVE FOR A LONG TIME, BILLY.
PTT
CRACK
SLISHHH
CLACK

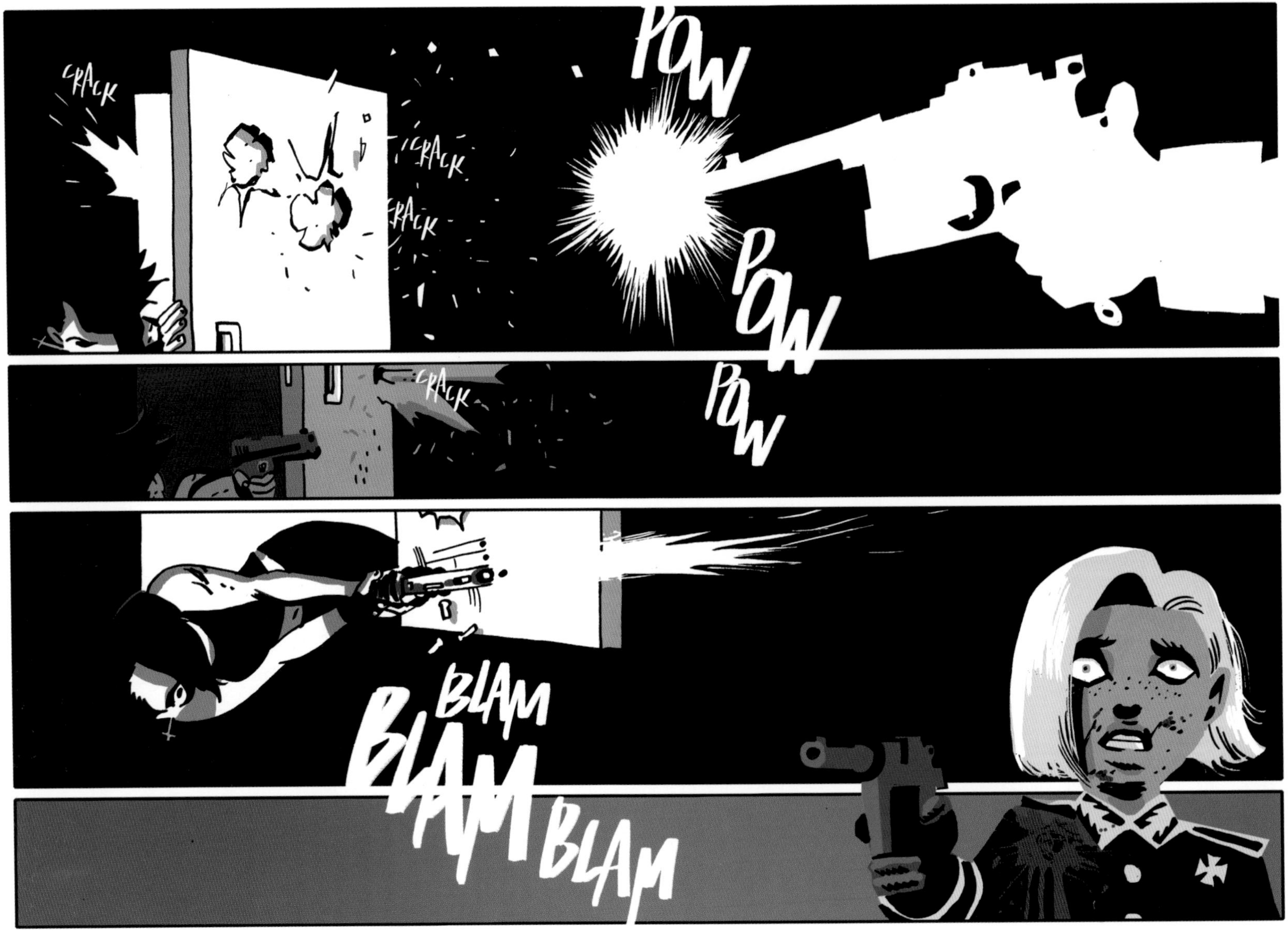
CRACK
CRACK
CRACK
POW
POW
POW
CRACK
BLAM
BLAM
BLAM
BLAM

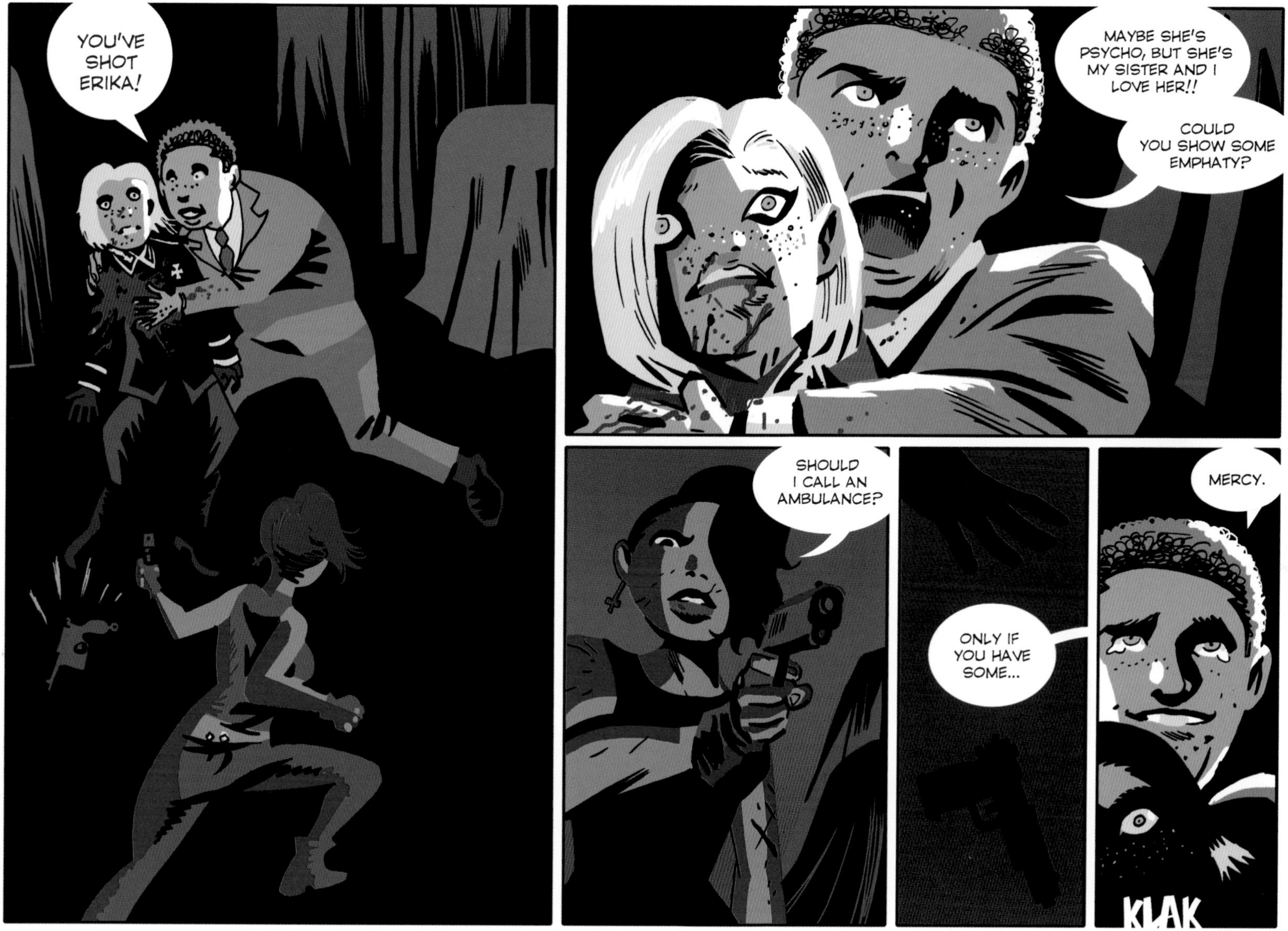
YOU'VE SHOT ERIKA!
MAYBE SHE'S PSYCHO, BUT SHE'S MY SISTER AND I LOVE HER!!
COULD YOU SHOW SOME EMPHATY?
SHOULD I CALL AN AMBULANCE?
ONLY IF YOU HAVE SOME...
MERCY.
KLAK

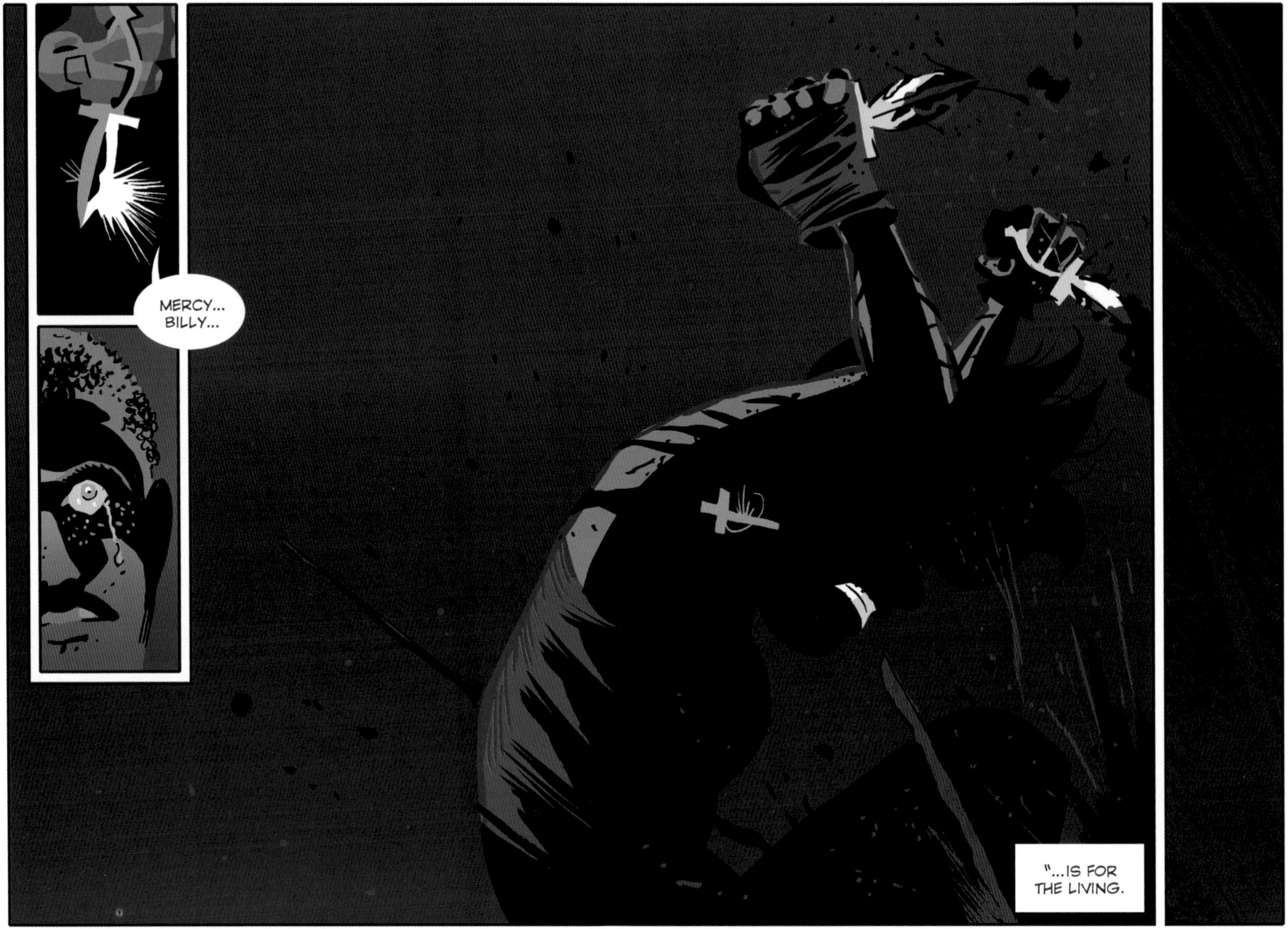
MERCY... BILLY...
"...IS FOR THE LIVING.

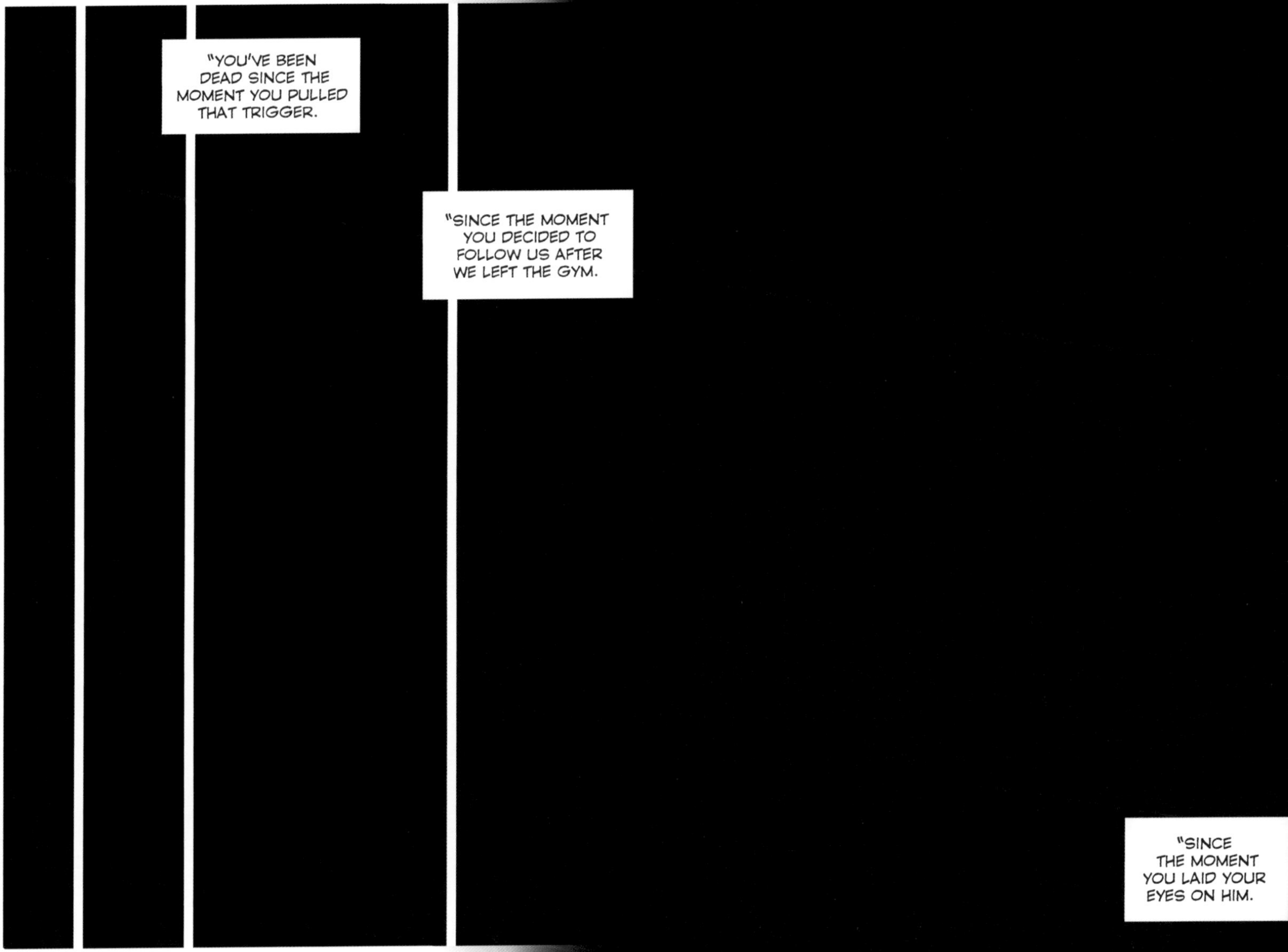
"YOU'VE BEEN DEAD SINCE THE MOMENT YOU PULLED THAT TRIGGER.
"SINCE THE MOMENT YOU DECIDED TO FOLLOW US AFTER WE LEFT THE GYM.
"SINCE THE MOMENT YOU LAID YOUR EYES ON HIM.

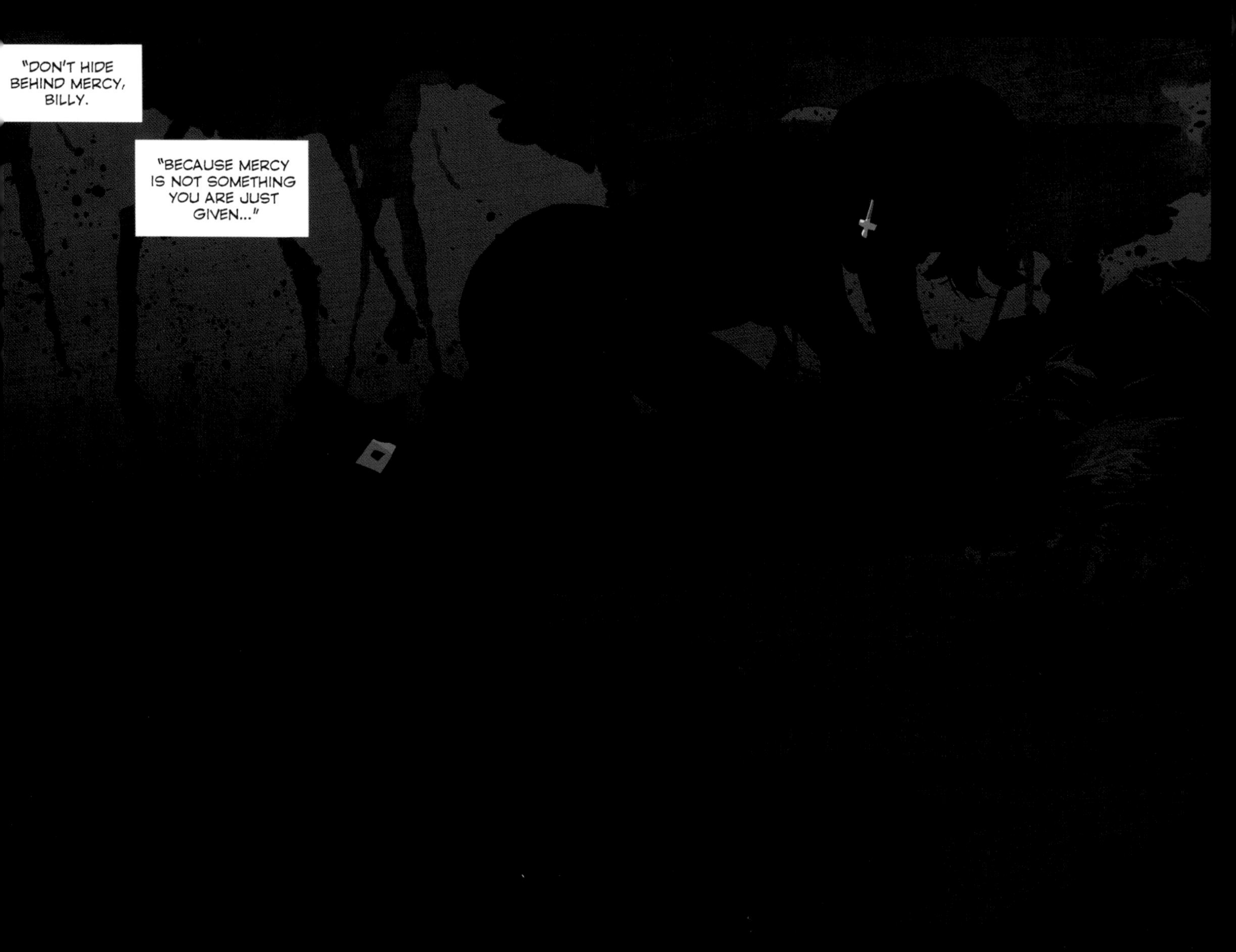
"DON'T HIDE BEHIND MERCY, BILLY.
"BECAUSE MERCY IS NOT SOMETHING YOU ARE JUST GIVEN..."

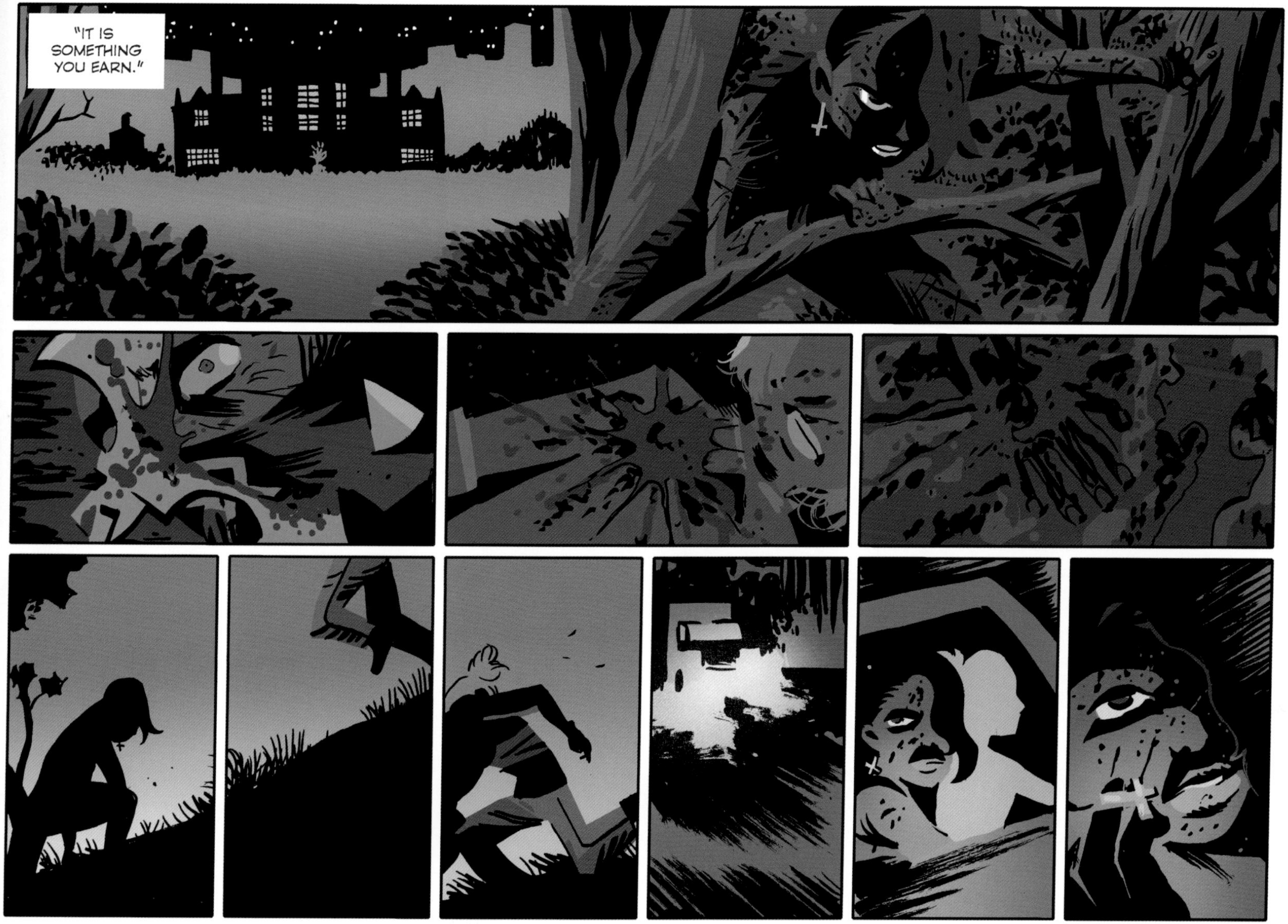
"IT IS SOMETHING YOU EARN."

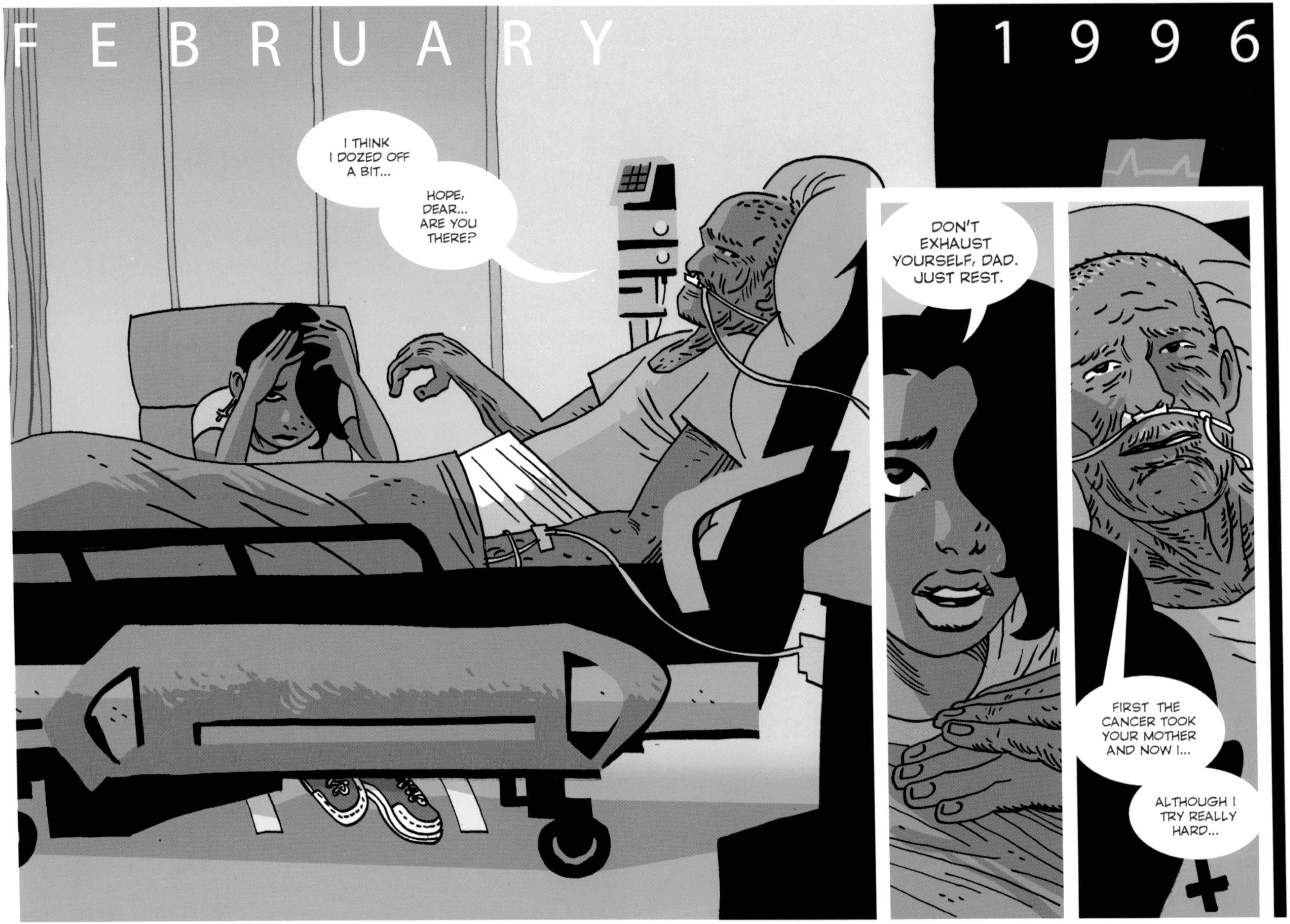
FEBRUARY 1996
I THINK I DOZED OFF A BIT...
HOPE, DEAR... ARE YOU THERE?
DON'T EXHAUST YOURSELF, DAD. JUST REST.
FIRST THE CANCER TOOK YOUR MOTHER AND NOW I...
ALTHOUGH I TRY REALLY HARD...

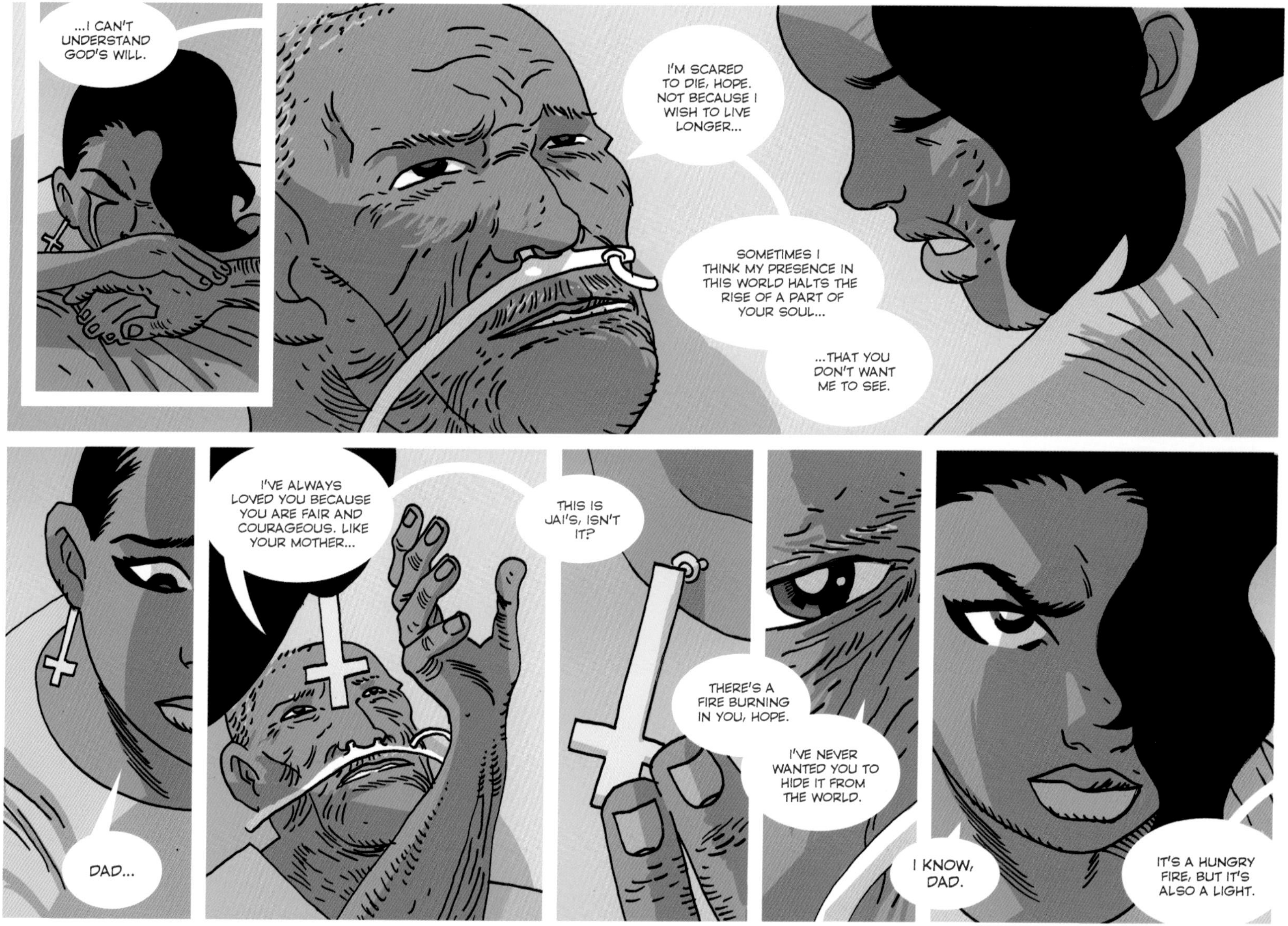
...I CAN'T UNDERSTAND GOD'S WILL.
I'M SCARED TO DIE, HOPE. NOT BECAUSE I WISH TO LIVE LONGER...
SOMETIMES I THINK MY PRESENCE IN THIS WORLD HALTS THE RISE OF A PART OF YOUR SOUL...
...THAT YOU DON'T WANT ME TO SEE.
DAD...
I'VE ALWAYS LOVED YOU BECAUSE YOU ARE FAIR AND COURAGEOUS. LIKE YOUR MOTHER...
THIS IS JAI'S, ISN'T IT?
THERE'S A FIRE BURNING IN YOU, HOPE.
I'VE NEVER WANTED YOU TO HIDE IT FROM THE WORLD.
I KNOW, DAD.
IT'S A HUNGRY FIRE, BUT IT'S ALSO A LIGHT.

"LET EVERYBODY ELSE SEE IT SHINE."

**END**

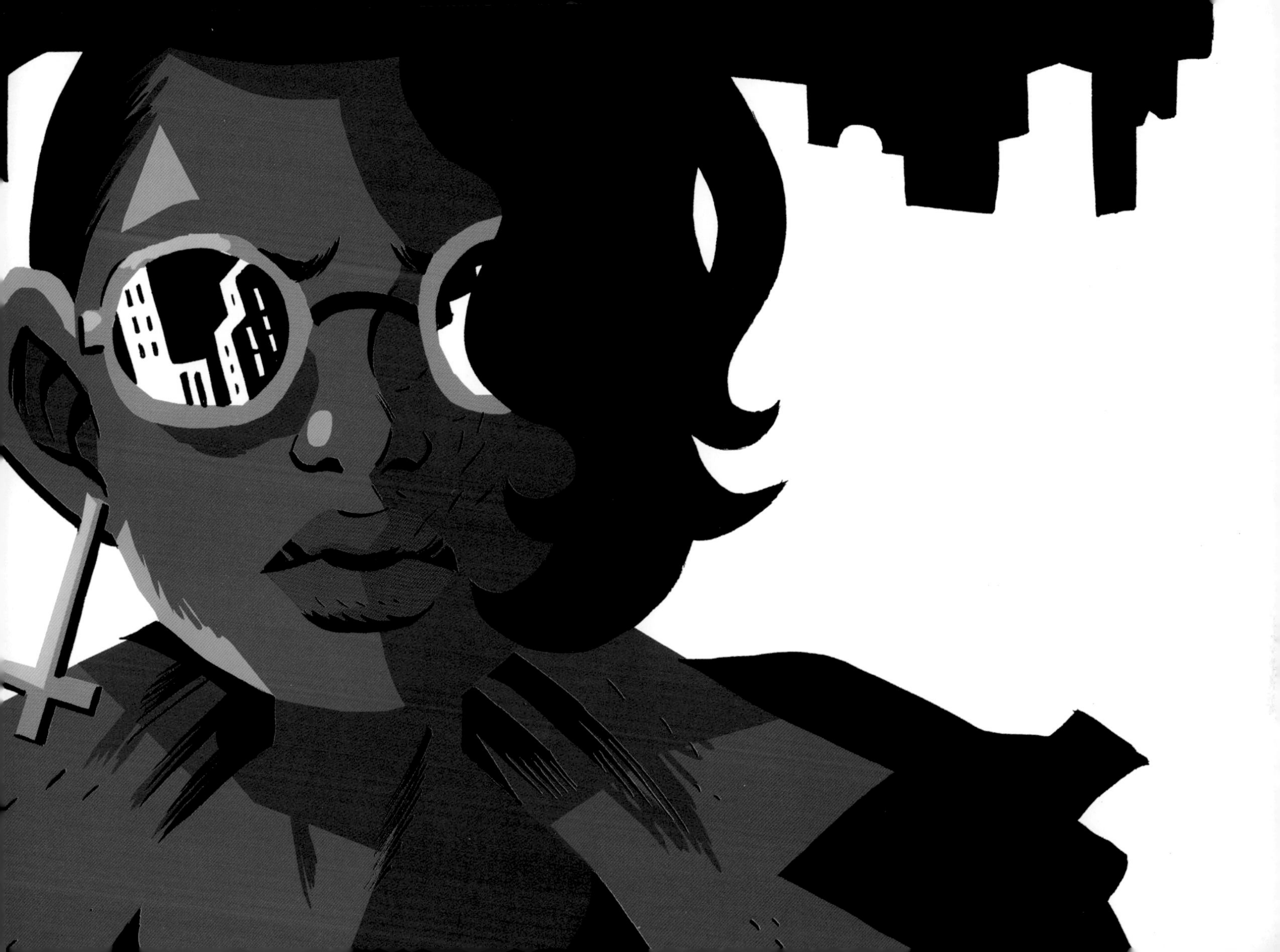

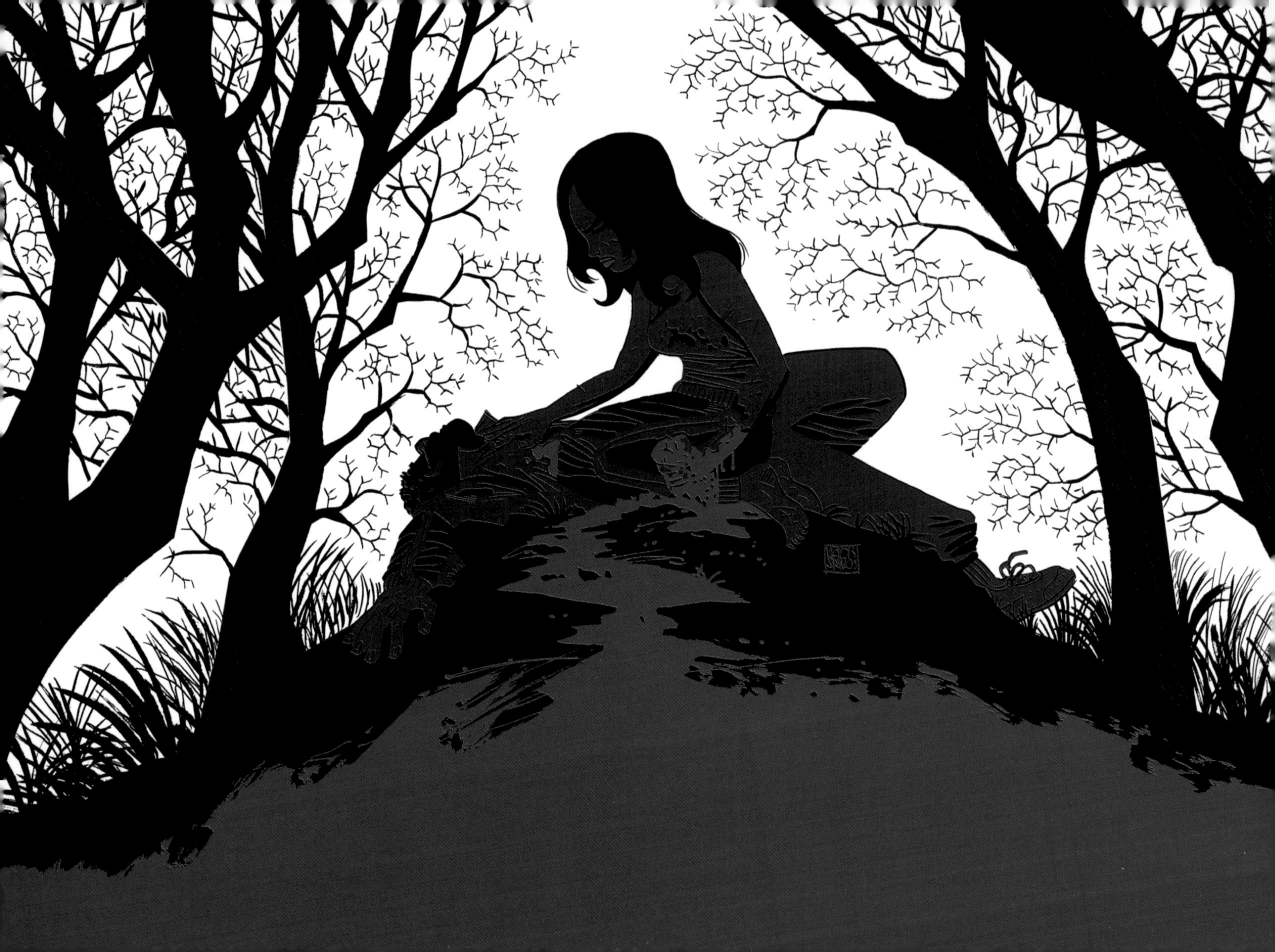

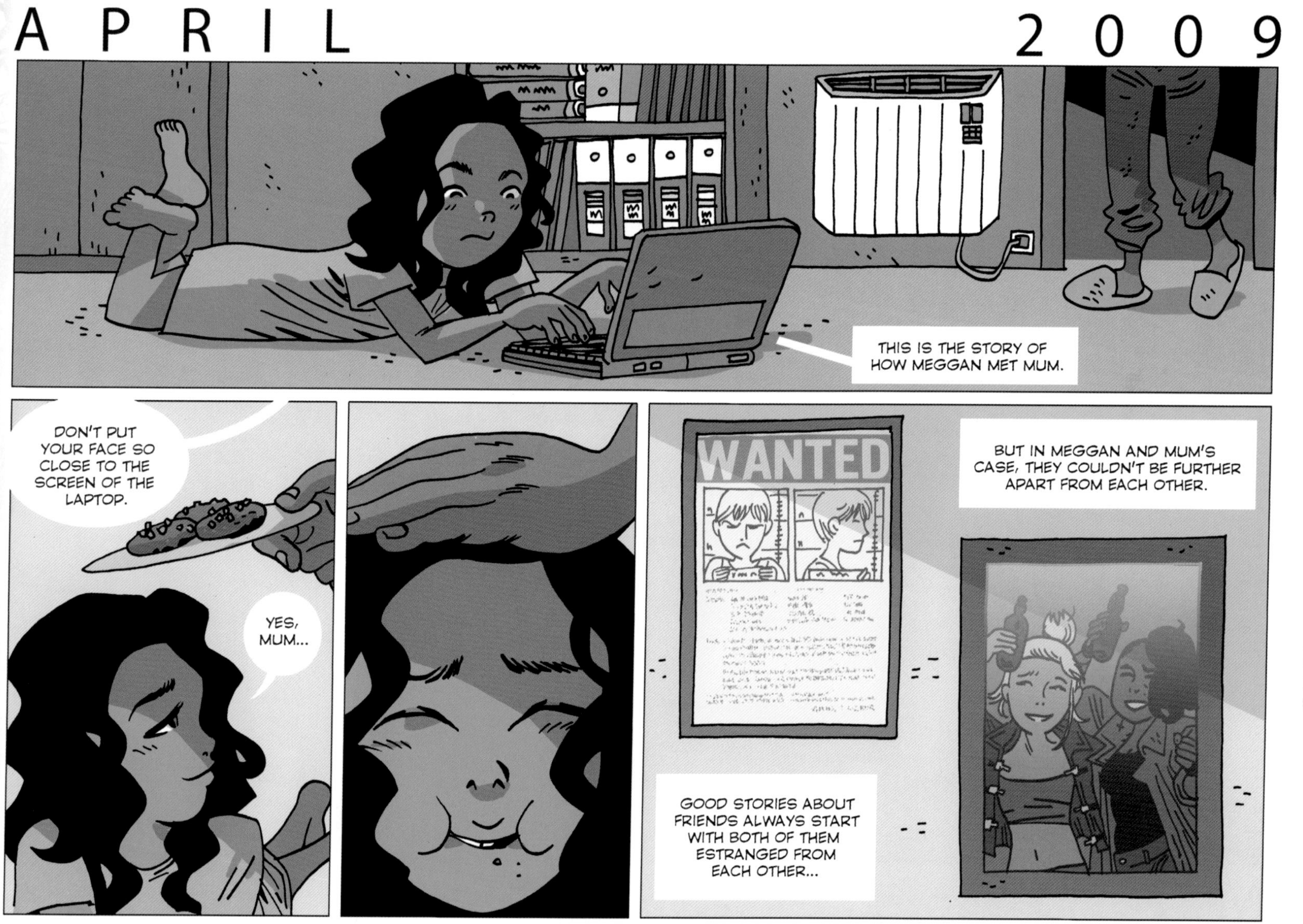

APRIL 2009
THIS IS THE STORY OF HOW MEGGAN MET MUM.
DON'T PUT YOUR FACE SO CLOSE TO THE SCREEN OF THE LAPTOP.
YES, MUM...
BUT IN MEGGAN AND MUM'S CASE, THEY COULDN'T BE FURTHER APART FROM EACH OTHER.
WANTED
GOOD STORIES ABOUT FRIENDS ALWAYS START WITH BOTH OF THEM ESTRANGED FROM EACH OTHER...

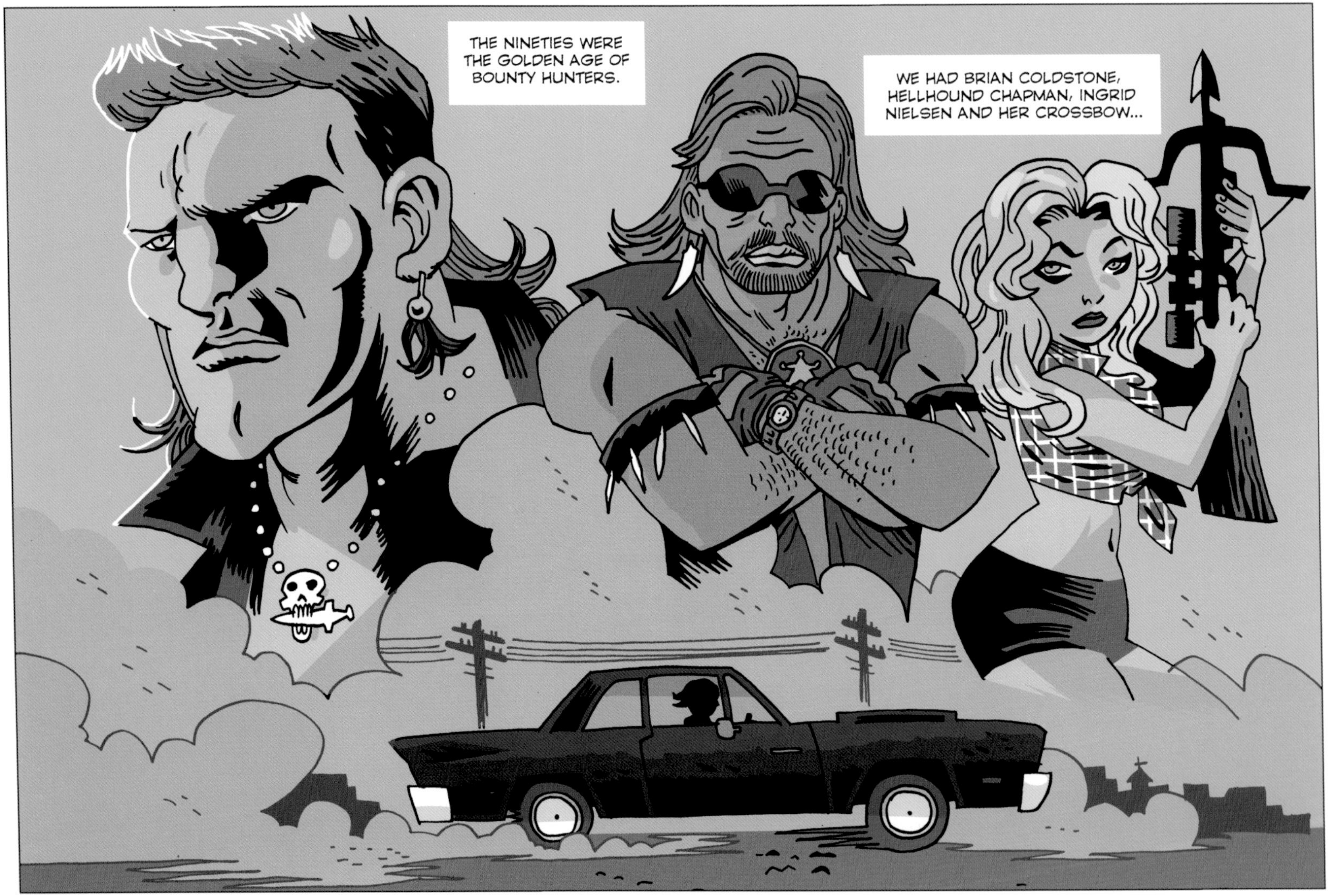
THE NINETIES WERE THE GOLDEN AGE OF BOUNTY HUNTERS.
WE HAD BRIAN COLDSTONE, HELLHOUND CHAPMAN, INGRID NIELSEN AND HER CROSSBOW...

M A Y

AND THEN HOPE WALKER, MY MUM, WITH HER REVOLVER AND HER OLD 64 PLYMOUTH ROAD RUNNER.

1 9 9 4

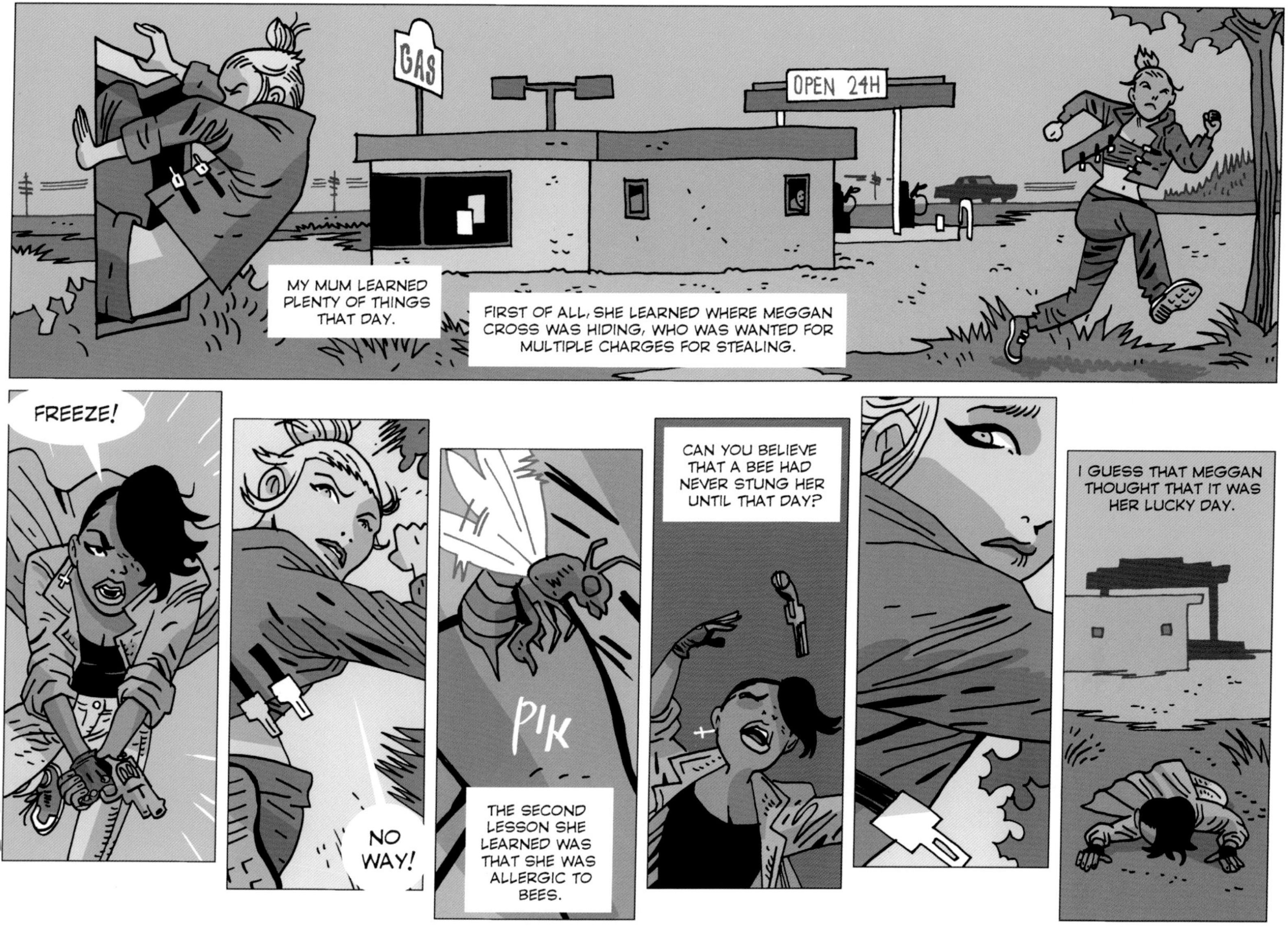
GAS
OPEN 24H
MY MUM LEARNED PLENTY OF THINGS THAT DAY.
FIRST OF ALL, SHE LEARNED WHERE MEGGAN CROSS WAS HIDING, WHO WAS WANTED FOR MULTIPLE CHARGES FOR STEALING.
FREEZE!
NO WAY!
PIK
THE SECOND LESSON SHE LEARNED WAS THAT SHE WAS ALLERGIC TO BEES.
CAN YOU BELIEVE THAT A BEE HAD NEVER STUNG HER UNTIL THAT DAY?
I GUESS THAT MEGGAN THOUGHT THAT IT WAS HER LUCKY DAY.

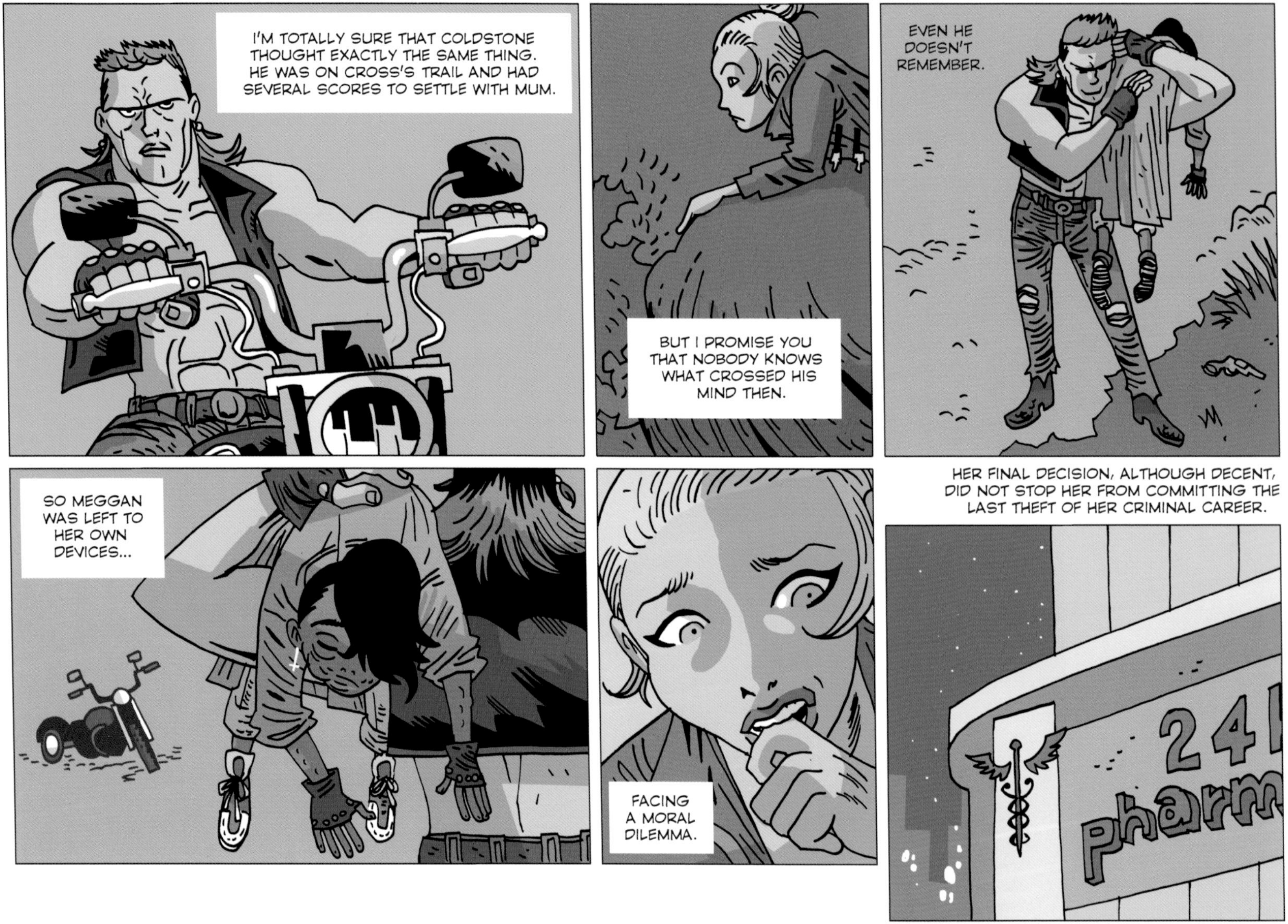
I'M TOTALLY SURE THAT COLDSTONE THOUGHT EXACTLY THE SAME THING. HE WAS ON CROSS'S TRAIL AND HAD SEVERAL SCORES TO SETTLE WITH MUM.
BUT I PROMISE YOU THAT NOBODY KNOWS WHAT CROSSED HIS MIND THEN.
EVEN HE DOESN'T REMEMBER.
SO MEGGAN WAS LEFT TO HER OWN DEVICES...
FACING A MORAL DILEMMA.
HER FINAL DECISION, ALTHOUGH DECENT, DID NOT STOP HER FROM COMMITTING THE LAST THEFT OF HER CRIMINAL CAREER.
24
pharm

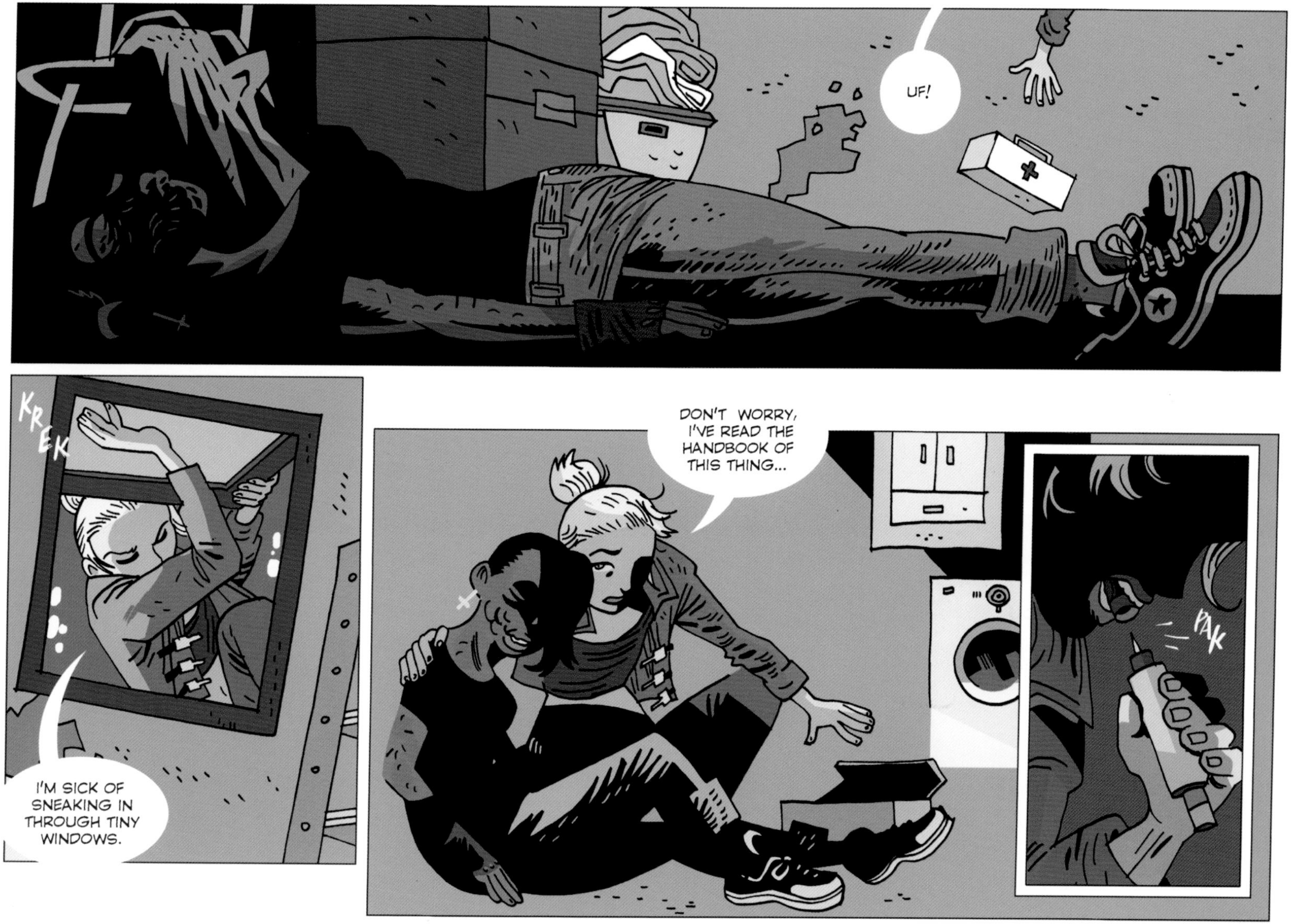
UF!
KREEK
I'M SICK OF SNEAKING IN THROUGH TINY WINDOWS.
DON'T WORRY, I'VE READ THE HANDBOOK OF THIS THING...
PAK

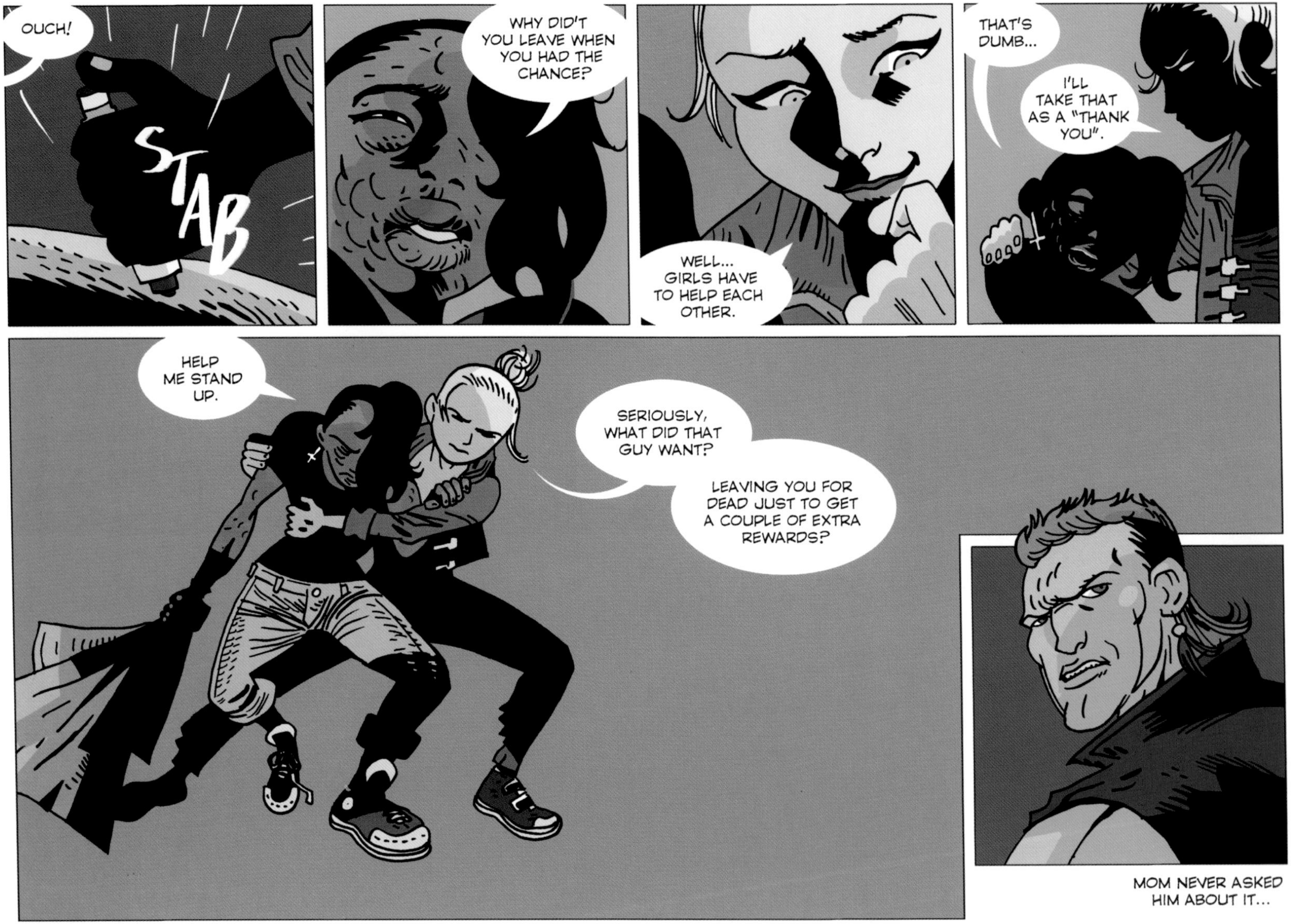
OUCH!
STAB
WHY DID'T YOU LEAVE WHEN YOU HAD THE CHANCE?
WELL... GIRLS HAVE TO HELP EACH OTHER.
THAT'S DUMB...
I'LL TAKE THAT AS A "THANK YOU".
HELP ME STAND UP.
SERIOUSLY, WHAT DID THAT GUY WANT?
LEAVING YOU FOR DEAD JUST TO GET A COUPLE OF EXTRA REWARDS?
MOM NEVER ASKED HIM ABOUT IT...

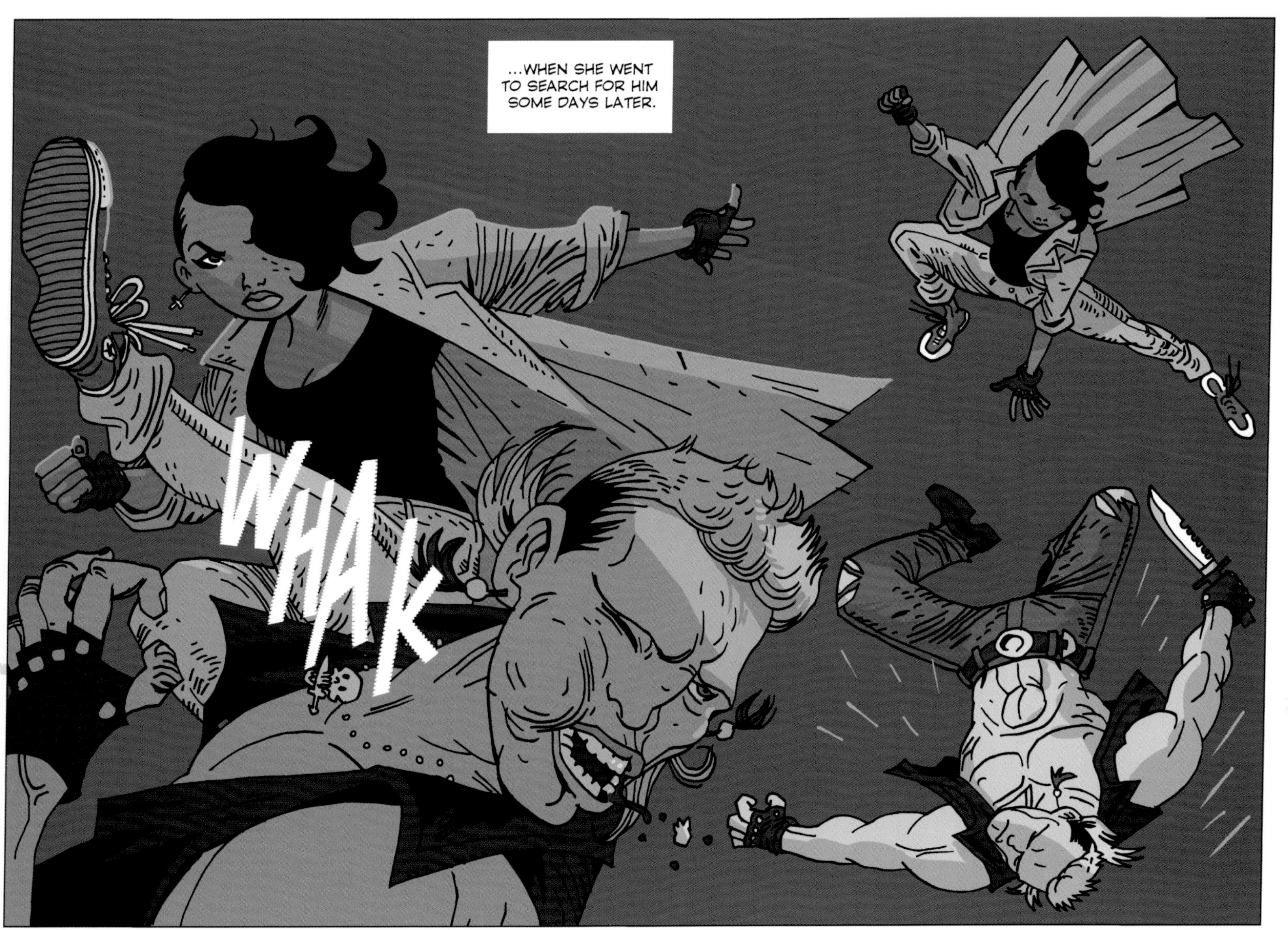
...WHEN SHE WENT TO SEARCH FOR HIM SOME DAYS LATER.
WHAK

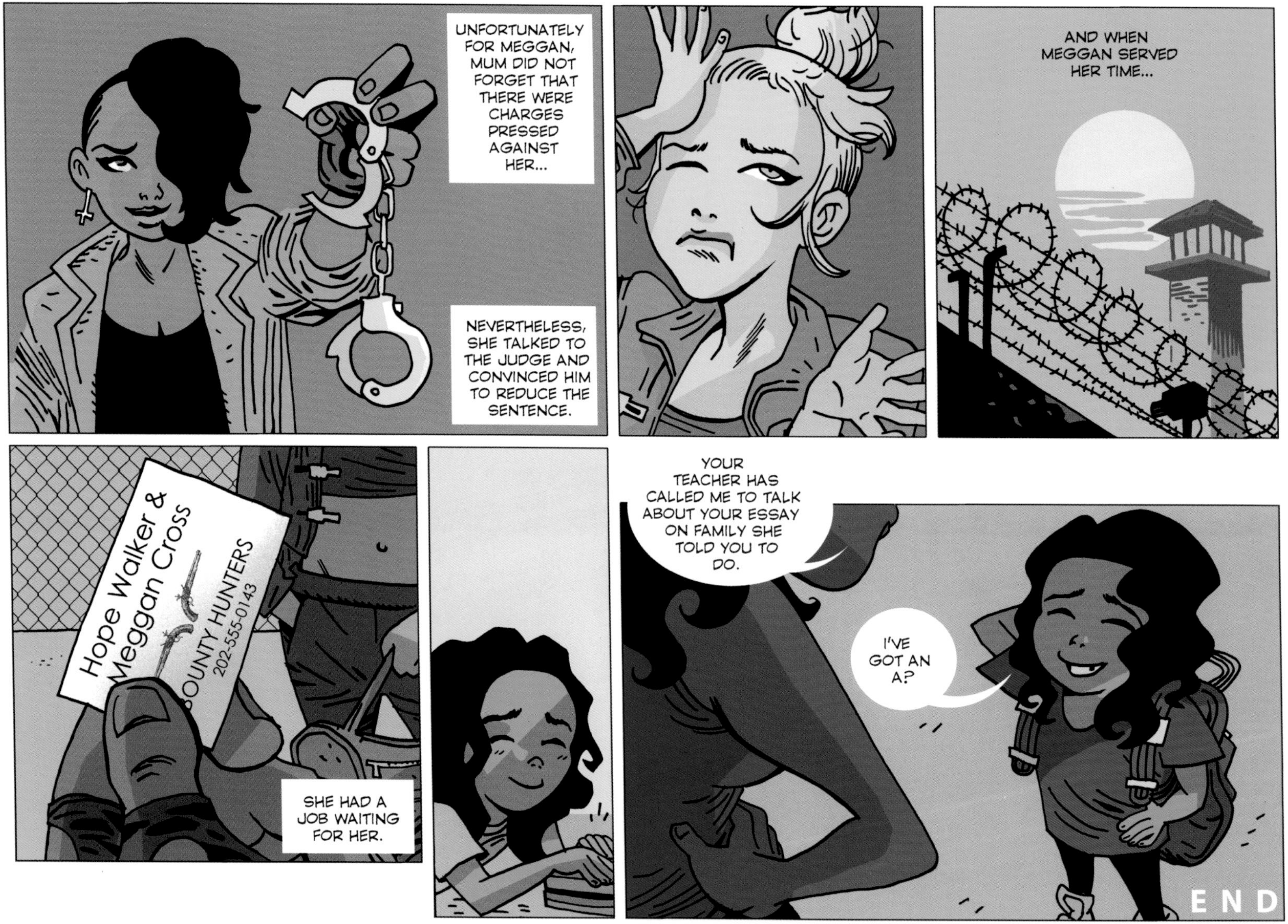
UNFORTUNATELY FOR MEGGAN, MUM DID NOT FORGET THAT THERE WERE CHARGES PRESSED AGAINST HER...
NEVERTHELESS, SHE TALKED TO THE JUDGE AND CONVINCED HIM TO REDUCE THE SENTENCE.
AND WHEN MEGGAN SERVED HER TIME...
Hope Walker & Meggan Cross
BOUNTY HUNTERS
202-555-0143
SHE HAD A JOB WAITING FOR HER.
YOUR TEACHER HAS CALLED ME TO TALK ABOUT YOUR ESSAY ON FAMILY SHE TOLD YOU TO DO.
I'VE GOT AN A?
END

# AGAINST HOPE™

## SKETCHBOOK

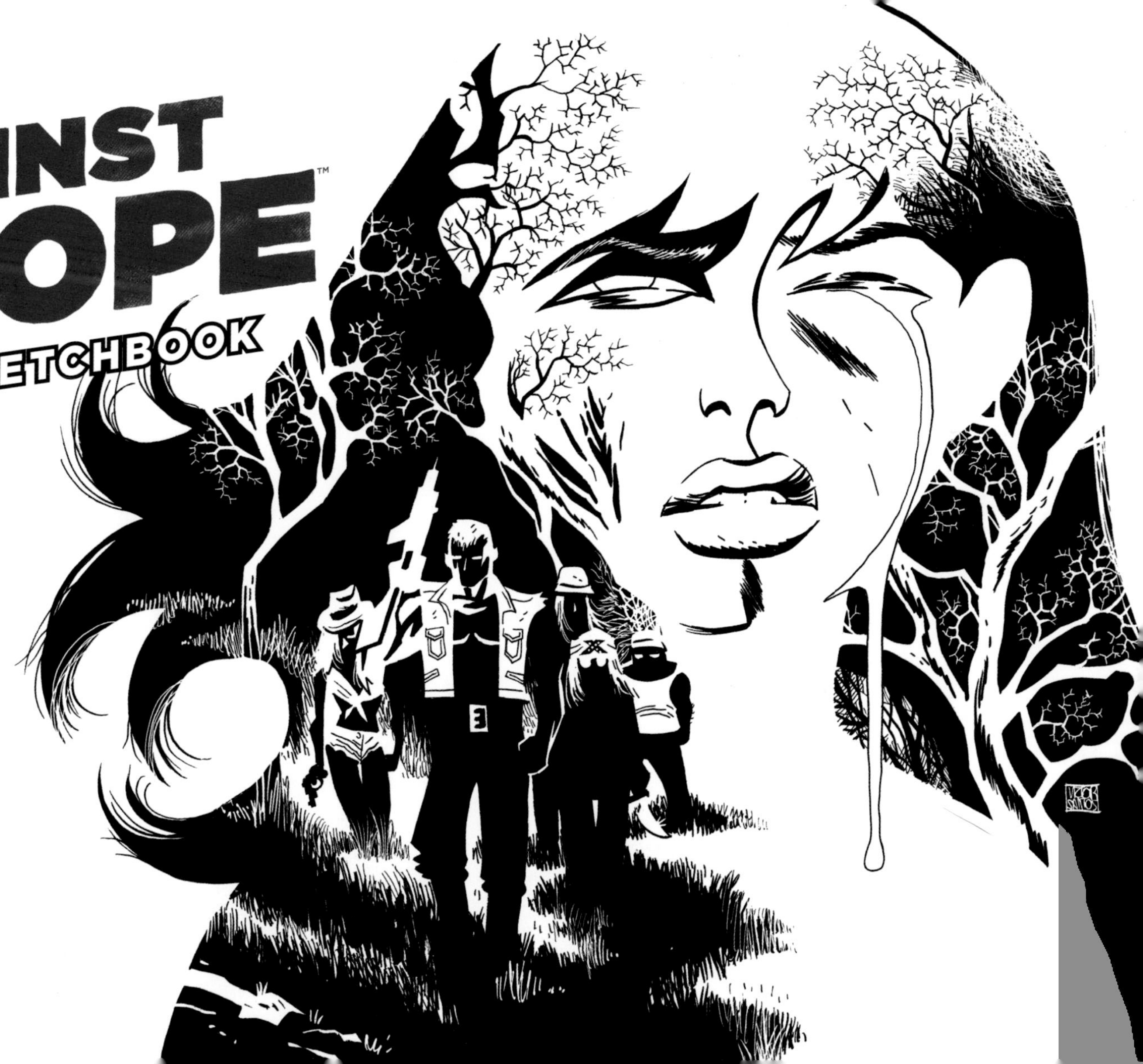

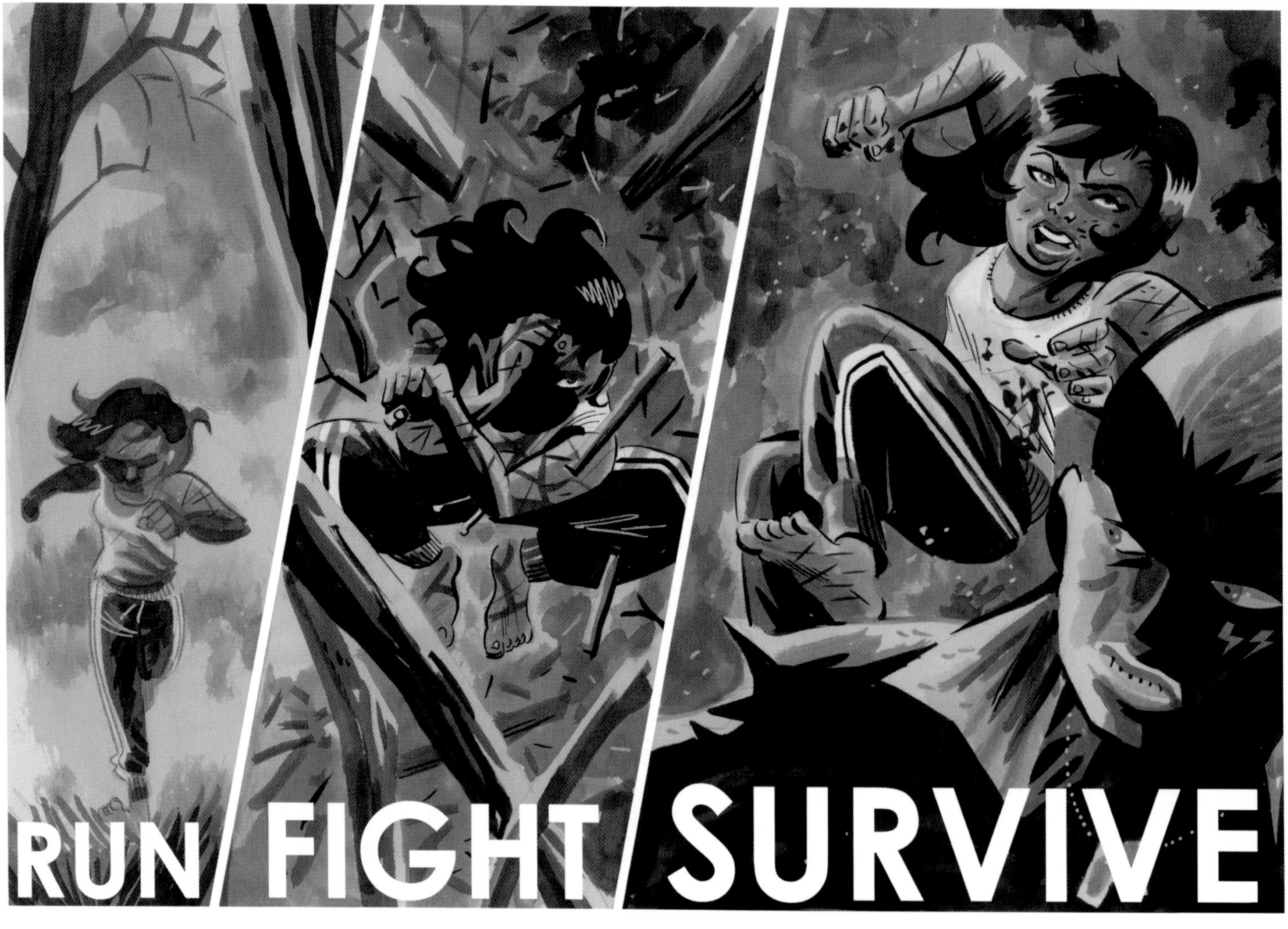
RUN
FIGHT
SURVIVE

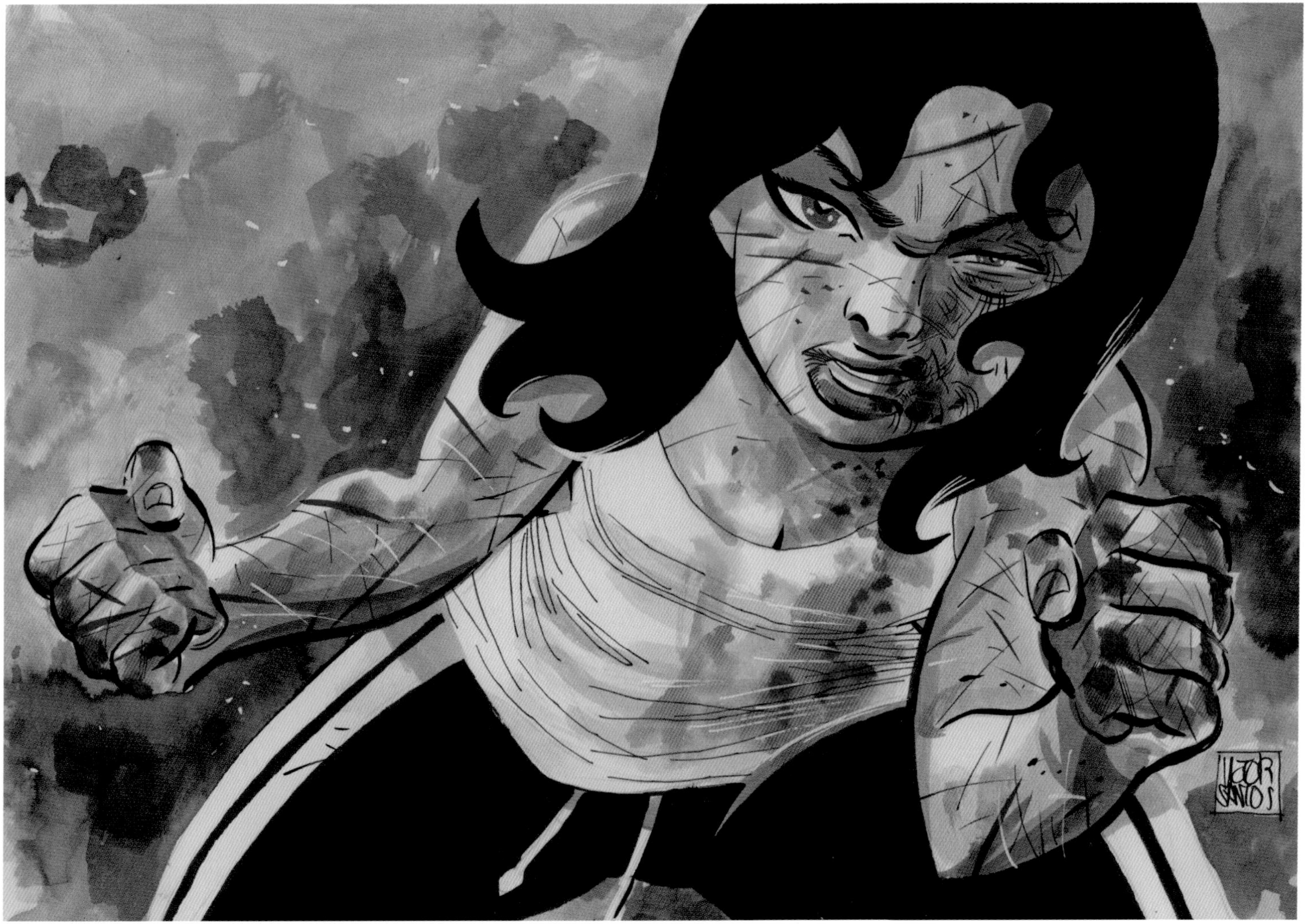

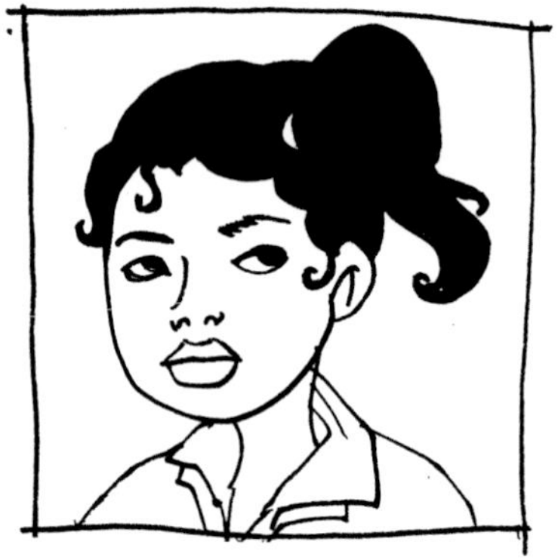

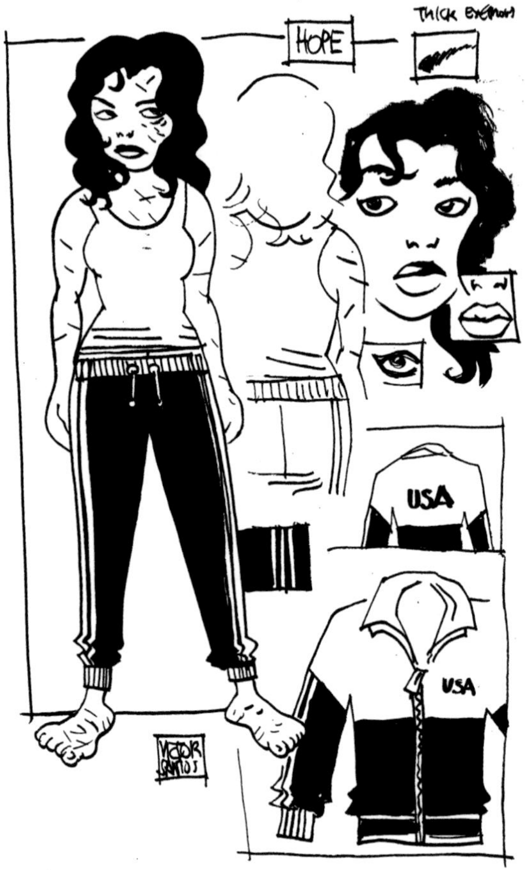
THICK EYEBROW
HOPE
USA
USA
VICTOR SANTOS

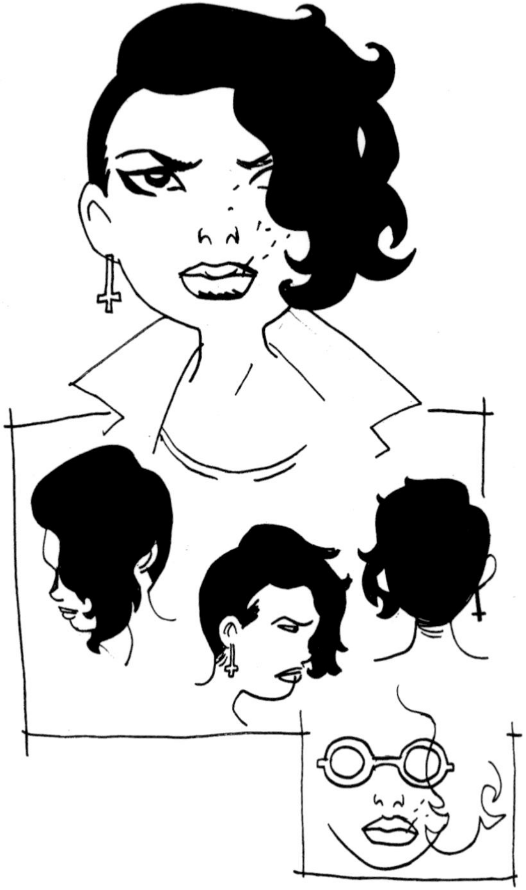

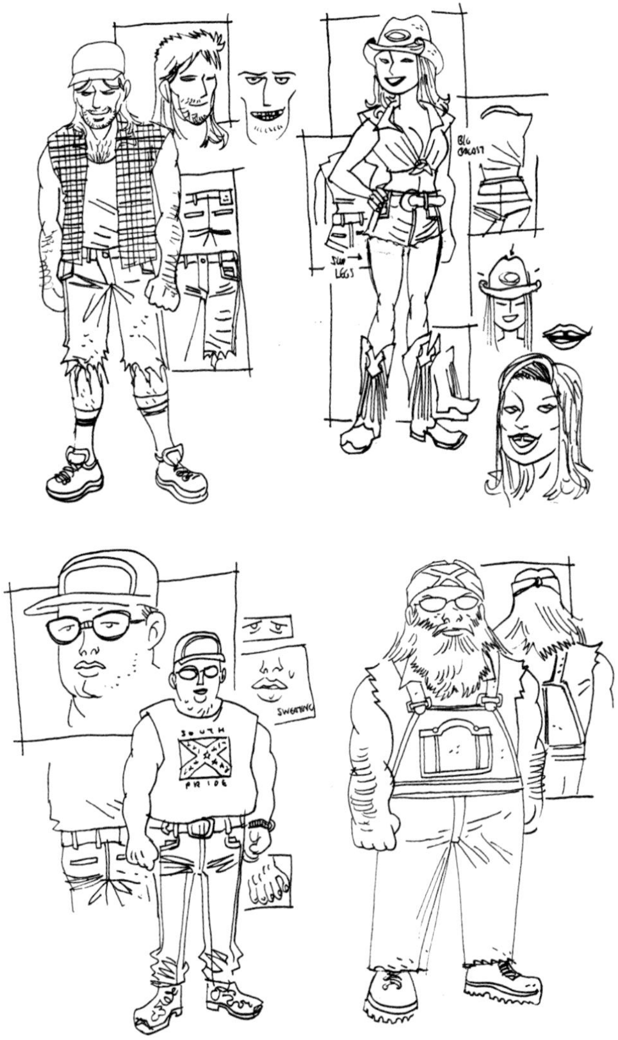
SLIM LEGS
SOUTH PRIDE
SWEATING

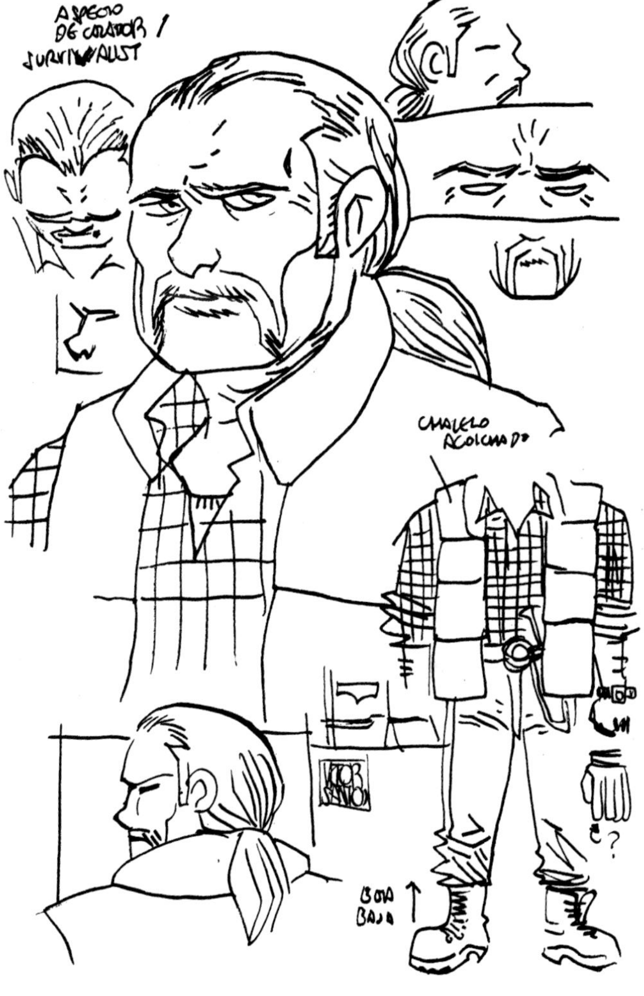
ASPECTO DE CAZADOR / SURVIVALIST
CHALECO ACOLCHADO
BOTA BAJA
¿?

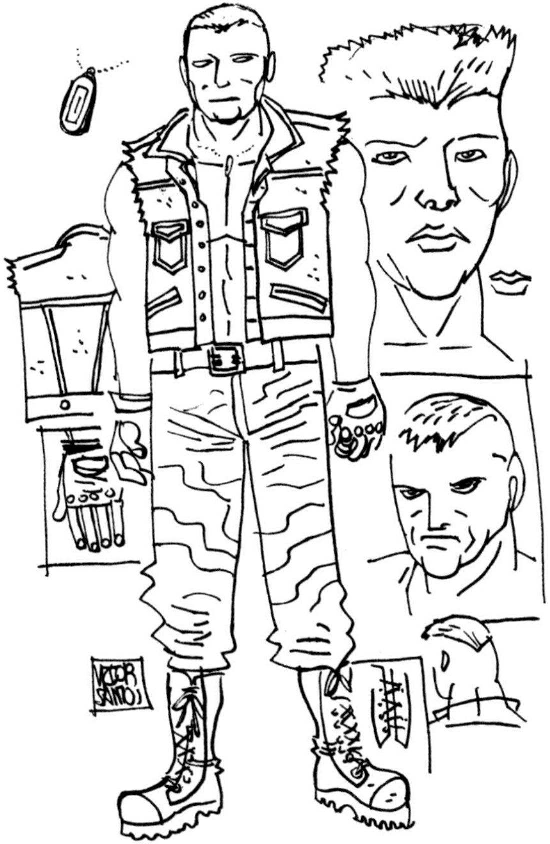
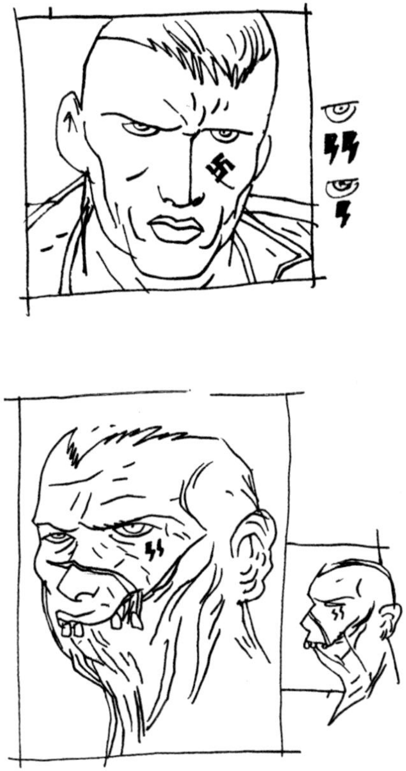
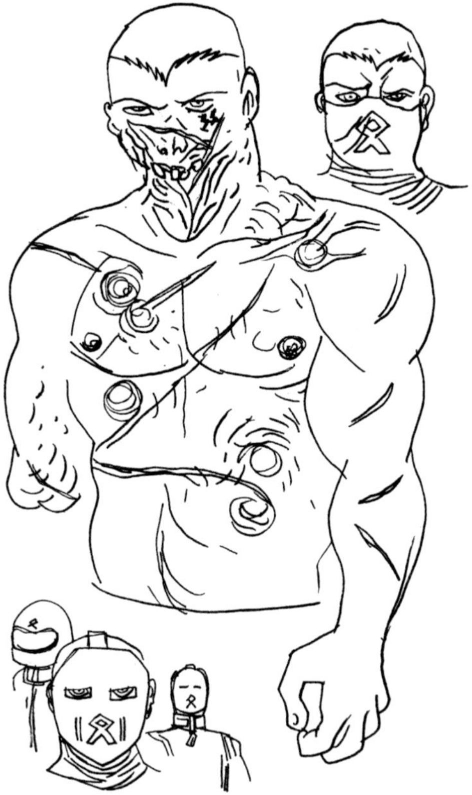

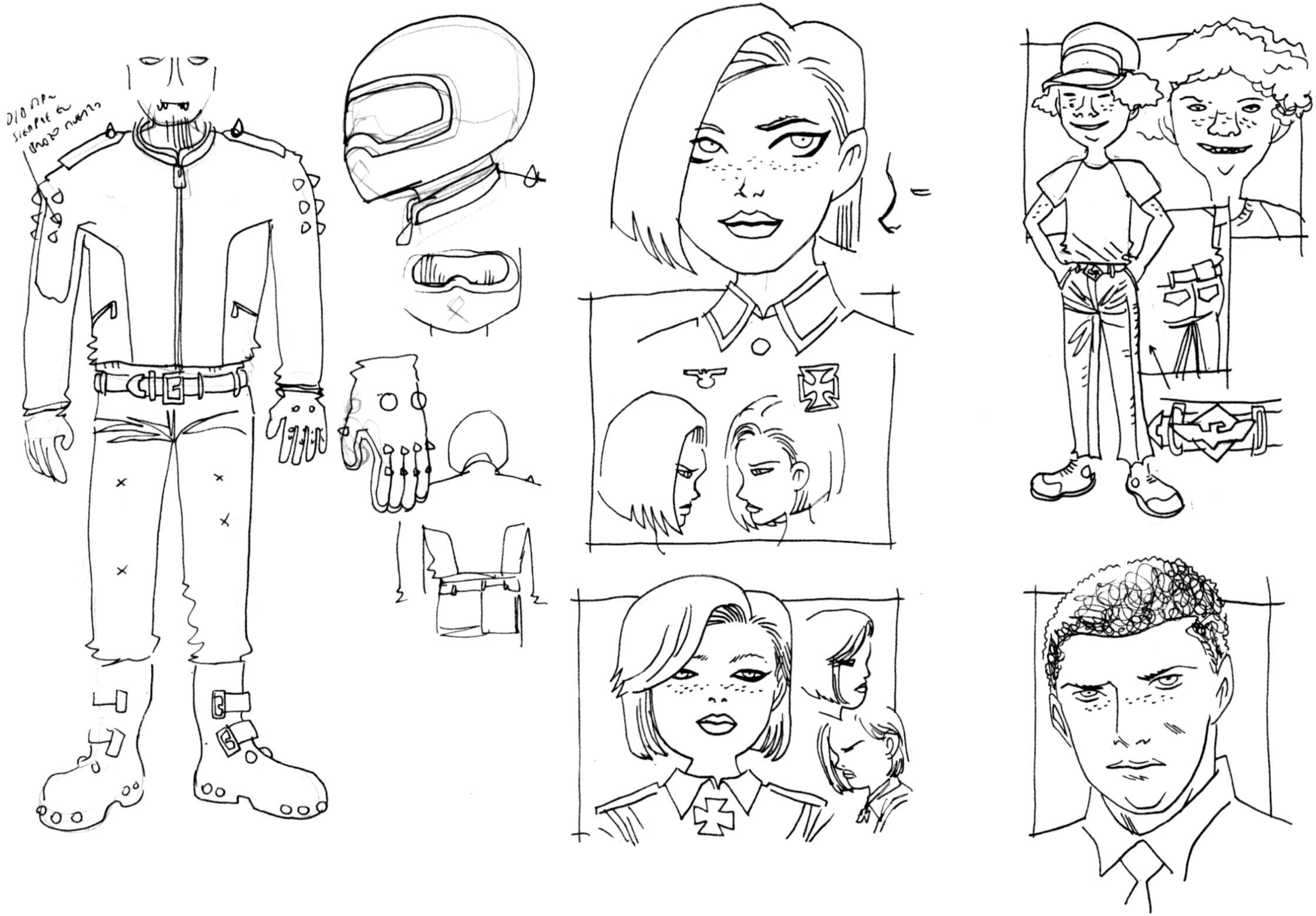

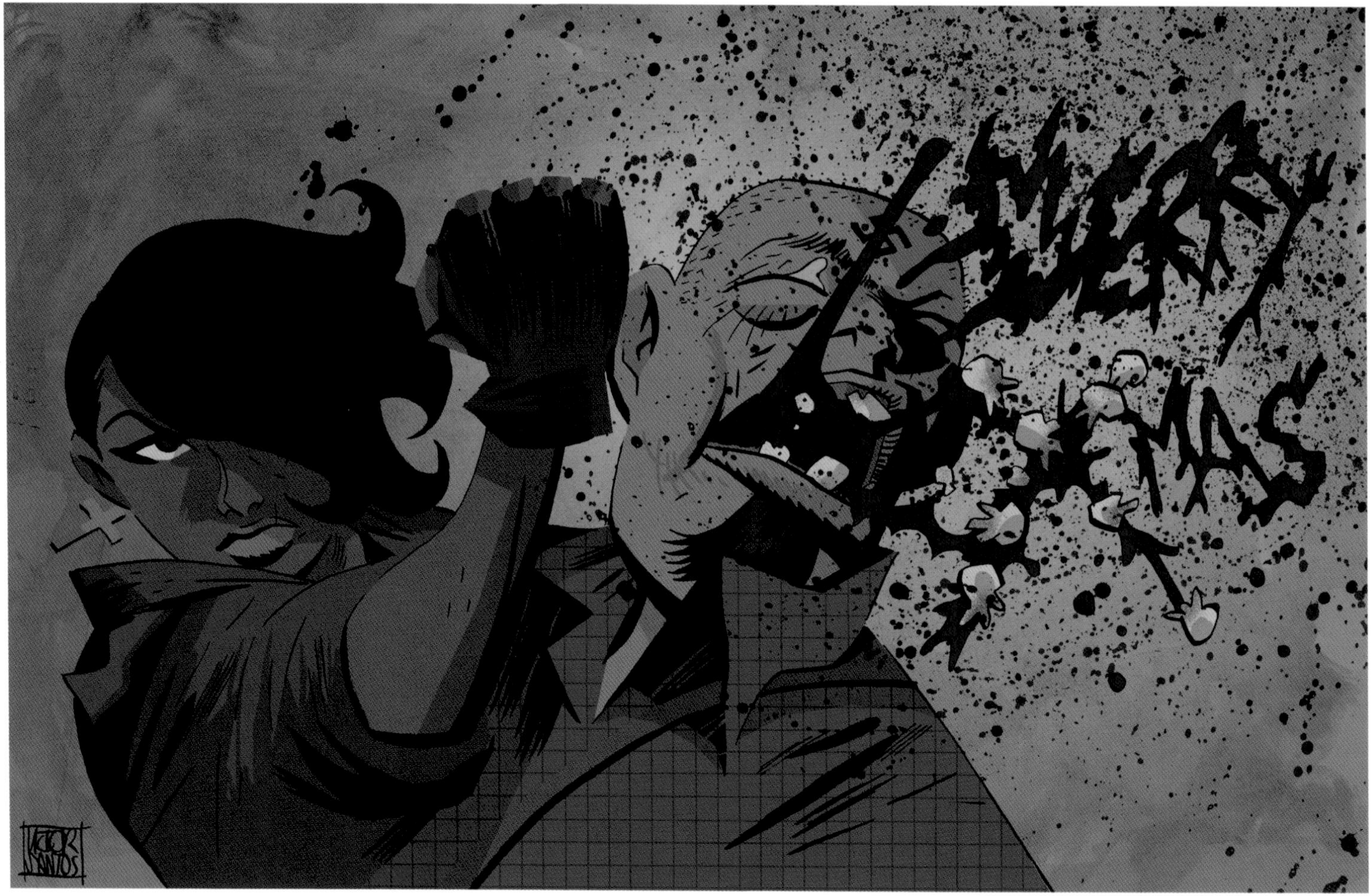
MERRY
XMAS

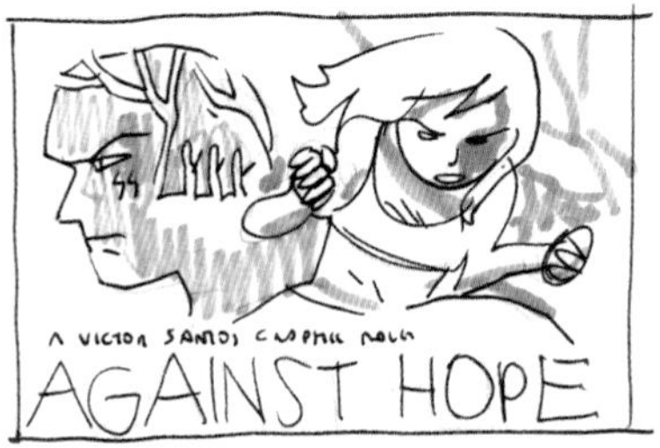
A VICTOR SANTOS GRAPHIC NOVEL
AGAINST HOPE

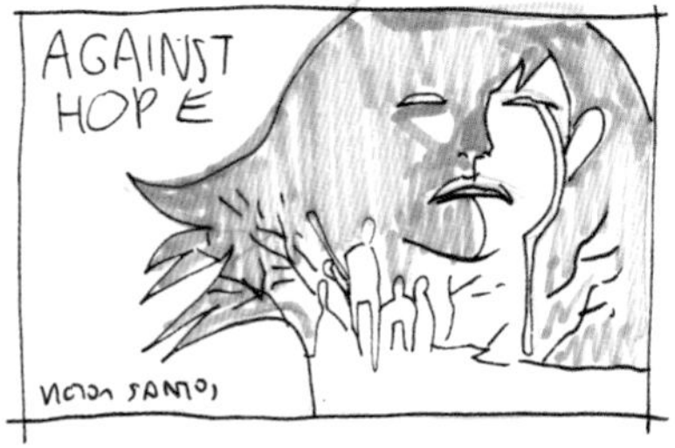
AGAINST
HOPE
VICTOR SANTOS

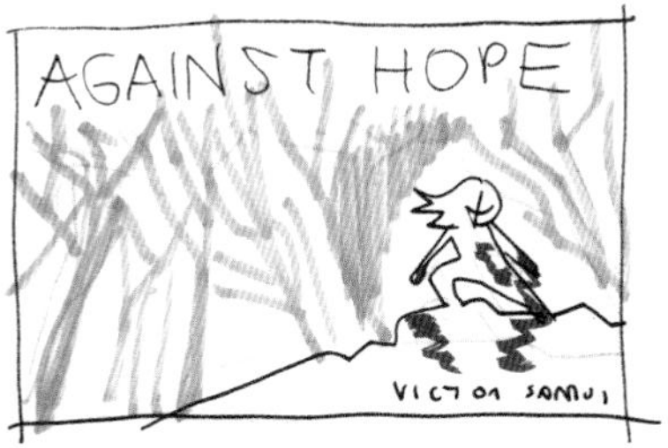
AGAINST HOPE
VICTOR SANTOS

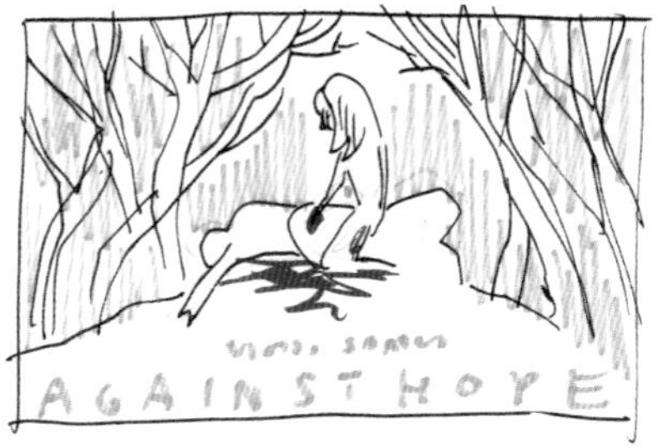
VICTOR SANTOS
AGAINST HOPE

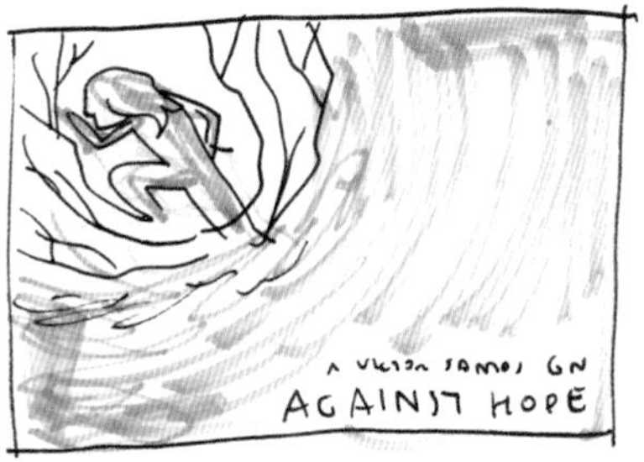
A VICTOR SANTOS GN
AGAINST HOPE

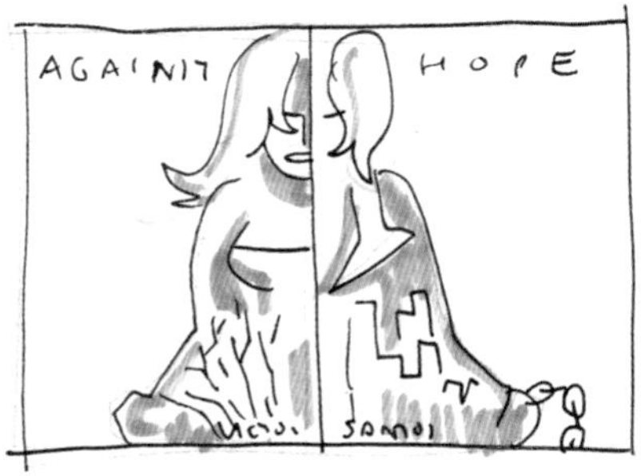
AGAINST
HOPE
VICTOR
SANTOS

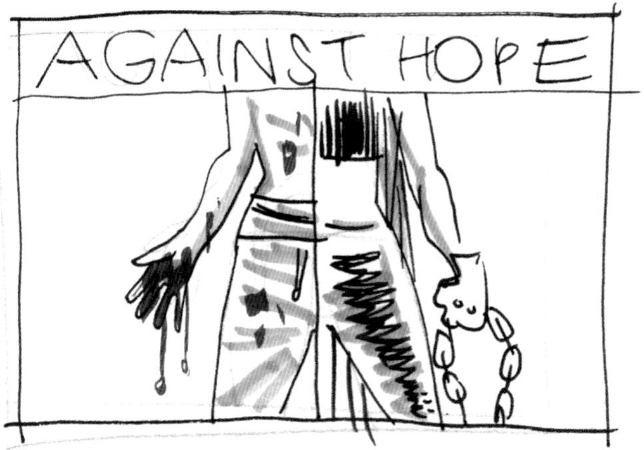
AGAINST HOPE

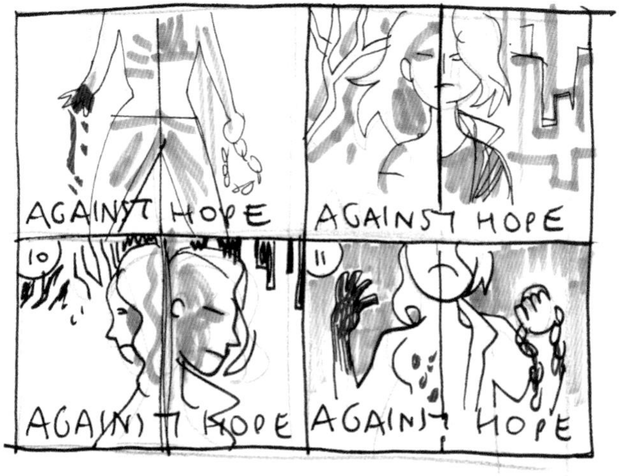
AGAINST HOPE
AGAINST HOPE
10
11
AGAINST HOPE
AGAINST HOPE

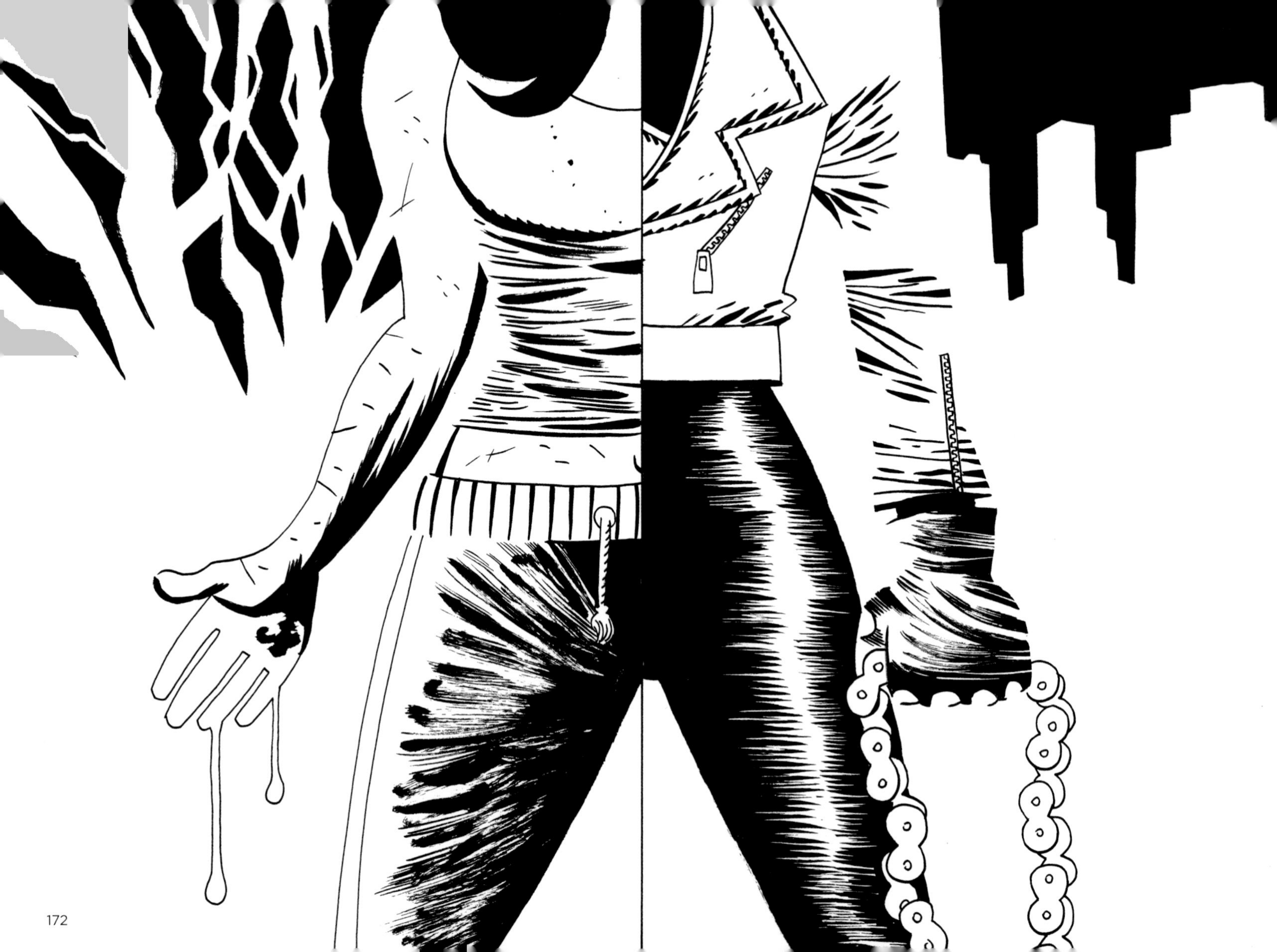

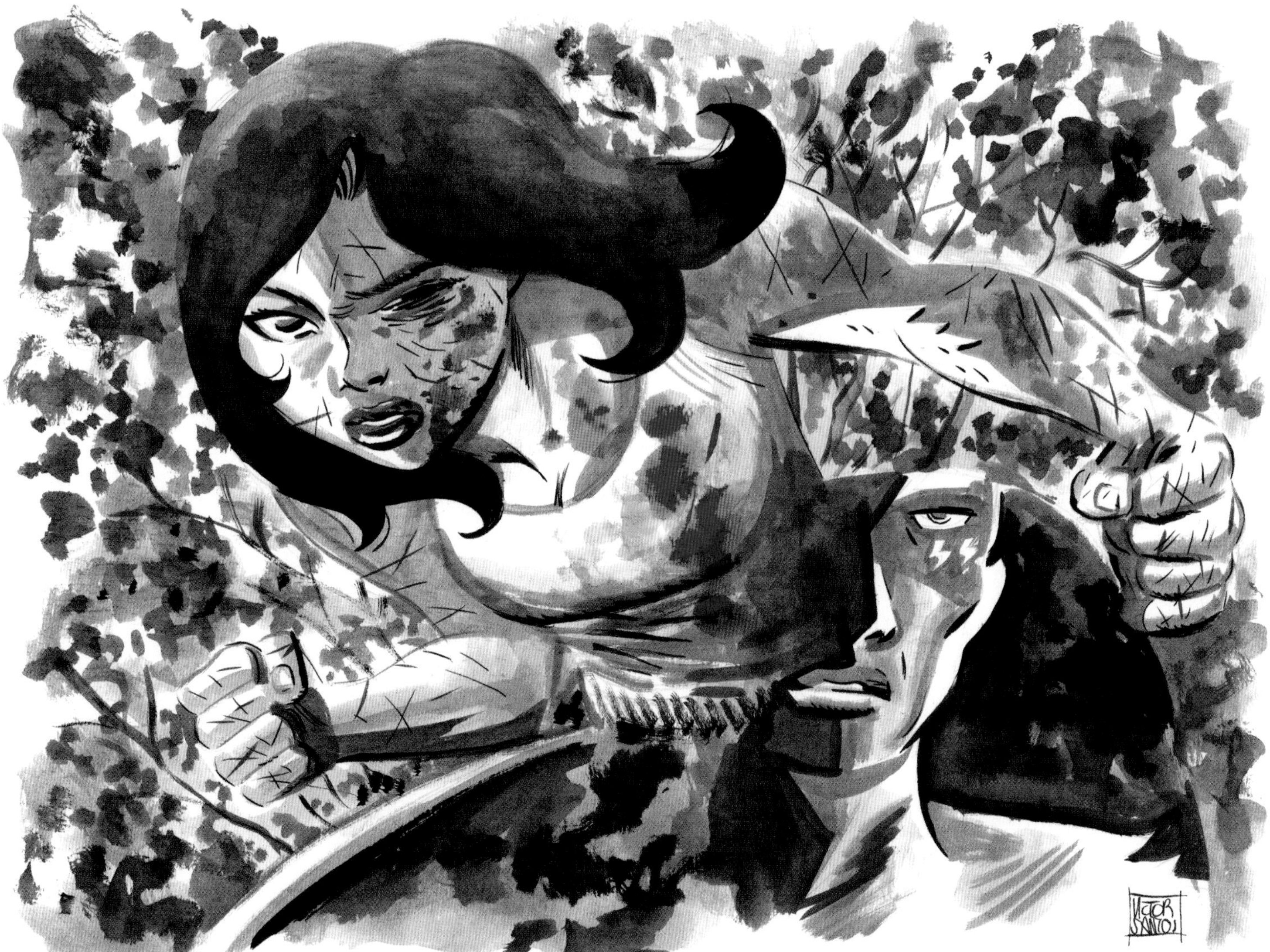

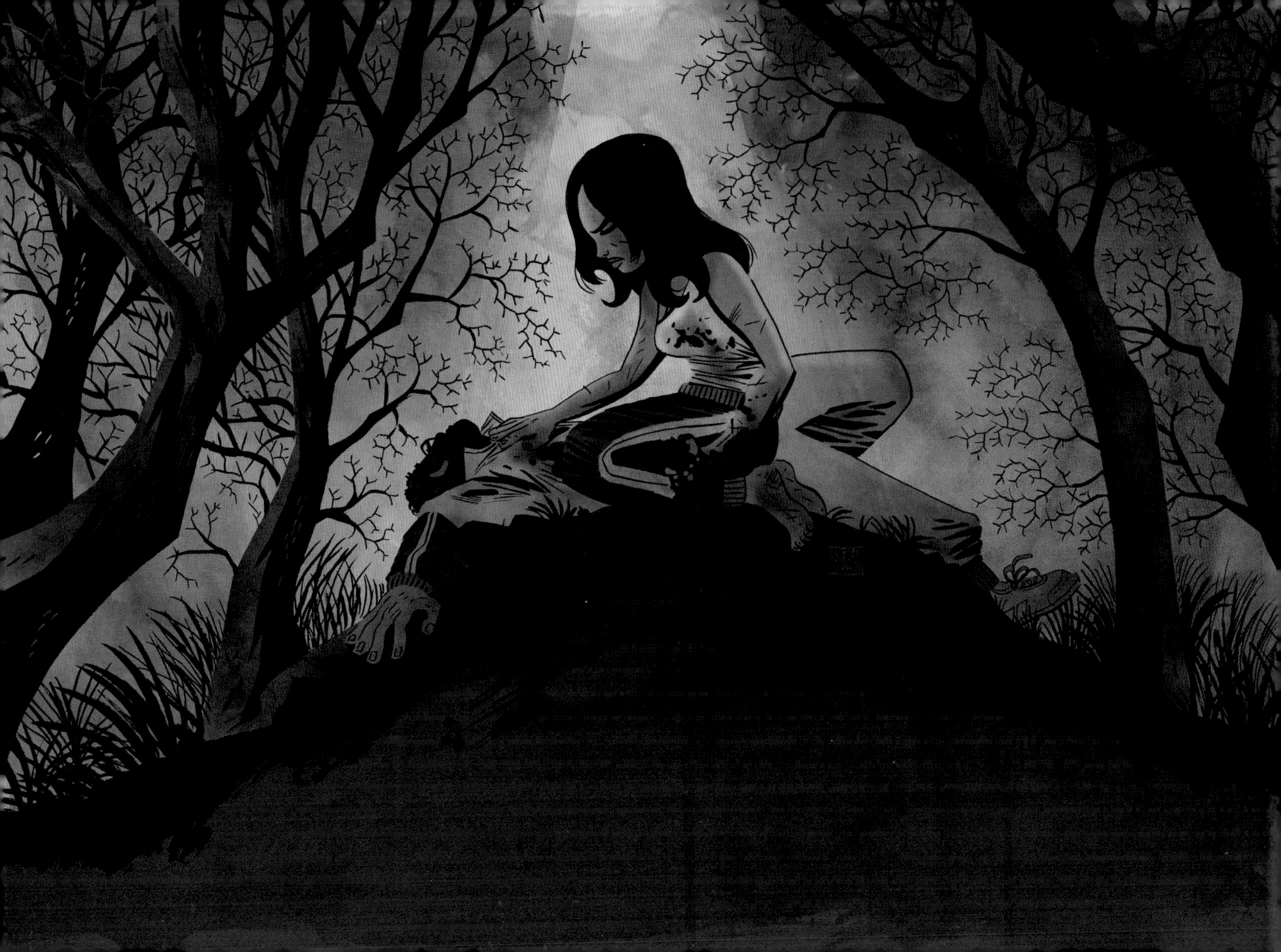

Born in Valencia in 1977, Victor Santos began his career writting and drawing a variety of comics published in Spain and France, including Los *Reyes Elfos* (*The Elf Kings*), *Pulp Heroes*, *Young Ronins and Infinity: Outrage*.

Santos has illustrated numerous comics in the United States, including the fantasy epic *The Mice Templar*, written by Bryan J. L. Glass and Michael Avon Oeming, James Patterson's New York Times best-selling *Witch & Wizard* series, written by Dara Naraghi, and DC Comics'*Filthy Rich with Brian Azzarello*.

His last works are the Image comics series *Violent Love*, written by Frank Barbiere, the graphic novel *Bad Girls*, written by Alex de Campi for Simon & Schuster, and his solo project *Rashomon*, a noir story placed in the feudal Japan revisiting the Ryūnosuke Akutagawa´s classic novel.

His most personal work, the noir/spy graphic novel series *Polar* has been adapted as a major motion picture by Constantin Films and Netflix, with star Mads Mikkelsen as the main character, Black Kaiser.

Santos has won six awards at the Barcelona international comic convention and three at the Madrid comics convention. In 2014 he was nominated for the prestigious Harvey Award for his work in *Polar: Came from the Cold* and for the Eisner Award in 2019 for *Bad Girls*. The original art of the *Polar* graphic novels had two successful exhibitions in the Glénat Gallery in Paris in 2016 and 2019.

He lives in Bilbao, Spain.

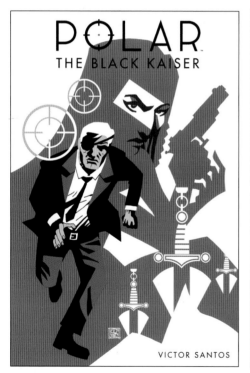
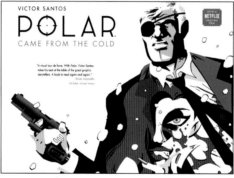